COMMON MARKET
CARTEL LAW

A Commentary on
Articles 85 and 86 of the EEC Treaty and
Regulations Nos. 17, 27, 26, 19/65, and 67/67
Second Edition

by

Conrad W. Oberdorfer, LL.B., LL.M., Dr. iur.
Member of the Firm of Choate, Hall & Stewart
Practicing Attorney in Boston

and

Alfred Gleiss, Dr. iur., Martin Hirsch, Dr. iur.
Members of the Firm of Gleiss, Lutz, Hootz,
Hirsch & Partners
Practicing Attorneys in Stuttgart

COMMERCE CLEARING HOUSE, INC.,
PUBLISHERS *of* TOPICAL LAW REPORTS
NEW YORK   CHICAGO   WASHINGTON
BOSTON   PHILADELPHIA   LOS ANGELES   SAN FRANCISCO

c C

Preface to Second Edition

The Rome Treaty, the treaty establishing the European Economic Community, or "Common Market" as it is still commonly called in the United States, took effect on January 1, 1958, and thus has now been in force over a decade. Its positive provisions as well as its general philosophy have taken root in economic and legal thought so deeply that notwithstanding certain continuing strains and stresses, largely of a political nature, and notwithstanding a number of remaining shortcomings and inadequacies, the European scene can scarcely be imagined any longer without this new economic order. Administrative and judicial precedents are developing and accumulating. In this respect the Treaty does not suffer by comparison with the Sherman Act which was passed in 1890 but did not receive significant implementation until the *Northern Securities* decision of 1904, or perhaps not even until the *Standard Oil* and *American Tobacco* cases of 1911.

Readers familiar with American antitrust developments, especially those of the more recent past, will be able to discern and appraise many other and more specific parallels in the historical development and substantive features of the two systems of business regulation. Nevertheless, there remain striking dissimilarities, some of an institutional nature, e.g., administrative v. judicial control, some in basic antitrust policy, e.g., "abuse of dominant position"—a cautious approach—v. "monopoly power,"—much stricter and more far-reaching —and many in the treatment of specific problems, for instance in the recently very active fields of exclusive distributorships, agency agreements and resale price control.

The German *Kommentar* by Messrs. Gleiss and Hirsch appeared in 1965 in its second and much enlarged edition.

The present second American edition, being the third version of the work in the English language, takes account of significant legal

v

developments through the fall of 1970. The authors have endeavored to preserve the character of the work as an easily comprehensible text written in clear and simple language so far as the frequently refractory subject matter allows.

A list of previous versions of this work includes the following:

First German Edition Gleiss/Hirsch, EWG-Kartellrecht, Verlag "Recht und Wirtschaft," Heidelberg, October 1962.

First American Edition Oberdorfer/Gleiss/Hirsch, Common Market Cartel Law, Commerce Clearing House, Chicago, March 1963.

English Edition Honig/Brown/Gleiss/Hirsch, Cartel Law of the EEC, Butterworth's, London, Autumn 1963.

Second German Edition Gleiss/Hirsch in cooperation with Dr. Christian Hootz, EWG-Kartellrecht, Verlag "Recht und Wirtschaft," Heidelberg, August 1965.

French Edition Antoine Braun/Gleiss/Hirsch in cooperation with Ludovic de Gryse and Bernard Francq, Droit des Ententes de la CEE, published jointly by Larcier, Brussels, and Dalloz, Paris, January 1967.

Italian Edition Gleiss/Hirsch, translation by Aurelio Pappalardo, Il Diritto Communitario della Concurrenza, Giuffré, Milan, November 1968.

A parallel work in domestic German cartel law is Gleiss/Hootz, Gesetz gegen Wettbewerbsbeschränkungen, Verlag "Recht und Wirtschaft," Heidelberg, January 1966.

Conrad W. Oberdorfer

Alfred Gleiss

Martin Hirsch

Boston and Stuttgart

January, 1971

Common Market
Cartel Law

Preface to First Edition

This American version of the *Kommentar zum EWG-Kartellrecht* originally published by Drs. Gleiss and Hirsch in October of 1962 (Verlagsgesellschaft "Recht und Wirtschaft" mbH, Heidelberg) is designed primarily to serve as a working tool for the American lawyer and corporate executive dealing with operations of American business establishments or their foreign subsidiaries or of joint American-European undertakings in one or more of the Common Market countries. It has retained virtually all of the substance and arrangement of its prototype; yet, it is not a mere dictionary translation which would leave it to the reader to accomplish a meeting of the minds between different legal systems, but has been adapted to the concepts and jargon of the American antitrust practitioner, with frequent side glances on analogues or contrasts from his indigenous law. And, of course, it takes account of developments which occurred since the German *Kommentar* appeared.

Even the original version is a "German" work only in a limited sense. Of course, it was written by German authors in their language, against the background of German legal institutions and with copious references to German literature. Nevertheless, it deals with a newly created supra-national field of law which has no accumulated body of jurisprudence or experience to draw on and must of necessity be interpreted against the background of national law of the member countries of the EEC. Within that broad frame of reference, the German legal scene plays a particularly important role because, in addition to the common element of civil law concepts and institutions which it shares in varying degrees with the other EEC countries, it was, on the one hand, profoundly influenced by the impact of post-war occupation, and it served, on the other hand, as a major source for the provisions now governing the Common Market as a whole. Surely, any attempt to by-pass the European roots of the subject matter and to relate it directly to the jurisprudence of the Sherman Act would ignore its nature and setting.

As in most matters of foreign law, translation is a major problem, not merely in the sense of transposing one or the other of the four official texts of Treaty and regulations into the English language, but even more in the sense of conceptual faithfulness to the originals. This task is complicated by the presence of a fair number of substantial discrepancies among the official texts themselves. For the basic provisions of the Treaty we therefore prefer to offer our own translation. For the regulations we have, for the user's convenience and to facilitate coordination with other English-language literature, used existing translations.

As already indicated in the preface to the German original, the practical orientation of the book has resulted in relatively more intensive treatment of substantive topics such as exclusive distributorships and license contracts, as well as of procedural requirements, and relatively less emphasis on academic analysis and jurisprudential refinements. At the same time, however, we believe that the work as a whole reflects the structure and those basic principles of the economic order in the Common Market which are likely to remain its permanent features regardless of the rapidity and extent of changes and new developments in specific directions. For information on the latest state of affairs from time to time, the American practitioner is referred to the "Common Market Reporter" (English-language looseleaf Reporter by Commerce Clearing House, Inc.), in particular to its extensive sections on the rules of competition.

The Authors

Boston and Stuttgart

March, 1963

Table of Contents

Article 85

Article 86

Regulation 17: First Regulation Implementing Articles 85 and 86

Regulation 27: First Regulation Implementing Regulation 17

Regulation 26: Application of Rules of Competition to Agricultural Products

Regulation 19/65: Application of Article 85, Paragraph 3, of the Treaty to Groups of Agreements and Concerted Practices

Regulation 67/67: Application of Article 85, Paragraph 3, of the Treaty to Exclusive Dealing Agreements

Table of Court and Agency Decisions Cited

Table of Other Authorities Cited

Text of Pertinent Treaty Provisions

Translation used in CCH Common Market Reports

There is no official English-language translation of the Treaty of Rome. The author, Dr. Oberdorfer, has supplied his own translation of Articles 85 and 86 for the purposes of this book and these appear on pages 7 and 107.

For the convenience of the reader the British Foreign Office translation, as published by Her Majesty's Stationery Office and as reproduced, by permission, in the CCH COMMON MARKET REPORTS, is also included here because of its widespread use. The pertinent provisions, Articles 85 and 86, from this translation, follow.—CCH.

Article 85

1. The following practices shall be prohibited as incompatible with the Common Market: all agreements between undertakings, all decisions by associations of undertakings and all concerted practices which are liable to affect trade between Member States and which are designed to prevent, restrict or distort competition within the Common Market or which have this effect. This shall, in particular, include:

(a) the direct or indirect fixing of purchase or selling prices or of any other trading conditions;

(b) the limitation or control of production, markets, technical development or investment;

(c) market-sharing or the sharing of sources of supply;

(d) the application of unequal conditions to parties undertaking equivalent engagements in commercial transactions, thereby placing them at a competitive disadvantage;

(e) making the conclusion of a contract subject to the acceptance by the other party to the contract of additional obligations, which, by their nature or according to commercial practice, have no connection with the subject of such contract.

2. Any agreements or decisions prohibited pursuant to this Article shall automatically be null and void.

3. The provisions of paragraph 1 may, however, be declared inapplicable in the case of:

—any agreement or type of agreement between undertakings,

—any decision or type of decision by associations of undertakings, and

—any concerted practice or type of concerted practice

which helps to improve the production or distribution of goods or to promote technical or economic progress, while allowing consumers a fair share of the resulting profit and which does not:

(a) subject the concerns in question to any restrictions which are not indispensable to the achievement of the above objectives;

(b) enable such concerns to eliminate competition in respect of a substantial part of the goods concerned.

Article 86

Any improper exploitation by one or more undertakings of a dominant position within the Common Market or within a substantial part of it shall be deemed to be incompatible with the Common Market and shall be prohibited, in so far as trade between Member States could be affected by it. The following practices, in particular, shall be deemed to amount to improper exploitation:

(a) the direct or indirect imposition of any unfair purchase or selling prices or of any other unfair trading conditions;

(b) the limitation of production, markets or technical development to the prejudice of consumers;

(c) the application of unequal conditions to parties undertaking equivalent engagements in commercial transactions, thereby placing them at a commercial disadvantage;

(d) making the conclusion of a contract subject to the acceptance by the other party to the contract of additional obligations which by their nature or according to commercial practice have no connection with the subject of such contract.

Introduction

A.   The Organs of the Community

On April 8, 1965, the governments of the member states decided to merge the executive organs of the three European Communities.[1] This merger came into force on July 1, 1967.[2] Since then the three Communities have had the same organs. Even prior to the merger, the European Court, the Parliament and the Economic and Social Committee were the same for all three.[3] Work on the merger of the three Treaties is being carried out.[4]

I.   The Council

The Council consists of representatives of the member states; each government delegates to it one of its members (Article 2 of the Merger Treaty[5]). In the Council the member states have the opportunity to exercise a direct influence on the Community's development. The Council's decisions need not be ratified by the member states.

According to Article 145 of the EEC Treaty, it is the Council's task to see to it that the aims of the Treaty are reached and that the economic policy is in harmony with the Treaty's provisions. For this purpose the Council has the power to take decisions (Article 145).

In substance this competency of the Council means that it is the Community's legislator (not the European Parliament as laymen often believe); thus, it also decides political questions. The large scope of the Council's discretion is limited in that the Council must act only according to the Treaty (Article 145); this, in practice, means that in most cases it can act only on the Commission's initiative[6] (note that here again the European Parliament is not involved).

---

[1] Eighth General Report on the Activities of the Community, 1965, p. 19.

[2] First General Report on the Activities of the Communities, 1967, p. 25; publication of the German Federal Government, July 27, 1967, BGB1 II, p. 2156.

[3] Agreement on the European Communities' Joint Organs, March 25, 1957, BGB1 II, p. 1156.

[4] First General Report on the Activities of the Communities, 1967, p. 30.

[5] Treaty on the Establishment of a Joint Council and a Joint Commission of the European Communities, April 8, 1965, BGB1 II, p. 1454 ff. (CMR ¶ 5115).

[6] See, for example, Articles 21, 43, 44, 49, 54, 63, 69, 75, 87 of the EEC Treaty; here the Council may act only "on a proposal of the Commission."

II. The Commission

Since July 1, 1970, the Commission has had nine members who are appointed by the member states' governments, acting in concert, for a term of four years. No more than two members may belong to one of the six states. The president and the three vice-presidents are chosen from among the Commission's members and are appointed by the member states, acting in concert, for a term of two years (Articles 10, 11 and 14 of the Merger Treaty). They may be re-appointed.

The Commission must, among other things, see to it that the EEC Treaty is applied and enforced. It has to issue recommendations or opinions insofar as the Treaty provides for them or the Commission itself considers them necessary. It has to take steps on its own and cooperate in actions taken by the Council. Finally, it must exercise the powers that the Council confers upon it to enable it to enforce the Council's provisions.

The Commission's right to make suggestions, already mentioned, must be emphasized. The Council, for the most part, may not act without such suggestions. This right to cooperate in most decisions taken by the Council assures the Commission considerable influence.

The Commission's structure is as follows:

Secretariat

Legal Service

Official Spokesman's Group

Statistical Office

Directorate-General for External Relations

Directorate-General for Economic and Financial Affairs

Directorate-General for Industrial Affairs

Directorate-General for Competition

Directorate-General for Social Affairs

Directorate-General for Agriculture

Directorate-General for Transport

Directorate-General for Aid to Development

Directorate-General for Personnel and Administration

Directorate-General for Press and Information

Directorate-General for Foreign Trade

Directorate-General for General Research and Technology

Directorate-General for Dissemination of Information

Directorate-General for Internal Market and Harmonization of Legislation

Directorate-General for the Joint Research Agency

Directorate-General for Regional Policy

Directorate-General for Energy

Directorate-General for Credit and Investments

Directorate-General for Budget

Directorate-General for Financial Control

Supply Agency

Directorate-General for Supervision of Security

Security Office

The Commission makes use of these agencies to fulfill its tasks, but the power of decision remains with the Commission alone.

III. The Court

The Court, as is now true of the Council and the Commission, is a joint organ of the three European Communities—namely, the European Coal and Steel Community, Euratom and the European Economic Community. It consists of seven judges, appointed by the governments of the member states, acting in concert, for a term of six years (Articles 165, 167). Every three years, three or four judges are replaced (Article 167), but they may be reappointed. The judges elect from among their members the president of the Court for a term of three years; he too may be re-elected.

B. The System of Articles 85-86

I. Immediate Validity

Articles 85 ff. constitute valid domestic law that directly creates rights and duties for the enterprises subject to it. All regulations issued by either the Council or the Commission in order to enforce or implement Articles 85 and 86, i.e., Regulations 17, 26, 27, 99/63, 19/65, 67/67 and 1017/68, are also directly applicable. They are all self-executory, i.e., directly effective inside the member states and must be applied as such; this follows from Article 189, paragraph 2.

II.   Scope of Application of the Substantive Cartel Law

Articles 85 and 86 are what German lawyers call the Community's "materiell" (substantive as opposed to formal or procedural) cartel law.

Articles 85 (1) and 86 contain self-executory prohibitions. Everything within the scope of these articles is automatically prohibited without a special statement or decision to this effect, e.g., by the Commission, being required. The prohibition in Article 85 (1), however, in contrast to Article 86, is limited by the possibility that an exemption may be granted under paragraph 3 of Article 85 (for details, see Article 85, ¶ 87 ff., infra).

III.   Function of Formal Cartel Law

It is the content and task of the Community's formal cartel law, i.e., the above-mentioned Council and Commission regulations, to apply or enforce the two general clauses in Articles 85 and 86.

IV.   Relationship Between National and Community Cartel Law

The relationship between national and Community cartel law has been much discussed. The prevailing opinion was that EEC and national cartel law regulate different matters because they have different aims—viz., the protection of competition in interstate trade, on the one hand, and the protection of competition in the national market, on the other. Consequently, both legal systems were thought to be applicable if a restraint affected both interstate and intrastate trade, even potentially.

In its *Tar-Colors* decision of February 13, 1969,[6a] the Court has ruled that, in principle, Community cartel law prevails. National authorities may proceed against a cartel, even if the Commission is examining whether the cartel is compatible with Community law, but this scope of national law should not encroach upon either the unlimited and uniform application of Community law or on the measures already taken or to be taken in the future to put it into practice.

Consequently, a national cartel authority must not contradict a decision by the Commission. If a decision of the Commission is pending, the national authorities have to take into account that there must not be any conflict.

[6a] Case No. 14/68, Recueil Vol. XV, 1969-1, p. 1; English translation in CMR ¶ 8056; annotations by Schumacher, AWD 1969, p. 85; Gleiss/Hootz, WRP 1969, p. 218; Hootz, Europarecht 1969, p. 151; Niederleithinger, BB 1969, p. 1185.

Nevertheless, the co-existence of both national and Community cartel law will, in practice, lead to difficulties, if only because more than one proceeding will be necessary.

With regard to the relationship between national and Community law in general, the French Conseil d'Etat has ruled in a decision of March 1, 1968, that later national law can abrogate prior Community law. This decision was generally considered to be contrary to the Rome Treaty, but the Commission refrained from taking any action against the French Republic under Articles 155 and 169 of the EEC Treaty because it might violate the independence of the judicature.[6b]

V. Competent Authorities

It is primarily up to the Commission to enforce the Common Market cartel law.[6c] It is true that even the national authorities are entitled to apply the prohibitions contained in Articles 85(1) and 86, so long as the Commission has not opened a procedure to eliminate a contravention or to grant a negative attestation (or clearance) or an exemption. This competence does not, however, mean much in practice.

It is, therefore, primarily up to the Commission to prosecute violations of Articles 85(1) and 86. The Commission alone can grant (Articles 2 and 9(1) of Regulation 17) negative clearances and exemptions under Article 85 (3). Thus, it is the Commission's task to apply the EEC cartel law. Decisions can be made only by the Commission as such, i.e., by the 9 Commissioners acting together as an entity. The main work in this field, however, is done by Directorate A, "General Policy with Regard to Competition"; Directorate B, "Cartels, Market-dominating Enterprises and Private Discriminations" (except the energy and steel sectors); and Directorate C, "Cartels, Combinations (particularly mergers) and Private Discriminations" (energy and steel). These three Directorates form the Directorate-General for Competition.

According to Article 173, a suit may be filed against the Commission's decisions. The Court in Luxembourg has jurisdiction for such suits. It guards the correct application of cartel law in the Common Market.

[6b] Decision published in Recueil Dalloz-Sirey 1968, Jurispr., p. 286; cf. also the inquiries put to the Commission by Deringer and Westerterp, and the answers given by the Commission: OffJour No. C 71 (July 17, 1968), p. 1; and No. C 20 (February 14, 1970), p. 3.

[6c] On the Commission's cartel policy from 1962 through 1967, see Mok, CMLR Vol. 6, No. 1, November 1968, p. 67 ff.; in 1968 see Kirschstein, WRP 1969, p. 223; Gutzler, WRP 1969, p. 220; on recent developments see Ulmer, AWD 1970, p. 193.

In the field of Article 86 the Commission has not yet made any decisions. With regard to Article 85, however, it made five decisions in 1964, three in 1965, one in 1967, eight in 1968, and eleven in 1969 (for a survey, see the Table of Court and Agency Decisions Cited). Not all the early decisions contain matters worth presenting in detail here, since they are either self-evident or do not even reflect a restraint of trade.

VI. Scope of Application

The term Common Market includes the six member states (Article 227(1)) and the French overseas departments (France d'outremer). For details it is necessary to refer to Article 227 (1), (2) and (3), particularly with regard to other overseas territories (Netherlands Surinam and Antilles). The situation as to Algeria has become doubtful following its independence. Monaco, San Marino and Andorra did not sign the Rome Treaty; they are considered as belonging to the Common Market in fact, but not in law. Associated territories do not belong to the Common Market.

The Commission has extended the scope of application of Community law to enterprises domiciled outside the Common Market. From this it follows that such enterprises also may be punished if they violate Articles 85 ff. Service in such cases may be performed on subsidiaries inside the Common Market. The Commission did so with regard to Ciba, Geigy and Sandoz, of Switzerland, and ICI of Great Britain, in the tar-colors case.[7] Thus, the Commission extends the applicability of Community law in a way similar to U. S. antitrust practice.[8]

---

[7] Decision of July 24, 1969, OffJour No. L 195 (August 7, 1969), p. 11; CMR ¶ 9314.

[8] For details from the viewpoint of non-American firms, compare Gleiss, AWD 1969, p. 499.

Article 85

(Author's Translation)

(1) Incompatible with the Common Market and prohibited are all agreements between or among enterprises, decisions of associations of enterprises and concerted practices which are apt to affect adversely trade between member states and which have as their purpose or effect a prevention, restriction or distortion of competition within the Common Market, in particular:

    (a) direct or indirect fixing of purchase or sales prices or of other terms and conditions of doing business;

    (b) limitation or control of production, distribution, technical development or investments;

    (c) allocation of markets or sources of supply;

    (d) application of unequal terms to parties furnishing equivalent considerations, whereby they are placed at a competitive disadvantage;

    (e) subjecting the conclusion of contracts to the condition that the other parties to them accept additional goods or services which are unrelated to the subject matter of the contract either by their nature or by commercial custom.

(2) Agreements or decisions prohibited by this Article are null and void.

(3) The provisions of paragraph (1) may, however, be declared inapplicable to any of the following:

    —agreements or categories of agreements between or among enterprises,

    —decisions or categories of decisions of associations of enterprises,

    —concerted practices or categories thereof,

which contribute to the improvement of production or distribution of goods or to the promotion of technical or economic progress, while reserving to consumers an equitable participation in the resulting profit, and which do not

    (a) subject the enterprises concerned to restrictions which are not indispensable to the achievement of these objectives, or

    (b) open up possibilities to the enterprises concerned to eliminate competition for a substantial portion of the goods involved.

A.   ARTICLE 85 (1)—GENERAL PROHIBITION

I.   Enterprises

¶ 1   Article 85 (1)[1] is addressed to "enterprises" (and associations of enterprises); however, it does not define this term but simply assumes a meaning for it. Since Article 85 (1) speaks of agreements between enterprises, it presupposes that they are legally capable of entering into contracts, i.e., of being the subjects of rights and obligations.[2] Only a *unit with legal capacity* can therefore be an enterprise; mere economic unity will not suffice.[3] Legally dependent establishments, such as branch undertakings and mere business divisions, are not enterprises within the meaning of Article 85 (1). The individual plants of an enterprise, such as production facilities, often called "works," branch sales offices of a manufacturer, and stores in a grocery chain, are thus not "enterprises."[4] A concern ("Konzern") is not a legal but an economic unit; under the literal tenor of Article 85 (1) it is thus not an enterprise.[5] Whether it may nevertheless be treated as such will depend upon the spirit and object of this provision as well as upon the circumstances of the particular case (compare V, infra).

It should be noted that the word "concern" is used herein neither in its ordinary Anglo-American sense, in which it is as generic a word as "enterprise" or "business organization," nor as a technically adequate translation of the German word "Konzern," itself a word of greatly varying application. As here employed, it is to express the

---

NOTE: For list of authorities cited, see page 269; for abbreviations, see page 289.

[1] Kleemann, p. 18 ff. expresses the view that Articles 85 ff., in particular Article 85 itself, are contrary to the Basic Law (Constitution) of the Federal Republic of Germany and have therefore not become valid law for the Federal Republic. The German Federal Constitutional Court, by decision of October 18, 1967 (Vol. 22, 1968, p. 293 ff.), has stated that regulations of the Council and of the Commission of the European Communities cannot, in contrast to purely German laws, be assaulted directly by the so-called appeal against constitutionality (Verfassungsbeschwerde). The practical result is, in our opinion, that the laws of the EEC are considered to be of a higher rank, supranational. Cf. the annotations to this decision by Ipsen, EuR 1968, p. 137; Deringer, NJW 1968, p. 338; Fischer, NJW 1968, p. 322; and Immenga, NJW 1968, p. 1036.

[2] Accord: von Gamm, p. 22; Wohlfarth/Everling/Glaesner/Sprung, Article 85, note 1; also apparently the BKartA in its Annual Report 1961, p. 61; contra: von der Groeben/von Boeckh, Article 85, note 15, who do not regard legal capacity as necessary.

[3] Accord: Wohlfarth/Everling/Glaesner/Sprung, *ibid.*; von Gamm, pp. 22, 23.

[4] Chains (e.g. SPAR in Germany or Centra in Belgium), however, are separate independent enterprises.

[5] Accord: von Gamm, p. 23.

broad concept of economically affiliated enterprises under common management underlying the definition of "Konzern" in § 18 of the Aktiengesetz 1965, which reads in translation as follows:

"(1) If a dominant and one or more dependent enterprises are joined under the uniform management of the dominant enterprise, then they constitute a concern; the individual enterprises are concern enterprises. If there is a contract of domination between enterprises (§ 291) or if one enterprise is integrated into the other (§ 319) they are to be considered joined under a uniform management. It is presumed that a dependent enterprise forms a concern with the dominant enterprise.

(2) If legally independent enterprises are joined under a uniform management without one enterprise being dependent on the other, then they also constitute a concern; the individual enterprises are concern enterprises."

According to the decisions of the Court of Justice under the European Coal and Steel Treaty, the term "enterprise" means only a natural or legal person. Thus, according to these decisions, several legally independent enterprises do not constitute an "enterprise," even when they comprise an integrated economic unit.[6]

¶ 2   The *legal form* of the enterprise is not determinative.[7] Included within the purview of this provision are *inter alia* legal entities such as corporations, limited liability companies, etc., but also enterprises operated as general or limited partnerships or carried on by the owner as an individual.[7a] Nor does it make a difference who owns the enterprise (concerning public enterprises, see ¶ 4, infra).

¶ 3   Article 85 (1) protects the commercial intercourse between the member states of the EEC against restraints on competition; it follows from this objective that the enterprise must be active in commerce. Its activity consequently must be directed to produc-

---

[6] Compare the decision of March 22, 1961, Cases Nos. 42 and 49/59, Recueil Vol. VII, p. 101.
[7] Accord: Wohlfarth/Everling/Glaesner/Sprung, *ibid.;* von Gamm, p. 22; BKartA Annual Report 1961, p. 61.
[7a] Compare Antoine Braun/Gleiss/Hirsch, p. 50, second paragraph, *inter*

alia: les sociétés de personnes à responsabilité limitée (s. a. r. l. en droit français, s. p. r. l. en droit belge), les unions de crédit, les associations momentanées, les associations en participation, etc.

tion or exchange of *goods*[8] or to *commercial services*[9].[10] Private activity
serving to supply personal demand will not suffice.[11] An intention to
realize gain is not necessary.[12] Thus, a nonprofit organization is not
excluded from classification as an enterprise. The size of the enterprise is immaterial here; thus, even one-man businesses are enterprises
within the meaning of Article 85 (1).[13] An enterprise outside the
Common Market is, of course, an enterprise within the meaning of
Article 85 (1); the location of its seat or domicile is immaterial in
this regard.

¶ 4   *Public* enterprises too are enterprises within the meaning of
Article 85 (1), as seen indirectly from the treatment of "public
enterprises" in Article 90 (1) and of the enterprises in Article 90 (2).[14]
For them, also, legal form is immaterial. They can be public corporations, public federations, or the like. Also considered enterprises are
organizations such as the German State Match Monopoly, or stock exchange associations, technical control associations (for example, for
the supervision of automobiles), as well as other associations under
public law such as guilds. Organs of the state which act with sovereign immunity do not belong here since they do not engage in commerce in private law forms.

¶ 5   The Bundeskartellamt[15] considers members of the *liberal professions* also as "enterprises" within the meaning of Article 85
(1). However, this view, thus generally stated, is subject to the same
objections as in the case of the German Gesetz gegen Wettbewerbsbeschränkungen (Law against Restraints on Competition, effective since

---

[8] This term has, however, a meaning different from the legal definition in § 1, paragraph 2, No. 1 of the HGB, which equates goods with movable property. Goods within the purview of Article 85 (1) also include, e.g., real estate, magazines, industrial protective rights.

[9] The definition of "services" in Article 60 of the EEC Treaty cannot, in our view, be taken over for purposes of Article 85; it cannot be divorced from the context of Part II, Title III (free movement of services and capital). Article 60 enumerates as services specifically industrial, commercial and artisan activities and those of the liberal professions.

[10] Accord: von Gamm, *ibid.*; BKartA, *ibid.*

[11] Accord: BKartA, *ibid.*

[12] Accord: BKartA, *ibid.*; also compare the definition of "enterprise" there and further in von Gamm, *ubi supra;* Wohlfarth / Everling / Glaesner/Sprung, *ubi supra;* von der Groeben/von Boeckh, *ubi supra.*

[13] Contra: von Gamm, p. 23. However, on the question whether a contract is apt to affect trade between member states, the size of an enterprise may be a material factor.

[14] Accord: von Gamm, *ibid.;* Wohlfarth/Everling/Glaesner/Sprung, Article 90, especially note 3.

[15] *Ibid.*

¶ 4

January 1, 1958, hereinafter referred to as GWB).[16] Liberal professions do not as a rule render "commercial services"; it may possibly be different in individual cases. The definition of "services" in Article 60 of the EEC Treaty lends no support to the view of the BKartA (compare footnote 9); on the contrary, a distinction is there expressly made, among other things, between industrial activities and those in a liberal profession.

¶ 6 *Federations* of enterprises are not as a rule themselves "enterprises" within the meaning of Article 85 (1),[17] because their activity is not directed to production or exchange of goods nor to commercial services, but to representing the interests of their members, to giving them advice, etc. (typically so in the case of trade and professional associations). However, if they also engage in commercial activities, e.g., by procuring joint purchases for their members, they will be enterprises to that extent.[18]

¶ 7 One who performs *work controlled by others* (an employee) is not an enterprise within the meaning of Article 85 (1). Agreements regarding terms and conditions of work thus do not come within this provision. The same legal situation prevails in practically all states with legislation against restraints on competition.[19] Wage and salary agreements between parties to collective bargaining are therefore not reached by Article 85 (1), nor are agreements by motion picture producers regarding the compensation of actors since the latter are also, at least according to the German legal view, employees.[20] This is true even where such agreements have restraining effects upon competition.[21]

A shareholder without his own firm is not an enterprise under Article 85, even if he acts as an entrepreneur to influence the company's market strategy.[21a]

---

[16] Compare on this subject Baumbach/Hefermehl, § 1 GWB, margin No. 13, and the references there. The Appeals Section of the BKartA and the Court of Appeals (Kammergericht in Berlin), however, in their decisions of May 9, 1959, and January 12, 1960, regarded, e.g., certified public accountants as enterprises within the meaning of § 1 GWB; WuW/E OLG 322 ff.

[17] Compare on this problem also BKartA Annual Report 1961, p. 31.

[18] The Commission's decisions offer some interesting, although not always clearcut examples, e.g., the negative clearances granted SOCEMAS and Limeburners (¶ 321 D and 321 H, infra), or the exemptions granted the Transocean Marine Paint Association and CECIMO (¶ 119 and 121, infra).

[19] As to the GWB compare, e.g., Gemeinschaftskommentar, § 1 GWB, margin No. 42; decision of the Court of Appeals (Kammergericht) of January 12, 1960, WuW/E OLG 323 ("Public Accountants"); also further BKartA in its letter of August 6, 1962, BB 1962, p. 978, No. 1617.

[20] Thus the court decisions and the uniform view of commentators; contra only Müller in UFITA, vol. 28, p. 134 f., for so-called star performers, but his view has not prevailed.

[21] Accord as to § 1 GWB: BKartA, *ubi supra*, footnote 17.

[21a] Würdinger, Aktien- und Konzernrecht, 2nd ed., 1966, p. 261 ff.

II. Associations of Enterprises

¶ 8   This term also is not defined by Article 85 (1). In any event,
it necessarily refers to associations of "enterprises" within the
meaning of this provision. Federations of employers and unions of
employees are not associations of enterprises. The legal form of the
"association" is immaterial under the unqualified wording of this provision: The association may be organized as a business corporation
or as an unincorporated association or otherwise.[22] There must be
an association in some fashion between at least two enterprises; a
mere participation by one enterprise in another will not make the
two an association of enterprises.[23]

Associations of enterprises include in particular federations, etc.,
but also cartels, "ad hoc" cartel organizations, etc. Whether holding
federations, i.e., associations composed of associations of enterprises,
come within the provision is doubtful. The wording argues against it,
but they, too, may well be covered by the spirit and object of the
provision, according to the circumstances of the particular case.[24]

III.   Cooperation: Agreements and Decisions

¶ 9   We place the concepts "agreements," "decisions," and "concerted practices" in the category of "cooperation." Every restraint of competition must be based on such cooperation in order to
fall within the prohibition of Article 85 (1); the individual conduct
of an enterprise does not suffice. Only Article 86 deals with individual
conduct of a single firm. If a French enterprise, for example, decides
not to market its product in Germany, there is no cooperation, merely
autonomous conduct. This principle was confirmed by the European
Court's *Parke, Davis* decision of February 29, 1968, in Case No. 24/67:
If the holder of a patent exerts and enforces the rights granted him
by a member state, this does not fall under Article 85, paragraph 1,
because it is not based on an agreement, decision or concerted practices.[24a]

---

[22] Accord: von Gamm, p. 23; Baum-
bach/Hefermehl, margin No. 14 to § 1
GWB (as to § 1 GWB).

[23] Contra: von Gamm, p. 23, who
therefore—in our view erroneously—
regards concerns also as associations
of enterprises. It is, however, difficult
to see how concerns would make "decisions." For examples in the Commission's decisions, see footnote 18, supra.

[24] Kleemann, p. 30, includes them in
any case among the associations of
enterprises; contra—not reached by
Article 85 (1)—Baumbach/Hefermehl,
Article 85, margin No. 4. As to the
term "industrial or professional associations" in Article 27 GWB, compare
Frankfurter Kommentar, TZ 6 to 19.

[24a] For the full text of this decision,
together with the conclusions of the
Advocate General, see CMR ¶ 8054.

¶ 8

If the conduct of a number of enterprises is based on public law, e.g., a statute or administrative measure, there is no cooperation within the meaning of Article 85 (1); mere sovereign permission by a member state does not suffice. Consequently, if French enterprises are prohibited by statute or administrative order from exporting to Germany, their conduct is not cooperative action even if they agree, in addition, not to violate this government export prohibition. If a member state prescribes the sales prices of milk, dealers of milk can make agreements to the same effect as the law with impunity. The other prerequisites of Article 85 (1) are probably met, especially those of a restriction or distortion of competition; however, they are not caused by cooperation but by sovereign act.[24b] Whether such conduct of a member state violates the Rome Treaty is a question that is not germane here.

"Agreements" is the same as "contracts" within the meaning of the civil law of Germany.[24c] In this respect it seems narrower than the term "contract" in Section 1 of the Sherman Antitrust Act, which has not been confined to agreements with legally binding effect; but its complementation by the concept of "concerted practices" should be kept in mind.

Article 85 (1) does not, as does the GWB, distinguish between contracts for a common purpose and other contracts. Agreements within the meaning of Article 85 (1) include, therefore, not only cartel agreements properly speaking, but all contracts with legally binding effect upon the parties. The law mentions only contracts between "enterprises"; in spirit, however, it is applicable also to agreements between associations of enterprises as well as those between such associations and individual enterprises.[25]

Decisions must be made by the association of enterprises or by its competent organs and must be binding for the member enterprises[26]—apart, of course, from nullity pursuant to Article 85 (2). Mere recommendations by the association or other suggestions without commitment do not fulfill the concepts of "agreement" and "decision"[27] (see ¶ 13, infra). A specific form, for either contracts or decisions, is not determinative under Article 85 (1). Consequently, they need not be in writing or even, for example, be notarized; mere oral agreements or decisions suffice.

[24b] As to the legal situation in the Netherlands, Belgium and France, compare Antoine Braun/Gleiss/Hirsch, p. 57, particularly footnote 27 bis.

[24c] It is the same under French and Belgian law, Antoine Braun/Gleiss/Hirsch, p. 58, ¶ 11.

[25] Accord: Baumbach/Hefermehl, Article 85, margin No. 3, and Kleemann, p. 31.

[26] Contra: Kleemann, who regards binding effect as unnecessary.

[27] Accord: von Gamm, p. 23; compare further Nissen, WuW 1960, p. 250 ff.

IV.   Concerted Practices

¶ 10   In contrast to § 1 GWB, which mentions only contracts and
decisions, Article 85 (1) reaches in addition cooperation by
"concerted practices." The novelty and artificiality of the German
term "aufeinander abgestimmte Verhaltensweisen," which is linguis-
tically not a pleasing phrase, betray its origin in another jurisprudence and its jargon. Article 85 (1) speaks of agreements between
enterprises and decisions of *associations of enterprises,* but mentions
neither enterprises nor associations thereof in connection with concerted practices. This, however, does not signify any substantive
difference; rather, the legislator (i.e., the parties to the EEC Treaty)
merely deemed a repetition of these terms superfluous. The concerted
practices are alternative to agreements between two or more enterprises and are treated the same as agreements insofar as the nature
of the subject matter permits.[27a] Similarly, concerted conduct takes
the place of decisions in the case of associations of enterprises.

¶ 11   The concept of "concerted practices" stems from the *concerted
practices* (or acts) known to the Anglo-American legal system
(compare the "pratiques concertées" in the French text), which in
turn are connected with the concept of "conspiracy."

A further refinement of the notion of an agreement implicit in
conduct, which is a degree more ephemeral than the "concerted practices" and has not found equal favor with the American courts,[28] is
"conscious parallelism." The German terminology in Article 85 (1)
may be literally re-translated as "mutually attuned modes of conduct"
and does not necessarily connote agreed-upon action. Both the German and the French "pratiques concertées" would appear to exclude
the application of Article 85 (1) to mere consciousness of paralleling
the conduct of others, without some consensual element.

¶ 12   The term "concerted practices" is intended to reach even
informal states of fact and situations where the participants
remain *without commitment.* An intent on the part of the participants
to bind themselves legally is not required; herein lies the difference
between concerted practices and legally binding agreements and decisions. Necessary, however, is some conduct pursuant to a conscious
mutual meeting of minds.[29] Two (or more) enterprises must mutually

---

[27a] For differences see ¶ 22, infra.

[28] See, e.g., *Theatre Enterprises, Inc.
v. Paramount Film Distributing Corp.,*
346 U. S. 537, 541 (1954). For a
treatment of this subject, see Donald F.
Turner, "The Definition of Agreement

under the Sherman Act: Conscious
Parallelism and Refusals to Deal," 75
Harvard Law Review 655 (1962).

[29] Accord in result: BKartA in its
Annual Report 1961, p. 61.

adjust their future market behavior one to the other, consciously and intentionally.[30] "Concerted practices" therefore are not present where several enterprises merely act identically in the market[31] or where an enterprise merely adapts itself to the market behavior of one or more of its competitors;[32] such conduct need not be based on mutual concert of action, but can be the result of keen competition. It is such competition that forces an enterprise to observe its competitors' behavior and to make allowance for their future actions in planning its own conduct. This mutual influence does not constitute "concerted practices" within the meaning of Article 85 (1). There are "concerted practices" where the participants establish a common plan for a particular market behavior and act (even without a gentlemen's duty) according to the plan. In our opinion, this "common plan" stands somewhere between a gentlemen's agreement and mere conscious parallelism. The participants need not establish direct contact with one another; whether the common plan is communicated by one of them or by a third party is immaterial. Of course, concerted practices also must have as their purpose or effect the restraint of trade.[32a]

"Concerting" alone never suffices for Article 85 (1); the law requires *conduct* based on this "concert." If an enterprise concludes a series of independent contracts, all with the same content, as, e.g., in a resale price maintenance system, the other contracting parties are not engaging in concerted conduct, not even if each of them binds himself with the tacit expectancy that his competitors will do likewise. It is dubious whether the same is true for the so-called "star contracts" (*Sternverträge*) by which competitors replace a (horizontal) contract between them with single contracts concluded by each competitor with a third party, which may be an *ad hoc* creation. In any event, if there is concerted conduct, it does not matter whether it is uniform or varied pursuant to "assigned roles."

It is difficult to say when conduct is "concerted"; some authors require an agreement without obligation, i.e., a gentlemen's agree-

---

[30] Accord: Baumbach/Hefermehl, Article 85, margin No. 5; Frankfurter Kommentar, introductory note TZ 6 to Article 85, which Commentary also regards as sufficient a "concert" implied from conduct permitting such an inference. Contra: Kleemann, who would require conduct pursuant to a non-committal arrangement arrived at in advance. If so, concerted practices would mean the same as gentlemen's agreements.

[31] Accord: Guenther, WuW 1957, p. 279; Baumbach/Hefermehl, *ubi supra;* Wohlfarth/Everling/Glaesner/Sprung, Article 85, note 3; BKartA, *ubi supra;* Kleemann, p. 31.

[32] Guenther, *ibid.,* and the authors quoted by Antoine Braun/Gleiss/Hirsch, p. 61, footnote 36.

[32a] See ¶ 22 ff., infra.

ment,[32b] despite the fact that the drafters of the Rome Treaty did not, presumably intentionally, adopt the term "verabredete Praktiken" (agreed-upon practices) from the European Coal and Steel Treaty. Others see concerted conduct also where recommendations are followed; finally, for a third group, every intentional, conscious cooperation would suffice. In our opinion, it is immaterial for Article 85 (1) whether the concerting is based upon a gentlemen's agreement, recommendations, or whatever else. Article 85 (1) is directed, not against the means, but against the result, i.e., the concerted conduct. The manner of "concerting" is immaterial; the law leaves this matter open.

The European High Court in its *Grundig* decision of July 13, 1966 (CMR ¶ 8046), prohibited the Consten firm of Paris from using its rights to the GINT trademark, derived from Grundig International, registered for Consten in France, to prevent parallel imports into France. The GINT trademark was affixed to all Grundig products and by contract had been registered for Consten in France. The High Court held that the agreement between Grundig and Consten concerning registration of the trademark constituted a violation of Article 85 (1), adding that the prohibition of that article would be of no effect were Consten permitted to take measures against parallel imports, i.e., imports by third parties into France. The reasoning of this holding, in our opinion, is misconceived since the action of Consten against such imports was not countenanced by the agreement with Grundig; rather, it was the result of an autonomous decision made by Consten. It would have been systematically better to have viewed Consten's measures as a part or result of a concerted practice having a common objective (see Gleiss, WRP 1967, p. 165). Certainly the agreement and registration for Consten of the GINT trademark constitute part of the concerted practice, but the primary element which gave Consten the opportunity to prevent imports by third parties was the fact that Grundig marked all its products in Germany with GINT (as well as "Grundig"). The culmination of the concerted practice occurs when Consten uses its opportunity under the trademark to proceed against parallel imports. Thus viewed, the arrangement is not concerted behavior of two enterprises followed by a violation by one (Consten), but, on the contrary, it is a concerted practice by *two* enterprises. This view is shared in substance by the High Court when it states that the Commission rightly weighed the overall effect of Grundig's distribution system. However, it is to be contradicted when the Court holds the agreement concerning the registration of GINT, standing alone, to be a violation of Article 85 (1).

[32b] For an example of concerted practices following a gentlemen's agreement, see the quinine cartel, ¶ 459, infra.

¶ 12

¶ 13   This presents an important *difference from the prohibition of recommendations* in § 38, paragraph 2, second sentence, of the GWB, whose place thus is taken only in part by the prohibition of cooperation through concerted conduct. The GWB denounces the means, viz., the recommendation, and not its consequence (uniform conduct), as unlawful; however, it requires such conduct for the unlawfulness of the recommendation.

Where a recommendation, horizontal or vertical, is heeded, there is, as a rule, merely uniformity of conduct; the "concerting together" among the addressees of the recommendation, or between any of them and the party making the recommendation will usually be missing, so that Article 85 (1) is not applicable to such uniform conduct.[33] The situation may be different where, e.g., the members of an association of enterprises first agree upon the recommendation, resolve that it be given, and thereafter follow it. The Commission of the EEC at one time seemed inclined to equate recommendations with concerted conduct,[34] in our opinion wrongly.

V. Restraint on Competition

¶ 14   The words *prevention, restriction* or *distortion* cannot be clearly differentiated. "Prevention" probably is stronger than "restriction," meaning a complete tying-up of competition. "Distortion," however, evidently is weaker or milder. All three terms together are equivalent in substance to "restraint on competition" in the GWB.[35] Compare also the tests of "injure, destroy or prevent competition" in Section 2 (price discrimination) and to "substantially lessen competition" in Section 3 (tying and exclusive dealing contracts) and Section 7 (acquisitions of stock or assets) of the Clayton Antitrust Act, all of which, however, refer to potential effects ("may be") rather than to actual effects or purpose.

According to German doctrine, a contract or decision must contain a legal obligation to refrain from competition ("content theory").[35a] Under EEC law, however, the restraint on competition can be based on concerted conduct as well. There is no requirement that the restraint be legally binding on the participants. Consequently, a legal obligation is not essential under Article 85 (1); restraints on freedom

---

[33] Contra: Deringer in GRUR AIT 1962, p. 293, footnote 76.

[34] Guide Lines in their provisional form; the reference to "recommendations" was, however, omitted in the final version, CMR ¶ 2801 ff.

[35] Accord: Baumbach/Hefermehl, Article 85, margin No. 14; Deringer, GRUR AIT 1962, p. 292.

[35a] For Article 85 see ¶ 22, infra.

of action accomplished by legal obligation (contract or decision) and
by measures in fact (concerted behavior) are equated with one another (unlike the GWB). The Commission perceives as the decisive
criterion in a contract, not the contractual obligation to refrain from
competition, but the actual effects of the contract on competition
("result theory"). The European Court, by decision of July 13, 1966,[35b]
in the *Grundig-Consten* case lets mere purpose to restrain competition[36] suffice.

The law does not define the term "competition." There are
very many definitions of the word; space does not permit a detailed
discussion of them here. In a ruling on § 3 (2) GWB, the German
Federal Supreme Court[37] defined competition as the attempt of one
enterprise to enlarge its market by its own efforts, such as better
quality or price, at the expense of another enterprise. The comparison between the "competitors" in the market was deemed to
be a necessary feature.

This definition is not entirely convincing: Of course an enterprise is competing if it tries to sell goods of lesser quality, even at
a higher price. It may attempt to compensate for this inferiority
by more advertising, better service, etc. According to a plausible
view held by the court below (Kammergericht Berlin),[37a] but reversed by the BGH, competition need not take place at somebody
else's expense. In an expanding market all may gain. Furthermore,
there is competition if an enterprise merely tries to hold its position.
According to the BGH, even such business conduct is at the expense
of others. In our opinion, the same would be true if the enterprise
for some reason decides to tolerate an annual loss in its market
share of, e.g., 10 percent.

The concept of competition does not require any particular
degree of intensity, nor any intensity at all, nor does it require
actual existence. There is "competition" even if it is merely latent
(potential competition).

[35b] OffJour No. 170, September 29, 1966, p. 3015; CMR ¶ 8046.

[36] Accord: OffJour 1964, p. 2545; con-tra: Deringer/Tessin, AWD 1964, p. 332. See also Rittner, MA 1965, p. 97; Ewald, MA 1965, p. 113.

[37] Decision of February 5, 1968, ("Fensterglas") WuW/E BGH 907; accord: Fikentscher, WuW 1961, p. 788; Brugger, WuW 1959, p. 467; Meyer-Cording, WuW 1962, p. 461; Picker, WuW/E BGH 929 (annota-tion to the BGH decision); contra:

Kirschstein, WRP 1968, p. 211; Knöpfle, NJW 1968, p. 1037; Knöpfle, Der Rechtsbegriff 'Wettbewerb' und die Realität des Wirtschaftslebens, 1966, p. 222; Deringer, EWG-Wettbewerbs-recht, Art. 85 (1), note 27; cf. also Scheufele, Über den sogenannten rele-vanten Markt (On the So-Called Rele-vant Market), AWD May 1969, p. 169, and the authors cited there.

[37a] Decision of May 4, 1962, WuW/E OLG 469, BB 1962, p. 859.

The European High Court in its *Grundig-Consten* decision does not clearly state whether the restraint must affect competition between a) parties to an agreement, b) such parties and third parties, c) one of them and third parties, or whether d) simply a restraint of the third parties' freedom of activity is enough. It may, however, be inferred from the opinion that the last alternative, i.e., the broadest construction, would suffice.

The High Court found the first type of restraint in Grundig's obligation not to supply, directly or indirectly, third parties with goods intended for the protected territory, France. This is merely a restraint of one party, namely Grundig. But the High Court continued: "The restrictive effect of this obligation is patently evident from the fact that not only was the Plaintiff Consten prohibited from exporting, but all other exclusive distributors of the Plaintiff Grundig as well." A weakness in this argument is that the Court did not determine that Grundig was obligated to impose such a restriction on the others and that it did so by reason of such obligation. It appears from the facts of the case that this restraint was imposed on other dealers years before the conclusion of the agreement between Grundig and Consten.

Nevertheless, the above criticism merely applies to the facts forming the basis for the decision; the High Court professed to deal with the case on the basis of the legal restrictions imposed, a theme from which it soon departed. For the Court, it was enough that third parties were, in fact, restricted in their freedom of action, not that they were limited by a legal obligation. This is evident from the remainder of the Court's opinion: The registration of the GINT trademark in France for Consten, naturally with the approval of Grundig, was intended to strengthen the protection of the exclusive distributor against parallel imports by the additional weapon of a trademark right. "In this manner, no third party could import Grundig products from other member states into France without encountering grave risks," i.e., a claim of infringement from Consten. The Court perceived this arrangement as an isolation of the French market. Thus, in the Court's opinion, competition was restrained not because the ability of Grundig or Consten or even only third parties to compete was restrained by an agreement, but because in fact third parties were excluded from the French market.[38]

---

[38] The Court's language at this point is obscure: the fact that Grundig prohibited its dealers from exporting to France does not necessarily mean that Grundig was under an obligation to do so; a contrary conclusion is not compelled either by logic or by actual business practice. For more on this case, see ¶ 16, infra.

¶ 15   Competition need not necessarily be in price, quantity and
        quality, but may concern terms, discounts, service, advertising,[38a]
etc. Restraints on one of these *media of competition* may therefore
come within Article 85 (1), even if competition continues to exist
in other respects,[39] since this provision (unlike Article 65, § 1, of the
Coal and Steel Treaty) does not cover merely restraints on "normal"
competition or on competition customary in the particular industry.

¶ 16   Article 85 (1) reaches not only *horizontal* restraints on com-
        petition between competitors, but also *vertical* ones,[40] e.g., re-
straints imposed by a supplier upon his customers; exact delimitations
of terms are therefore not necessary, and, in the last analysis, are also
very difficult to formulate.

This is the view also of the Court of Justice of the European
Communities in Luxembourg in its decision of April 6, 1962,[41] which
concerned a vertical restraint on competition. Thus, vertical prohibitions against export (involved in that case), exclusive dealing contracts, exclusive distributorship arrangements, etc., are not exempt
in principle from the prohibition of Article 85 (1). Boycott agreements, too, come within this prohibition if they are apt to affect interstate trade adversely, regardless of whether the participants are on
the same market level or not.

The opinion that the prohibition of Article 85 (1) also covers
single and individual agreements, particularly vertical ones, met with
opposition from some legal writers. Support for their position was
seen in, *inter alia,* the legislative history of Articles 85 ff., the language
of Article 85 (1), and the relation of this provision to Article 86.
The European Court in its *Grundig* decision of July 13, 1966,[41a]
declined to adopt the Italian government's contention that vertical
or single agreements did not fall under the prohibition of Article
85 (1). The Court rejected the Italian government's petition against
the Commission and Council of Ministers to have Articles 1 ff. of

[38a] For an example of joint advertising, see ¶ 321N, infra.
[39] So held under § 1 GWB in a decision
of the BGH of October 26, 1961, NJW
1962, p. 247 ff. (also BB 1962, p. 7 ff.),
in a case involving restraint on advertising; with annotation by Gleiss/Hootz,
NJW 1962, p. 391 ff.; compare also
BKartA Annual Report 1961, p. 62.
Accord: van Damme, cah. dr. eur.
1966, p. 300.
[40] Compare the survey of earlier court
decisions, practice of the BKartA and
literature, by Sölter, WuW 1961, p. 670
ff., and by Schlieder, BB 1962, p. 307
footnote 10.
[41] BB 1962, p. 467 ff., as also AWD
1962, p. 108 ff.; see the discussion of this
decision herein under Article 1 of Regulation 17, ¶ 301 ff. The full text of this
decision in the matter of *de Geus v.
Bosch,* Case No. 13/61, together with
Conclusions of the Advocate General and
Report of Hearing by the Reporting
Judge, may be found in CMR ¶ 8003.
[41a] See ¶ 14, supra.

Regulation 19 declared void and to have Article 5 (2) of Regulation 17 as well as Regulation 153 declared inapplicable to the agreement in that case. Even before the *Grundig* decision, the Court indicated in the *Société Technique Minière v. Maschinenbau Ulm* case (Case No. 56/65, Recueil Vol. XII-4, p. 337; CMR ¶ 8047) that it would not accept the theory that exclusive distributorships were not "agreements between enterprises" within the meaning of Article 85 (1) because the parties to the contract were on different levels of distribution. In the *Grundig* decision the Court also held that Article 85 (1) did not extend solely to horizontal agreements.[41b]

We regard the legislative history as inconclusive on this point. The language of this provision is susceptible of both interpretations. Furthermore, the comparison between Article 85 (1) and Article 86 does not support the view that single and individual contracts are not covered by Article 85 (1). The argument based on the illustrations is faulty: the examples in subparagraphs (a) and (b) of both articles are not in agreement with one another; subparagraph (c) of Article 85 (1) is completely lacking in Article 86. True, examples (d) and (e) in Article 85 (1) do correspond to those in subparagraph (c) and (d) in Article 86, but in our opinion it does not follow that Article 85 (1) does not at all cover single and individual agreements, especially vertical ones. On the contrary, the correspondence of these last two examples leads to the conclusion that Article 85 (1) does not prohibit discrimination in single contracts and individual tying transactions, but rather is aimed, first, at discrimination achieved by co-operation and, second, at agreements to insert tying clauses in contracts with third parties (compare also ¶ 66 and 71).

In any case, the Council of Ministers proceeded on the basis that Article 85 (1) also covers restraints on competition in individual contracts. This is evident, e.g., from Regulation 17 which, in Article 4 (2) (ii), exempts certain single and individual contracts from the notification requirements, thus presupposing that they could come within Article 85 (1) (compare also below, Article 4, Regulation 17). That the Commission shares this view is evidenced, e.g., by its "Official Notice Concerning Exclusive Representation Contracts with Commercial Agents."[42]

[41b] As to the legal aspects of these two basic decisions, see Gleiss/Hootz, comments on the Court's *Grundig-Consten* decision of July 13, 1966, AWD 1966, p. 307 ff., particularly p. 310-312; Gleiss, "Zwei bedeutsame Urteile des EuGH" (Two Important Decisions of the European Court), WRP 1967, p. 163, 176.

[42] December 24, 1962, OffJour 1962, p. 2921, Appendix No. 1, CMR ¶ 2697; followed in the Commission's *Grundig-Consten* decision, OffJour 1964, p. 2545; CMR ¶ 2743.

¶ 16

Whether the restrained enterprise is engaged in selling or in purchasing is not determinative; consequently, the view that Article 85 (1) does not cover those vertical agreements that restrain the parties in their capacities as purchasers is erroneous. The answer to the question "Which competition?" is, in our opinion, that between goods of different producers. It may be different in isolated circumstances, but not as generally and axiomatically different as the Court stated in its *Grundig* decision.

It is, in our opinion, axiomatic that competition between different products, or more precisely, between different producers, must not be restrained. This sort of competition would seem to be at least the starting point in any construction of Article 85 (1). However, the Commission and the High Court in the *Grundig-Consten* case took a different view. The Court stated that a restraint of competition in Grundig products sufficed. This holding is surprising and unconvincing; it is hoped that in the interest of predictability and development of a cogent Common Market cartel law, the High Court will have occasion to deal with and lend clarity to these basic questions and their answers.

The High Court's thesis that the isolation of the French market allowed prices for Grundig products to be set at levels that reflected a lack of competition is misconceived.

Just prior to the above statement, the Court held it completely unnecessary to determine the effects of the agreement under consideration on competition between like but different brand products. That is, even if similar or inferior quality radios, television sets, tape recorders and dictating machines of French, Dutch, or American manufacturers retailed at twice or ten times the price of comparable Grundig products, such circumstances need not be investigated or noticed by the Court since they are irrelevant. The essence of competition, however, is in the struggle between different producers and their goods, and on all levels of distribution. The notion that Consten could realize prices for Grundig products as it fancied is patently incorrect: no businessman can obtain prices at will simply because the goods are trademarked.

The above holding of the Court is also in conflict with its statements in the same opinion to the effect that all economic and legal circumstances are to be considered. It earlier had expressed the same view in the *Maschinenbau Ulm* case.

Hence, we deem it necessary that the High Court reconsider its narrow view that for Article 85 (1) a restraint on competition merely

¶ 16

between goods of one brand is sufficient without taking into consideration like goods of other producers.[43]

Meanwhile, the European Court has pronounced that not every exclusive (sole) distribution agreement with absolute territorial protection contravenes Article 85 (1) of the EEC Treaty.[43a] Absolute territorial protection will not be a contravention if the parties have an insignificant share of the market. But the case the Court had to decide was a petty one, as the two enterprises together had a share of only 0.6 percent in the Common Market. Therefore, it remains to be seen whether this decision will gain greater significance in the future.[43b]

¶ 17   By no means all forms of cooperation between enterprises lead to restriction or distortion of competition. This view is shared by the Commission of the European Communities, pronounced in its "Notice concerning agreements, decisions and concerted practices in cooperation between enterprises," the so-called "Cooperation Primer" or "Spelling Book."[43c] According to this Notice the following agreements are not to be considered as restricting competition:

(1) those having as their sole object:

(a) Exchange of opinions and experience,

(b) Joint market research,

(c) Joint comparative studies of enterprises and/or industries,

(d) Joint statistics and calculation models;

(2) furthermore:

(a) Cooperation in accounting,

(b) Joint securing of credits,

(c) Joint debt-collecting,

(d) Joint business or tax collecting agencies;

(3) furthermore:

(a) Joint research and development,

---

[43] I.e., for the four groupings of Grundig products, in all their types and variations, none of which are differentiated in the decision.

[43a] "Konstant" case. Decision of July 9, 1969, Recueil Vol. XV, 1969-4, pp. 296 ff.; CMR ¶ 8074.

[43b] Cf. the Commission's "Notice... Relating to Agreements, Decisions, and Concerted Practices of Minor Importance Not Coming within Article 85 (1) of the EEC Treaty," ¶ 17, infra.

[43c] OffJour No. C 75, July 29, 1968, page 3; CMR ¶ 9248. On this notice, cf. Hootz, WRP 1968, p. 383; Benisch, WuW 1969, p. 1; Spormann, AWD 1968, p. 285.

(b) Joint placing of research and development orders,

(c) Sharing out of research and development projects among the participants;

(4) furthermore:

Joint use of production, storing and transport facilities;

(5) furthermore:

Working partnerships for the common execution of orders where the participants do not compete with each other in the work to be done or where each by himself is unable to execute the orders;

(6) furthermore:

(a) Joint selling arrangements,

(b) Joint after-sale and repair services if the participants do not compete in the respective products or services;

(7) furthermore:

Joint advertising;[43d]

(8) finally:

Use of a common label to designate a certain quality, if the label is available to all competitors under the same conditions.[43e]

None of these agreements is considered to restrain the participating enterprises in their freedom to compete. The exclusion of "joint selling arrangements" in (6) (a) of the Notice seems at first glance to go surprisingly far. The negative clearance in the French Machine-Tool Manufacturers case (¶ 321C, infra) seems to be a good example of what is meant: a sort of joint sale by non-competitors. Compare, however, the Commission's other decisions dealt with at ¶ 321E, 321F, 321M, 321Q, infra.

In its "Notice of May 27, 1970, Relating to Agreements, Decisions, and Concerted Practices of Minor Importance Not Coming within Article 85, Paragraph 1, of the Treaty Establishing the European Economic Community,"[43f] the Commission took a further step toward defining the field of application of Article 85 (1). In order to promote cooperation between small and medium-size enterprises, only agreements with "perceptible effects"[43g] on market conditions are deemed to come within the cartel prohibition, "i.e. agreements through which the market position of third parties (enterprises) and consumers, that is, their sales potential and sources of supply, is perceptibly altered. . . . The Commission believes that agreements

---

[43d] For an example, see ¶ 321N, infra.

[43e] For an example of a joint trademark used as a joint quality mark, see ¶ 321L, infra.

[43f] OffJour No. C 64 (June 2, 1970), p. 1; CMR ¶ 9367; on further measures taken by the Commission to facilitate cooperation, see below ¶ 360.

[43g] The German word "spürbar" may also be translated by "noticeable." The Commission has already used the term in the Grosfillex case; cf. ¶ 22 below.

between enterprises engaged in the manufacture or distribution of goods do not come within the prohibition of Article 85, paragraph 1, of the EEC Treaty:

—Where the products involved, in the part of the Common Market covered by the agreement, account for no more than five percent of the turnover in the same products or products considered to be similar by consumers on the basis of their properties, usage or price, and

—Where the total annual turnover of the enterprises that are parties to the agreement does not exceed 15 million units of account[43h] or, for agreements between enterprises engaged in trade (distribution, as opposed to manufacture), 20 million units of account."

The share of the market and the turnover may even in two consecutive fiscal years be exceeded by up to 10 percent.

There may be a restraint of trade only if the freedom to compete is restrained beyond these limits, expressly or by means of concerted practices. The notice of May 27, 1970 can be deemed to be a "general negative clearance," which does not, however, exclude the right to apply in doubtful cases for individual clearances according to Article 2 of Regulation 17.[43i]

Thus, the Commission is inclined to consider it a restraint of competition if certain recommendations or conclusions are pronounced in such a way that they lead to uniform conduct in the market of at least some of the participants. With regard to price information arrangements, the Commission believes that it is particularly difficult to differentiate between neutral information and behavior restraining trade. Especially in an oligopolistic market with homogeneous goods, exchange of information might restrain competition.

We do not think this belief to be legally correct. The information is intended to enable the enterprises to draw correct conclusions for their market conduct. If they, on account of the information, all arrive at the same results and, in consequence, behave uniformly, this is not yet a case of Article 85(1). Such case would be involved only if the participants had concerted their conduct. Thus, we consider mere exchange of information to be unobjectionable. If, however, the participating enterprises agree on a common behavior or arrange their behavior expressly or tacitly, a restraint of competition may or will be present.

This also holds true for the other agreements mentioned by the Commission.

[43h] I.e., U. S. dollars.
[43i] Benisch, DB 1970, p. 1363 f.

With regard to joint research, the extent to which the participants may agree to divide tasks and evaluate results is particularly interesting. Here, the Commission speaks extremely cautiously.

The participants are perfectly free to divide tasks and activities provided only that they grant each other access to the results. Restraint of competition may, however, occur if the results are not made known to all of them, if the enterprises are restrained in exploiting the results, if they are, outside the joint proceeding, restrained in their own research or development, if they agree or concert exclusively to manufacture goods or types of goods jointly developed or to divide production between themselves, or, possibly, also if they are precluded from granting licenses to third parties. On the other hand, the participants may agree to exploit the results according to the extent of their participation. If, for example, an enterprise makes only a modest financial contribution, competition is not restrained if this enterprise is confined to a corresponding share of the results.

Finally, we think it permissible to stipulate that the exploitation of the results arrived at jointly must be decided upon by all the participants or by each participant for a specific product or in a certain area only,[43j] provided the results of the research are the joint property of all the participants, since joint owners may decide when, by whom and how their results are to be used.

By a *most-favored-client clause* a supplier obligates himself to grant the entitled person the lowest price which he concedes to any customer. This agreement merely relates to the price the entitled person has to pay; it does not legally restrict the supplier in his relations with third partners and is therefore not a restraint of competition : The entitled person does not intend to prevent the supplier from offering better prices to others. But competition will be restricted if the supplier is obligated not to grant others better prices or conditions.

¶ 17A   The principle of cartel prohibition is considerably restricted by the term *perceptible* read into Article 85 (1) by the Commission and the European Court. Restriction of the parties' freedom to purchase and demand is not a perceptible restraint, but restriction of third parties' right to supply and sell is.[43k] No final definition can be drawn from decisions so far[43l] (cf. *Grundig/Consten* and *Konstant* decisions, ¶ 14, 16, 22, 25; Commission's negative clearances, ¶ 321D, 321G, 321H, 321L).

¶ 18   Moreover, restriction or distortion does not exist where there is no competition. Article 85 (1) cannot, therefore, be applied

---

[43j] Deringer/Tessin, DB 1964, p. 870, are more critical.
[43k] 8th General Report of Commission No. 67.

[43l] Cf. Spormann, WuW 1970, p. 459 with further references.

to horizontal agreements between enterprises which cannot possibly enter into competition with each other;[44] it can, however, be applied where competition between them, while not actually existing at the moment, might spring up at any time (potential competition) and where this potential competition is being restricted (see ¶ 14, supra). The delimitation is difficult in the individual case.[44a]

¶ 19   Restriction or distortion within the meaning of Article 85 (1) furthermore does not exist where what is being restrained is *competition not deserving of protection.* Which kinds of competition are, and which are not, deserving of protection may, just as under the German GWB, be doubtful in the particular case. Unfair and, more generally, any kind of unlawful competition is certainly not deserving of protection.[45] In its "Official Notice Concerning Patent Licensing Agreements" of December 24, 1962,[46] one of the two so-called Christmas Messages, the Commission recognized the view that the restraint of competition not deserving protection does not come within Article 85 (1), and at the same time deemed lawful only certain tie-in restrictions regarding the quality of the product or supply requirements imposed on a patent licensee. The proposition that undeserving competition should not be protected by Article 85 (1) has, nevertheless, general validity.[47] Under this view it can, for instance, be lawful for a purchaser of an enterprise to forbid the seller to compete with him.[48] Similarly, it may in narrow limits, e.g. for a transitional period of five years, be lawful if in the case of an enterprise being split and partly sold, the purchaser agrees not to compete with the seller in the market left to him.

¶ 20   *Consolidation* of enterprises, even if they are competitors, is not a restriction, etc., of competition within the meaning of Article 85 (1). This provision is not directed against mergers and similar concentrations. It would be theoretically possible to extend Article 85 (1) to cover consolidations, e.g., a merger agreement between two enterprises, as in the United States where mergers in some instances may also violate the restraint of trade prohibition in Section 1 of the

---

[44] Accord: The Commission's negative clearance granted Machines-Outils, July 17, 1968 (¶ 321 C, infra), and Christiani & Nielsen, June 18, 1969 (¶ 321 J, infra).

[44a] See the examples given in footnote 44 and the negative clearance granted the Limeburners, May 5, 1969, ¶ 321 H, infra.

[45] It seems too general a statement, however, to say (as does Kleemann, p.

40) that vertical prohibitions of exports or re-imports designed to protect a vertical price-fixing or exclusive distributorship arrangement restrict merely competition not deserving of protection.

[46] OffJour 1962, p. 2922; CMR ¶ 2698.

[47] See Gleiss/Hootz, NJW 1963, p. 233.

[48] Compare in this regard the negative clearance in Nicholas/Vitapro, OffJour 1964, p. 2287.

Sherman Act.[49] However, a provision against consolidations such as in Article 66 of the European Coal and Steel Treaty is omitted in the Rome Treaty, presumably intentionally. This means, in our opinion, that Article 85 (1) does not apply to consolidations of enterprises and thus not to the underlying agreements.[49a] This does not mean that such agreements might not contain prohibited restraints on competition. Application of Article 85 (1) to consolidations would, in addition, lead to insoluble complications; since Article 85 (2) provides that prohibited agreements shall be void, one would have to employ, e.g., the presumption of the existence, not in law but in fact, of the enterprises that were merged.

¶ 21   It is not yet clear whether Article 85 (1) is to be applied to agreements between enterprises which belong to the *same concern* (for definition, see ¶ 1, supra).[49b]

The BKartA[50] takes a rather extreme position. In its view, competition protected by Article 85 (1) between enterprises of the same concern ceases to exist only where the concern's management or the dominant enterprise actually prescribes certain conduct *in an obligatory manner,* i.e., makes use of the right to issue directions. Consequently, the BKartA infers from contracts between enterprises of the same concern that they are not deprived of their own life by the head of the concern and that, on the contrary, there exists between them competition protected by Article 85 (1).

This view, in our opinion, is erroneous: *Legally* binding directions (apparently intended by the BKartA) to the management of a corporation exist in German law only if a contract of domination pursuant to § 291 AktG is concluded between the dominant enterprise and the dependent corporation, or if the dependent corporation, maintaining its legal personality, is integrated into another corporation (having its domicile within the country) pursuant to § 319 AktG.

[49] E.g., the *Lexington Bank* case, CCH 1964 Trade Cases, ¶ 71,072; see also, Markert, AWD 1964, p. 186.

[49a] Accord: v. d. Groeben, Die Wettbewerbspolitik als Teil der Wirtschaftspolitik im Gemeinsamen Markt (The Policy of Competition as Part of the Economic Policy in the Common Market), Speech in the European Parliament in Strasbourg on June 16, 1965, published as separate print by the Commission, p. 20; cf. also Fikentscher, DB 1966, p. 689. The Commission stated its view in: Das Problem der Unternehmenskonzentration im Gemeinsamen Markt (The Problem of the Concentration of Enterprises in the Common

Market), ed. by the European Communities, series "competition," Vol. 3, 1966, see ¶ 207, infra.

[49b] Mainly on German law: Mulert, Die Wettbewerbsbeschränkung zwischen verbundenen Unternehmen, 1970.

[50] In BKartA Annual Report 1961, p. 61. Similarly, as to the GWB: Fikentscher, Festschrift für Alfred Hueck, 1959, p. 543 ff., esp. 548, and in the annotation to the decision of the BGH of October 26, 1959 (WuW/E BGH 359, also BB 1959, p. 1274 f.), WuW/E BGH 365; Würdinger, WuW 1956, p. 775 ff., esp. 782; Zeitler, WuW 1959, p. 621 ff., esp. 627, 635.

According to § 18, paragraph 1, third sentence AktG[50a] it is, however, presumed that dependent enterprises form a concern with the dominant company within the meaning of § 17, paragraph 1 AktG. In the case of this form of concern there are no legally binding directions (see § 76, paragraph 1, and § 111, paragraph 4, first sentence AktG). It is only the management that decides whether and, if so, which managerial measures are to be taken. To be sure, the board of supervisors (Aufsichtsrat) may prevent a particular measure by refusing to consent to it (to the extent to which the bylaws furnish a basis for this— see § 111, paragraph 4, second sentence, of the AktG), but may not prescribe affirmatively that the management is to take a certain measure, and thus may not give it "directions" in a legally binding manner. Nor may the general meeting or the stockholders do so.[51] The thesis of the BKartA therefore does not fit the situation where the dependent enterprises are corporations that are not connected with the dominant enterprise either by contract of domination or by integration. Whether a restraint on competition falls under Article 85 (1) or not depends in no case upon the legal form of the enterprises involved;[52] the BKartA, however, in postulating legally binding directions, will have to distinguish between the "normal" corporation and other forms of organization.[53]

If the BKartA, by the words ". . . actually prescribes certain conduct in an obligatory manner," refers to the binding effect of the directions *in fact* rather than in law, then everything depends on the circumstances of the particular case and in the final analysis on the question of how tight the union through the concern is. But even in the case of a tightly-knit union, the management of the concern "governs" in practice not only by directions. At any rate, no strict tests are to be employed in the application of this view; one ought in that case to regard as factually binding such directions as may be implemented (only) by discharge of the management of the dependent enterprise, for it is only in this way that factually binding directions to the management of a corporation are possible. The BKartA still, in our opinion incorrectly, attempts to solve the problem of restrictive contracts within a concern by the test of whether the directions have actually been issued or not.

[50a] For the text see ¶ 1, supra.

[51] Compare Würdinger, Aktien-und Konzernrecht (Law of Corporations and Concerns), 2nd edition, 1966, p. 120 ff.; Baumbach/Hueck, Kommentar zum Aktiengesetz (Commentary on Law of Corporations), 13th edition, 1968, § 111, marginal note 9.

[52] Accord: BKartA in its definition of "enterprise": ". . . irrespective of the legal form . . .," Annual Report 1961, p. 61.

[53] The thesis of the BKartA involving "*prima facie* evidence" is untenable. Contractual form may be necessary or desirable for a variety of reasons, e.g., on account of tax or foreign exchange laws, personal considerations, etc.

Finally, the presumption that the BKartA attaches to the mere conclusion of a contract within a concern is untenable; the use of a contract may be desirable or necessary for a variety of reasons, e.g., for tax, tariff, foreign exchange regulation, personal, etc., purposes.

In our opinion, the following analysis is determinative:

The aim of Articles 85 ff. of the EEC Treaty, as evident from its Article 3, paragraph f, is the protection of commercial intercourse between the member states against restraints on competition.[54] Where there is a genuine concern relationship, Article 85 (1) is not applicable to agreements between enterprises of the same concern, for the reason that economically they constitute a single unit and have no life of their own. Even if there exists in fact a certain degree of competition among them, this is not based upon their free determination as entrepreneurs, but depends upon the will of the concern's management, which may restrict or suppress this competition whenever it wishes to do so. In practice there are cases where a concern's management artificially stimulates competition between concern enterprises, or at least attempts to keep it alive. For instance, in case of a secret purchase of an interest in an enterprise, the personnel of the enterprises may not be informed that the firms belong to the same concern. This competition is merely a method of operation of the concern and not the kind of competition protected by Article 85 (1). Therefore, there can be no restraint on competition within the meaning of Article 85 (1) between enterprises of the same concern, whether by contract or in any other manner.[55] Of course, one will have to examine in each particular case whether a genuine concern relationship exists.

The Commission, on June 18, 1969, issued an important decision with regard to intra-concern restraints in the *Christiani & Nielsen* and *Kodak* cases (for a detailed discussion, see ¶ 321 J and P, infra).

---

[54] Accord: BKartA in its Annual Report 1961, p. 62.

[55] Accord: Kleemann, pp. 29, 39. This view also represents the majority opinion among legal writers; cf. also Rasch, Deutsches Konzernrecht, 4th ed., 1968, p. 357. It should be noted, however, that these views rest in part upon § 23 of the GWB and that a similar provision is missing in the EEC law. In the two cases Scott Paper-Continental and Scott Paper-Burgo Scott, the Commission announced its intention to decide favorably with regard to the restraints in licensing contracts between parent and subsidiary. Scott Paper, in the first case, holds a 100% interest in its subsidiary and, in the second case, holds a 50% interest. For details see ¶ 465A, infra, under Article 19 (3) of Regulation 17.

See also the Commission's (unpublished) letter (according to the Press Release issued by the Commission June 11, 1969), in the Sperry Rand-Remington (Italy) case, ¶ 48A, infra.

¶ 21

It should be remembered that under the Coal and Steel Treaty, also, the problem of restraint on competition by agreements within a concern had not been fully clarified.[56] Judging from prior holdings of the European Court in cases under the European Coal and Steel Treaty, it is quite possible that the Court will afford the same treatment to restrictive agreements between enterprises of the same concern as it does to those between economically independent enterprises. This result is indicated by the reasoning of the Court in a case (*Schrottausgleichskasse*)[57] with extraordinary facts: since the parties to the consolidation had intentionally chosen the particular legal form (legally separate companies forming a concern) most advantageous to them, they were not in a position to petition successfully for the disregard of this form when it resulted in disadvantages. This pronouncement could well be an adaptation from American antitrust decisions.

Under the antitrust laws of the United States, agreements between enterprises of the same concern are treated in principle just like those between economically independent enterprises. The doctrine of "intra-enterprise conspiracy" is one of wide scope and applies to all types of dependent or affiliated relations between legally independent units regardless of the closeness of economic ties—logically even to the relation between parent and wholly-owned subsidiary. Here, American antitrust law seems to aim its thrust at legal form rather than, as it does more normally, at economic substance, although the courts purport even in this connection to be concerned with substance.[58]

VI.   Have as Their Purpose or Effect

¶ 22   It is necessary only that the enterprises involved *effect* the restraint on competition; intent is not required. The restraint on competition need not be contained in the agreement.[59] Whether

---

[56] Compare, e.g., Krawielicki, Monopolverbot, pp. 11, 12. The European Court of Justice, in Cases Nos. 32 and 33/58—Recueil Vol. V, p. 275—did not regard the fact that two enterprises belonged to the same concern as sufficient, but this was a special case (payments into the scrap equalization fund). The Court meanwhile decided likewise in the (connected) Cases Nos. 42 and 49/59, decision of March 22, 1961, Recueil Vol. VII, p. 101.

[57] Scrap equalization fund, decision of March 22, 1961; see footnote 56.

[58] See, e.g., *United States v. Yellow Cab Co.*, 332 U.S. 218, 227 (1947); *Kiefer-Stewart Co. v. Seagram & Sons,* *Inc.*, 340 U.S. 211, 215 (1951). See also Sprunk, "Intra-Enterprise Conspiracy," ABA Antitrust Section Reports, vol. IX, p. 20 (1956); Graham, "Antitrust Problems of Corporate Parents, Subsidiaries, Affiliates and Joint Venturers in Foreign Commerce," *ibid.* p. 32; Kathleen Devine, "Foreign Establishment and the Antitrust Law: A Study of the Antitrust Consequences of the Principal Forms of Investment by American Corporations in Foreign Markets," 57 Northwestern University Law Review 400, 420 ff. (1962); also the survey by P. Ulmer in WuW 1960, p. 163 ff.

[59] Contra: Kleemann, p. 44. Compare the "content theory," ¶ 14, supra.

a restraint on competition which is actually accomplished is not to be attributed to the participating enterprises where—and only where —it has materialized "contrary to all probability and in contradiction to the experiences of daily life,"[60] may be seriously questioned.[61] According to the wording of the law, it suffices as well that the restraint on competition is only intended, although not effected.[62] The two prerequisites of Article 85 (1) are apparently alternatives, i.e., equivalent (but see below). It is not necessary that the parties expressly state this purpose in the contract or decision; it suffices that it is evident from the circumstances. Furthermore, according to the law it is not necessary that a restraint on competition be the only purpose; Article 85 (1) also covers the situation where in addition to the restraint on competition, other aims, as is often the case, are pursued (e.g., uniform standards and types).[63] In concerted practices, the purpose, i.e., the "concert" or "plan," is the primary element, the actual conduct, i.e., the "practice," being only secondary (see ¶ 10 ff., supra).

Radical conclusions from the literal text could lead to absurd results (see footnote 62). In practice, therefore, the literal interpretation will have to be limited in certain respects, at least where restraint on competition, while intended, is not accomplished. For the economic intercourse between the EEC countries protected by Article 85 (1), a restraint on competition which is merely intended, but not realized, is without significance. To prohibit this kind of behavior as well, would be a sanction against mere anti-competitive attitudes, which is not the task of Article 85 (1). Certainly in most cases of the intended, but not effected, restraint, the requisite aptness to affect adversely interstate trade will be lacking. This prerequisite is a corrective factor, but the result serves only to emphasize that the intended, but not realized, restraint on competition is of no significance for the law. Thus, it would be erroneous to conclude simply from the language of Article 85 (1) that the intended restraint on the one hand, and the realized restraint on the other, are to be treated as having equal importance. On the contrary, in our opinion it follows from the wording of Article 85 (1) that a realized restraint on competition does not need also to be intended by the parties to the contract.[64] This means that purpose as a separate prerequisite has no significance in practice. The High Court does not share this view as is evident

---

[60] This is the formula regarding causality found in BKartA Annual Report, 1961, p. 61.

[61] For the negative see also Kleemann, p. 45, who, differently from the BKartA, demands probability that the restraint of competition will materialize, in our opinion rightly so.

[62] Wohlfarth/Everling/Glaesner/Sprung, Article 85, note 5, and Kleemann, p. 44, would not apply Article 85 to a wholly vain attempt, and in our opinion rightly so.

[63] BKartA Annual Report, 1961, p. 61.

[64] See Gleiss/Hirsch, NJW 1964, p. 1605.

from the following misconceived statement in its *Grundig* decision:[64a]
"On the other hand, the actual effects of an agreement need not be
taken into consideration when applying Article 85 (1) if it is evident
that it aims at a prevention, restriction or distortion of competition."[65]

The prerequisites of Article 85 (1) are not met by a contract, etc.,
effecting a restraint on competition only theoretically or remotely.[65a]
On the contrary, according to the "negative" clearance issued by the
Commission in *Grosfillex-Fillistorf*, the restraint must have a *noticeable*
or *perceptible* (as the French wording of the Commission's decisions
now has it) effect.[66] According to the Commission's reasoning in this
negative clearance, there is no restraint on competition where the
parties to the agreement, manufacturer and dealer, are competing with a
considerable number of enterprises, i.e., are in keen competition. In
our opinion, the reasoning of the Commission is not confined to the
facts of *Grosfillex-Fillistorf,* but has general application. The European
Court's decision of June 30, 1966, in the *Maschinenbau Ulm* case (see
¶ 16, supra) follows similar reasoning; in its *Grundig* decision of July 13,
1966, however, the same Court lets intrabrand competition suffice,
in our opinion again motivated by the extreme nature of the case.
Concerning noticeable effects of a restraint of interstate trade, see
¶ 14 and 17, supra and 25, infra.

The competitive restraint must take effect *within the Common
Market.* If this is the case, it makes no difference whether it was
caused within or outside of that Market. Thus, even restraints in an
agreement between an American and a Swedish enterprise may fall
under Article 85 (1) if the agreement has repercussions on trade
between member states. On the other hand, restraints lacking such
effects are not reached by Article 85 (1) even if they originate within
the Common Market. (Compare also ¶ 29 f., infra.)

The parties cannot circumvent the prohibition of restraints on
competition in Article 85 (1) by stipulating that some foreign law,
e.g., Swiss, shall govern their agreement. Articles 85 ff. are obligatory
public law provisions, the application of which cannot be avoided by

---

[64a] See ¶ 14, supra.

[65] Compare Gleiss, WRP 67, 163-76.
But cf. the negative clearance granted
to Rieckermann/AEG-Elotherm, ¶ 321 G,
infra.

[65a] The European Court seemingly held,
particularly in the *Grundig* case that
mere purpose suffices; but this actually was an obiter dictum because in
that case the Court considered factual
effects to be present. In this connection
it is, by comparison, of interest that the

Swiss Cartel Act of December 20, 1964
(Article 2), contains the prerequisite that
a contract, etc., influence the market or
be apt to do so.

[66] Decision of March 11, 1964, Off-
Jour No. 58, April 9, 1964, p. 915. In
this case, a French manufacturer of
plastic household appliances had made
a Swiss firm his exclusive dealer, cf.
¶ 45, infra. For *perceptible*, see ¶ 321D,
infra.

¶ 22

a private agreement. Thus, for instance, a Swiss judgment validating
an agreement that violated Article 85 (1) could not be enforced inside the Common Market since it would be a breach of the *ordre public*.[66a]

VII. Apt to Affect Adversely

¶ 23   Article 85 (1) reaches only those agreements, decisions and
        concerted practices "which are apt to affect adversely trade
between member states . . ." The agreements, etc., in restraint of trade
must be causal, i.e., the reason for the hampering of trade between
member states. The High Court also presumes this, as is evident
from its *Grundig* decision. There it stated that interstate trade was
affected adversely since the agreement between Grundig and Consten
hindered other enterprises in importing into and exporting to France.
The contract and the adverse effect have a causal relation.[67] If the
enterprises involved *effect* a restraint on competition, the restraint is
logically the cause of the restriction. The same should be true where
the parties intend a restraint. If, contrary to our view, mere intent is
allowed to suffice, there will be no effect on competition to be determined and, thus, no causality. A kind of subjective causality would
have to do, and the criterion would become a matter of semantics.
Furthermore, the degree of an intended, but not effected, restraint is
not susceptible of precise measurement. Actual adverse effect thus is
unnecessary, *aptness being sufficient*. Aptness to have an adverse effect
exists, however, not only in the case of those agreements, etc., which
relate to trade between member states.[68] Nor is a relatively high
degree of probability required;[69] possibility, unless too remote, is
sufficient. Whether it exists must be judged according to the circumstances of each particular case.

¶ 24   It should be pointed out here that the difficulties inherent in
        the interpretation of the German term for "apt to" (geeignet),
and the terms used in the other three official languages of the EEC
Treaty, are compounded by the difficulties of translation into English.
Among terms variously used by translators, "likely to" denotes too
high a degree of probability, whereas "can" goes to the other extreme
by including almost any degree of possibility, and "may" would be
similarly broad and indefinite. "Liable to," which has also been used,
is ambiguous; in its more modern usage, it is interchangeable with

---

[66a] Accord: BGH, decision of February 27, 1968, BB 69, 692, *Fruchtsäfte*
(Fruit Juice) case.
    [67] Contra: Kirschstein, WuW 1966,
779.

[68] Contra: Spengler, WuW 1958, p. 78;
Kleemann, p. 38.
    [69] Contra: Frankfurter Kommentar, in-
troductory note TZ 11 to Article 85;
Kleemann, *ibid.*

"likely to," whereas its older meaning, equivalent to "apt to," is now obsolete. We therefore employ "apt to" as the relatively best translation.

The Dutch term for *"affect adversely"* (the German "beeinträchtigen") is "ongunstig . . . beinvloeden," the Italian, "pregiudicare," all versions which have the connotation of "injure." The French text, however, employs the neutral word "affecter." This difference in the terms chosen has led to doubts in the interpretation of this concept. The majority opinion has been (in our opinion rightly) that it should be understood as meaning to affect "unfavorably" or "adversely."[70]

Here, again, one faces a translation problem or, more accurately, the problem of which of the official versions to follow. Without attempting here to weigh various arguments in favor of one view or the other, we are including the "adversely" on the basis that three of the official texts so require, while the fourth leaves the matter open. Too much significance need not, however, be attributed to this matter as, for reasons presently to be discussed, there will be no radical differences in result, whichever view is adopted.

What is meant by unfavorably or adversely is left open. That question must be answered in the light of the spirit and object of Articles 85 ff. As indicated by Article 3, paragraph f, of the EEC Treaty, these provisions are to bring about an economic system free from distortions of competition; their purpose is to protect the commercial intercourse between the members of the EEC from restraints on competition. This protective aim is endangered, according to one theory, not only where trade between the member states (interstate trade) is diminished by a restraint on competition, but whenever a concerted restraint on competition deflects "the current of goods between the member states from its normal and natural course."[71] It is immaterial whether the concerted action in question leads or may lead to an artificial diminution or to an artificial increase in interstate trade.[72] An artificial increase of interstate trade results in an adverse effect

---

[70] In accord, e.g., Sölter, WuW 1961, p. 666 f.; Antoine Braun/Gleiss/Hirsch, p. 80 with more recent references; contra, e.g., Wohlfarth/Everling/Glaesner/Sprung, Article 85, note 4.

[71] Thus BKartA Annual Report 1961, p. 62. Note the close resemblance of this phraseology to American concepts of interstate commerce and restraints thereon: see, e.g., *Swift & Co. v. United States*, 196 U.S. 375, 399 (1905); *United States v. Socony-Vacuum Oil Co.*, 310 U. S. 150, 221-224 (1940). Less severe, the Court in the *Grundig* case, see be-

low; now also the Commission in its exemption granted to the Transocean Marine Paint Association on June 27, 1967, ¶ 119, infra.

[72] Accord: Baumbach/Hefermehl, Article 85, margin No. 13; Steindorff in Kartelle und Monopole, vol. I, p. 162 f.; Schlieder, BB 1962, pp. 305, 306; Advocate General Lagrange in his Conclusions in the *Bosch* case (see footnote 41, supra); similarly Spengler in Gemeinschaftskommentar, Appendix to § 101 No. 3 GWB, margin No. 10; see ¶ 26, infra.

¶ 24

thereon, e.g., when a quota cartel of Dutch producers fixes contractual penalties for goods which a member enterprise sells beyond its quota in the Dutch market, and grants bounties to those enterprises which do not exhaust their quotas for the domestic market. In this way the cartel "presses" more and cheaper goods, e.g., into the Federal Republic, than would otherwise go there (and, to illustrate, this will make sales in Germany more difficult not only for German but also, e.g., for French and Belgian producers). The total volume of trade between the six states may remain the same. However, the comparison to the deflection of a current from its natural course should not be carried too far. For instance, it is of no legal relevance for interstate trade, i.e., for the flow of commerce within the Common Market, if an English producer, acting under an agreement, ships his goods into the Common Market by way of Rotterdam or Hamburg instead of Antwerp, or if an American firm bases its subsidiary in Stuttgart instead of Paris. Adversely affecting covers, according to the High Court's *Grundig-Consten* decision, more than diversion of commerce from its natural course, a neutral circumstance as shown in the above example. The High Court requires an endangering of the goals of the Common Market. The Court's understanding of such danger is stated in the *Maschinenbau Ulm* decision: Whether a contract falls within the purview of Article 85 or not depends on whether it erects barriers to trade between member states, thus impeding desirable multilateral economic penetration.[73]

However, "adversely affecting" includes not only unfavorably influencing the *quantity* of goods or services in interstate trade, but comprises also unfavorably influencing such trade in a *qualitative* sense; e.g., poorer quality or higher price for goods or services brought or rendered from one country into the other.[74]

¶ 25   The literal text of Article 85 (1) does not differentiate between proximate and remote, nor between *direct* and *indirect*, effects of cooperative restraints upon interstate trade. Nevertheless, not every influence upon interstate trade constitutes an adverse effect thereon. Purely theoretical effects do not amount to an unfavorable influence; they leave interstate trade untouched. Nor will remote effects suffice. We deem it incorrect to hold that prohibitions from selling competing lines, tying agreements, and export prohibitions imposed upon a dealer by his supplier always affect adversely, or even

---

[73] For details, see ¶ 42, infra, footnote 6.
[74] Gleiss/Hirsch, AWD 1962, p. 123. Regarding ¶ 24, cf. Antoine Braun/

Gleiss/Hirsch, p. 82, where the DRU-Blondel exemption (OffJour No. 131, July 17, 1965, p. 2194) is quoted.

directly, interstate trade. Here again, whether there is a restraint depends upon the particular facts and circumstances of the case.

Only that kind of restraint on competition affects interstate trade adversely which influences it unfavorably to an appreciable and not merely negligible degree.[75] The High Court fails to mention this element in its *Grundig* decision.[76] This should not be taken to mean, however, that there need not be perceptible effects, since undoubtedly the Court merely took them for granted. On the other hand, it is not necessary that a substantial part of the volume of interstate trade be affected. Aptness to have an adverse effect need not be of such magnitude that not only the interests of individuals or classes of participants in the market are injured, but also the economic interests of at least one member state. This position would be too extreme. Nor is it necessary that regulation of the commercial intercourse between states be as such the object of the concerted restraint on competition.[77] Where there is an appreciable and unfavorable influence upon interstate trade, i.e., where there is adverse effect, it is immaterial whether this influence upon economic intercourse is direct or indirect;[78] such a test would be inconsistent with the purpose of the law.

There is a parallel here to the problems of aptness "to influence market conditions . . . through restraint on competition," in §1 of the GWB. The BGH, in its decision of June 7, 1962,[79] did not demand any particular minimum degree, but regarded as sufficient any effect upon the conduct of the participants in the market which is appreciable according to general economic experience (not, however, aptness imaginable merely in theory).

Applying this, e.g., to a purely domestic (intrastate) vertical price agreement,[80] this means that such an agreement restrains in a

---

[75] Accord: BKartA Annual Report 1961, p. 63; Advocate General Lagrange in the *Bosch* case (see footnote 41, supra); similarly, von Gamm, pp. 21, 22; undecided: BKartA in its Declaration of December 12, 1960, WuW/E BKartA 337, 338; Schlieder, BB 1962, p. 306; cf., most recently, Scheufele, AWD 1970, p. 385.

[76] See ¶ 14, supra; for the *Konstant* decision of July 9, 1969, see ¶ 16, footnote 43a, and for the Commission's Notice of May 27, 1970, see ¶ 17, footnote 43f.

[77] Contra: Spengler, WuW 1958, p. 78; Kleemann, p. 38.

[78] Accord: Antoine Braun/Gleiss/Hirsch, p. 84, with further references.

[79] BB 1962, p. 936 f. ("SPAR"). This involved an agreement dividing markets between the only two SPAR wholesalers in West Berlin. There are 400 food wholesalers doing business in that city. Unfortunately, the market share of the SPAR wholesalers and retailers is left open in the decision.

[80] In this connection, compare Gleiss/Hirsch, AWD 1962, p. 123.

¶ 25

direct sense only competition within the country in question. Indirectly, however, it may affect interstate trade also: If the price
fixer sets the resale price at a low level, competing products from the
other EEC states might then no longer enter in the same volume.
If the resale price is set high, there may possibly be an increase in
imports of competing products from the EEC area. Nonetheless, the
price agreement is not reached by Article 85 (1) because it cannot,
at least as a rule, influence interstate trade to an appreciable degree
and is, therefore, not apt to "affect it adversely."[81] The same applies
to similar restraints on intrastate competition, e.g., a price observance
agreement by a licensee. It would normally apply to a vertical price
agreement even where the price-fixing supplier and his price-bound
distributors are located in different EEC countries, although there is
the additional factor that the sales volume of the distributor, and
thus the volume of his orders from the country of the supplier,
naturally are influenced by, among other things, the level of the
fixed price.

¶ 26   Not every kind of concerted restraint on competition will in-
        fluence interstate trade merely unfavorably; on the contrary,
interstate trade will often be *promoted* at the same time. Article
85 (1) is, however, applicable even in that case, and its applicability
does not depend upon a balancing of unfavorable and favorable effects
(which would mean a kind of rule of reason). Rather, it is only under
Article 85 (3), i.e., in granting exemptions, that there may be an
examination of the question whether the concerted action involved will
also promote interstate trade and whether this will outweigh or at
least balance the adverse effects.[82]

VIII. Interstate

¶ 27   It has to be interstate trade that the restraint on competition
        is apt to affect adversely. This does not necessarily mean
trade among all of the member states; trade between any *two* EEC
members is sufficient.[83] Restraints on trade between Germany and
Luxembourg, for example, are also covered by Article 85 (1), despite

---

[81] Accord, e.g., Frankfurter Kommentar, introductory note TZ 12 to Article
85.

[82] Contra: Sölter, WuW 1961, p. 669
f., who regards the "net balance" as decisive; in accord with our view: BKartA
Annual Report 1961, p. 62; Kleemann,
pp. 36, 37; see also footnote 72, supra.

[83] Accord: Spengler in Gemeinschaftskommentar, Appendix to § 101 No. 3
GWB, margin No. 10, although he premises a Treaty text which contains an
error in this regard ("between *the* member states")—an error (interpolation of
the article) which is frequently made in
English translation also. On the interstate clause in general, see Teichmann,
WuW 1969, p. 671.

the fact that Luxembourg's population comprises only .5% of the Common Market's and its trade with other states constitutes only a negligible part of the total volume of interstate trade within the Common Market. Likewise, the trade between Luxembourg and Italy comes within Article 85 (1), even though it may be trifling for Italy. Nevertheless, this trade may be significant for Luxembourg and Luxembourg is a full member of the Community. Since, however, the relevant goods or services are always determinative, it is possible in a given case that the restraint on competition is not apt to affect adversely the particular interstate trade to a noticeable degree.

The prerequisite of aptness to affect adversely trade between member states is by some authors understood merely to be a jurisdictional rule;[83a] if the prerequisite is fulfilled, then the Commission would have exclusive jurisdiction (disregarding Article 9 (3) of Regulation 17). In our opinion, this view is erroneous. The jurisdiction of the Commission is derived not from the prerequisite in Article 85 (1), but rather from Article 89. If the Commission had jurisdiction solely over contracts, etc., that are apt to affect adversely interstate trade, then it could not issue a negative clearance in cases where this prerequisite was not met (e.g., the clearances for Grosfillex and DECA, see below Article 2, Regulation 17, footnote 27), since the power to issue a clearance presupposes jurisdiction over the matter. In such cases the Commission would have to reject the application for negative clearance because of lack of jurisdiction, an absurd result. The High Court has not so concluded on the basis of the above theory. In the *Maschinenbau Ulm* case it avoided the issue and in the *Grundig* case it stated: "The concept of agreements apt to affect adversely trade between member states," serves to distinguish the respective scopes of the cartel laws of the Community and of the member states. But this formulation contains only a pertinent description of the area of protection, not an approval of the above competence theory. The next sentence of the Court confirms our view: only insofar as an agreement may affect adversely trade between member states, is such restraint subject to the Community's prohibition in Article 85. The Court is stating, in essence, nothing novel in this regard, but is merely reiterating that the above is another requirement, like "contract" or "enterprise," which must be met before the law may be applied.

Previously it was considered incorrect to conclude from the prerequisite "interstate" that only EEC law could be applied to the

---

[83a] Schumacher, AWD, November 30, 1965, p. 405; Kirschstein, WRP 1965, p. 80.

¶ 27

exclusion of national cartel law. But now the Court in the *Tar-Colors* decision of February 13, 1969, has decided that Community law prevails. Still EEC cartel law, because of its different scope of protection, will not, however, always take precedence over the national laws (for details, see the Introduction).

¶ 28   The criterion "interstate" does not mean that *intrastate* cartels could not also come within this provision.[84] Rather, it depends only upon the question whether and to what extent the action of the participants is apt adversely to affect trade between member states of the EEC. Included here are, e.g., export or import cartels of German enterprises which concern export or import of goods from or into other member states of the EEC.[85] As a further example, a domestic cartel for discounts and terms may artificially make importation from other EEC countries more difficult.[86] Thus, a discount cartel based on total volume, which covers the territory of a member country and which does not include supplies from other EEC states, may, in some instances, violate Article 85 (1),[87] depending upon the circumstances of the case. At present, the Commission is considering whether or not a total volume cartel (Gesamtumsatzkartell) permitted in one member state violates Article 85 (1) even if it takes into account every import from outside of the country. This seems to go too far because, as a rule, interstate trade will not be affected.

¶ 29   According to the wording of Article 85 (1) it suffices also that only the party bound to the restraint is located in one of the six EEC countries whereas the party entitled to the benefit of the contract is *situated outside of the Common Market,* e.g., in England or one of the Scandinavian countries. In an even more far-reaching manner, the literal text reaches agreements, none of the parties to which is located in an EEC country. The prerequisite in both of these cases is only that the agreement is apt adversely to affect trade between member states of the EEC.[88] (Compare also ¶ 22, supra.) In principle, the legislative jurisdiction thus exerted over otherwise extraterritorial states of fact, on the basis of intraterritorial consequences, is in accord with antitrust jurisprudence in the United

---

[84] Contra: Deringer, WuW 1962, p. 82; not clear: Kleemann, pp. 34, 40.

[85] Koch, BB 1959, p. 243; Baumbach/Hefermehl, Article 85, margin No. 13.

[86] Accord: Koch, BB 1959, p. 244; Baumbach/Hefermehl, Article 85, margin No. 13.

[87] Compare, May 4, 1962, decision of the Kammergericht, BB 1962, pp. 859-60.

[88] On the problem of applicability of the EEC cartel law in such cases, compare Seidl-Hohenveldern, AWD 1960, p. 225 ff., esp. 229 f.; Hug, Kartelle und Monopole, vol. II, p. 603 ff., esp. 618; I. Schwartz, Kartelle und Monopole, vol. II, p. 673 ff.

States: see, e.g., *United States v. Aluminum Co. of America*, 148 F. 2d 416, 443-444 (C. C. A. 2, 1945). Conversely, the "effects" test under Article 85 (1) will reach, e.g., agreements made by American corporations on American soil, provided only that they have the proscribed effect upon trade between member states.

¶ 30   "Interstate character" is, however, absent where what is involved is not trade between member states of the EEC, but that between outside countries and the *EEC area as an economic bloc.* A German producer, therefore, may bind, e.g., his Swedish or Japanese customer not to import the goods supplied to him (or other goods) into the Common Market, since what is involved is only trade between one member state and a third country which is not protected by Article 85 (1). Likewise, the producer may prohibit his Swedish or Japanese customer from importing competing products from the Common Market or from a member country, since again trade between member states is not involved. For this reason, the combination of this prohibition against import with a reexport prohibition on the customer in a third country is permissible. If he has given the Swedish customer an exclusive distribution franchise for the latter's country, he furthermore may, in order to protect this right, also bind his customers in the EEC countries not to export his products to Sweden. Thus, agreements restraining competition, in particular, export cartels for countries outside of the Common Market, are also permitted, provided that competition within the Market among the participants remains unrestricted.[89] If such export cartels also have effects on trade between member states, then to this extent they will be covered by Article 85 (1).[90] As another example, a licensee in Argentina may be prohibited from manufacturing certain products there; again, trade between member states within the meaning of Article 85 (1) is not involved. Further, it is also permissible for a German producer to prohibit his French competitor from manufacturing and distributing in South America and for the French producer to impose the same restriction on the German for the territory of Eastern Asia. Likewise, and on the same condition, restraints upon American exports to or imports from member states are not reached by the prohibition of Article 85 (1). Their status under the antitrust laws of the United

---

[89] Accord: Wohlfarth/Everling/Glaesner/Sprung, Article 85, note 5; Spengler, *ubi supra.*

[90] See reply of the Commission, Off-Jour 1961, p. 736. Cf. also the negative clearances in the VVVL and "Kodak" decisions, ¶ 321 L and ¶ 321 P, infra.

States is, of course, an entirely different matter and is beyond the scope of this book.[91]

IX. Trade

¶ 31   Trade means broadly economic intercourse.[92] A similarly broad concept underlies restraint of "trade" (or commerce) and restrictive trade practices in American law, although—just as under Article 85 (1)—there must be involved "some form of competition in the marketing of goods or services," at least as far as the Sherman Act is concerned (*Apex Hosiery Co. v. Leader*, 310 U. S. 469, 495 (1940)). For a restraint on services, which was exempted under Article 85 (3), see ¶ 121 (CECIMO), where jointly organized exhibitions were concerned.

B. ARTICLE 85 (1)—LIST OF ILLUSTRATIONS

X. General Observations

¶ 32   The examples given in the lettered subparagraphs (a)-(e) illustrate the situations to which the general prohibition of Article 85 (1) applies;[92a] they have no independent legal significance. The "in particular" introducing the list of illustrations indicates that this list *does not exhaust the general clause* of Article 85 (1). Thus, it is immaterial if a set of facts does not fit within one of the illustrations, so long as it is covered by the general prohibition.

The examples serve to clarify only the criterion "prevention, restriction or distortion of competition." We shall discuss only this prerequisite in connection with the individual examples. Of course,

---

[91] On this subject the reader is referred generally to Brewster, "Antitrust and American Business Abroad," New York 1958; Fugate, "Foreign Commerce and the Antitrust Laws," Boston 1958; Van Cise, "The Application of the United States Antitrust Laws to the European Community," Institute on Legal Aspects of the European Community, Federal Bar Association, Washington 1960, p. 140; Haight, "Some Aspects of United States Antitrust Laws and Foreign Commerce," in "Doing Business Abroad," Practising Law Institute, New York 1962, vol. 1, p. 266.

Compare the negative clearance granted to Rieckermann (a Hamburg exporter to Japan) and AEG, November 6, 1968; the details are discussed at ¶ 321 G, infra.

[92] Accord, e.g., Wohlfarth/Everling/Glaesner/Sprung, Article 85, note 4; BKartA, *ubi supra*; Koch, BB 1959, p. 243; Baumbach/Hefermehl, Article 85, margin No. 11; von Gamm, p. 25.

[92a] Four of the illustrations, (a), (b), (d), and (e) are similar or identical to those in Article 86 (2)(a)-(d). Hence, compare our comments there (¶208 ff., infra).

for a case to come within Article 85 (1), the other prerequisites, e.g., aptness to affect adversely trade between member states, must be met. We shall not always refer to these criteria in the following treatment.

¶ 33   *None* of the restraints on competition mentioned in the examples is *prohibited per se*, but rather only if it fulfills all the prerequisites of Article 85 (1).

In the literature on the subject,[93] certain types of restraints on competition, e.g., those which are tantamount in effect to quantitative limitations on imports (quotas), are being designated as prohibited *per se* and as not capable of receiving an exemption under Article 85 (3). However, there are no such restraints on competition which would be prohibited *per se*. This view is approved by the High Court in the *Maschinenbau Ulm* case (¶ 16, supra). Sentence 3 of the court's syllabus states that Article 85 (1) requires a consideration of the effects of agreements from an economic standpoint and, thus, may not be construed as extending only to certain types of contracts and not to others, both without exception. The concept of *per se* violations would be misconceived in Common Market law since it belongs to, and indeed, may not be severed from, the law which nurtured it, that of the United States. In any case, it would then be necessary also to borrow the "rule of reason" for Article 85 (1), since the concept of the *per se* violation has been developed as a counterpart to what, under the rule of reason, may be regarded as reasonable restraints. More accurately speaking, the *per se* violation is a type of restraint which is categorically unreasonable, or else it is a type of restraint to which the rule of reason will not be applied, the choice between these two theories being largely a matter of semantics. These two concepts—rule of reason and *per se* violation—are linked from a substantive point of view and cannot be considered separately without distorting their meaning. This is true particularly since the borderline between reasonable and unreasonable restraints on competition, including those which are prohibited *per se,* has not yet been clearly drawn in the half century since the rule of reason was first pronounced in *Standard Oil Co. v. United States,* 221 U. S. 1 (1911).

¶ 34   To be sure, Article 85 (1) requires reasonable interpretation, as do all laws, but it does not call for the *"rule of reason"* with its specifically American connotation. Even its legislative history argues against its application here. It was developed essentially because United States antitrust law does not permit administrative

---

[93] Steindorff, BB 1958, p. 89 ff.

exemption in individual cases or groups of cases, so that the courts
had to remedy the situation. This need evidently does not exist to
the same degree for Article 85, where the exemption provisions of its
paragraph (3) are available;[94] it is this consideration which has led
to Article 85 (3) being called a legislative "rule of reason."[95] The
policy of letting minimal "violations" pass (cf. ¶ 17, supra, on the
term "perceptible") is related to the de-minimis concept.

XI. Article 85(1)(a)

¶ 35   This illustrative category comprises *price* and *terms* cartels,
         i.e., agreements, decisions and concerted practices directed to
these factors. Definition of the line between elements of price on the
one hand and terms and conditions on the other is unnecessary since
subparagraph (a) (differently from § 2 GWB) makes no distinction
in this respect.

¶ 36   More specifically, the illustration in (a) covers the following
         restraints on competition of the *horizontal* type: Price and
discount cartels (including discounts based on total volume) and,
since even "indirect" fixing of purchase or sale prices suffices, calculation cartels which fix elements of price calculation (and not merely
methods or formulas therefor); furthermore, terms cartels regardless
of whether they regulate all terms in the industry or only some of
the terms such as payment dates and discounts, liability for defects,
warranties, etc.[96] The "indirect" fixing of prices or terms need not
be intended;[97] this is immaterial under the clear language of Article
85 (1) which the example in subparagraph (a) merely illustrates.
However, not every direct or indirect influence on prices or terms is
covered; they must be "fixed"[98] (see also ¶ 38). Compare the Anglo-
American concept of "price-fixing" which, at least in current antitrust
jurisprudence in the United States, may be said to include broadly
any consensual determination of price derogating from the play of
ordinary market forces.

---

[94] Kleemann, p. 36, also deems the rule of reason inapplicable to Article 85. In favor of its application is E. Wolf, Basel, in his report of August 23, 1962, delivered before the International Law Association at Luxembourg.

[95] See Ladas, 23 Ohio St. L. J. p. 713.
[96] See also von Gamm, p. 27.
[97] Contra: Wohlfarth/Everling/Glaesner/Sprung, Article 85, note 5.
[98] See Kleemann, p. 45.

¶ 35

¶ 37   As for *vertical* restraints on competition, the example in sub-
         paragraph (a) includes vertical tying of prices and terms,[99]
regardless of whether or not trade-marked or branded merchandise
is involved and—at least in principle—regardless of whether these
restraints extend only to one or to several countries.[1]

¶ 38   Since prices and terms have to be fixed by agreement, decision
         or concerted practice, simple unilateral *recommendations* re-
garding prices and terms are *not reached*, whether they are made
horizontally or vertically. Article 85 (1), before giving the illustrative
situations, lists the instruments of "fixing" in an exhaustive manner;
specifically, such recommendations do not amount, by themselves and
without more, to concerted action (compare ¶ 13).[2]

XII.   Article 85(1)(b)

¶ 39   This illustration is substantially parallel to Article 65, § 1 (b),
         of the Coal and Steel Treaty. It is very far-reaching in its
scope; any limitation or control (Kontrolle)[3] suffices. Because of its
broad and at the same time imprecise wording this provision may
become harmful, and generous application of Article 85 (3) by the
Commission is necessary. It seems to follow this line.

¶ 40   The illustrative category comprises, e.g., specialization and
         other rationalization cartels (i.e., cartels designed to affect
overall economies by division of product lines among the participants
or by other methods), as well as agreements, etc., on unified development and application of product standards and types (but cf. Article
4 (2) (iii) (a) of Regulation 17), on formation of joint purchase and

[99] It should be noted, however, that such vertical restraints would not normally be apt to affect adversely trade between member states: compare discussion supra, ¶ 25; also Wohl-farth/Everling/Glaesner/Sprung, Article 85, note 6; G. Schwartz, MA 1959, pp. 322, 325; Obernolte, "Europäische Wirtschaft" (The European Economy) 1960, p. 465; OLG Düsseldorf, decision of October 21, 1958, BB 1958, p. 1110 No. 1933, also in WuW/E OLG 262 ff.

[1] This may, however, be material in connection with aptness to affect adversely: see G. Schwartz, *ibid.;* Obernolte, *ibid.* An example of forbidden joint resale price maintenance is to be found in the former ASPA statute (see ¶ 321 Q, infra). As for terms creating

vertical distribution systems and thus, independent national markets, see ¶ 327, infra.

[2] Under § 38, paragraph 2, second sentence of the GWB, however, such recommendations may be improper if they lead to uniform conduct of the addressees in the Federal Republic.

[3] Here one should take account of the likelihood that the Anglo-American concept of "control" was drawn upon —a term having a connotation different from the German "Kontrolle." Where-as "control" in the antitrust context means domination or power over the subject matter, "Kontrolle" would ordi-narily refer to supervisory or checking functions.

sales organizations (syndicates, in a somewhat more enduring as well as special sense than the normal American one of *ad hoc* groups for the pursuit of individual financial or industrial projects), on joint research (but cf. Article 4 (2) (iii) (b) of Regulation 17) to the extent that freedom of competition is restrained thereby, which will not be the case with mere common research activities (see ¶ 17, supra). Quota cartels, for example, also limit the market. Cartels designed to meet structural crises in industry (compare § 4 GWB) may, among other things, result in restrictions on the market and on investments. Recommendations suggesting, for example, that certain standards should be applied are not covered (see ¶ 13, supra).

XIII.   Article 85(1)(c)

¶ 41   Among *horizontal* restraints on competition, there are covered by this illustrative category,[4] first of all, regional cartels, even though they may not coincide with the tariff boundaries of one or more EEC countries, and, depending on the particular circumstances, also export and import cartels, to the extent that they concern imports into and exports from EEC countries. An illustration of a horizontal allocation (or division) of markets in the sense of Article 85 (1), subparagraph (c), is an agreement between a German and a French manufacturer of safety nuts to the effect that the French manufacturer will distribute solely in France, the German only in Germany.[5] There is further the possibility of application to specialization cartels (market-sharing in the technological sense) ; but exact classification is unnecessary here also since, as is true of the other lettered paragraphs of Article 85 (1), only an illustrative category is involved.

¶ 42   As for *vertical* restraints on competition, one could imagine applicability of this illustration to certain situations which are permitted under national law, e.g., § 18 of the GWB, viz., to exclusive franchises, especially for exclusive distributors, importers, etc., and to export, reimport or re-export prohibitions and the like; compare the Belgian law of July 27, 1967, Antoine Braun/Gleiss/Hirsch, p. 95, and the High Court's decisions in the *Grundig* and *Maschinenbau Ulm* cases (¶ 14 and 16, supra).[6]

---

[4] Compare also Article 65, § 1(c), of the Coal and Steel Treaty.
[5] In such a case (Julien/Van Katwijk), the Commission refused exemption: decision of October 28, 1970, OffJour No. L 242 (November 5, 1970), p. 18.

[6] Cf. ¶ 16, footnote 41b. An example of forbidden vertical export prohibitions is to be found in the Agfa-Gevaert recommendation, ¶ 327, infra.

¶ 43   *Exclusive distributorship agreements:* In exclusive distributor
        or importer contracts, etc., there ordinarily are involved three
typical restraints on competition, viz., obligating the customer to deal
only in goods of the supplier and to distribute them only in a designated territory, and obligating the supplier to deal only with the customer in that territory.

¶ 44   Agency contracts with *employees* (compare here § 84, para-
        graph 2, of the HGB) may be put aside here; employees are
not "enterprises" within the meaning of Article 85 (1).[7]

¶ 45   Apart from employees, a distinction should be made between
        commercial agents, commission houses and commission men
on the one hand, and independent traders on their own account
on the other.

It is characteristic of *commercial agents,* etc., that they act in
the interest of their principal. It is the principal who derives rights
from, and is obligated under, contracts made by them, either legally
(in the case of true agents) or economically (in the case of commission houses and commission men); it is he who may determine
when, where, how and with whom business is done. Commercial
agents, etc., are subject to his directions and are bound by a special
degree of loyalty to him. The obligations of the commercial agent,
etc., are justified by this high degree of loyalty and, thus, do not come
under Article 85 (1). The principal, too, owes a higher degree of
loyalty than usual. His obligation to supply only the commercial
agent in a particular territory and to protect the latter's territory
against sales by other domestic or foreign customers or agents of
the principal, is also justified by the high degree of loyalty owed
and likewise is outside of Article 85 (1). The Commission as well
sees no restraint on competition within the meaning of Article 85 (1)
in these obligations of the commercial agent and the principal,[8]
reasoning that they are "the consequence of the special duty of
mutual protection of interests." This presents the interesting idea
of the justification of restraints on competition by virtue of a special

---

[7] See the discussion under I, supra. Under the cited provision of the HGB, a person who is entrusted on a continuous basis with the negotiation or conclusion of transactions for or in the name of another enterprise, and who is not himself an independent entrepreneur, is deemed to be an employee. If he is independent in the sense that he is substantially free to determine his own activities, including working hours, he is a "commercial agent" (non-employee) pursuant to § 84, paragraph 1.

[8] See the Commission's "Official Notice Concerning Exclusive Representation Contracts with Commercial Agents," OffJour 1962, p. 2921; CMR ¶ 2697.

duty of loyalty,[9] an idea which could lead, *inter alia,* to the justification of prohibitions of competition between partners in the articles of association or statute.

These special considerations do not apply to exclusive distributorship contracts with *independent traders.* Thus, these contracts come within the language of Article 85 (1); so do the obligations of a supplier since the Rome Treaty does not contain special rules *for distribution or other agreements* of the type in Section 18 GWB. The above applies, of course, only if the remaining prerequisites of Article 85 (1) are met (see ¶ 32, supra). Such considerations are reflected in the Commission's Regulation 67/67 (¶ 701 ff.) which exempts, until December 31, 1972, certain types of simple exclusive distributorship agreements, but only those not containing absolute territorial protection.

One of the latest decisions of the European Court of Justice concerning exclusive dealing arrangements is *Brasserie de Haecht v. Consorts Wilkin Janssen* of December 12, 1967.[9a] The plaintiff, a Belgian brewery, sued the owners of a small tavern for damages and repayment of a loan. They had concluded a contract obligating the plaintiff to furnish the defendants with trade equipment and to grant loans, and requiring the defendants to buy beer exclusively from the plaintiff. The brewery alleged a breach of contract by the defendants because they had bought beer from another supplier, a violation which the defendants admitted. However, they contended that the tying agreement was void as violative of Article 85, basing their argument on the Court's decisions in the *Grundig, Maschinenbau Ulm* and *Noordwijks Cement Accoord* cases (CMR ¶ 8046, 8047 and 8052). The controversy in the Belgian court reached an impasse on the question whether the agreement alone was to be considered or whether it was to be viewed as part of an existing pattern of such agreements throughout the Belgian beer industry for the purpose of judging its aptness perceptibly to affect adversely trade between member states. The particular agreement, standing alone, it was clear, could have no perceptible impact on interstate trade since the turnover of the defendants' tavern was infinitesimal in relation to that in the Belgian market as a whole. The defendants apparently argued, though, that the agreement was not to be considered apart from "the simultaneous existence of numerous analogous contracts concluded either by a single brewery . . . or by several

---

[9] See Gleiss/Hootz, NJW 1963, p. 233.
[9a] Case No. 23/67, Recueil Vol. XIII (1967), p. 543 ff.; CMR ¶ 8053. For the latest German decision on a similar beer contract and the European Court's de Haecht decision, see BGH decision of February 26, 1970, WuW/E BGH 1081.

¶ 45

breweries established in the same member state." (Adv. Gen'l Roemer's Submissions to the Court, CMR ¶ 8053.) The Belgian court referred the question to the European Court because it could rightly find no language in Article 85 that was dispositive of the point. The Court answered by stating that the existence of parallel agreements must be taken into account in assessing the adverse effect of such an agreement but that even if an overall pattern is established, it is only one element to be considered in the ultimate determination of validity or invalidity under Article 85. Although a contrary result would have been impossibly restrictive of judicial review of anti-competitive agreements, the burden thrust upon national courts is onerous. They must weigh and assess numerous other similar agreements to determine if they are relevant, thus posing substantive and procedural problems for local courts. Adv. General Roemer alludes to these and others in his Submissions.[9b] Should parties wish to clarify the legal validity of an agreement which is doubtful in view of the *Brasserie de Haecht* decision, it would be well to consider an auxiliary application for negative clearance, perhaps even of a standard form contract.

Great caution must be used in drawing the line between commercial agents and independent traders. In economic reality there exists every transitional form between them. This reality, rather than the legal classification, is determinative. The Commission has adopted its own criteria to distinguish between commercial agents and independent traders in its "Official Notice Concerning Exclusive Representation Contracts with Commercial Agents" of December 24, 1962 (CMR ¶ 2697); whether the European Court will follow this line remains an open question.

Before discussing the contents of the Official Notice, it should be pointed out that it has no constitutive effect such as that, e.g., of a group exemption pursuant to Article 85 (3) (compare ¶ 86, infra). Rather, the Official Notice represents only the legal view of the Commission. It is a "notice of intention" *(Absichtsankündigung)*. While it is of import, it is not binding on the European Court.

In broad terms, the test of distinction, which is the determinative one in the eyes of the Commission, as stated in the Official Notice referred to above, is the *incidence of the financial risks* connected with the transactions of the distributor: Apart from the frequently found "del credere" guaranty (under which the agent guarantees payment by customers to whom he extends credit), assumption of any of those risks by the distributor will disqualify the relation as one of agency.

[9b] For details, see Gleiss' review, WuW 1968, p. 206, 207; Gleiss/Helm, NJW 1968, p. 1553. For this question, cf. also the recent BGH decision, WM 1970, p. 1188, referred to in ¶ 310, footnote 13b, infra.

Factors specifically mentioned by the Commission as indicating the status of an independent trader are present where the distributor is required to maintain or in fact maintains a substantial inventory of the goods concerned, to which he has legal title, or where he is required to furnish or in fact furnishes substantial free service to customers at his own expense, and also where he is free to determine or in fact determines prices and conditions of his transactions with customers. In all such cases, so states the Commission, it will regard the reduction of supply or demand, or both, resulting from the exclusive distributorship contract, as effecting a competitive restriction within Article 85 (1). The question in each individual case will then be whether trade between member states is adversely affected thereby, whereas similar effects on supply or demand in the case of a true agency in the legal or at least economic sense may be considered as merely incidental to the special relationship of the parties. Under the latter, the agent performs but a vicarious or auxiliary function for the principal and therefore, it may be added, he may be ignored in the present connection as an economic unit in his own right.

Since the Commission views the distribution of the financial risks, not the characterization chosen by the parties, as determinative, in our opinion the same test applies in deciding whether a trader denominated as independent by the contracting parties is, in economic reality, independent. Thus, contracts with independent traders whose contractual positions, judged by the incidence of financial risks, are the same as those of commercial agents are, in our opinion, not subject to the prohibition of Article 85 (1). This is not the same view as that propounded by the plaintiff in the *Grundig-Consten* decision to the effect that exclusive dealers were to be considered agents, an argument rejected by the Court in its July 13, 1966 decision (¶ 16, supra).

The Commission's view of the anti-competitive aspects of exclusive distributorship agreements with independent distributors is reflected in its first "Official Notice" of December 24, 1962 (CMR ¶ 2697). The Commission listed various obligations of the independent distributor for which it wished to grant a general exemption from the prohibition of Article 85 (1) : the obligation to advertise, observe the market, maintain an inventory of goods, develop and maintain a sales or service network, guarantee goods, buy minimum quantities, and not distribute or sell competing products. From this it can be seen that the Commission's definition of "restraint on competition" is very broad, in our opinion, wrongly so. On the other hand, it can be presumed from this Notice that the Commission will grant exemptions for these restraints on competition unless special circumstances militate against it.

¶ 45

The Commission and the Court, in the *Grundig-Consten* litigation (¶ 14 ff., supra), differentiate between exclusive distributors with "absolute" and those with "relative" territorial protection. There is "relative" territorial protection where a producer obligates himself directly to supply only one distributor in a given area; the protection is "absolute," if he undertakes even to omit indirect deliveries into this area, and further to prevent his other distributors from selling there. The Court in its *Grundig* decision maintained that Grundig was thus bound to obligate his other customers, besides Consten, but the facts did not really bear out this thesis.

While the Commission did not commit itself regarding contracts with "relative" territorial protection, it did determine in its *Grundig-Consten* decision that it will issue an exemption under Article 85 (3) for contracts with "absolute" territorial protection only under exceptional circumstances and for compelling reasons, e.g., where a technically complicated product is involved, or for a limited time if the costs of introducing a new product are great. Certainly, a weighty factor for the Commission in its *Grundig-Consten* decision was the difference in price between Germany and France for Grundig products which allowed the "parallel importer" to underprice the exclusive distributor Consten. The European Court declared the question of these price differences to be legally irrelevant since it deemed, in our opinion incorrectly, the restraint of competition in Grundig products (intrabrand competition) sufficient itself to constitute a violation of Article 85 (1). It is regrettable that the Commission's decision did not elucidate and adduce more evidence concerning these price differences between Germany and France and between Consten and the "parallel importer," so that it is impossible to form a clear and conclusive picture of the actual situation of these price differences on the various levels of trade.

In the Commission's opinion, the absolute protection was not "indispensable" within the meaning of Article 85 (3); it would have been sufficient had Grundig in France supplied only Consten since parallel importers would have had to buy from other distributors instead of from the manufacturer. But the initial investment might have been so great that the small percentage margin of Consten was insignificant when compared to those of the parallel importer. Furthermore, the parallel importer might establish his own firm in Germany, buy directly from the producer, e.g., Grundig, and forego all profit. In our opinion, all these economic factors are germane to a proceeding under Article 85 (3), as well as, *inter alia,* the relation between investment and risk on the one hand, and the amount of profit within a given period on the other. There are no substantial references to

¶ 45

these elements in the Commission's *Grundig-Consten* decision, nor to Grundig's competition and the strength thereof. The Commission was satisfied with its observation that the consumer is not able to judge concerning such technical products. This is insufficient for a decision of such legal and economic import, especially since the negative clearance issued in *Grosfillex-Fillistorf* (¶ 22, supra) made reference to the competition from other brands. These critical views were also propounded by Advocate General Roemer in his final brief in the *Grundig* case, a circumstance which did not prevent the High Court from reaching a result favorable to the Commission on these points.

The Commission's decision in *Grundig-Consten* did not, due to its nature, examine the question of alternative solutions, e.g., whether the parallel importer may be obligated to pay a profit pass-over to the exclusive distributor in whose territory he makes deliveries. In our view, this could be permissible, but perhaps objectionable if the pass-over were prohibitive. An agreement whereby the producer prohibits his exclusive distributor in one member country from enticing away customers from another exclusive distributor in another country, or prohibits any such sales, would, despite the *Grundig-Consten* decision, in our opinion, qualify for exemption. The European Court in its decision of July 13, 1966 (CMR ¶ 8046), affirmed the Commission's decision except for the invalidation of the whole contract between Grundig and Consten, declaring void only those clauses which made absolute the rights of Consten as an exclusive dealer. This is regrettable in view of the inconsistencies and gaps in the reasoning of both the Commission and the Court.

For a more lenient view on absolute territorial protection in case of insignificant market shares, see ¶ 16, supra, and for notification of exclusive distributorship agreements with independent traders, see below, Regulation 17, Article 4.

¶ 46   *Prohibitions of export and reimport:* According to the High Court's *Grundig* decision, whether the supplier may, for the protection of an exclusive (independent) distributor, impose an *export prohibition* upon his customers without violating Article 85 (1) is a disputed question.[10] This question has, however, been clarified in principle by the *Bosch* decision of the European Court (see ¶ 16,

---

[10] In its decision of October 28, 1970, the Commission, after the export prohibitions were terminated by the parties to the exclusive distributorship agreements, granted an exemption for the clause under which only a limited number of retailers were to be supplied (OffJour No. L 242 (November 5, 1970), p. 22; CMR ¶ 9396).

supra).[11] To what extent other export and reimport provisions come within the scope of Article 85 (1) is a matter to be examined in each particular case. The Court has an unmistakable tendency to view all such provisions violative of Article 85 (1). Nonetheless, it is in our opinion incorrect to assume, as did the Landgericht in Munich,[12] on a theoretical basis and without an examination of the surrounding circumstances, that an export prohibition would result in a forbidden division of markets and would be apt to affect adversely interstate trade, and consequently violates Article 85 (1). The decision of this court immediately evoked deserved criticism from commentators. The court did not perceive that the European Court in the *Bosch* decision did not hold export prohibitions "per se" illegal, but only stated that it was possible that they violated Article 85 (1).

¶ 47   The *Bosch* decision says nothing about *reimport prohibitions,* e.g., for the protection of a vertical price agreement. The Commission regards export and reimport prohibitions to be generally violative of Article 85 (1).[12a] In our opinion, they are not generally immune;[13] but, whether they do come within Article 85 (1) is again a matter for individual examination. The purposes served by the reimport prohibition[14] may be important in this connection, at least for an exemption under Article 85 (3).

¶ 48   If the owner of a *trademark* sells merchandise under that mark himself, according to German court practice he may not, without violating Article 85 (1), impose a contractual prohibition upon his customers against exports into countries where he has an identical trademark. He may not combat such exports with his trademark in the country of import since the trademark has been "consumed." The decisions of the Bundesgerichtshof affirm such consumption on the theory that the product was lawfully trademarked and sold, that the trademark

---

[11] BB 1962, p. 467 ff. with annotation by Weyer; see also ¶ 16, footnote 41, supra. Bosch had granted to the Dutch firm van Rijn an exclusive distribution franchise for its refrigerators and had imposed an export prohibition on its customers in Germany. The European High Court stated that it would not be out of the question for such export prohibitions to be violative of Article 85 (1). According to the BGH decision of November 12, 1969 (*Auto-Entfroster*), WuW/E BGH 1054, absolute territorial protection, under German law, needs explicit agreement.

[12] Decision of January 14, 1963, BB 1963, p. 167, set aside by the Munich Court of Appeals. See ¶ 342, infra.

[12a] Commission's press announcement IP (69) 214.

[13] Accord: WuW/E BKartA 333, 338; decision of the OLG Frankfurt a.M. of January 19, 1962, BB 1962, p. 735, which is, however, dubious in its part concerning EEC law; apparently of different opinion Kleemann, pp. 34, 40.

[14] Compare, e.g., G. Schwartz, MA 1959, p. 325 ff.; Hans Lutz/Basson, NJW 1961, p. 385 ff.

becomes exhausted in performing the function of indicating origin and that no one is deceived as to the source of the merchandise where the trademark owner himself has put the merchandise into circulation.[14a] According to these decisions (which expressly point out the differences between trademarks and patents), a contractual prohibition of exports imposed by the trademark owner upon his customers is not protected by the trademark and consequently may fall within Article 85 (1).

The European High Court has looked with disfavor on a contractual export prohibition buttressed in the importing country by possible trademark infringement claims against importers. The Court in fact feels, as in its *Grundig* decision (¶ 14 ff., supra), that an action based on such trademark rights constitutes a violation of Article 85 (1). This means that a citizen of one member nation is obligated not to press a claim granted him by his own national laws. Such a prohibition is justifiable only in select circumstances, as perhaps those of the *Grundig* case.

In any case, trademark infringement actions are, in our opinion, permissible according to cases decided by the European High Court as well as the German Supreme Court.

The situation is different, in our opinion, even on the basis of those decisions, where the *licensee* under a trademark puts out goods produced by him under that mark. Here, trademark owner and producer of the merchandise are different persons; there is deception regarding the source of the goods if the customers of, say, a French licensee-producer export them into the Federal Republic. If the German trademark owner uses the identical mark in this situation, then the trademark on the imported merchandise points to him and not to the French licensee as the producer. The identical and unlicensed mark of the licensor thus has not been consumed, so that an export prohibition for the licensee and his customers does not come within Article 85 (1) (see also ¶ 50, infra). This applies even more if the goods of the licensor and those of the licensee are not identical.[15]

Licensor and licensee, in our opinion, are not to be legally distinguished if both belong to the same concern, e.g., corporate parent and subsidiary; it is questionable whether in this case there can be a legally relevant deception as to the source of the goods. The Oberlandesgericht Düsseldorf considers the concern relation significant and deems the right to prevent import of trademarked goods unavailable in such a case.[16] Since the national laws of the

---

[14a] Thus, the German Federal Supreme Court in its *Maja* decision of January 22, 1964, see ¶ 48A, footnote 18b, infra.

[15] This point was deemed material by the Bochum Landgericht's decision of April 20, 1964, AWD 1964, p. 369.

[16] Decisions of March 29, 1963, BB 1963, p. 489 and July 14, 1964, AWD 1964, p. 262.

member states in which the trademark is registered are determinative here, there is the possibility of conflicting results in particular cases. Thus, in the Netherlands a subsidiary located there can defend itself against undesired imports if, e.g., the German parent corporation has assigned (not just licensed) the Dutch trademark to it.[17]

If the assignment of the trademark from a producer to his general importer in another country serves to secure a territorial protective scheme prohibited under Article 85 (1), the view of the Commission and the European Court was that the voidness of the latter extends to the assignment of the trademark as well.[18]

The European High Court does not make clear its position in this regard. In its *Grundig* decision (¶ 14 ff., supra), it characterizes the agreement concerning registration of the GINT trademark for Consten as violative of Article 85 (1), but concludes only that Consten should not be permitted to prevent or hinder parallel imports by use of its trademark right, as that would constitute misuse of its legal right. Employment of the concept of misuse of right is not necessary and not desirable due to its generality and dangerously imprecise meaning. It would, in our view, be better to use the construction we have outlined above whereby the infringement action brought by Consten is regarded as part of Grundig and Consten's concerted practice. The registration of the GINT trademark for Consten would remain legally valid and could be the basis for claims against "normal" infringers.

It does not fall under Article 85 (1) if the holder of an industrial protective right or of a trademark makes use of these rights. The European Court decided this, it is true, only with regard to the holder of a patent (*Parke, Davis* decision of February 29, 1968, Case No. 24/67[18a]); however, the Court's argument that there was no agreement, decision or concerted practice holds true generally, not only for patents, but also, e.g., for registered designs, design patents (fancy designs) and trademarks.

¶ 48A   In the case involving the American *Sperry Rand Corp.* ("Sperry"), and its wholly owned subsidiary, formerly *Remington* Rand Italia, now Sperry Rand Italia, Milan ("Remington") the Commission has not taken a decision, but, according to a Press Release

---

[17] See Czapski, DB 1963, p. 406 and the decision cited therein of the Hoge Raad of January 12, 1939, Nederlandse Jurisprudentie 1939, No. 535; see also, decision of the Gerechtshof te 's-Gravenhage of February 20, 1963. For Germany, however, compare the holding of the OLG Düsseldorf, AWD 1964, p. 262, rejecting trademark claims in such a case. Cf. also Wertheimer, National Trademark Law and the Common Market Rules of Competition, CMLR, Vol. 4, No. 3, p. 308.

[18] OffJour, 1964, p. 2545.

[18a] OffJour No. C 42, May 6, 1968, p. 1; CMR ¶ 8054; for details, see ¶¶ 50, and 205, infra.

issued on June 11, 1969, has written a letter to the interested parties. Although this letter has not been published, the matter is of sufficient importance to warrant discussion here.

Sperry had, by contract, transferred to Remington the trademark rights that it held in Italy with respect to electric shavers. An Italian enterprise, Electro Market *Innovazione,* Milan, imported Remington shavers, among others, from other member states. Sperry's Italian subsidiary, Remington, filed an action in Milan against the parallel importer, based on a violation of trademark rights and unfair competition. Innovazione appealed to the Commission, whereupon the national court suspended its proceedings.

The Commission took the view that the way in which the parties had interpreted and applied the contract was objectionable under Article 85, because their objective was to hinder imports of authentic Remington shavers—i.e., not those fraudulently marked "Remington" —from other EEC countries into Italy. Thus, according to the Commission, interstate trade was affected adversely and competition was restrained, since Remington was granted absolute territorial protection, an objective that is outside the proper function of trademark rights.

Because of the Commission's intervention, Sperry and Remington have agreed to desist from using the trademark rights to hinder parallel imports. The lawsuit in Milan was settled amicably.

In our opinion, this is an extension of the Court's *Grundig-Consten* decision (see ¶ 16) which we feel is not entirely convincing. In that case, it was a matter of whether a contract between a manufacturer (Grundig, Nuremberg) and an independent importer/distributor (Consten, Paris) could go so far as to grant absolute territorial protection. In the *Sperry Rand-Remington* case, the problem is not how far a contract between a parent company and its wholly owned subsidiary can go. The two companies concerned needed no contract to do what they did. They could have achieved the same result without any contract, e.g., if Remington had registered the trademarks in Italy in its own name and Sperry did not object. We mention this to indicate that the contract regarding title to the Italian trademark right is irrelevant under cartel law. The real problem is whether the owner of an Italian trademark, be it Sperry or Remington, does indeed violate Article 85 (1) merely by using his rights to block "parallel" importers. We believe the answer to this question is no. The solution of such cases is to be found in trademark law.

¶ 48A

The German Supreme Court indicated this in its well-known decision in the *Maja* case.[18b] In that case, the Spanish manufacturer and owner of the mark "Maja" sold his soap to wholesalers in Spain who then exported it to Germany. The German enterprise, authorized by the manufacturer to use his German trademark rights, filed an action to stop the parallel importer. Without applying cartel law at all, the court in Karlsruhe turned down this action, arguing that the sole purpose of a trademark was to indicate the manufacturer and, in that way, to protect the buyer. In this case, according to the court, the buyer was not misled, and the soap had become "free"; the trademark rights were consumed because the manufacturer himself had placed his product on the market.

In connection with the *Grundig* case we have maintained[18c] that the core of the matter was not the transfer of trademark rights from Grundig to Consten, and Consten's acquisition of these rights. Quite logically, the Commission and the Court in that case did not even require the parties to cancel Consten's trademark rights. What they really attacked, whether rightly or not, was the concert of action by which Grundig and Consten tried to stop parallel imports.

In the *Sperry Rand-Remington* case, we believe that the Commission could have, at most, directed its attack at the misuse of a dominant position—if one is involved; in other words, the Commission might have tried to apply Article 86 if the conditions of that provision were present. We do not have enough information to judge whether this is the case, but we do not believe that the approach which the Commission took in the *Sperry Rand-Remington* case was legally correct. If a similar case arises in the future, the Commission's objections may be contested in the Luxembourg Court, which in its *Parke, Davis* decision (see ¶ 50, ¶ 205, infra) followed the same views as we do.

These views are shared by the President of the Arrondissements Rechtbank (court), Breda, in the *OMO* case, which was finally decided on December 31, 1968.[18d] The President stated that the import into Holland of a German manufacturer's products, legitimately branded with his trademark and sold in Germany, violates the trademark right of a legally independent Dutch manufacturer who is entitled to the corresponding trademark in the Netherlands. The fact that both the German and Dutch enterprise are subsidiaries of the same parent

---

[18b] January 22, 1964, BGH [Official Reporter] 41, p. 84-88; see ¶ 48, supra.

[18c] Gleiss, Zwei bedeutsame Urteile des EuGH (Two Important Decisions of the European Court), WRP, May 1967, p. 163-176; Gleiss/Hootz, Comments on the Court's *Grundig-Consten* decision of July 13, 1966, AWD 1966, p. 307 ff., particularly p. 310-312.

[18d] GRUR AIT, June 1969, p. 203 ff.

¶ 48A

does not affect this statement. The President went on to say that
if in such a case "interstate" trade is hindered as a result of the fact
that there are two different trademark owners, one German and one
Dutch, this does not constitute a violation of Article 85, because it
does not follow from an agreement, decision or concerted practice,
but from the territorial nature of a trademark right. In this connection, the President was justified in quoting the Luxembourg Court's
Parke, Davis decision.[18e]

¶ 49   *License agreements regarding industrial protective rights:* Ac-
        cording to the prevailing opinion, there is no general im-
munity for such agreements, and Article 85 (1) applies.[19] This was
confirmed by Regulation 17, which in its Article 4(2)(ii)(b) designates
certain license agreements as not requiring notification and thus presupposes that Article 85 (1) may be applicable to them. The European
Court determined, in its *Grundig* decision, that industrial protective
rights are not exempted from the Community's cartel law by Articles
36, 222 and 234. The Court came to a somewhat different conclusion
in its *Parke, Davis* decision of February 29, 1968 (for details, see ¶ 50,
infra).

        Article 85 (1) is applicable only to commitments of the licensee
which *lie outside the scope of the legal protection* of the licensed protective right.[20] Article 36 of the EEC Treaty reserves the matter of
industrial property ("propriété industrielle") for the legislation of the
member states;[21] Articles 85 ff. have to respect these laws. Restraints
on the licensee within the range of legal protection are therefore not
reached by Article 85 (1). Articles 222 and 234 of the Rome Treaty, as
well as the fact that no national cartel law derogates from this scope of
protection, all point in this direction. To that extent, restraint on

---

[18e] The Commission also intervened
and caused a restraint of trade to be
terminated in a case involving a Dutch
tractor agreement (see CMR ¶ 9305 regarding its Press Release of May 29,
1969).
[19] Accord, e.g., Spengler, GRUR AIT
1958, p. 321 ff. and MA 1960, p. 888;
G. Schwartz, MA 1959, p. 317 ff.;
Jannse/Oudemans/Wolterbeek, GRUR
AIT 1961, p. 276; von Gamm, pp. 20,
28; Deringer, GRUR AIT 1962, p. 293;
contra only Gotzen, GRUR AIT 1958,
p. 224, in reliance upon Articles 36 and
90 of the EEC Treaty, whose reasoning, however, is not persuasive. For
introduction, see Gambrell, Patents and
Antitrust: An Integrated Approach in
the European Economic Community,
Boston College Industrial and Commercial Law Review, Vol. VI, No. 3,
Spring 1968, p. 541; Schatz, Die Erschöpfung des Patentrechts im Recht der
Mitgliedstaaten der Europäischen Wirtschaftsgemeinschaft, GRUR AIT 1970,
p. 207.
[20] Contra: Schlieder, BB 1962, p.
306. Magen, pp. 79 ff. considers the
extent of the monopoly position of the
owner of the protective right decisive,
not the statutory limits; in our opinion, this test is too broad.
[21] Accord: Bodenhausen, GRUR AIT
1958, p. 218 ff.; Gotzen, *id.* p. 224 ff.;
Spengler, *ubi supra.*

competition does not rest upon agreements, etc., but follows from the rights of the proprietor to exclusivity, i.e., from the law. Were Article 85 (1) to apply to restraints covered by the contents of the licensed protective right, it would mean that this provision would intrude directly into the protected area of industrial property rights. That area, however, is defined by the national laws, from which Article 85 (1) must not derogate. Thus, there may be, and presently are, disparities in the range of Article 85 (1) since the scope of protection can vary from country to country. These disparities are to be accepted. They should not be disposed of by extensive application of Article 85 (1). That is the task of the harmonization of national patent, trademark, etc., laws, called for in Articles 100 and 101 of the EEC Treaty.

Restraints on the *licensee* can therefore fall within Article 85 (1) only to the extent that they are *not* covered by the legal scope of the protective right under license.[22] The Commission recognized this in principle in its Official Notice Concerning Patent Licensing Agreements of December 24, 1962.[23] How far the protected area extends must normally be gathered from the national law of the state that has granted the protective right. In its Notice, the Commission attempts to clarify, independent of the national laws. which restrictions imposed on a licensee are included in the scope of a patent grant (for particulars, see ¶ 51, infra). If it is doubtful whether a specific restriction falls within the scope, it is a matter to be determined under the pertinent national law.

Restraints on the *licensor*, on the other hand, cannot, of course, be covered by the protective scope of the licensed right, since that scope includes only prohibitive rights on the part of the owner. There is, therefore, no aggregate of restraints on the licensor which would automatically be excepted from Article 85 (1). Rather, any restraint of the licensor in competition may come within that prohibition. This constitutes a substantial aggravation in comparison to the GWB, under which restraints on the licensee are governed by Sections 20 and 21, but those on the licensor only by Sections 15 ff., in practice especially Section 18.[24]

---

[22] Accord: Bodenhausen, *ibid.;* Spengler, *ibid.;* Kunschert, DB 1960, pp. 487, 488; von Gamm, p. 28; Deringer, *ubi supra,* and Bericht No. 101; Kleemann, p. 47; Schumacher, WuW 1962, p. 481; undecided, as yet, Gleiss/Hirsch, AWD 1962, p. 124. The cartel laws of all countries respect industrial protective rights in principle, although the courts of the United States have progressively narrowed their scope vis-à-vis the public policy expressed in the antitrust laws.

[23] OffJour 1962, p. 2922; CMR ¶ 2698. See ¶ 51, infra.

[24] Such restraints are therefore effective and may merely be declared to be ineffective by the cartel authority, under rather narrow conditions.

¶ 49

¶ 50   *Restraints on the licensee within the protected area:* Under general principles, the validity of an industrial protective right is limited to the territory of the state where it exists (territorial principle).[24a] For instance, if an enterprise has patents for the same invention in all of the six EEC countries, the licensee under the German patent cannot sell in the other EEC countries because he is excluded by the local patents there. The territorially limited effectiveness of industrial protective rights thus may result in export prohibitions for the licensee. They do not, however, come within Article 85 (1) since it is not the agreement between licensor and licensee that is the efficient cause for the adverse effect upon interstate trade,[25] but rather the patent situation in the several EEC states. The same applies to licenses under trademarks (but see ¶ 48), registered designs, utility models (process patents), and plant patents.

If the licensee is prevented by the patent situation from exporting into the other EEC states, so too, of course, are his customers. Therefore, the licensor may also obligate the licensee to impose a corresponding export prohibition on the latter's customers. Here, too, it is not the consensual restraint on competition that is the cause of the adverse effect upon interstate trade. There is, however, reason to believe that the Commission will adopt a contrary position, namely that an export prohibition imposed on customers of the licensee is impermissible. We believe this position to be incorrect under the principle of territoriality, at least where patents are concerned.

The licensor is not under any legal duty to lift this export prohibition for the licensee (and his customers) by means of granting licenses under his protective rights in the EEC states for the entire Common Market as a unit; that would in effect be a compulsory license and thereby an impermissible interference with the applicable local laws. In principle, the European Court confirmed this thesis in the *Parke, Davis* decision of February 1968.[25a] The Detroit firm Parke, Davis and Co., holder of two Dutch process patents on drugs (biochemicals), was held to be entitled to file suit against a Dutch firm, Centrafarm, based on these patent rights, to stop imports of drugs manufactured in Italy by using the procedure not patented there (because there is no patent protection for pharmaceutics in Italy). In spite of the obvious consequences of a national court's cease and desist order for interstate trade the European Court did not consider the prohibition

---

[24a] Cf. Samwer, GRUR AIT 1969, p. 1; Alexander, Article 85 of the EEC Treaty and the exclusive license to sell patented products, CMLR, Vol. 5, p. 465.
[25] Accord: Gleiss/Hirsch, *ibid.*

[25a] See ¶ 48, footnote 18a, supra and ¶ 205, infra.; annotations by Gleiss, WRP 1968, p. 143; Kirschstein, Europarecht 1968, p. 306; Alexander, Cahiers de droit Européen 1968, p. 307; cf. also BGH, "Voran" decision of February 28, 1968, p. 152.

of imports to Holland from Italy to be a violation of Article 85, paragraph 1. The Court argued that the rights granted to a patent holder by a Member State must not be endangered by application of Articles 85 and/or 86. To make use of such rights did not violate Article 85 (1) because there was no agreement, decision or concerted practice; one of these three elements had to be present in order to fulfill the requirements of this article.[25b]

Support for this view is found also in the Coal and Steel Treaty. The High Authority was of the opinion[26] that restraints due to the territorially limited effectiveness of protective rights do not contravene Article 65 of the ECSC Treaty. True, this expression of opinion of the High Authority should not be overvalued for the purposes of Article 85 (1) of the EEC Treaty, but it still is useful as a guide in the latter's interpretation.[27]

¶ 51   Since the *scope of protection* depends upon the applicable *national law*, Section 20, paragraph 1, of the GWB should be consulted for the German law. The restraints upon the licensee enumerated (in the second sentence) keep within the area of protection.[28] For details we must refer to the literature and practice under Section 20, GWB. Of special importance is the "Commission's Official Notice Concerning Patent Licensing Agreements."[29] In it the Commission lists obligations imposed on a licensee which, in its opinion, do not fall under the ban of Article 85 (1) of the Rome Treaty. Before discussing the particulars of the Notice, it should be pointed out that it, just as the other one, also dated December 24, 1962,[29a] has no constitutive effect, such as that of a group exemption under Article 85 (3) of the Rome Treaty (see ¶ 86, infra). What is involved is only an enumeration of restrictions which, in the opinion of the Commission, are prima facie not within the prohibition of Article 85 (1), thus, a type of group negative clearance (see ¶ 317, infra). It is therefore theoretically possible that the European Court is of a different opinion and perceives a violation of Article 85 (1) in one or another restriction.

On the other hand, the Official Notice referred to above does not mean that all restrictions not enumerated therein automatically fall within Article 85 (1). They are to be scrutinized in each particular case to determine whether they meet the prerequisites of this

---

[25b] Cf. ¶ 65, infra.
[26] In its Fourth General Report on the Activities of the Coal and Steel Community, April 11, 1955—April 8, 1956, p. 156.
[27] Accord: Spengler, GRUR AIT 1958, p. 330.

[28] See, e.g., Baumbach/Hefermehl, § 20 GWB, margin No. 11.
[29] December 24, 1962, OffJour 1962, p. 2922; CMR ¶ 2698.
[29a] See ¶ 16, footnote 42, and ¶ 45, supra.

prohibition or not. This will not be the case for many restrictions, primarily because they are within the scope of the patent grant, even though not mentioned in the Official Notice. The Commission itself expressly points out that the enumeration is not exhaustive.

Details of the Official Notice: Restrictions on the licensee pertaining to certain types of utilization of the patent do not come under Article 85 (1) (Paragraph IA1 of the Official Notice). (The German Patent Law recognizes four so-called "types of utilization": manufacture, offer to sell, distribution, use; see Section 6 Patent Act.)

Thus, it is permissible, e.g., for the licensee to be granted only a license to manufacture, but not a license to sell; he must then sell the merchandise manufactured under the license to the licensor. It is also permissible to grant one licensee the right to manufacture, another the right to sell, so that the former must distribute his goods through the latter.

Furthermore, restrictions on the licensee allowing him to utilize the patented invention only for specified technical *fields of application* are included within the scope of the patent grant (Paragraph IA2 of the Official Notice). If a patented invention can be employed, e.g., for gasoline as well as diesel motors, the licensee may be obligated to utilize it only with diesel motors, only with diesel motors over 500 horsepower, or only with stationary, not truck, motors, etc.

Moreover, the licensee may be restricted as to the quantity of the products he may manufacture, or as to the number of "acts of use" (*Benutzungshandlungen*) (Paragraph IA3 of the Official Notice). This type of restriction, too, is within the scope of the patent grant. Consequently, the licensee may be obligated, e.g., not to produce under the patent more than 20,000 units per year or for the duration of the licensing agreement. According to the language of the Official Notice, one might be led to believe that the licensee could be limited only in the maximum amount he may produce. But also the duty of the licensee to produce a specified minimum quantity within a period of time, e.g., a year, is within the scope of the patent grant. The licensor can have an interest in a minimum quantity if, e.g., he has granted the licensee only the right to produce the goods, reserving to himself the distribution, and thus must assure himself of an adequate supply. The obligation to produce a minimum amount is most often found where the license is an exclusive one; in this way the licensor can be assured that the licensee will not allow the license to lie idle. This interest of the licensor is most obvious where the royalty agreed upon is measured by the number of goods produced by the licensee. The obligation of the licensee to exercise the patent right, most often found in connection with an exclusive license, also belongs in this grouping, although it is not mentioned in the Official Notice. In our opinion, this obligation lies within the scope of the patent grant and is therefore manifestly permissible.

Finally, restrictions on the licensee in *time, space, or in alienability* are within the scope of the patent grant (Paragraph IA4 a-c of the Official Notice). It is thus allowable to conclude a licensing agreement for a period less than the life of the patent (for agreements extending beyond this time, see ¶ 59, infra), to limit the license to a specified part of the area in which the patent is valid, to stipulate that the patent be used only in a certain firm, or to prohibit the assignment of the license and/or sublicensing.

For further details of the "Official Notice Concerning Patent Licensing Agreements," see ¶ 58, for patent marking obligation of the licensee; ¶ 54 for obligations of the licensee with respect to quality of product and sources of supply; ¶ 58, for the obligation to exchange know-how and cross-license; and ¶ 60 and 61, for the exclusive license.

¶ 52   Sections 20 and 21 GWB deal with contracts concerning acquisition and use of patents, registered designs, plant patents, and secret know-how, and thus deal only with a segment of Article 85 (1). The latter reaches in addition contracts regarding acquisition or use of *other industrial protective rights,* as shown by Article 4 (2) (ii) (b) of Regulation 17, which expressly mentions also utility models and trademarks, but those too merely as examples. The protective scope of those rights also must be gathered from the applicable national law.[30] The Commission's Official Notice of December 24, 1962 (see ¶ 51, supra), is limited, regrettably so, to licensing agreements concerning patents. In our opinion, however, its basic principles can be applied analogously, but with caution, to other industrial protective rights.

This applies especially for licensing agreements concerning registered design patents and trademarks, and for licensing agreements concerning secret know-how (called Betriebsgeheimnisse—trade secrets— in Section 21 GWB).

It is within the scope of the trademark protection when the licensee, e.g., is obligated to use the licensed mark only with goods of a specified quality and to submit to quality-control inspection for this purpose.[31] We also believe it unobjectionable if the licensee is obligated not to contest the trademark (no-contest clause). But it is

---

[30] See also Deringer, GRUR AIT   [31] Ladas, 52 TMR, pp. 1165 f.
1962, p. 293.

outside the scope of trademark protection if a licensee is obligated not to compete with the licensor for the duration of the agreement or after its expiration.

In contrast to patents, there is no publication and no expiration of the protection for *secret know-how* within a period specified by statute. This alone is not sufficient reason to treat licensing agreements concerning secret know-how more strictly under the cartel law than agreements concerning patents: in reality, unprotected know-how will not remain secret longer than 18 years (the duration of a German patent), seldom more than 14 years (the duration of a French patent), not to speak of 20 years (Belgian patents). Moreover, it will be made obsolete by technical developments much before the end of this time, if it is not developed more fully by its possessor, in which case it may well have become a completely different trade secret. For know-how licensing agreements,[32] all provisions that serve to protect the trade secrets against unauthorized use or betrayal are without legal objection.[33] This means foremost that the licensee may be obligated to manufacture certain articles with the know-how, but is forbidden to make others,[34] or that he may use the know-how only in a specified plant, etc. If the licensor is unable to determine, because of factual circumstances, e.g., great distance, technical impossibility, or economic infeasibility, whether the licensee is using the know-how in a manner contrary to the agreement, he may then impose a clause prohibiting the licensee from competing with him in order to exclude unauthorized utilization.[35] In this case the agreement not to compete protects the licensed trade secrets; thus, the parties' concern is still only the licensed protective right. This theory, to be sure, was developed for German cartel law; in our opinion, however, it is valid in general, i.e., also for Article 85 (1). Restrictions of the licensee pertaining to duration and alienability (prohibition of assignment of the license) as well as the obligation to mark those articles produced according to the secret process, are also permissible under Article 85 (1). The same is true for obligations concerning the quality and sources of supply, in any event if such obligations are necessary for technically unobjectionable exploitation of the process; it is certainly true for obligations of the licensee to communicate experience gained in the use of the process, or to grant licenses for patents on improvements, to the extent that such obligations are non-exclusive and reciprocal (see ¶ 58, infra).

---

[32] See Maddock's detailed examination, CMLR, Vol. 2, p. 36.
[33] Van Notten, 38 N.Y.L.R. p. 531.
[34] Ladas, 23 Ohio St. L.J. p. 746; Skaupy, GRUR 1964, p. 545 and van Notten 38 N.Y.L.R. p. 532.
[35] BKartA, September 2, 1963, WuW/E BKartA 741.

¶ 53   *Restraints on the licensee outside of the protected area:* Here, too,
it is true that no restraint falls *per se* within Article 85 (1).
Rather, one should examine the particular case to determine whether
or not Article 85 (1) applies to it.

¶ 54   Aptness for adverse effect upon interstate trade may be relatively easy to find where the licensee is under an *obligation* to
purchase certain raw materials and the like only from the licensor or
from a third party named by the latter. In the absence of this obligation it would be possible for the licensee to procure the raw materials
elsewhere, including other member states. However, such an obligation does not come within Article 85 (1) if procurement from third
parties would be an indirect infringement of a patent,[36] which depends again upon the national law. This is really another case where
the restraint is still covered by the scope of the protective right and
therefore is not reached by Article 85 (1). Such an obligation, in our
view, is permissible also where procurement from the licensor is
technically necessary for the exploitation of a patent[37] or is justified
for the purpose of its most beneficial utilization, taking account also
of the licensor's good will. This was recognized to a limited extent
by the Commission, in its Official Notice Concerning Patent Licensing
Agreements of December 24, 1962 (see ¶ 51, supra). According to the
Notice, commitments of the licensee concerning the quality of the
product and sources of supply do not violate Article 85 (1), "to the
extent that and so long as such obligations are indispensable to
technically unobjectionable exploitation of the invention" (Paragraph
IC of the Official Notice). The Commission's definition of technical
indispensability is very strict. Provisions imposed by the licensor
with regard to the quality of the product must not, according to the
Commission's views, which we think economically unsound, merely
lead to improvement in the quality, etc., of the products or ensure a
specified minimum standard; rather, according to the Commission's
opinion, such provisions are permissible only if their aim is to prevent
technically unsuitable, i.e., actually useless, application of the invention. Only in such a case, in the Commission's view, do the provisions
concerning quality restrain competition not "worthy of protection."

According to the Official Notice, there is a relation of priority
between provisions dealing with quality and those dealing with
sources of supply. The licensor must first set out quality provisions,
i.e., objective criteria, which the products made under the license, as
well as preliminary products, raw and supplementary materials, must

---

[36] See Heine, GRUR 1960, p. 265 ff.
[37] This is also the position of the Commission in its Official Notice Concerning
Patent Licensing Agreements (see ¶ 49,
supra); also in accord: Kleemann, p. 47.

satisfy. Only if it is not possible to prescribe such criteria may the licensor, according to the Official Notice, impose obligations on the licensee to purchase certain raw materials, etc., but again only if such obligations are necessary to prevent useless application of the inventions.

In our opinion, this limitation may be justifiable in the case of obligations to purchase raw materials, although there are possible individual exceptions, but it is not justifiable to prohibit the licensor from imposing abstract provisions concerning quality. We believe it erroneous to apply the same standards to them as used for obligations to purchase raw materials, since the latter deprived the licensee of the freedom of choice, *inter alia,* of supplier. The legitimate interest of the licensor does not extend merely to assuring that the licensee markets products which are technically just barely usable; in our opinion, he may also provide that they shall meet higher standards. Commercial considerations, such as the good will of the licensor, should also be allowed for, but the Commission evidently does not choose to do so. To refer the licensor instead to the thorny and, as experience has shown, time-consuming path of Article 85 (3) is unsatisfactory and unnecessary.

Whether a license which, e.g., allows the patented process to be utilized only in connection with those materials that the licensee purchases from the licensor, may be spoken of as an obligation to purchase from the licensor (*Bezugspflicht*) can be seriously questioned. To be sure, in such case, use of the licensor's materials is required for the exercise of the license, but the licensee is not legally obligated to purchase from the licensor.

¶ 55   Aptness for the described effect will frequently be present where the licensee must not make or distribute *competing products.*[38] In our opinion, in exceptional cases the agreement not to compete must also be counted as being within the protected area if, by reason of actual circumstances, the licensor cannot supervise the licensee or otherwise prevent him from also using the patent outside the scope of the license. In this case the agreement not to compete still protects the licensed right. Although this theory was developed for trade secrets,[39] we believe it may be applied correspondingly to licensing agreements concerning patents and other protective rights.

---

[38] See WuW/E BKartA 29; accord: Kleemann, p. 47.

[39] See September 2, 1963, decision of the Federal Cartel Authority, WuW/E BKartA 741-42; accord: Magen, p. 177.

¶ 56   As to prescribing the licensee's *prices* for the protected objects,
       see ¶ 25, supra.[40] This would not normally be apt to affect
adversely interstate trade, even if one does not assume at the outset
that it would fall within the scope of the patent grant. The licensee's
obligation comes closer to an undue restraint of trade where he must
observe fixed prices also in selling other, unprotected goods. If, as
will mostly be the case, the product brought to market by the licensee is composed of protected and of unprotected parts, it depends
upon the particular case to what extent price-fixing is permitted.

¶ 57   An agreement by the licensee *not to contest the validity of the
       protective right* will as a rule be permissible.[40a] It is true that a
successful attack upon the licensed right, particularly in countries
where there is no examination before registration or where the examination is less stringent than in Germany, might further interstate
trade and that the no-contest clause thus might affect it adversely.[41]
However, such an attack in many cases is possible not only on the
part of the licensee but also from other quarters, e.g., from competitors
of the licensor. The latter are not precluded from attack. If, then,
the licensee is not the sole nor the principal potential party contesting
the right, the no-contest clause does not come within Article 85 (1)
since it cannot appreciably influence interstate trade, not even if it
continues in force after the termination of the license agreement. More
of a problem is presented where the licensee is put under an additional
obligation not to contest other protective rights not licensed to him.
Here, applicability of Article 85 (1) suggests itself more definitely.

     To be taken into account, in our opinion, is the consideration
that the licensee often comes to know the strengths and weaknesses
of the licensed right only through the license. For this reason, it does
not restrain competition worthy of protection and it is consequently
permissible for the licensee to be prevented from defeating the rights
of the licensor with the knowledge thus acquired. The OLG Karlsruhe[41a] deemed an agreement not to contest the validity of a protective right to be in accord with Article 85 (1), since it came under
Article 4 (2) (i) of Regulation 17 (see ¶ 339 ff., infra).

---

[40] Kleemann, p. 47, regards tying the licensee to a price as permitted.

[40a] Recently the U. S. Supreme Court abolished the doctrine of the patent licensee's "estoppel," with or without an agreement not to contest: *Lear, Inc. v. Adkins*, 395 U. S. 653 (1969).

[41] We regard as not supportable the theory that no-contest clauses ought to be immune from the prohibition of Article 85 (1) by virtue of the very language used in its subparagraph (e), because they are usual ones by trade custom: thus von Gamm, p. 28; cf. Gleiss/ Hirsch, AWD 1962, p. 124. This pro- vision is directed at "tying clauses" and contemplates situations where the parties agree to insert tying clauses in contracts with *third parties*. It is not applicable to license agreements.

[41a] Decision of April 23, 1968, WuW/E OLG 951.

¶ 58   As for the obligations of a patent licensee to *exchange know-how* and to *grant licenses for improvements or new uses* to his licensor, the applicability of Article 85 (1) depends on the provisions of the particular agreement. Aptness for adverse effect upon inter-state trade is missing where the licensee is not prevented from passing on his know-how and from giving licenses under his inventions to others also, i.e., where he need grant the licensor only a non-exclusive license; it is true that this obligation can be a restraint on competition, but the licensee is free to grant as many licenses as he desires, thereby furthering competition and trade even more. For this reason, the obligation to grant the licensor non-exclusive licenses for *parallel inventions* may also be permissible. It may be different where the licensee is bound to give know-how and licenses only to the licensor or to transfer rights in improvements and the like to him; but here it depends upon the circumstances of the particular case.

The Commission's view on this subject is more severe (see its "Official Notice Concerning Patent Licensing Agreements" of December 24, 1962, ¶ 51, supra). In its opinion, the obligations of the licensee to exchange know-how and to license his inventions regarding improvements and new uses are unobjectionable only if such obligations are non-exclusive and reciprocal on the part of the licensor (Paragraph ID of the Official Notice). The Commission requires such corresponding obligations of the licensor, in our judgment, wrongly, since this requirement does not lessen the obligation of the licensee and the latter still has the opportunity, even without this "counterweight," to communicate his know-how to third parties and grant them licenses for his inventions regarding new uses and improvements.

That the Commission's theory of the "reciprocal obligation of the licensor" as a justification for a restriction of the licensee is logically untenable is demonstrated by the consideration that the licensor never needs to put himself in the position of finding new uses and/or improvements. Thus, his "reciprocal obligation" is in many cases completely worthless. The Commission's requirement of a corresponding obligation of the licensor finds no basis in the Rome Treaty. It was evidently borrowed from the German GWB (Section 20, paragraph 2, no. 3); the theory there, however, is equally unsound since the relevant GWB provision likewise is not concerned with the question of equality of considerations. One might just as well permit a restraint on competition if and because compensation was paid for it, a proposition which has found application in English law in some circumstances.

¶ 58

It is permissible to obligate the licensee to mark the products made under the license *with a reference to the patent or license*. This does not restrain him in competition. It may be different if he may not add his own name or trademark. Such an obligation prevents him from developing his own good will and thus limits him competitively. Whether this obligation violates Article 85 (1) or not is a question for the individual case. Our opinion in this regard corresponds with the view of the Commission in the "Official Notice Concerning Patent Licensing Agreements" of December 24, 1962 (see ¶ 51, supra).

¶ 59   Finally, it should be noted that Article 85 (1) may be applicable to all obligations of the licensee which are imposed upon him beyond the *duration of the licensed protective right*. Notoriety of the secret know-how is analogous to the expiration of a protective right. This is true even of restraints which were covered by the scope of the protective right during its existence. Whether all the prerequisites of Article 85 (1) are fulfilled must be determined for each particular case.

The Commission is of the opinion in its "Official Notice Concerning Patent Licensing Agreements" of December 24, 1962 (see ¶ 51, supra), that the licensee may never be bound longer than the licensed protective rights last. As a categorical proposition, this is too extreme. For instance, continued payment of license royalties after expiration of the protective right or notoriety of the secret know-how is not automatically a restraint on competition of Article 85 (1) in every case;[42] it may also be remaining remuneration for the general advantage received under the license by the licensee, and is then permissible. It is conceivable, e.g., that the contracting parties might set the royalties intentionally low for the first five years in order to enable the licensee to "get on his own footing" economically, and that the higher royalties to be paid in equal installments during a period of, say, three years after expiration of the protective right and of the license would therefore be reasonable. Thus, for continued payments of royalties, just as for the continued existence of other restraints, it must be determined whether all prerequisites of Article 85 (1) are fulfilled.

The Commission may grant group negative clearances under Regulation 19/65 for restraints of the licensee outside the scope of protection, for the licensed right and for restraints on the licensor.

---

[42] Graupner, 1962 Law Gazette, p. 381.

¶ 60   *Restraints upon the licensor:* Article 85 (1) does not apply
         where the owner of the protective right grants a license under
it *to the exclusion of his own right to exploit it,* i.e., where he remains
the owner only in form. Such a license is legally less than an assignment of the protective right involved, which would automatically bar
the licensor (assignor) from further exploitation. An assignment,
however, does not come within Article 85 (1), and the same must be
true of a partial alienation which excludes the licensor from use.

The Commission, in its Official Notice of December 24, 1962,
recognized this reasoning regarding the licensor's obligation not to
exploit the licensed patent any further; in its opinion this obligation
of the licensor comes so close to being a full assignment of the right
that it is therefore unobjectionable. Under the language of the Official Notice, this holds true for the exclusive as well as the non-
exclusive license; to make a differentiation here would not be justified.

¶ 61   Again, an *exclusive license,* in the sense that it prevents the
         licensor from granting similar licenses to third parties, is not within
the purview of Article 85 (1). Thus, the licensor under a simple
license may also incur the contractual obligation not to grant further
licenses to third parties.

This, too, is recognized by the Commission in its "Official Notice Concerning Patent Licensing Agreements," although for unsatisfactory reasons. The Commission does not follow the "from the
greater to the lesser" reasoning advocated here; on the contrary, it
merely states that the obligation of the licensor not to grant further
licenses to third parties would not be apt to affect adversely trade
between member states under the present situation in the Common
Market. This ground is unsatisfactory because it introduces criteria
which offer no prospect of predictability and protection of reliance on
the present state of the law. The Commission should at least be
required to make known when, in its view, such an obligation can
affect adversely trade between member states.

On the other hand, in our opinion, it would not, without more,
be excepted from Article 85 (1) if the licensor granted an exclusive
license for his French patent, and, in addition, obligated himself to
the licensee not to license third parties under an identical German
patent or another French patent. Such an obligation has nothing to
do with the exclusive license under the first patent.

Article 85 (1) will not apply to an undertaking by the licensor
not to grant to other licensees more favorable conditions than to the
first one, or to extend more favorable conditions conceded to other

¶ 60

licensees also to him *(most favored treatment clause).* On the other hand, a more serious problem is raised by an obligation to grant licenses to third parties only on certain more onerous terms; here Article 85 (1) applies, in our opinion, if the other prerequisites are fulfilled.

¶ 62   Thus, no Article 85 (1) situation is presented where, e.g., a German licensor has given an exclusive license under his French patents and consequently may not export into the licensee's territory, France, even though this results indirectly in an export prohibition for the licensor (and his customers). The same ought to be true, in our view, where he has granted only a simple license under the French patents but has obligated himself contractually not to export patent-protected goods to France. In either case, the customers of the German licensor cannot, unless they have a license under the French protective rights, export the protected goods produced by him into France, since marketing of the goods in the Federal Republic does not consume the French protective rights (territorial principle). It is therefore also permissible, in our opinion, for the licensor in such a case to agree to impose an export prohibition on his customers.

¶ 63   Article 85 (1) does apply to an obligation of the licensor *not to undersell* the licensee or to sell the protected goods only at a *fixed price.* This is true particularly where the licensor concurrently prescribes for the licensee prices for the sale of the protected goods.

¶ 64   Article 85 (1) is not applicable to an obligation on the part of the licensor under a patent to *inform the licensee of his further experience* and to *grant further licenses for improvements.* This is the position taken by the Commission *(ibid.),* without the qualification of non-exclusiveness and reciprocity made by it for similar obligations of the licensee.

¶ 65   Article 85 (1) is to be applied to an obligation of the licensor not to manufacture or market *competing products.*

Regarding *patent pools, cross-licensing* and *multiple parallel licenses,* the Commission, in its Official Notice of December 24, 1962 (cf. ¶ 51), takes no position. However, the mere formation of a patent pool does not violate Article 85 (1). The participants bring their patents and licenses into the pool. Legally there is no restraint of competition in doing so; what is involved is permissible alienation. Restraints on competition may, however, lie in the agreement concerning the formation of the pool; here it depends on the individual case. In any case,

¶ 65

the general rules do apply to licensing agreements concerning individual patents that the pool later concludes with participants or third parties.

The Commission's reticence regarding reciprocal or multiple parallel licensing is not readily understandable. In our opinion, neither reciprocal nor multiple parallel licensing as such violates Article 85 (1); the content of the agreement is decisive. Here the general rules find application. If the content does not go beyond, e.g., the scope set by the Commission in its Official Notice, then such agreements are certainly permissible.

A claim of patent infringement is not a "decision" or "agreement" within the meaning of the prohibition of Article 85 (*Parke, Davis & Co. v. Centrafarm,* ¶ 48, ¶ 50, supra). That case considered the action of Parke, Davis, holding patents in the U. S. and Holland, in attempting to prohibit the import of infringing products from Italy, where it had no patent protection, into Holland where its licensee did business. The Court carefully avoided making a statement with regard to the problem of multiple parallel patent licensing.

XIV. Article 85(1)(d)

¶ 66   This provision contains *no general prohibition against discrimination*. What is prohibited here is only discrimination through cooperation by cartel agreement, decision or practice.[43] A (non-dominant) enterprise, then, may exact unequal terms, e.g., unequal prices, from its customers or suppliers in the same circumstances, but may not obligate itself (horizontally or vertically) to such action. Article 85 (1), therefore, should not be regarded as a price discrimination statute comparable to the Robinson-Patman Act (Section 2 of the Clayton Act), but rather, even in its subparagraph (d), as a somewhat more detailed analogue to Section 1 of the Sherman Act.

Only discrimination against parties with whom the discriminator does business, i.e., customers or suppliers, is prohibited. Contrary to the German GWB, Article 85 (1) manifestly does not cover discrimination against competitors.

[43] Compare, however, the prohibition in Article 86 (c), phrased identically, against discrimination on the part of enterprises having a dominant position in the Common Market, and our discussion there. Furthermore, there are provisions against discrimination contained in Article 7 (because of nationality), Article 37 (state trade monopolies), and Article 90 (public undertakings); cf. Zimmermann, Beiträge zum EWG Recht, Internationales Kartellrechtsforum in Brüssel 1960, p. 200. Compare also ¶ 71, infra.

¶ 66

¶ 67   The illustration given in subparagraph (d) does not differentiate between "terms" (or, as translated by others, "conditions"). Even agreements, etc., to apply only *subordinate terms* in a discriminatory fashion are therefore prohibited. It is probably true, however, that Article 85 (1) ought not to be applied to entirely inconsequential differences.

¶ 68   The literal text requires that the parties discriminated against be actually *put at a disadvantage* in competition. This is narrower than the general prohibition of Article 85 (1),[44] where mere purpose is enough. However, since subparagraph (d) is only an illustrative situation for the scope of that prohibition, it is sufficient also if the parties discriminated against are *intended* to be placed at a disadvantage, without any such actual result;[45] but if one shares our opinion that mere "purpose" in Article 85 (1) is not meant as an independent alternative (see ¶ 14, supra), then the detriment must actually occur. Indirect detriment is enough.

¶ 69   The application of different conditions is prohibited only where there is equality of consideration—the quid pro quo —furnished by the parties among whom the differentiation is made. ("Furnishing equivalent considerations" seems a preferable translation to the "undertaking equivalent engagements" used by others, since the German "Leistungen" and the French "prestations" are by no means limited to executory undertakings.) As far as the wording is concerned, this is not the same thing as the "intrinsically justified reason" of Section 26, paragraph 2, GWB, where personal or subjective reasons for a differentiation (e.g., a family relationship with a dealer) may also be thus justified. Beyond the literal text of Article 85 (1)(d), however, which, one must remember, is merely an illustrative situation, one ought to assume here too that different conditions are permissible in spite of equivalent counter-values if they are *intrinsically justified otherwise*.

¶ 70   Discrimination on the basis of *nationality* is prohibited in any event and independently from cooperation by cartel. This prohibition against discrimination in Article 7 of the EEC Treaty applies also to individual enterprises. As to Article 7, the European Court has ruled[45a] that it also constitutes a discrimination to treat unequal situations equally. This does not apply to Article 85 (1) (d), as the wording shows.

---

[44] Accord: von der Groeben/von Boeckh, Article 85, note 10; Baumbach/Hefermehl, Article 85, margin No. 20.

[45] Accord: Baumbach/Hefermehl, *ibid.*
[45a] Decision of July 17, 1963 (Case No. 13/63, Italian refrigerators, Recueil Vol. IX, page 335; CMR ¶ 8014).

XV.   Article 85(1)(e)

¶ 71   It is not *tying transactions* as such that are prohibited, but
agreements, etc., regarding them.[46] This results again from
the fact that the cooperative restraint of competition required for the
application of Article 85 (1) qualifies all of the illustrative situations
given in its lettered subparagraphs. As far as subparagraph (e) is
concerned, the prohibition thus extends only to agreements, etc., to
insert tying clauses in contracts with third parties and not to individual tying transactions. This construction is compelled, among
other things, by a comparison with the prohibition of tying in Article
86 (d) for enterprises having a dominant position: Were Article 85
(1)(e) to apply to individual tying transactions, it would, of course,
prohibit such transactions by dominant as well as by other parties,
and Article 86 (d) would then be a superfluous and incomprehensible
repetition of Article 85 (1)(e) without any substantive significance.
The relation of these two provisions thus is the same as that between
Article 85 (1)(d) and Article 86 (c) (see footnote 43 at ¶ 66) and
supports a parallel argument. Again, just as Article 85 (1)(d) is no
Section 2 of the Clayton Act, so Article 85 (1)(e) is no Section 3 of
that statute (the tying-clause section), but merely presents a specific
situation of consensual restraint of trade which would be dealt with
in the United States under Section 1 of the Sherman Act, at least as
far as direct applicability is concerned.

The German GWB also covers individual tying transactions only
in connection with market domination (Section 22, paragraph 3, no. 2
GWB); tying agreements as a result of cooperation are dealt with in
Section 18, paragraph 1, no. 4 GWB which applies for all enterprises.
In Section 18 GWB, as in Article 85 (1)(e), a tying transaction as
such (the *Zweitvertrag* or secondary contract) is not banned, but only
the antecedent underlying obligation.

Restraints on competition in individual (e.g., licensing) contracts
cannot, therefore, in our view, be justified by analogy to Article
85 (1)(e), on the basis that they may be a matter of commercial
custom. In our opinion, Article 85 (1)(e), directed as it is to a nar-
rowly limited situation, does not lend itself to such an analogous
application (compare also footnote 41 at ¶ 57). In addition, it should
be noted that subparagraph (e) is merely an illustration. Consequently, the fact that a restraint does not fall under this example does not
compel the conclusion that it is altogether exempt from Article 85 (1);
rather, it is still possible for it to come within this article (see ¶ 32, supra).

---

[46] Compare, however, the prohibition against tying by enterprises having a dominant position in the Common
Market, in Article 86 (d) of the Treaty.

C. ARTICLE 85 (2)—LEGAL CONSEQUENCES

XVI. On the Criminal Side

¶ 72   Culpable (intentional or negligent) violations of Article 85 (1) may be punished by the Commission under Article 15 (2)(a) of Regulation 17 (see our discussion there) through the imposition of fines that are not of a "penal character" (compare Article 15 (4) of Regulation 17).

XVII. On the Civil Side

¶ 73   Paragraph (2) declares contracts and decisions in violation of Article 85 (1) void. "Concerted practices" are not mentioned in this connection. They are omitted for a good reason: they are patently not legally binding, so that such a sanction against them would be ineffective.

The European Court has stated in the *Grundig* decision (¶ 16, supra) that only specific prohibited clauses of an agreement in violation of Article 85 (1) are automatically void; the agreement in its entirety is void only if its void parts cannot be severed from it. The result is that the Commission must indicate in its opinion whether only parts are void and whether these parts are inseparable from the remainder of the agreement. The Court stated that not all clauses of the agreement in the *Grundig* case violated Article 85 (1); partial invalidity was evident from "particular clauses of the agreement . . . which provided for absolute territorial protection, as well as the supplementary provision concerning the GINT trademark." Such language still does not clarify exactly which clauses were deemed to be invalid. The Court further contributes to this lack of clarity when it states that the clauses of the Grundig agreement "which go beyond the grant of an exclusive dealership and touch upon the foundation of interstate trade" in order to prevent parallel imports, thus securing absolute territorial protection, are violative of Article 85 (1). Under French law an exclusive dealer may enforce his rights against third parties not privy to the dealership agreement *(opposabilité aux tiers)*; thus, every "simple" exclusive dealership is to some extent "absolute" according to French law. The solution to the problem would not be to regard relevant provisions of the contract, if severable, as void and invalid, but rather to deny the exercise of any rights under such an agreement against third parties. Thus seen, the question of partial invalidity and the resultant quagmire could be avoided.

¶ 73

The concept of voidness in Article 85 (2) is equivalent in general to that in the German civil law; the desired results of the transaction (agreement or decision) are not affected. Nevertheless, a declaration of voidness under Article 85 (2) is capable of interpretation to a limited extent; in some circumstances this can lead to contingent invalidity.

The effective date of Regulation 17, March 13, 1962, is highly important for the content of the declaration of voidness.

¶ 74   *Before March 13, 1962* (the effective date of Regulation 17), violations of Article 85 (1) resulted in voidness of an agreement or decision if (and, contrary to the wording of Article 85 (2), only if) *either* the agreement, etc., in question had been declared void by the national authorities pursuant to Article 88 of the Treaty and at the same time had been denied an exemption pursuant to Article 85 (3), *or* the Commission had declared pursuant to Article 89 (2) that the agreement, etc., contravened Article 85 (1).[47] That has not happened in any case. All agreements, etc., which violated Article 85 (1) were therefore legally valid until March 12, 1962.

¶ 75   For the time *since March 13, 1962,* one has to distinguish between old (concluded earlier) and new (concluded since that date) agreements, etc., and furthermore between those requiring notification (Articles 4 (1) and 5 (1) of Regulation 17) and those that do not (Articles 4 (2) and 5 (2) of Regulation 17). For details see the discussion under Article 1 of Regulation 17.

¶ 76   The *legal consequences of voidness* are governed by the applicable national law.[47a] As far as the Federal Republic is concerned, this means:

¶ 77   Section 139 of the BGB determines the question whether invalidity of an agreement, etc., on account of violation of Article 85 (1) goes to the transaction in its entirety or only to the part restraining competition. Under that provision, voidness affects in principle the entire transaction; there is an exception where the transaction would have been concluded even without the void part. This legal consequence from Section 139 BGB may be avoided if the agreement stipulates in advance that voidness of individual provisions shall not affect the validity of the remainder (separability clause). The risk on the civil side attendant upon a violation of Article 85 (1) may to that extent be reduced.

---

[47] So conclusion No. 1 of the *Bosch* decision, *ubi supra*, footnote 41 at ¶ 16.   [47a] Accord: BGH, July 10, 1969, WuW/E BGH 1039 (*Auto-Lok*).

The presumption of invalidity of Section 139 BGB should not be rigidly upheld in every case. Especially with regard to agreements restraining competition, it will often, if not as a rule, be the intention of the parties to retain the remaining portions of the transactions in effect. If, for instance, an export prohibition violates Article 85 (1) because it prevents the obligee from supplying customers in other member states, it will probably correspond to the parties' intentions if the prohibition remains effective for third countries. German court decisions concerning licensing agreements have long held to this effect; for such agreements, the presumption of invalidity holds true only in obviously exceptional cases.

If, e.g., a vertical export prohibition that a producer imposes on his customers to protect his vertical price maintenance system, were not timely (before January 31, 1963) registered with the Commission and consequently void,[48] it does not necessarily follow that the vertical price maintenance scheme is also void. An export prohibition is not an indispensable component of a vertical price maintenance scheme. Apart from this, to be taken into consideration here, as in all other cases, is the principle that Section 139 BGB is not as a rule applicable where part of a contract becomes invalid due to a change in the law subsequent to conclusion of the contract.[49]

If the Commission grants an exemption for only part of an agreement but denies an exemption for the remainder, the exempted portion may be ineffective according to Section 139 BGB. A provision similar to Section 19, paragraph 2, GWB, where the BKartA may exempt from invalidity portions of an agreement that violate Section 18 GWB, is lacking in Community law. It may be different when the participants secondarily apply for an exemption for a part (the rest) of an agreement. If the Commission then denies an exemption for the whole agreement, it must grant exemption for the rest if it fulfills the prerequisites of Article 85 (3). Problems under Section 139 BGB do not occur in such a case since the intention of the parties is apparent from the secondary or auxiliary application *(Hilfsantrag).*

The *Grundig* decision of the European High Court contains nothing contrary to our recommendation above, viz., application for exemption of a part of an agreement or, under Regulation 17, Article 8, conditional or restricted exemption.

---

[48] Contra: LG Munich, January 14, 1963, BB 1963, p. 167, reversed by OLG Munich, May 30, 1963, BB 1963, p. 744.

[49] Compare BGH, January 8, 1952, NJW 1952, p. 299, March 18, 1955; see also, e.g., RGZ 146, p. 366.

¶ 78   In principle, invalidity does not attach to *separate individual contracts* which may have been concluded on the basis of the cooperative restraint on competition prohibited by Article 85 (1).[50] Exceptions are possible either where the individual contracts contravene Article 85 (1) by themselves, or where they have been made between parties to the prohibited cooperation by cartel and serve its implementation or performance.[51] For instance, the export prohibitions that Grundig imposed on its German customers could have come within one of these exceptions if the Commission's decision had not expressly included them. Whether such separate individual contracts, where they are of a continuing nature, may in every case be terminated for important cause or may, after the cessation of the basis for the transaction, be adapted to the changed circumstances,[52] we regard as a doubtful question.[53] Nevertheless, their validity does not preclude damage claims by the contracting party on whom the agreed-upon cartel restrictions were imposed, against the other party.[54]

Under American law, while the effect of illegality under an act of Congress is a matter of federal rather than state law, and while approach and terminology ("intrinsic" vs. "collateral" illegality) are different, actual results reached by the courts seem to be generally in accord with those produced both by the rules and the exceptions just stated in the text (probably not including, however, the same degree of respect for a separability clause as such in this field). See, for instance, *Kelly v. Kosuga*, 358 U. S. 516, 519 ff. (1959); *Bruce's Juices v. American Can Co.*, 330 U. S. 743, 754-755 (1947).

¶ 79   Whether a violation of Article 85 (1) may give rise to injunction and damage claims, perhaps by third parties affected thereby, depends in Germany upon the question whether the prohibition of Article 85 (1) is a "law for the protection of another" within the meaning of Section 823, paragraph 2, of the BGB. Article 85 (1) does serve the purpose of protecting economic intercourse between the EEC states against restraints on competition (see ¶ 21, supra) and thereby protects the general public, but not individuals or particular groups of persons. Advantages for the latter may be only incidental and are not necessarily indicative of a "law for the protection

---

[50] Accord: Baumbach/Hefermehl, Article 85, margin No. 25; von Gamm, p. 33; compare also the German decisions and literature in Kracht, WuW 1959, p. 546, footnote 1.

[51] Accord: Baumbach/Hefermehl, *ibid.*

[52] This is argued by von Gamm, p. 33.

[53] The BGH decision cited by von Gamm, of June 1, 1951, NJW 1951, p. 836, also in BB 1951, p. 623 No. 1616, in our view involved a special case and can scarcely serve as a precedent generally.

[54] Compare OLG Celle, February 15, 1963, BB 1963, p. 1113.

of another."[55] It therefore is not a protective law within the meaning of Section 823, paragraph 2, of the BGB.[56] Nevertheless, one cannot predict with any certainty what the course of judicial decisions will be. There is a conflict of opinion whether Article 85 (1), in its illustrative situations (d) and (e), is or is not aimed also at protecting individuals and is or is not, to that extent, a protective law.[57] The right of application of interested persons and associations of persons in Article 3 (2) (b) of Regulation 17 is not conclusive one way or the other.

This is a complex of questions which, while requiring judicial solution in many EEC countries, does not arise under the antitrust laws of the United States since they expressly (Section 4 of the Clayton Act) confer on parties injured by a violation the right to seek injunctive relief and (treble) damages in court. Belgian law apparently does recognize damage claims by third parties, provided that the damages are certain and that their causal relation to the violation of Article 85 (1)—or Article 86—can be demonstrated (see van Hecke/Suetens, Journal des Tribunaux, 1962, p. 364)—conditions reminiscent of, but probably in practice more stringent than, those for treble damage actions under the American antitrust laws. In German cartel law there is a special statutory provision (Section 35 GWB) concerning damage claims which, however, refers to a protective law and thereby leads back to Section 823, paragraph 2, BGB.

D.   ARTICLE 85 (3)—EXEMPTIONS

XVIII.   Introductory Remarks

¶ 80   Under certain generally defined conditions, the prohibition of Article 85 (1) may be declared inapplicable pursuant to Article 85 (3). Like (1), paragraph (3) is a *general clause,* so that the general prohibition of cooperative restraints on competition in (1) is matched by the equally broad and general possibility of exemption under (3). The proceedings before the Commission to obtain an exemption are free of charge (cf. also ¶ 321, infra).

---

[55] The same is true of Section 1 GWB. Benisch, Gemeinschaftskommentar 63, Section 35 GWB, marg. n. 5.

[56] See also Wohlfarth/Everling/Glaesner/Sprung, Article 85, note 14; von der Groeben/von Boeckh, Article 85, note 12; Baumbach/Hefermehl, *ubi supra;* von Gamm, p. 33; Kleemann, p. 60.

[57] The affirmative is taken by Wohlfarth/Everling/Glaesner/Sprung, *ibid.,* and by von der Groeben/von Boeckh, *ibid.;* the negative by von Gamm, *ibid.,* and by Kleemann, *ibid.* The BGH has denied the character of a "protective law" to the prohibition of discrimination in Article 60, Section 1, of the CST, in its decision of April 14, 1959, BB 1959, p. 576, especially 578.

¶ 81   Article 85 (3) does not distinguish between types of cooperative restraints on competition. Rather, the prohibition of Article 85 (1) may be declared inapplicable for *every agreement*, etc.,
which fulfills its prerequisites. A declaration of non-applicability or
exemption may therefore be available in the case of cartels for which
there is no possibility of legalization under the GWB, e.g., genuine
price cartels (see also ¶ 33), or vertical price maintenance prohibited
under French law. Removal of the prohibition of Article 85 (1)
through exemption under the "double fence theory" did not also lift
the ban under national laws (this theory now modified by the Court's
Tar-Colors decision of February 13, 1969, see the Introduction).

Not only agreements and decisions, but also *concerted practices*
may be exempted from the prohibition of Article 85 (1), as expressly
stated in (3).

XIX.   General Matters

¶ 82   There is a conflict of opinion on the question whether Article
85 (3) constitutes a reservation in favor of (administrative)
exemption grants, or constitutes a statutory exception.[58]

If it is a *reservation of exemption*, then every cooperative restraint
on competition falling within Article 85 (1) would be prohibited until
exempted from this prohibition pursuant to paragraph (3). The exemption would in that case be an operative act and would in principle
be effective only for the future. If Article 85 (3), on the other hand,
is in itself a *statutory exception*, then any cooperative restraint on
competition fulfilling the requirements of the exception would be
lawful and effective *ab initio*. The exemption would in that case be
merely declaratory of existing legality and would therefore quite
naturally relate back to the time of the exempted transaction.[59]

The European Court held in the *Bosch* decision that for the period
before March 13, 1962, agreements would be considered void only if
they were expressly declared so by the Commission or a national authority; this occurred in no case. Consequently, the disputed question
remains of practical importance only for the time since that date and
then only for old agreements, etc., requiring notification. For new

---

[58] See Antoine Braun/Gleiss/Hirsch, p.
146 ff., particularly p. 146, footnote 234
ter dealing with French theory and
French law, and footnote 245 *bis* on
Italian law.

[59] For details on the disputed question see, e.g., Sölter, WuW 1961, p.
665 ff., especially 674-676, with further

references; von Gamm, p. 28. Article 85
(3) has been construed as a statutory
exception, e.g., by the Commerce Court
of the Seine, decision of May 21, 1962,
AWD 1962, p. 206; but that decision
was reversed by the First Chamber of
the Cour d'Appel of Paris (see Handelsblatt of February 6, 1963).

agreements, Article 85 (3) is undoubtedly to be considered as a reservation of exemption; this is also the practice of the Commission. In our opinion, this interpretation should also be valid for old agreements.[60]

In its *Portelange* decision,[60a] the European Court held that the answer to the question of whether an agreement is really prohibited by Article 85 (1) presupposes the evaluation of the economic and legal context. It must be expressly stated that in a certain case not only Article 85 (1) is fulfilled but, in addition, that the exemption under Article 85 (3) is out of the question. "So long as this statement has not been made, each notified agreement must be regarded as valid."

¶ 83   The character of Article 85 (1) as a general prohibition could result in the following *allocation of the burden of proof:* The authorities would have to prove that the facts come within the terms of the prohibition; and the participants in the restraint on competition, that the prerequisites to a declaration of non-applicability under Article 85 (3) exist. To be sure, Article 85 raises no questions of burden of proof in the ordinary sense, since public law rather than a civil action is involved, but the above theory is sound in substance. The European High Court makes it clear in the *Grundig* decision (¶ 16, supra) that the Commission may not limit itself to requiring proof of satisfaction of the criteria for exemption, but rather must itself contribute to a clarification of the factual circumstances of the case according to general principles of effective administration.

¶ 84   *Jurisdiction:* Since March 13, 1962, *exclusive* jurisdiction for exemption grants pursuant to Article 85 (3) rests with the Commission of the EEC. Its decisions are subject only to review by the Court in Luxembourg[61] (see also Article 9, Regulation 17). An exemption binds the national authorities and courts.

Before March 13, 1962, the competent national authorities could also issue declarations under Article 85 (3) (see Article 88 of the Treaty). The BKartA has done so in several cases.[62] Where the BKartA did not limit its exemptions to a shorter period, they lost their effectiveness on March 13, 1965 (Article 23 (1) of Regulation 17).

---

[60] Guide Lines, p. 18; accord: Ellis/Heuvel, p. 424.
[60a] Decision of July 9, 1969, Recueil Vol. XV, p. 309 ff.; CMR ¶ 8075.

[61] See Article 9 (1) of Regulation 17, and Article 173 of the EEC Treaty.
[62] See, e.g., WuW/E BKartA 28 ff., 250.

¶ 85   *Application:* As far as the text of Article 85 (3) is concerned,
the Commission could grant an exemption on its own motion,
and exemption would thus not depend upon an application therefor.
However, at least for those agreements, decisions and practices which
come within Article 85 (1) and for which the benefits of paragraph
(3) are to be claimed, Articles 4 (1) and 5 (1) of Regulation 17 prescribe notification, and that, in practice, means an application to the
Commission. The Commission may grant exemptions for agreements,
etc., not requiring notification without application of the participants
having been made (see discussion under Article 4 of Regulation 17,
¶ 334).

The application is to be filed with the Commission on Form A/B
(Regulation 27, Article 4). Applications which do not use this form
are improper, except for those filed before May 11, 1962, the effective
date of Regulation 27 (Article 5 (1) thereof). Even the latter, however, must be re-filed on Form A/B if the Commission demands it, as
has occasionally happened (Article 5 (2) of Regulation 27).

¶ 86   *Group Exemptions:* Pursuant to the text of Article 85 (3),
exemptions may be granted also for categories of agreements,
decisions or concerted practices. The term "categories" (Gruppen)
needs interpretation.[63] We understand it to mean agreements, etc., of
a certain type.[64] This meaning is also conveyed by the "categorie"
in the French version. These types must be classified according to
abstract characteristics,[65] e.g., license agreements which go beyond
the scope of the licensed protective right only by obligating the licensee to exchange know-how and not to contest the validity of the
right; distribution agreements which stipulate that the distributor
sell only to specialty stores in the branch of business involved; vertical
price-fixing contracts for brand-name articles which compete with
others; agreements for terms and conditions regarding reservation of
title, liability for defects and scope of warranties, etc. "Categories of
agreements," therefore, is not limited to those made by a certain enterprise recurrently and regularly (i.e., merely contracts following the
same sample or pattern), e.g., vertical price-fixing contracts for the
bakery products of Company X.

---

[63] On the history of the word "Gruppen" in German business law see
Sölter, WuW 1961, p. 677 ff.

[64] Accord: Sölter, *id.,* p. 678; Gleiss,
Handelsblatt (Journal of Commerce)
of December 15/16, 1961.

[65] Accord: Wohlfarth/Everling/Glaes-
ner/Sprung, Article 85, note 15; Frankfurter Kommentar, introductory remarks
to Article 85, TZ 16; Sölter, *ubi supra,*
p. 676 ff.; probably also Günther,
WuW 1957, p. 281.

This interpretation of "categories" is in our opinion virtually compelled by Article 4 (2) of Regulation 17, which exempts certain agreements, etc., from the requirement of notification. All of these agreements are described by generic characteristics, e.g., as imposing "restraint on the rights of any person acquiring or using industrial property rights" (Article 4 (2) (ii) (b)); and these classes of agreements are elsewhere (e.g., in Regulation 17, Articles 5 (2) and 22 (1)) referred to under the same term, "categories," as is used in Article 85 (3) of the Treaty. In the absence of any reason for giving the term a different meaning here, the latter provision thus must be presumed to refer also to classes defined by abstract criteria.

A group exemption may be granted only if the agreements of the type involved fulfill the prerequisites of Article 85 (3). In the nature of things, this cannot be examined in advance for each agreement of the general type. It is necessary, rather, to describe the category in abstract terms, but so that fulfillment of the conditions is guaranteed as much as possible under the circumstances.

The Council of Ministers has, in Regulation 19/65, granted the Commission the power to issue group exemptions for specified restrictions in exclusive distributorship agreements and contracts concerning the assignment or use of industrial property rights, manufacturing processes, and technical know-how.[66]

While Regulation 1017, dated July 19, 1968 (OffJour No. L 175, July 23, 1968, p. 1; CMR ¶ 2761), does not grant a general exemption as regards transport, it does exempt certain types of agreements, decisions and concerted practices involving transport on railways, roads and inland waterways. These agreements, etc., are those that merely aim at or effect the application of technical improvements or technical cooperation. Furthermore, they are agreements, etc., of certain small and medium enterprises that pertain to the formation and activities of joint enterprises engaged in transport on roads and inland waterways, or to the joint financing and joint acquisition of "transport material" (apparently, e.g., lorries or ships) or accessories.

The regulation introduces a kind of "objection procedure" (in German cartel law known as "Widerspruchsverfahren"), for agreements contributing to the improvement of transports or to the promotion of greater continuity and stability on markets in which supply and demand fluctuate. The procedure also applies to agreements increasing the productivity of enterprises or promoting technical or

---

[66] For the Commission's first act granting a group exemption, see Regulation 67/67, ¶ 701 ff., infra.

economic progress. All this presupposes that the customers' interests are adequately taken into account, that the participating enterprises are not unnecessarily restricted, and that it is impossible to eliminate competition for an essential part of the relevant transport market.

Enterprises participating in such agreements, etc., may request the Commission to exempt them from the prohibitions contained in Article 85. The essential point is that if the Commission does not, within 90 days from the date the request was published in the Official Journal, notify the applicants that it objects, the agreements, etc., are considered to be exempted for the past and for the future. This exemption, however, is good for no more than three years from the date of publication.

XX. Requirements for Exemption: General Observations

¶ 87   Article 85 (3) contains four conditions (two of them of an affirmative and the other two of a negative nature) which must be fulfilled for an exemption to be granted.

The *affirmative* conditions are:

(1) equitable participation by consumers in the profit resulting from the benefits achieved by the cooperative restraint, *and* (in the conjunctive)

(2) some contribution to the improvement of production or distribution or (in the alternative) to the furtherance of technical or economic progress;

and the *negative* conditions are:

(3) no restraints on competition which are not indispensable to the achievement of the objectives described in (2), *and* (in the conjunctive)

(4) no opening of the possibility for the participants to eliminate competition for a substantial portion of the goods involved.

Positive and negative prerequisites must be given at the same time.

¶ 88   These conditions are phrased in such a manner that their letter fits only certain types of competitive restraints (e.g., syndicate agreements), but is not really appropriate for many others (e.g., license agreements, contracts for exclusivity, etc.). Therefore, the Commission ought not to be overprecise in construing the requirements for exemption. Overcautious and narrow interpretation and application would render the prohibition of Article 85 (1) not only rigid but unrealistic.

Both positive prerequisites are not rigid but elastic: the less the significance of the restraint on competition, the less is required to fulfill the prerequisites, and *vice versa*.

XXI.   Equitable Participation by Consumers in the Profit

¶ 89   *Consumer* does not refer only to the ultimate consumer. Rather, the term includes every customer for the goods or commercial services involved.[67] The word "utilisateur" in the French version indicates this more clearly. Equitable participation of the consumer is thus present even where only the immediately subsequent trade level enjoys the advantages concerned. It is not required, nor in many instances even possible, that these advantages be passed on from there, possibly as far as to the ultimate consumer.[68]

¶ 90   The term *profit* is not employed in its technical meaning so as to require participation in the net gains shown on the books of the enterprises. Profit rather means any economic advantage brought about by the cooperative restraint on competition.[69] Such advantages need not necessarily be lower price[70] or better quality, but may consist of larger choice, better customer service, better delivery terms, etc.[71]

¶ 91   Whether the consumers' participation is *equitable* or not must be examined in each particular case. E.g., if a given cooperative restraint on competition leads to a profit for the participants which would make price reductions possible,[72] but no such reductions are

---

[67] Accord, e.g., Wohlfarth/Everling/ Glaesner/Sprung, Article 85, note 17; Sölter, WuW 1961, p. 681; Kleemann, p. 51.

[68] Accord: Court's *Grundig-Consten* decision, ¶ 14 and 16, supra.

[69] Accord: Wohlfarth/Everling/Glaesner/Sprung, *ubi supra;* von der Groeben/ von Boeckh, Article 85, note 16; Baumbach/Hefermehl, Article 85, margin No. 28; Günther, WuW 1957, p. 281; Koch, BB 1959, p. 246; Kellermann, GRUR 1959, p. 576; von Gamm, p. 30; BKartA Annual Report 1959, p. 55; WuW/E BKartA 30, 250.

[70] Accord: Baumbach/Hefermehl, *ibid.*

[71] Accord: Günther, *ibid.;* Koch, *ibid.;* von der Groeben/von Boeckh, Article 85, note 6; Baumbach / Hefermehl, *ibid.;* BKartA Annual Report 1959, *ibid.;* WuW/E BKartA, *ibid.* Good examples of "profit" are to be found in Antoine Braun/Gleiss/Hirsch, p. 154, ¶ 122.

[72] Compare, e.g., BKartA, decision of November 29, 1961, WuW/E BKartA 400 ff., also in BB 1962, p. 77 f. ("Süddeutsche Zementwerke," South German Cement Works).

made, the question may arise whether the consumers' participation in other advantages is still "equitable."[73]

It might be noted here that the German word, "angemessen," is possibly narrower than the French "equitable," in the sense that at least its literal meaning is, "fitting" or "adapted to the circumstances," perhaps even, "adequate" or "proportionate," rather than more generally "fair and reasonable"; but the distinction is so slight that it should not lead to different results in application.

It is immaterial whether, in the case of several advantages, consumers are sharing equitably in each of them, taken separately, the question being rather one of the aggregate advantages.[74] Nor is it material whether each individual consumer participates equitably, as long as consumers as a whole do.[75]

¶ 92   Whether consumers' participation must be of a *continuing* nature, or whether it suffices if they share in the advantages but once, will depend on the concrete case.[76]

¶ 93   It makes no difference whether equitable participation is intended or not. It is enough that the cooperative restraint is *objectively apt* to that end.[77] By the same token, mere good intentions alone will not suffice.

XXII.   Improvement of Production or Distribution of Goods . . .

¶ 94   The cooperative action resulting in restraint on competition must be appraised *as a whole.* Thus, it is not necessary that the competitive restraints themselves contribute to the improvement of production or distribution.[79] A license agreement may contribute to improvement of production by increasing the number of suppliers of patent-protected goods,[80] although in other respects it may restrain the licensee in his competition.

¶ 95   Only production or distribution of *goods* is mentioned, not *commercial services.* This, however, has no substantive significance; otherwise, the prerequisite now under discussion for admis-

---

[73] Accord: Baumbach/Hefermehl, *ibid.*
[74] Thus, WuW/E BKartA 250; also Sölter, *ubi supra.*
[75] Accord: Sölter, *ibid.*; Kleemann, p. 51.
[76] For details, see Sölter, *ibid.*
[77] Differently: Kleemann, *ibid.*, who demands a certain degree of probability;

accord with here: Baumbach/Hefermehl, *ubi supra;* Sölter, *ibid.*
[78] Reserved.
[79] Baumbach/Hefermehl, *ibid.*; Sölter, *ibid.*
[80] Such an assumption was made by the BKartA in WuW/E BKartA 30.

sibility of restraints on competition could never find application to commercial services. In our view, therefore, cooperative action in restraint of competition which leads to increased supply of commercial services, improvement of their quality and the like, complies with this condition.

¶ 96   In what respect the production or distribution of goods must be improved Article 85 (3) does not say. It therefore does not depend upon improvement of any particular type or in any particular direction. As an example, increased supply[81] due to the fact that a new kind of product is being offered in the market would be sufficient. Increased supply of existing products likewise would suffice, as would also savings in or rationalization of production by the use of uniform standards or types. Specialization, too, may contribute to the improvement of production. Improvement of distribution may be found, for instance, in the creation or the enlargement of a distributing organization through syndicates, in increase of quantity or assortment of merchandise in stock at local distribution centers, in the fact that a market for certain goods is created for the first time, etc.

Since, therefore, the *promotion of any aspect* of the production or distribution of goods is sufficient, it is not only rationalization cartels in the proper sense of the term that may contribute to the improvement,[82] but also any other type of trade-restraining cooperation. This is the reason why the term "rationalization cartels," frequently used as a convenient but loose characterization of all cartels eligible for an exemption under Article 85 (3), has not been adopted here for that purpose.

¶ 97   Whether there is an *"improvement"* must be determined relative to the state of affairs which would exist in the absence of the competitive restraint. This will in practice often mean a comparison with the state of affairs before the conclusion of the agreement, etc.,[83] but with the qualification that the effect of existing illegal cartels must be discounted in appraising the status quo. What counts here again is the aggregate or net effects. There may thus be an improvement where the number of suppliers is being diminished but output of the merchandise is increasing. There will also be improvement where a further drop in production is being prevented or at least retarded by cooperation through a cartel,[84] e.g., a cartel designed to combat a structural crisis in the industry (compare Section 4 of the GWB). An entirely negligible improvement will not suffice; on the

---

[81] Such a situation was involved in WuW/E BKartA 30.
[82] Accord: Sölter, *ibid.*
[83] Accord: Sölter, *ibid.*
[84] Accord: Sölter, *ibid.*; Kleemann, p. 51.

other hand, "perceptible" improvement (Article 65, Section 2, paragraph 2 of the Coal and Steel Treaty) is not demanded.

One difficulty in making the necessary comparison will often be encountered in the fact that the past and present state of affairs is known or at least ascertainable, whereas future conditions are unknown or less certain. The appraisal will be even more difficult where a competitive restraint has already existed for a long time. The Commission must envisage in such a case what would happen if it denied the exemption. Here, then, the comparison must be with theoretical, fictitious situations.[85]

¶ 98   It is not sufficient that the participants may subjectively intend improvement of production or distribution by their cooperation in restraint of competition. Likewise insufficient, on the objective side, is mere aptness to bring about the improvement, for this in itself is not to "contribute" as demanded by the law.[86] Rather is it necessary, objectively, that the improvement of production or distribution actually materialize. Subjectively, as indicated by the language of Article 85 (3) (a), this must be an *objective* of the cooperation, but it *need not be its main or sole objective.* The requirement of a contribution is fulfilled where the cooperation brings about an improvement of production or distribution as one factor among others, e.g., the general development of technology or of the economy (see ¶ 102, infra).

The above comments are largely supported by the opinion of the European Court in the *Grundig* decision (¶ 16, supra). There it is stated, *inter alia,* that not every advantage accruing to a contracting party out of an agreement concerning production and distribution is to be regarded as an "improvement." Some advantages are always discernible, but to constitute an improvement within the meaning of Article 85 (3), there must be objective, tangible advantages that are apt to counterbalance disadvantages wrought by the agreement.

Naturally, achievement of the improvement, etc., can be evidenced only where an agreement, etc., was already in force before exemption so that its effects are known, e.g., when there is an old cartel or application for renewed exemption (compare Article 8 (2), Regulation 17). If, on the other hand, the agreement was not in force before exemption so that the Commission knows as yet nothing concerning

---

[85] In this regard, compare Antoine Braun/Gleiss/Hirsch, p. 155, and the Commission's *DRU-Blondel* decision (OffJour No. 131, July 17, 1965, p. 2194; ¶ 116, infra) and its *Hummel-* *Isbecque* decision (OffJour No. 156, September 23, 1965, p. 2581; ¶ 117, infra).

[86] Contra: Baumbach/Hefermehl, *ibid.;* Kleemann, *ibid.* Accord: Sölter, *id.* pp. 680, 681.

its effects, the Commission must be content with a prediction. It suffices if, according to general experience, the improvement can materialize.

XXIII.   . . . or Promotion of Technical or Economic Progress

¶ 99   Use of the disjunctive in the text of the law means that there must be either improvement of production or distribution, or promotion of progress; there need not be both. These *alternatives* cannot be nicely separated from each other in scope; improvement of production or distribution will generally also promote economic progress. However, since the alternatives are of equal value, there is no necessity for an exact distinction.

¶ 100   As in the case of "improvement," etc., "promotion" also need not be effected through the competitive restraint in question; the agreement, etc., is to be appraised here also *in the aggregate*.[87]

¶ 101   This alternative condition is even less specific than that regarding improvement of production, etc. It therefore can accommodate any imaginable kind of agreement in restraint of competition. Promotion of progress need not be in any particular direction; *promotion in any aspect* is enough. E.g., license agreements under industrial protective rights will in principle serve technical and economic progress because they enable other enterprises to exploit a right otherwise reserved exclusively to the licensor.[88]

¶ 102   As with improvement (see ¶ 98, supra), here also it is not necessary that the participants intend the promotion of progress as their principal or sole objective. On the other hand, mere intention will not suffice if the agreement does not in fact promote progress.[89] The law demands a contribution; it must actually be rendered and the promotion *effectuated*[90] (but see ¶ 97, supra). A "contribution" toward this end will, however, suffice, and this very terminology justifies the conclusion that it is not necessary for the cooperation in restraint of competition to have promotion of progress as its principal effect.[91]

---

[87] Accord: Sölter, *id.* p. 680.
[88] Thus, the BKartA in WuW/E BKartA 30.

[89] Accord: Baumbach/Hefermehl, *ibid.;* Kleemann, *ibid.*
[90] Accord: Sölter, *ibid.*
[91] Sölter, *ibid.*

¶ 102

XXIV.   Indispensability of the Competitive Restraint
(Article 85(3)(a))

¶ 103   This condition involves the question of the extent to which
         an enterprise participating in an agreement, etc., may be
restrained in its competition, i.e., the *scope of the competitive restriction in the relations of the parties inter se* rather than its effect upon the
market[92] (as to the latter, see ¶ 106 ff., infra).

¶ 104   When a competitive restriction is indispensable can be de-
         termined only in each particular case. *Indispensability* requires,
first of all, that improvement of production, etc., could not, or at least
not with sufficient certainty, be achieved without the competitive restriction.[93] The latter thus must be indispensable for the accomplishment of one or the other of the legally required objectives. This must
be judged objectively and not according to the views of the participants in the cooperative restraint.[94] The Commission also holds this
opinion; in its recommendation[95] to the "Convention Faience," it
considers as significant the question of whether the cooperative restraints on competition were necessary according to an objective
viewpoint. Indispensable, in that sense, would be an exclusive distribution franchise, e.g., for a certain EEC country, if none of the
enterprises qualified by size, efficiency and similar factors would be
willing to take on the distribution of the goods concerned without
such a franchise.

Indispensability also requires that the competitive restrictions do
not go beyond what is necessary for the accomplishment of the required objectives.[96] This, too, must be determined by objective
standards.

¶ 105   It is *not necessary*, however, that the competitive restriction
         be *proportionate* to the desired objective.[97] Article 85 (3) (a)
does not demand proportionality between competitive restriction and

---

[92] Accord: Sölter, WuW 1961, p. 685.

[93] Accord: Baumbach/Hefermehl, Article 85, margin No. 30.

[94] This view was also approved by
the European Court in its *Grundig* decision (¶ 16, supra) : Consten's "absolute
protection" by Grundig was not necessary. In the cases *DRU-Blondel* (Off-
Jour No. 131, July 17, 1965, p. 2194;
¶ 116, infra) and *Hummel-Isbecque* (Off-
Jour No. 156, September 23, 1965, p.
2581; ¶ 117, infra), the Commission admitted that a restraint on competition in

case of "open" (not absolute) sole distributorship may be considered indispensable.

[95] Of July 24, 1963, WuW/E EV 60;
also in AWD 1964, p. 187; CMR ¶ 2741.

[96] Accord: Baumbach/Hefermehl, *ibid.;*
von Gamm, p. 31; Sölter, *ibid.*

[97] Contra: Günther, WuW 1957, p.
281; Baumbach/Hefermehl, *ibid.;* Wohl-
farth/Everling/Glaesner/Sprung, Article
85, note 17; von Gamm, p. 31; Koch, BB
1959, p. 247; accord: Sölter, *ibid.;* and
Kleemann, *ibid.*

success. It requires merely that the restriction not exceed the measure necessary for the accomplishment of the objective.[98] If it stays within that measure, it is immaterial whether the particular restriction is adequate to the desired objective or not, although the decisions of the European Court may indicate a contrary view.

Proportionality between competitive restriction and objective is advocated by some authors above all on account of the administrative law rule of proportionality of means, as well as on account of the basic principle of Article 85 which is to permit restraints of competition in interstate trade only when their positive effects are preponderant. According to administrative law, however, the principle of proportionality is binding only on administrative bodies, not on private citizens. Moreover, the economic effects of competitive restraints, i.e., the effects on the market, are not to be determined in this connection, but rather when answering the question of whether there is the likelihood of elimination of a substantial amount of competition (see ¶ 106 ff., infra).

The desired objective of the restraint on competition must be improvement in production or distribution, or technical progress, with equitable participation by consumers in the profit. Other objectives, e.g., social ones, do not justify the restraint on competition. On the other hand, the restraint does not need to be aimed exclusively at the statutory objectives; there may be other, additional goals (see ¶ 99 ff.).

In determining whether the prerequisites of Article 85 are fulfilled, an aggregate appraisal is again decisive for a number of restraints on competition; isolated examination of individual restrictions would not suffice. In making such an appraisal, those restrictions which are not expressly contained in the agreement, but which are evident from the surrounding circumstances, are to be considered.

XXV. Possibility of Elimination of Substantial Competition (Article 85(3)(b))

¶ 106   This condition, in contrast to the one under (a), goes, not to the extent of the competitive restraint as a matter of the internal relations between the parties, but to its *effects upon the market*.

¶ 107   Although the wording of the law refers only to *goods*, the condition applies equally to commercial services.[99]

---

[98] Accord: Sölter, *ibid.*   [99] Accord: Baumbach/Hefermehl, Article 85, margin No. 31; Kleemann, p. 53.

¶ 108   Competition must not—and the possibility thereof is suffi-
         cient: see ¶ 112—be eliminated in a substantial portion of
the "goods involved." It therefore is necessary first to identify the
goods to be considered in this connection; in other words, to define
the *relevant market*.

This includes, in the first instance, the goods for which the competitive restraint is being agreed upon ("contract goods"). It includes, furthermore, all goods which may reasonably be used interchangeably for the same purpose.[1] One must therefore take account
of the possibility of functional substitution. Decisive factors are the
use to which the merchandise is to be put, its durability, its price, its
special qualities, etc. Which goods are functionally interchangeable
and which are not must be examined for each particular case. Mere
substitute products that are not interchangeable do not fall within
the goods to be included here[2] (see also ¶ 206, Article 86).

Geographically, the relevant market comprises the territory in
which the goods concerned are distributed. This will generally, but
need not necessarily, be the entire Common Market. The relevant
market need not always be a "substantial" part of the Common
Market.[3]

¶ 109   What portion of the goods involved is *"substantial"* can like-
         wise not be laid down categorically. First, one will have to
determine the volume in which the goods concerned are distributed
in the Common Market, taking account also of supplies from outsiders and imports. The part affected by the competitive restraint
must then be considered in relation to this total volume.[4] The market
share of the participants is thus a crucial factor,[5] but market structure,
e.g., number and volume of outsiders, also plays a part. On these
points the *Grundig* decision of the European Court (¶ 16, supra) is lacking; nothing is said concerning the volume of Grundig products distributed
by Consten and parallel importers (such as UNEF and Leissner),
concerning the volume of such products sold in the entire Community,
nor concerning the amounts of competing products sold in any area.
Under the broad holding of the Court, the result would be the same

---

[1] See, e.g., Borchardt/Fikentscher, p.
53 ff.; Günther, Relevanter Markt, p.
17; Spengler, WuW 1961, p. 513;
Barnikel, WuW 1961, p. 249; BKartA,
decision of August 11, 1961, BB 1961,
p. 1255 No. 2389, also in WuW/E
BKartA 427; for a comparative law
view, Schwenk, WuW 1960, p. 3 ff.
Compare also the discussion under
Article 86, ¶ 206, infra.

[2] Contra: Kleemann, *ibid.*, who apparently includes such substitute products also; accord: Sölter, WuW 1961,
p. 688.
[3] Contra: Sölter, *id.* p. 687.
[4] Accord: Baumbach/Hefermehl, *ibid.*;
Kleemann, *ibid.*
[5] To that effect already the BKartA
in WuW/E BKartA 30; also Baum-
bach/Hefermehl, *ibid.*

if the amount of Grundig sales in France constituted but one-millionth of the market. It is in the interest of business certainty and proper development of the law that a decision of such importance be related more definitely to the economic facts of the case.

A parallel may be found in the Coal and Steel Treaty: Pursuant to Article 65, Section 2, the High Authority may approve certain cartels if it determines that they are not apt to control prices for a "substantial portion of the products involved" (paragraph 1 (c)). In this connection the European Court, in its Case No. 13/60 (Coal Syndicate for the Ruhr),[6] has expressed the view that the possibility of controlling "a substantial portion" of the goods involved exists in the case of a market share of 26%-47%. This surprising decision may come to play a certain role in the interpretation of Article 85 (3) (b). But no general rule can be deduced from it, since market share alone is not determinative. Our conviction is shared by the Commission (see ¶ 205 f.).

¶ 110   The restraint must not open up the possibility of eliminating *competition* in the described field. Article 85 (3) (b) refers here to competition in general and does not distinguish between competition in price, in discounts, in quality, in terms, etc. All of these aspects of competition come within that term. Competition thus will still exist where some forms of it, e.g., in terms and discounts, are suppressed by the restraint in question, but others are preserved, e.g., price competition,[7] or vice versa. Material here is not only the competition among the participants in the restraint, but also that offered to them by third parties, although they may be located outside of the Common Market.[8]

¶ 111   *Elimination* means total suppression of the competition[9] so that it ceases to be a governing factor in the market concerned.[10] This will be the situation even though some inconsequential competition in secondary respects, or competition in substitute products, may remain.[11]

¶ 112   Under the unambiguous language of the law, it is only the *possibility of eliminating competition* that needs to be opened up. Competition need not, therefore, actually be eliminated, nor is it

---

[6] Decision of May 18, 1962, Recueil Vol. VIII, p. 165 ff.

[7] Accord: Sölter, *id.* p. 688.

[8] Accord: Sölter, *id.* p. 687.

[9] Accord: Sölter, *id.* p. 688; Deringer, GRUR AIT 1962, p. 293.

[10] Accord: Baumbach/Hefermehl, *ubi supra.*

[11] Accord, with respect to competition by substitutes, Sölter, *ibid.,* with further references.

necessary that such a result be intended. Objective aptness of the cooperative restraint to that end will suffice.[12] If this aptness exists, good intentions on the part of the participants will not save the situation. On the other hand—and herein lies an important limiting qualification of this condition which could hardly ever be complied with otherwise—there must be the possibility of *substantial* elimination.

XXVI. Granting of the Exemption, Effect, etc.

¶ 113   If the requirements of Article 85 (3) are met, the Commission must declare the prohibition of (1) inapplicable to the agreement, etc., involved. It is true that Article 85 (3) says only that the Commission "may" make the declaration of non-applicability. However, this wording expresses merely the legal authority of the Commission (it can or may grant exemptions); it does *not* mean that the issuance of an exemption is within the Commission's *discretion* where the conditions therefor are fulfilled. If the prerequisites are met, the party making the application thus has a legal claim to the exemption.

If an exemption is requested for an agreement as a whole and the prerequisites are fulfilled for only a part thereof, the Commission may grant the exemption only for such part and deny it for the remainder, but it does not have to do so. It may limit itself to a denial of the exemption for the contract as a whole since as far as the Commission is concerned, it is not at all certain that the contracting parties desire an exemption for only a portion of the agreement. An expedient solution for them may be a secondary or auxiliary application for partial exemption (see ¶ 77, supra).

¶ 114   As to the time from which a declaration of non-applicability is effective, see Article 6 of Regulation 17. For the period of effectiveness and revocation of the declaration, see Article 8 of Regulation 17.

¶ 115   Regarding the legal remedies against the Commission's decision, see the discussion under Article 21 of Regulation 17.

Exemption gives relief from the prohibition of Article 85 (1). It results in complete *legal validity* of the agreement, etc., involved, with binding effect also upon the national administrative authorities and courts. Exemption pursuant to Article 85 (3) does not, however,

---

[12] Contra: Kleemann, *ubi supra,* who   Accord: Baumbach/Hefermehl, *ibid.;*
demands a certain degree of probability.   Sölter, *id.,* p. 690.

¶ 113

dispense with the obligation to obtain permissions, consents and the like, which may be required for the agreement involved by national cartel law or general national law.[13]

Exemption is not permitted where the agreement, etc., in question contravenes *other prohibitions* of the EEC Treaty, solely or concurrently with Article 85 (1).[14] There is no exemption, e.g., for violations of Article 86, or for violations of the prohibition against discrimination on account of nationality in Article 7.[15]

XXVII.   Exemptions Granted by the Commission

The first edition of this book had to be based on opinions expressed in the legal writings of the time. Using them as a point of departure, we developed a theoretical basis. In the meantime the Commission has granted quite a number of exemptions and negative clearances. The exemptions are dealt with in the following paragraphs, with some comments, and the negative clearances in ¶ 321A through ¶ 321Q, in connection with Regulation 17.

¶ 116   *DRU-Blondel:* In its decision of July 8, 1965,[16] the Commission issued its first exemption, in the case Diepenbrock en Reigers N.V. (*"DRU"*), Ulft, Netherlands, and Etablissements Blondel S.A. (*"Blondel"*), Paris.

DRU, a manufacturer of iron household goods, had granted Blondel a sole selling right in France. The right to export DRU products was available to Blondel and any other party. Similarly, dealers in other Member States were entirely free to import competing products.

The Commission stated that the object or aim of the contract was to restrict competition within the meaning of Article 85 (1) and that the contract was apt to affect "interstate" trade. The fact that,

---

[13] For the national cartel laws of the member states, the reader is referred generally to the article by Riesenfeld in "American Enterprise in the Common Market: A Legal Profile," University of Michigan Law School, Ann Arbor 1960, Chapter X, entitled "The Protection of Competition," vol. II, p. 197, especially 207 ff., and to the briefer surveys by Becker, "The 'Antitrust' Laws of the Common Market," American Bar Association Antitrust Section Reports, vol. XVII, p. 456 (1960), and Kelleher, "The National 'Antitrust' Laws of Europe," *id.* p. 506 (reprinted in "Doing Business Abroad," Practising Law Institute, New York 1962, vol. 1, p. 286). See also the surveys of competition rules in the "Doing Business" sections of CMR, ¶ 6400 ff.

[14] Accord: Baumbach/Hefermehl, Article 85, margin No. 32; Steindorff, BB 1958, p. 92.

[15] Accord: Baumbach/Hefermehl, *ibid.;* Steindorff, *ibid.;* Koch, BB 1959, p. 247.

[16] OffJour No. 131, July 17, 1965, p. 2194; for details, see CMR ¶ 9049.

in France, only Blondel could buy directly from DRU meant that, the position of other dealers, i.e., third parties, in the market was appreciably changed. The restraint on competition was perceptible and its influence on trade between member states was of some importance. Hence, the contract came within the prohibition of Article 85 (1). The Commission granted the exemption because all the prerequisites of Article 85 (3) were fulfilled. An exclusive licensee, responsible for imports, marketing facilities, etc., gives the manufacturer a better picture of the market and makes it easier for the consumer to obtain foreign products adapted to his habits.

The fact that there was no "absolute" territorial protection for the licensee, no ban on exports to isolate member state markets, was decisive for the Commission. This was the essential difference from the *Grundig-Consten* case.

The Commission stressed the fact that Blondel had not used the contract with DRU to oppose imports by third parties and had no intention of doing so. This means that Blondel did not try to make the licensee's rights absolute by means of the *opposabilité aux tiers*, a possibility under French law which also played a part in the *Grundig-Consten* case.

¶ 117   *Hummel-Isbecque:* The exemption granted September 17, 1965,[17] for the *Hummel-Isbecque* agreement is so much like the DRU-Blondel exemption that we need not dwell on it.

In this case Hummel, a manufacturer of agricultural and similar machinery, had his domicile in southwest Germany, and Isbecque, the sole distributor for Belgium, was domiciled in Brussels.

Cases of this type are now covered by Regulation 67/67.

¶ 118   *Maison Jallatte:* The same is true for the exemption granted December 17, 1965,[18] in the case of the French firm *Maison Jallatte,* Nimes, which granted exclusive distribution rights for its safety shoes to a German firm, Voss, and a Belgian firm, Vandeputte. Here again, as in the two preceding cases, the manufacturer was not bound to prevent "parallel imports" and the licensees were free to re-export. Only Vandeputte was bound under an exclusive purchase clause not to deal in competing goods, i.e., products similar to those manufactured by Jallatte.

---

[17] OffJour No. 156, September 23, 1965, p. 2581; for details, see CMR ¶ 9063.   [18] OffJour No. 3, January 6, 1966, p. 37; for details, see CMR ¶ 9083.

It would seem that Voss was not thus restricted and that the Commission found the restraint on Vandeputte to be necessary in order to reach the aim of the contract. In this, as in the two preceding cases, the licensees were free to set their selling prices to customers.

¶ 119   *Transocean Marine Paint Association:* The exemption in the *Transocean Marine Paint Association* case of June 27, 1967,[19] came after a period during which there had been no decision by the Commission in the field of Article 85 after 1965.

This exemption is one of the Commission's most detailed decisions, with regard both to facts and to reasons. The association, whose seat is in Rotterdam, consists of 18 medium-size manufacturers of marine paints in 18 countries, including Japan, Australia, Panama, and five of the six EEC countries.

The association's aim is to manufacture jointly, according to a uniform formula and apart from other marine paints sold by its members individually, special marine paints, making use of the members' collective experience, and to sell these special paints under the same trademark. This trademark is registered in each of the 18 states in the name of the member established there. The members may add their own name and trademark, but they may not manufacture paints of the same quality as Transocean paints. They must submit to quality controls, exchange information on experience, and keep such information secret. Those members who hold patents apt to further the sale of Transocean paints are required to grant licenses to members first. The 18 firms are free to set their own prices. If one member sells in the business area of another member, he must pay that member ". . . %" commission. The figures for the commissions are mentioned only as guides. The members must inform the association of their turnover both in Transocean and in other paints, indicating the customers and the ships for which the products were intended. There are also quite a number of other restraints (see CMR ¶ 9188). The period of time for which the agreement is concluded is considerable: 20 years, renewable for another 20 years unless a majority of the members vote for dissolution 12 months prior to expiration of the first 20-year period. Disputes regarding the agreement must be submitted to arbitration.

To justify the agreement, the association has told the Commission that the customers prefer to deal with suppliers that are able to offer in all important ports paints of the same composition, be-

---

[19] OffJour No. 163, July 20, 1967, p. 10; see CMR ¶ 9188.

cause new coats of paint applied over old coats do well only if the
new paint has the same qualities as the old.

The Commission gives four reasons for which the agreement is
apt to affect trade between member states, and determines that the
agreement aims at and effects a perceptible restraint of trade, in
particular, by procuring for each member a preferential position in
its area. The Commission adds that, by erecting these artificial
barriers, freedom of trade is endangered in a way that might be
detrimental to the realization of a single interstate market.

The Commission then states, in more detail than in its former
decisions, that the agreement, while coming within the ban of Article
85 (1), fulfills all the conditions for an exemption under Article 85 (3).
Among other things, it declares that the association enables the
members to rationalize and to increase the sale of their paints by
establishing contract territories in each of which one member is
responsible for offering these paints, stocking them, granting service,
etc., in many ports. Thus, the members can also satisfy those buyers
that insist upon being supplied with paints of uniform quality whenever and wherever they wish. Without the agreement the members
would have to establish individually their own network of facilities
in a large number of countries, which would entail costs too high for
medium-size firms. The agreement, however, enables them to compete intensely with larger manufacturers of paint already represented
in all important countries. The exemption was granted as of June
15, 1966 (the date on which the notified agreement was amended,
i.e., freed from excessive restraints so as to make the exemption legally
possible), for the period ending December 31, 1972. To enable the
Commission to supervise the application of the agreement and, if
necessary, to revoke or alter the exemption or to forbid certain actions
of the members, the following conditions were imposed:

(1) The Commission must be informed, without delay, of
    (a) all changes in the membership of the association,
    (b) all changes in and additions to the agreement,
    (c) all decisions of the administrative board and all arbitra-
        tion rulings, insofar as they concern the application
        and interpretation of the provisions of the agreement
        which were taken into consideration in this decision.

(2) An annual report—for the first time for 1967—must be sub-
    mitted to the Commission, on the activities of the association,
    showing separate information on the production and sale of
    Transocean and other marine paints manufactured by the
    members, on the volume of deliveries for which the members

¶ 119

having their domicile within the Common Market are mutually bound to pay commissions, and on the amount and rate of such commissions.

This was the first exemption granted to a horizontal agreement between enterprises located in various countries. Hence, this is— more so than the Maison Jallatte case, which basically involved an arrangement between retailers—of general interest for agreements between enterprises on the same level, in this case manufacturers who simultaneously act on the level of supplying and servicing ultimate consumers. The fact that the Commission this time gives a more complete picture of the facts in its decision must be appreciated. Important figures are, however, still missing. The Commission has found out the association members' share of the market, but, unfortunately, it merely states that this share is "only about . . . percent," so that the reader does not learn this essential figure. The same is true with regard to other percentages, e.g., that of the Commission mentioned above. Respect for trade secrets may have played a role.

The following is, among other things, of particular interest to lawyers:

Formerly the Commission had maintained that any contract, etc., diverting the flow of interstate trade from its natural bed was "apt to affect interstate trade." Since the European Court, in the *Grundig-Consten* case (see ¶ 16) did not support this theory, the Commission adopts the Court's view here, arguing that the agreement is apt to endanger free interstate trade in marine paints in a way that might be detrimental to the achievement of the aim of a single interstate market. In spite of this rather complicated language it is now clear that to "affect adversely" means more than to change the course of trade from what is otherwise its natural flow.

We note further that all four criteria mentioned by the Commission for aptness to affect adversely trade between member states are, at the same time, used by the Commission for a restraint on competition.

Furthermore, we wish to stress the following sentence in the Commission's argument:[20]

"There is no reason to believe that the above provisions as they are applied result in a greater restriction of the members' economic freedom than is indispensable to achieve the objectives of the agreement."

This statement shows that the Commission does not place too much emphasis on the words "which do not subject the enterprises

---

[20] Translation from CMR ¶ 9188, III-(2) (b).

concerned to restrictions not indispensable to the achievement . . ." in Article 85 (3).

Finally, we think it should be pointed out that the Commission states that there were no reasons to deny the retroactivity of the exemption under Regulation 17, Article 7. This may indicate that such retroactivity is normal and that it will be granted as far as is possible under Regulation 17, Article 6 (see ¶ 120).

¶ 120   *ACEC-Berliet:* On July 17, 1968,[21] the Commission, in the case *ACEC-Berliet,* granted an exemption for an agreement on cooperation in research, in development and perhaps also in the manufacture of a new motor coach equipped with an electric transmission.

In its decision the Commission presents the following facts:

The agreement divides between the Belgian partner (ACEC in Brussels, the sole manufacturer of transmissions of the type concerned) and the French partner (Berliet in Lyon) the tasks involved with regard to the research and development of an electric transmission[22] (ACEC) and other parts of the vehicle (Berliet) up to series production. The partners exchange the necessary technical information and are partially restricted in using such information in their relations with third parties. If series production should come about later on, Berliet is obliged to buy electric transmissions from ACEC exclusively. In France, ACEC may supply such transmissions only to Berliet and in the other EEC countries, apart from Belgium, only to one manufacturer in each country. Insofar as the prices for the transmission are concerned, Berliet enjoys a most-favored-client clause and is free to sell the coach equipped with the ACEC transmission wherever it wishes, but it is bound to add the ACEC mark in countries outside of France. Each partner remains sole holder of all protective rights.

In its reasons the Commission states that the obligations of the partners with regard to purchasing and supplying, which also restrict the freedom of third parties, *aim at* a restraint on competition within the Common Market and are *apt to impair* trade between member states. But this, according to the Commission, is not a restriction or distortion of competition within the meaning of Article 85 (1).

---

[21] OffJour No. L 201, August 12, 1968, p. 7; Second General Report on the Activities of the Communities, 1968, p. 49; CMR ¶ 9248 and 9251.

[22] The idea is to place small electric motors into the wheel axles, thus giving better performance and more comfort for passengers.

¶ 120

At this—generally very important—point, one might ask why the Commission did not grant a negative clearance.

The Commission, after mentioning the bond of confidence between the two enterprises and their common risk, goes on to state that there is the risk of failure in all technical research. This does not, however, conflict with the statement that cooperation in research contributes to the promotion of technical progress. Since an economic exploitation is not possible until later, only the future can tell whether the consumers have an adequate share in the resulting profit. In this case it is sufficient that there is a reasonable probability that this adequate share will result. This is probable since the partners will have to make great efforts just to introduce their new bus— if a bus should be produced—considering the strong competition offered by the traditional buses and coaches firmly established in the market and by others of a newer type.

In the Commission's opinion the exclusivity clause is indispensable for attaining the favorable results of the agreement, because it enables both parties to write off their investments in common research and development. Because of their general importance, we quote here two sentences from the decision:[23]

"One could not reasonably expect one of the parties to take the trouble to develop a new technique in collaboration with the other partner and then allow that partner to make use of the result of its research with a third party. The reciprocal exclusivity clauses are therefore essential to achieve the favorable results of the agreement."

It must be assumed that the agreement will not enable the partners to eliminate competition with regard to an essential part of the products concerned.

The exemption, according to Article 8, paragraph 1, of Regulation 17, is valid for the period from March 14, 1966, to July 1973. It imposes on the partners the obligation to submit to the Commission at the end of 1971, i.e. after a period of about two and a half years, a report on the results of the agreement. The retroactivity of the exemption is based on Article 6, paragraph 1, of Regulation 17 (see ¶ 119).

It must be pointed out that these statements with regard to future events are speculative. Such statements are necessary, however, if agreements on joint research and development are to be brought under Article 85 (3), and this is certainly desirable.

---

[23] Translation taken from CMR ¶ 9251 III(3).

¶ 121   *CECIMO:* On March 13, 1969, the Commission granted the following exemption :[24]

CECIMO (Comité Européen de Coopération entre les Industries de la Machine-Outil, i.e., European Committee for Cooperation in the Machine-Tool Industries) is an association of twelve trade associations of manufacturers of machine tools for metal working. These trade associations are located in Germany, Austria, Belgium, Denmark, France, UK, Italy, Holland, Sweden, Switzerland, Spain and Portugal, i.e., all EEC countries, except Luxembourg, and seven others. Most manufacturers in the countries concerned are members of these national trade associations. With regard to the organization of European Machine-Tool Expositions, the CECIMO has made decisions on the participation of manufacturers. It applied for an exemption for these decisions in case they should be considered as coming within Article 85 (1).

According to these decisions the CECIMO, every odd year, organizes a fair (in the following text the words "fair" and "exposition" will be used interchangeably) through the trade association of the country concerned. (The nine fairs organized so far have been held in Paris, Hanover, Brussels and Milan.) During the year of the fair the manufacturers may not exhibit their products in any other of the twelve countries, not even indirectly. During the remaining years, i.e., every other year, they are free to exhibit wherever they wish. Should a licensor or licensee of a manufacturer exhibit at other fairs, this manufacturer and the machines concerned are excluded from the common fair.

According to the Commission's reasons, the decisions of CECIMO come within Article 85 (1) as "cartel decisions" from four aspects, the two most important of which we have just mentioned (exclusion of manufacturers in odd years from all other fairs, clause on licensors and licensees).

The Commission considers the following points to be in restraint of competition :

(a) The restriction of the freedom of action of all organizers of fairs in the EEC countries during the years in which a joint fair takes place ;

(b) restriction of "middlemen," because their freedom to exhibit is also restricted by special clauses ;

(c) the restriction of the freedom of action of the manufacturers.

---

[24] OffJour No. L 69, March 20, 1969, p. 13 ; CMR ¶ 9295.

Competition is restricted perceptibly, both with regard to the organization of expositions and the sale of machine tools.

This may also affect trade between member states, because only one exposition takes place in only one of the member states "so that the integration of the markets for the services is impeded." Even the machine-tool trade between the countries may be hampered. The same is true, particularly, with regard to manufacturers intending to gain a foothold on a special market and for customers "for whom it is sometimes difficult to go to other countries to look at machine tools . . . of interest to them, and possibly to acquire them." Manufacturers whose names and brands are well-known are less restricted.

Hence, a negative clearance was out of the question.

The Commission granted an exemption, among others, on the following grounds:

"The expositions taking place only every other year in *one* country permit a concentration and comparison of almost the entire supply of machine tools . . . thus allowing a comprehensive survey . . . with minimum advertising efforts." These advantages outweigh the disadvantages of the restriction on the freedom to exhibit. Participation in the fairs of the association is expensive, but expenses are less because the manufacturers do not have to exhibit at a series of fairs. Thus, the total expenses for the machines are lower. The interests of the "middlemen," according to the Commission's reasoning, only in exceptional cases do not coincide with those of the manufacturers, because for some retailers it is more advantageous to participate annually in expositions permitting direct contact with their personal customers.

The Commission argues, therefore, that an improvement in the distribution of goods and a promotion of economic progress are evident.

These advantages also benefit the consumers because they need not attend as many fairs, but can gather information at one single exposition, in direct contact with the exhibitors. Even prices will, in view of the keen competition on the market of these machine tools, be kept low.

Finally, the Commission argues, no restrictions are imposed which are not indispensable for the achievement of the objectives mentioned.

Since the decisions of the CECIMO were notified within the time-limit of Article 5 (1) of Regulation 17, the Commission's decision may take effect as of March 13, 1962. The exemption is valid "for ten years," i.e., until December 31, 1978, as the Commission stated.

The exemption is subject to the condition that the Commission be informed, without delay, of all decisions under which the CECIMO withholds admission to one of its fairs. By attaching this condition, the Commission establishes the basis for a continuous control of abuse.

The Commission, in its preceding announcement, even asked the associations of countries that are not member states to submit their comments.

In this case it is not the sale and purchase of goods that are concerned, but services in the special field of fairs, jointly arranged for practically all the West European industrial countries. The Commission's approach promises understanding in similar cases, but it must be borne in mind that the economic importance of the case is not too great.

¶ 122   *Clima Chappée-Buderus:* On July 22, 1969, the Commission granted the following exemption:[25]

Clima Chappée S. A. at Labuissière, France, and Buderus'sche Eisenwerke A. G. at Wetzlar, Germany, in January, 1968, concluded an agreement on specialization and reciprocal sole distributorship which they notified on April 2, 1968. Under this contract

(a) Clima undertakes to manufacture, e.g., centrifugal-axial blowers, steel cooling towers, ventilators, exhaust fans, convectors and baseboard heating elements;

(b) Buderus undertakes to manufacture, either itself or through a subsidiary, e.g., automatic oil and gas hot air heaters of all sizes, certain hot air appliances, exhaust convectors, and plastic cooling towers.

Each party delivers its products in the other party's country exclusively to that party, which in turn agrees to sell them exclusively on its market, provided that it can meet competition there. Both parties are free as to sales in the other member states and as to resale by their customers, who may install the equipment outside of their own country. (With regard to six other clauses, among them some escape clauses, see CMR ¶ 9279.)

The Commission stated that the contract restrains each party's freedom of action, for an indefinite time, as to, e.g., any investment

---

[25] OffJour No. L 195, August 7, 1969; CMR ¶ 9316.

and production in the field in which the other one specializes. In certain respects the consumer's freedom of choice may also be restricted because potential competition between the two parties is eliminated and no other enterprise in the two countries can buy the articles manufactured by the parties directly from them. Thus, the agreement conflicts with Article 85 (1). But its clauses are inseparably connected or ancillary to each other, and there is no clause which does not serve the economically desirable aims of the agreement. Among its results will be, as is normal, the lowering of prices, and it is sufficiently probable that the consumers will profit by that. Since the parties are just beginning to specialize, the Commission assumes that the facts on which its decision is based will not change before ten years have passed. The exemption was granted for this period of time.

This decision depends on so many technical and commercial details, partly, but not exhaustively, rendered in the Commission's statements, that it is hardly possible to draw any general conclusions from it. Those interested in similar agreements will have to study and analyze these data first.

¶ 123   *Jaz-Peter:* On the same day, July 22, 1969, the Commission also granted the following exemption[26]—the last one since that date:

Jaz S. A., Paris, and Peter-Uhren, Rottweil, Germany, on January 11, 1967, concluded a specialization and reciprocal exclusive supply agreement (which Jaz notified on March 20, 1967) involving mechanical and electric wall clocks and electric alarm clocks. Under the contract Jaz is to manufacture electric wall clocks and electric alarm clocks, Peter large mechanical alarm clocks. Each partner is obliged to supply the products in which he specializes, in the other partner's country, to that party exclusively, at the lowest price that he would charge a third party under similar conditions. Both are obliged to buy fixed minimum quantities. Furthermore, the parties are to exchange technical knowledge and discuss and coordinate common problems. The contract is concluded for an indefinite period of time and may be terminated on 18 months notice. It is subject to arbitration.

The Commission stated that both parties are free to set the selling prices of their own products and the resale prices of those they buy from their counterpart. Peter does not in any way influence the resale prices of goods sold by it, whereas Jaz issues price lists

---

[26] OffJour No. L 195, August 7, 1969; WuW/E EV 260; CMR ¶ 9317.

with price recommendations. In West Germany there are 90 to 100 manufacturers competing with the parties, four of which, at least, are larger than Peter in terms of capital, turnover and number of employees. Jaz is the largest of the about 40 French competitors, but its share of sales in France does not surpass 30 percent in any of the products concerned. Its share in the Common Market is not higher than five percent. Considerable quantities are imported from third countries, among them some COMECON members, Japan, and Switzerland. The products of the parties are trademarked by the respective manufacturer. The Commission finds proof of the profit of the contract in the fact that Jaz lowered the recommended resale prices in France for Peter's alarm clocks by seven percent as compared with similar products which Jaz previously bought from French manufacturers. Furthermore, according to the Commission, the prices of Peter's products on the German market have remained unchanged since 1967, in spite of considerably higher production costs, particularly wages. In this case the Commission stresses that neither partner would have given up market shares in favor of its counterpart if it were not sure of being able to buy from the latter the products necessary to round out its line of goods offered.

Otherwise the Commission's reasoning is much the same as in the Clima case. The exemption was granted for approximately ten years, viz. from the date of notification, March 20, 1967, to January 10, 1977.

The facts of this case are simpler than those of the Clima case. The argument that we think is worth stressing is that, according to the Commission, the parties to the contract would not have given up market shares to their counterparts if it were not for this special agreement. Besides, the restraints in the Jaz-Peter case go beyond the Commission's Statement on Cooperation of July 1969 (see ¶ 17, supra; CMR ¶ 9248 and 9269, where reference is correctly made to the Commission's indications in favor of cooperation, particularly between small and medium-size enterprises).

¶ 123

Article 86

(Author's Translation)

Incompatible with the Common Market and prohibited is the abusive exploitation by one or more enterprises of a dominant position in the Common Market or in a substantial part thereof, to the extent to which trade between member states is apt to be adversely affected thereby.

Such abusive practices may consist, in particular, of the following:

(a) direct or indirect imposition of unfair purchase or sales prices or of other terms and conditions of doing business;

(b) limitation of production, distribution or technical development to the detriment of consumers;

(c) application of unequal terms to parties furnishing equivalent considerations, whereby they are placed at a competitive disadvantage;

(d) subjecting the conclusion of contracts to the condition that the other parties to them accept additional goods or services which are unrelated to the subject matter of the contract either by their nature or by commercial custom.

A. SCOPE OF APPLICATION

I. Enterprise

¶ 201   The concept of enterprise in Article 86 does not differ from that in Article 85 (see ¶ 1 ff.); neither Article 85 nor Article 86 furnishes sufficient reason to assume the contrary. For purposes of applying Article 86, it is immaterial where the enterprise has its headquarters. (The Civil Law concept of what is here translated as "headquarters" (Gesellschaftssitz, siège social) attributes nationality or domicile to a business organization in the same sense as "organized under the laws of . . ." does in American law.) Enterprises not located in the Common Market area are subject to the prohibition of abusive practices laid down in Article 86, to the extent that they have a dominant position in the Common Market within the meaning of that provision.[1]

---

[1] See Antoine Braun/Gleiss/Hirsch, p. 171.

II. Market Domination by More than One Enterprise

¶ 202   Besides the relatively rare case of market domination by a
single enterprise, Article 86 of the EEC Treaty also reaches
domination by *several* enterprises. The provision says nothing about
the relations which must exist among the latter. What comes to
mind first is market domination by several enterprises which, although independent legally, are connected for the purpose of carrying
on their business jointly in a *concern;*[2] the question whether these
enterprises are to be regarded as a unit because of their combination
in the concern need not be answered for purposes of Article 86.[3]
Apart from that situation, market domination by several enterprises
may exist where these are connected with each other by cartel agreement, association decision or concerted practices, in other words,
where there is cooperation in restraint of competition among them.[4]
Finally, Article 86 reaches also market domination by several enterprises which have no contractual or other relations with one another,
i.e., domination by *oligopolists.*[5] A finding of oligopolistic market
structure is, however, difficult;[6] mere uniformity of conduct among
several independent enterprises ought not to suffice for an inference
of market domination.[7] In practice, therefore, the situation is not
too different from that under Section 2 of the Sherman Act, which
does not appear to be properly applicable to "oligopoly" acquired by
non-related corporations unless there is some element of "combining
or conspiring to monopolize" (*American Tobacco Co. v. United States,*
328 U. S. 781 (1946)).[7a]

¶ 203   If the dominant position of several enterprises rests upon
cooperation in restraint of competition within Article 85 (1),
that provision must be applied in addition to Article 86; the prohibitions of these two provisions are independent of one another.[8] *Article*

---

[2] Accord: Spengler, WuW 1961, p.
519, 520. For an explanation of the
term "concern" (Konzern) as used
here, see ¶ 1, supra.
  [3] Accord: Langen, Marktbeherrschung,
p. 49.
  [4] Accord: Günther, WuW 1957, p.
283; Spengler, WuW 1961, p. 520;
Gleiss/Hirsch, AWD 1962, p. 121;
probably also Baumbach/Hefermehl,
Article 86, margin No. 2.
  [5] Accord: Spengler, *ibid.;* Baumbach/
Hefermehl, *ibid.*
  [6] This is emphasized particularly by
Spengler, *ibid.*
  [7] Accord: Spengler, *ibid.*

[7a] On the possibilities recently opened
up by the U. S. Supreme Court by its
making a distinction between "combination" and "conspiracy" (Albrecht v. Herald Co., 390 U. S. 145 (1968)), see James
E. S. Baker, Combinations and Conspiracies—Is There a Difference?, in 14 Antitrust Bulletin (Spring 1969), p. 71;
James L. Underwood, Combinations in
Restraint of Trade: Are They No Longer Synonymous with Conspiracies?, in 18
Journal of Public Law 135 (1969). Both
also in The Journal of Reprints for
Antitrust Law and Economics, Vol. 1,
(Spring 1970), p. 1275 and 1297.
  [8] Accord: Baumbach/Hefermehl, Article 86, No. 6.

85 has no primacy over Article 86.[9] A subsidiary character of Article 86 cannot be deduced either from the text or from the objects of the two provisions, for they have different application and effects: Article 85 (1) applies to restraint of competition by the cooperation of the several enterprises *inter se;* Article 86 to abuse of the dominant position by each single one of these enterprises, especially vis-à-vis suppliers and customers.[10]

III. Dominant Position

¶ 204   Article 86 does not define "dominant position"; it does not say what it must consist in and when it will exist. The illustrations of abusive practices in subparagraphs (a)-(d), at any rate, cannot be drawn upon for a definition. They demonstrate the concept of abuse, not that of a dominant position.

¶ 205   A definition of domination by a single enterprise is contained in Section 22, paragraph 1, of the GWB. According to that provision, an enterprise dominates the market if it is, "for a certain kind of goods or commercial services, without competitors or not exposed to substantial competition. . . ." This definition may serve as a contribution to the interpretation of Article 86 of the EEC Treaty.[11] The amendment to § 22 GWB, which is under discussion, contains the legal presumption that all enterprises have a dominant position in a market if three of them together have a market share of more than 60 percent, or six of them more than 80 percent (market shares of less than ten percent being disregarded). This definition of dominant position seems to be far too broad since—apart from the difficulties in defining the relevant market—it would in many lines of industry subject all producers to the inspection of the BKartA, although there might be heavy competition between them. Such a definition cannot be of any help in explaining Article 86 of the EEC Treaty. Under Article 66, Section 7, of the Coal and Steel Treaty, too, it depends on whether an enterprise is or is not exposed to "actual competition." It ought to be characteristic of a dominant

[9] Contra: Wohlfarth/Everling/Glaesner/Sprung, Article 86, note 2, according to whom Article 85 (1) has priority in such a case. Günther, *ubi supra,* also seems inclined toward that view.

[10] See Antoine Braun/Gleiss/Hirsch, p. 173 ff., particularly p. 174 on Belgian, French and Dutch law.

[11] Contra: Kleemann, pp. 54, 55, who uses the test of the Belgian and Dutch cartel laws whether an enterprise has a "predominant influence." Accord: Langen, Marktbeherrschung, p. 45; Baumbach/Hefermehl, Article 86, margin No. 2; Wohlfarth/Everling/Glaesner/Sprung, Article 86, note 1. See brief comparison of the various laws by Kartte, DB 1962, p. 1133 ff.

position within the meaning of Article 86 of the EEC Treaty that the pressure of competition is missing,[12] regardless of whether this is due to natural reasons or to restraint by cooperation. An enterprise occupies a dominant position if it can, in any one of the markets where it does business, adversely affect the competitive situation without paying substantial heed to competitors.[13]

Whether such a condition exists can be answered only after considering the circumstances of the particular case. Indicia: Market share of an enterprise,[14] number and strength of competitors inside and outside of the Common Market, intensity of competition between them and the putative dominant enterprise, extent of potential and substitute competition,[15] etc.[15a] The dominant position does not have to be based on factual circumstances; a firm also has a dominant position when its "monopoly" is based on a statute or a sovereign act (leaving aside the special regulation in Article 90 (2)). The absolute size of the enterprise (number of employees, turnover, capital) is not decisive, at least not when considered alone.

In its study on the applicability of Article 86 to concentrations of enterprises, the Commission stresses the fact that the dominant position in a market cannot be defined only by market shares of an enterprise and other quantitative elements of a given market structure. "It is primarily an economic power, namely the capability of exerting an influence on the market that is substantial and in principle foreseeable for the domineering enterprise. This economic capability of a domineering enterprise influences the behavior on the market and the economic decisions of other enterprises, regardless of whether it is used in a specific sense. An enterprise that can, at its convenience, oust a competitor from the market may have a dominant position and influence the actions of other enterprises decisively even if its own market share is still relatively small."[15b] The causes of the dominant position are said to be found in production, distribution or financial power. Therefore, it would be necessary to analyze an enterprise in the context of its economic relations. Thus, an enter-

---

[12] Accord: Baumbach/Hefermehl, *ibid.* Spengler, WuW 1961, p. 519, and Kleemann, p. 55, deny market domination even then if the dominant supplier is held in check by a dominant customer; and it is true, in fact, that in a state of equilibrium, neither will "dominate" the other. To use a term coined by John Kenneth Galbraith (*American Capitalism: The Concept of Countervailing Power,* Boston 1956), this is a situation of countervailing pressure for the economist—a concept, however,

which has not yet come to be generally recognized in Sherman Act jurisprudence.

[13] While the Commission has not yet articulated its views on these matters, it is likely that they will not be different in any important respects. See Guide Lines, CMR ¶ 2804.

[14] Accord: Wohlfarth/Everling/Glaesner/Sprung, *ubi supra.*

[15] Günther, *ubi supra;* Kleemann, p. 55.

[15a] In our opinion low profits are an indicium against domination.

[15b] See ¶ 20, footnote 49a.

prise that is the price leader in an oligopoly would, as a rule, have a dominant position.

The European Court in the *Parke, Davis* decision of February 29, 1968 (¶ 48 and 50, supra) stressed that a combination of three elements, i.e., that all three elements of Article 86 had to be present to make it applicable: the existence of a dominant position, the abusive exploitation of that position, and the possibility that trade between member states may be affected thereby. Market share alone will not be determinative, any more than under the Sherman Act (compare the lack of endorsement by the Supreme Court in *American Tobacco Co. v. United States,* 328 U. S. 781, 811-814 (1940), of the percentage point tests suggested in *United States v. Aluminum Co. of America,* 148 F. 2d 416, 424 (C.C.A. 2, 1945), significant in view of its otherwise strong approval of that decision). On the other hand, it cannot be said that market domination always begins with a share of at least 51%. That would not take into consideration, e.g., the possibility of securing a dominant position through prohibited cooperation. A significant indication may also be found in the market behavior of the enterprise, e.g., tying-in a less marketable product with another, which as a rule presupposes that there is market power for the latter product. "Domineering" market behavior is likewise no more than an indicium. Thus, it would be unjustified to draw the incontrovertible conclusion from such practices as price-cutting or a refusal to deal under certain conditions, that a firm has a dominant position.[16]

In *Parke, Davis & Co. v. Centrafarm,*[16a] the plaintiff attempted before a Dutch court to prohibit the import of certain pharmaceuticals from Italy into Holland. The plaintiff had patents on the products in the U. S. and Holland and had licensed manufacture in Holland. The Dutch court referred the following questions to the European Court under Article 177: (1) Whether Articles 85 (1) and 86, together with Articles 36 and 222, were violated when the holder of a patent under the law of one member state sued to prevent distribution of an infringing product that was manufactured in another member state which afforded the patentee no protective right, and (2) Whether the above articles were applicable because a licensee charged a higher price in the member state where his right was accorded protection than the price of a third party importing from the second member state.

The High Court held that, if a patent grants its owner special protection in a member state, it does not necessarily mean that the

---

[16] See, however, Deringer Article 86, margin No. 28.   [16a] See ¶ 48 and 50, supra.

three criteria of dominant position, misuse and possibility to affect interstate trade are met. Intrastate law controls the question of the validity and scope of patent protection; this area is governed by Community law only to the extent that patent protection could contribute to a dominant position and, in turn, misuse of that position and a restriction of trade between member states. To be sure, the Court stated, the selling price of a protected article could be used as one indication of misuse of a dominant position, but misuse was not established merely because the price of a patented product was higher than that of an unpatented one. Article 85 (1), according to the statement of the Court, was not violated because there was no agreement, decision or concerted practice. We agree, especially with the conclusion that a licensing contract is no such agreement, decision, etc.

IV. Relevant Market

¶ 206   Whether or not a position is dominant depends in each case upon the delimitation of the "relevant market,"[16b] for an enterprise cannot have a "dominant position" in general, but always only in respect of certain products or services. The dominated relevant market can be defined only in each individual case, and even then many difficulties will arise in correctly relating the various data. This is one of the greatest problems for the application of Article 86: The relevant market has to be defined by subject matter, geography and time. "The more the term 'relevant market' is narrowed, the greater the number of dominant positions."[16c] We feel, moreover, that the more the market is specified, the fewer the number of enterprises active in it.

In the first instance, it is thus necessary to define the market according to *subject matter*. This depends upon functional interchangeability, a concept familiar to American lawyers especially since the *du Pont* cellophane case (*United States v. du Pont & Co.*, 351 U. S. 377 (1956)). The relevant market consequently includes all products which are reasonably interchangeable, i.e., which may reasonably be

---

[16b] See Antoine Braun/Gleiss/Hirsch, p. 177 ff., particularly footnote 26.

[16c] The Commission's study on the "Problem of the Concentration of Enterprises" (see ¶ 20, footnote 49a), p. 25.

employed for the same purpose.[17] Significant factors here are, among other things, use of the goods, special qualities, durability, price, etc. (see also Article 85, ¶ 108, supra). If certain products are interchangeable according to these criteria, it is irrelevant whether there is further similarity in their production; such a test would be unworkable.

The OLG Stuttgart, in its decision of May 17, 1961, in the matter of fines against a coal dealer on account of price recommendations,[18] distinguished between interchangeability "of coal, wood and oil generally and *in abstracto,*" which it acknowledged to exist, and interchangeability *"in concreto* under present economic conditions in this market," which it denied; but the decision entirely fails to make clear why this should be so and what the difference between abstract and concrete consists in. "Abstract interchangeability" is relevant in cartel law at most as a preliminary question; it depends always upon interchangeability under the particular circumstances of the case.[19]

Theoretically, it is true that an enterprise can be called dominant if it has a strong position in the market for a single product only. Still a cautious approach seems necessary if it manufactures thousands of articles and dominates only in a few of them.

Geographically, the dominant position must exist in the "Common Market" or in a "substantial part" thereof. The term "Common Market" includes only member states, not associated territories (see Introduction). What part of the Common Market would be "substantial" cannot be stated generally. That depends not only upon the spatial share in the Common Market; even the territory of a large member state of the EEC is not necessarily a "substantial part,"[20] nor even the territories of two or more of these states.[21] The decisive element is, rather, the significance of the dominated part of the market in relation to the entire EEC market for the goods or services involved.[22] For this reason, if, for instance, production of or trade in certain goods is concentrated in a single member state, domination of the market in that state may at the same time be domination of a "substantial" part of the Common Market; conversely, domination of the relatively unimportant market in other states would not suffice

---

[17] Compare Borchardt/Fikentscher, p. 53 ff.; Günther, Relevanter Markt, pp. 17, 19; Spengler, WuW 1961, p. 513; Barnikel, WuW 1961, p. 249; BKartA, decision of August 11, 1961, BB 1961, p. 1255, No. 2389, also in WuW/E BKartA 427; comparative law treatment by Schwenk, WuW 1960, p. 3 ff.

[18] WuW/E OLG 426 ff.

[19] Accord: Kartte, DB 1962, p. 1134.

[20] Accord: Baumbach/Hefermehl, Article 86, margin No. 2.

[21] Contra: Wohlfarth/Everling/Glaesner/Sprung, Article 86, note 3; Spengler in Gemeinschaftskommentar, appendix to Section 101, No. 3; Spengler, WuW 1961, p. 515.

[22] Accord: Baumbach/Hefermehl, *ibid.*

¶ 206

in that case.[23] The question whether the part subject to domination is a substantial part, like the question of dominant position itself, can therefore be answered only on the basis of the factual circumstances of the particular case. On the other hand, it is not necessary (see ¶ 201, supra) that the dominant enterprise have its headquarters within the Common Market. Here, too, the "effects test" (see ¶ 29, supra) applies. Decisive is where the products are marketed or the services rendered. Consequently, in analyzing the competition between enterprises within the Common Market, imports from outside have to be taken into account.[23a] On the whole, it may be said that the "substantial part" test is not likely to be applied with anything approaching the all-inclusiveness of "any part of the trade or commerce among the several States" in Section 2 of the Sherman Act, construed to be satisfied if merely "some *appreciable* part of interstate commerce is the subject of a monopoly" (*United States v. Yellow Cab Co.,* 332 U. S. 218, 225 (1947) (emphasis supplied) ; compare also the comprehensive construction of "any section of the country" in Section 7 of the Clayton Act: *Brown Shoe Co. v. United States,* 82 S. Ct. 1502, 1530 f. (1962)).

V. Prohibition of Abuse

¶ 207   A dominant position in the Common Market within the meaning of Article 86 of the Treaty does not as such entail sanctions or other legal consequences. Herein, of course, lies a most important difference from Section 2 of the Sherman Act: Originally thought to ban only "bad (predatory) trusts" as distinguished from "good (well-behaving) trusts" (compare, e.g., *Standard Oil Co. v. United States,* 221 U. S. 1 (1911), and *United States v. American Tobacco Co.,* 221 U. S. 106 (1911), with *United States v. United Shoe Machinery Co.,* 247 U. S. 32 (1918), and *United States v. United States Steel Corp.,* 251 U. S. 417 (1920)), Section 2, as now construed (see, as representative of the turning point, especially *United States v. Aluminum Co. of America,* 148 F. 2d 416, 427 ff. (C.C.A. 2, 1945), and *United States v. Griffith,* 334 U. S. 100, 107 (1948)), reaches power to exclude competition even where not attended by any abuse (*United States v. United Shoe Machinery Corp.,* 110 F. Supp. 295, 345 (D. Mass. 1953), affirmed *per curiam,* 347 U. S. 521 (1954): "Probably few monopolies could produce a record so free from any taint" of predatory practices).

---

[23] Contra: Spengler, WuW 1961, p. 515, and Kleemann, p. 56, in whose view dominant position in a single member state would never be sufficient unless it extends to at least a part of another member state. Accord: Baum-bach/Hefermehl, *ibid.;* von der Groeben/von Boeckh, Article 86, note 6.

[23a] The Commission's study on the "Problem of the Concentration of Enterprises" (see ¶ 20, footnote 49a), p. 25.

Article 86 of the Treaty, furthermore, does not subject a dominant enterprise to preventive control directed against abuse of its position, nor is such an enterprise prevented from further strengthening its position, be it by enlarging production capacities or by acquiring other enterprises. Nor does Article 86 expressly require notification of mergers, as does Section 23 of the GWB; even less does it provide for the necessity of previous approval of mergers or for any possibility of undoing them after the fact.

The question of whether Article 86 provides the means of a merger control is one of the major problems and political questions articulated in recent years.

In its 1966 study on "Problems of the Concentration of Enterprises within the Common Market"[24] the Commission rightly points out that Article 85 might be applied in certain cases of concentration if its prerequisites are fulfilled, but that there are various practical reasons against a general application, such as the inapplicability of the "positive" preconditions for an exemption to concentrations, the question of voidness under Article 85 (2), or the uselessness of the periodical review of exemptions under Article 8 of Regulation 17, since the transfer of property in an enterprise once achieved has to be final and cannot be allowed or forbidden for a limited time. Some of the disadvantages of applying Article 85 could be avoided by issuing an implementing regulation according to Article 87 which might, however, lead to the difficulty of having clearly to define the difference between restrictions of competition by cartels and those by concentration.[24a]

The Commission, following the opinion of an advisory board of professors,[24b] holds that the application of Article 86 to mergers does not meet similar difficulties, that it is of no relevance whether a concentration in which a dominant enterprise is involved is effected by agreement between two enterprises, or by acquisition of a competing enterprise by buying its shares at the stock exchange. In applying Article 86 (instead of Article 85), the admissibility would not depend on a positive evaluation of a single case of concentration but would be defined by the negative criterion of abusive exploitation of a dominant position. The prohibition would apply only in exceptional cases, and if the legality of a merger is doubtful, a negative clearance (Article 2 of Regulation 17) might be requested.

---

[24] See ¶ 20, footnote 49a, supra; cf. also von der Groeben's speech mentioned there.
[24a] Opposing this view of the Commission on Article 85: Canellos/Silber, Concentration in the Common Market,
CMLR 1970, p. 138 ff. They advocate a broad, "teleological" interpretation of Articles 85 and 86, but without any basis in the Treaty.
[24b] Doc. 14 190/IV/64-D.

According to the Commission's study, the exploitation is abusive if the conduct of an enterprise objectively is misbehavior with regard to the aims of the Treaty. The abusive practices can be related to present or potential competitors, to suppliers or consumers. "Since there is no general term of abuse, the yardstick to measure the abusive action in each case has to be taken from the aims of the law in which the term is used."[24c] In interpreting the examples given in Article 85 (a) to (d), the Commission finds that Article 86 is not merely directed against certain types of abusive behavior on the market. Article 86 (b), e.g., refers to a disadvantageous conduct which alters the "structure of offers" ("Angebotsstruktur") although it does not concern the behavior of the enterprise on the market but only internal operations. "A merger between two enterprises, one of which has a dominant position by means of which the otherwise continuing competition is excluded and a monopoly is created, can have the same negative effect as the conduct described in Article 86 (b). A monopoly actually removes the stimulus for technical progress. It often leads to a limitation of production in order to reach maximum gains by prices higher than those on a market with oligopolistic competition and greater production."[24d] For these reasons, the Commission holds a concentration of enterprises which is monopolizing the market generally to be an abusive exploitation of a dominant position according to Article 86. The merger is already deemed to be an abuse because it completely excludes competition. "The closer a domineering enterprise is (by means of mergers) to becoming a monopolist and thereby to limiting the choice of buyers, distributors, and consumers, the greater the probability of entering into the field of abuse."[24e]

In June 1969, Sassen—at that time the one of the 14 Commissioners in charge of competition matters—stated at a Brussels meeting that his office was considering establishing a duty to notify mergers in advance. As an alternative, Sassen said that the Commission was contemplating a procedure of prior consultation, or hearing, for mergers in those lines of industry where there is a high degree of concentration.[24f]

[24c] Commission's study (see ¶ 20, footnote 49a), p. 26.
[24d] Ibid.
[24e] Ibid.
[24f] Cf. also Sassen, Competition Policy: More Than "Anti" Trust, lecture given to the Federal Bar Association on September 10, 1969; as early as 1965, von der Groeben stated similar ideas, cf. ¶ 20, footnote 49a, supra. Agreeing with the Commission's view: De Jong, Concentration in the Common Market, CMLR, Vol. 4, 1966, p. 166, 175 f., who criticizes the Commission's reasoning but advocates the application of Article 86 to mergers, accusing the Commission of being too tolerant of concentration. Fikentscher, DB 1966, p. 689-692, and "Festschrift Böhm," (1965) p. 261 ff., wants to apply Article 86 even in cases where the dominant position is created by the merger. Cf. also Mestmäcker, Festschrift Hallstein 1966, p. 322.

¶ 207

Apart from the question of whether such a control of mergers in the Common Market is desirable or not, the Commission's legal reasoning cannot be upheld. Merger control is not an instrument that can be created unilaterally by the Commission but would have to be granted to it by the member states. This has not been done in Articles 85 and 86 of the EEC Treaty: Article 86 is not directed against mergers as such.[24g] The wording is quite clear in prohibiting an abusive exploitation of a dominant position in the Common Market by one or more enterprises. Thus, it clearly distinguishes between the structure of the market and behavior in the market. Only behavior can be prohibited, if a dominant position is exploited abusively. With regard to the structure of the market Article 86 is neutral.[24h] Even a merger which completely extinguishes competition, i.e., which leads to a monopoly in the relevant market, is therefore not *per se* an abusive exploitation of a dominant position. The question of abuse is only the second prerequisite of Article 86; it has to follow from the dominant position and has actually to be proved; Article 86 does not imply any presumption that a strong or even dominant position as such is an abuse. If shares of an enterprise are bought at the stock exchange this cannot possibly be a transaction in the relevant market, i.e., the one in which the enterprise is doing business. Thus it cannot be an abuse of the dominant position in that market. For example, the English *Dunlop Co. Ltd.* and the Italian *Pirelli S.p.A.* plan

[24g] Von der Groeben/von Boeckh, Kommentar zum EWGV, 1958, Art. 86, No. 2; Deringer, Art. 86, No. 1; Baumbach/Hefermehl, Wettbewerbs- und Warenzeichenrecht (1960) GWB, Appendix, Art. 86 of the EEC Treaty, No. 1; Hefermehl, Unternehmenszusammenschlüsse im Lichte der Art. 85 and 86, Studienvereinigung Kartellrecht, Kooperation und Konzentration im Gemeinsamen Markt, 2. Kartellrechtsforum Brüssel, 1967 (1968), p. 59 ff.; Hefermehl, Festschrift Nipperdey (1965), p. 771 ff. For the interpretation of Article 86, see, in particular, Samkalden/Druker, Legal Problems Relating to Article 86 of the Rome Treaty, CMLR, Vol. 3, 1965/66, p. 158 ff.; Schmidt, Relevanter Markt, Marktbeherrschung und Missbrauch in § 22 GWB und Art. 86 EWGV, WuW 1965, p. 453.
[24h] Burki, Le problème de l'abus des positions dominantes des grandes entreprises dans le marché commun (1968); Catalano, Manuel de droit des Communautées Européennes (2nd ed., 1964), p. 421 f. and 454 f.; Dabin, Les concentrations d'entreprises et le droit de la concurrence (Paper issued by a seminar held in Rome); Thiesing, Concentrations dans le Marché Commun, RMC 1968, p. 289; Bollack, Das marktbeherrschende Unternehmen im EWG-Recht, Kartellrundschau, Vol. 8, p. 223 ff.; Langen, Marktbeherrschung und ihr Missbrauch nach Artikel 86 des EWG-Vertrages, 1959, p. 49 ff.; Spengler, Das marktbeherrschende Unternehmen im EWG-Vertrag, WuW 1961, p. 509 ff.; von Gamm, Das Kartellrecht der EWG (Kartellrundschau, Vol. 3, 2nd ed., 1969), p. 76 ff.; Omneslaghe, Anwendung der Art. 85 und 86 des Rom-Vertrages, Beiträge zum EWG Kartellrecht, 1967, p. 41 ff.; Homburger/Jenny, Internationalrechtliche Aspekte des EWG-Wettbewerbsrechts, 1966, p. 41; van Themaat, Competition and Restrictive Business Practices in the European Economic Community. Proceedings of the 1960 Institute on Legal Aspects of the European Community, Washington, D. C., 1960, p. 99 ff.

to merge[241] (by exchanging between 40 and 49 percent of the shares of each enterprise), since only multinational groups on a European basis (of American size) are deemed to have a future in the industry involved. By this merger, the two enterprises will enlarge their production programs—Dunlop in the field of electric cables and Pirelli in sports equipment and fine mechanics. At present, the two enterprises together have a total turnover of nearly one billion pounds sterling, with 200 plants all over the world and nearly 200,000 employees. The mere exchange of shares, in our opinion, cannot possibly be an abuse of any dominant position that the two enterprises might have.

To put these arguments into a more concrete form: The language of Article 86 is classically clear; it says that a dominant position must be used and exploited, i.e. applied as an instrument. Fikentscher's thesis[24j] that a merger of, e.g., two medium-size enterprises, neither of which enjoys a dominant position but which only together create this position, violates Article 86 is an extreme example of what the law does not say: In our opinion, it is not logical to say that a dominant position is misused by creating it. It is impossible to misuse it before it exists. Therefore, even buying all the shares of a corporation that has a monopoly cannot be a misuse, much less an abusive exploitation, irrespective of whether the buyer already owned some shares or had nothing to do with the enterprise bought prior to the acquisition. On the contrary, this is an internal process and not the behavior that Article 86 is directed against, viz. an external way of using a strong market position "on the outside," i.e. toward customers and suppliers. Whether X or Y is the owner of the shares of a dominant enterprise is purely an internal question; X may today sell his shares to Y, and Y may resell them to X tomorrow: it is absurd to maintain that both X and Y misused their dominant position.

Our interpretation is strengthened by the fact that Article 86 not only speaks of an abuse of the dominant position but adds a second very clear word: *exploitation*. Logically, this accumulation of two different phrases with the same meaning would be unnecessary. It goes to stress, cumulatively, that the strong position must be used and exploited before the prohibition can apply.

It is not permissible to reason, as the Commission does, that a merger as such is an abuse because it excludes competition and limits the choice of buyers or suppliers. This may be wishful thinking but is not in the law. All these objections hold true even if a monopoly can be called an abuse of a liberal free market system. The

---

[241] Press report in Handelsblatt of May 20, 1970.   [24j] See ¶ 207, footnote 24f, supra.

¶ 207

results may be absolutely undesirable but they are not hit by the law as it stands. Such "teleological" interpretation is not legitimate since it is clearly contrary to the language of the Treaty. To show in an example what the law's objective is: A strong enterprise must not undercut its competitors' prices systematically until they surrender unconditionally, e.g., offer themselves to be bought cheaply.

The words in the corresponding § 22 GWB are exactly the same: "abusive exploitation of a dominant position." From the beginning, the vast majority of legal authors and all German cartel authorities in the "Länder," the Bundeskartellamt in Berlin, and the Federal Ministry of Economics consistently have interpreted these words in the same way as we do. This is one of the declared reasons for endeavoring to get the provisions of the GWB changed[24k] in order to make them applicable to mergers, in other words, to get a pre-merger control enacted. Even this has been met with considerable resistance in Germany.

It is also significant that the Commission, from the date the Rome Treaty became law on January 1, 1958 (the same day as the GWB), never said anything to the contrary, until in 1965/66 it released the theories dealt with above. It is a fact that during these more than twelve years the Commission has not made a single decision against any one of the vast number of mergers which have been carried out. It is fair to assume that the Commission, like the German authorities, feels that the legal provisions at its disposal do not suffice for what it considers desirable to achieve. Therefore, it may in a test case try to show either that its theory is supported by the European Court or that the Treaty has to be amended and strengthened by the same kind of legislation as is envisaged in Germany.

In its report to the European Parliament on "The Rules of Competition and the Position of the European Enterprises in the Common Market and in the World Economy" (Berkhouwer Report), dated March 9, 1970 (Doc. 242) the Economic Committee made the following statement:

"It is considered necessary to introduce obligatory notification preceding mergers exceeding a certain market share or a certain size. Such mergers shall be considered to be permitted only if the Commission does not object within a certain deadline to be fixed."

This statement and the report as a whole show that the European Parliament, too, does not believe that Article 86 contains any provision preventing mergers, even of the greatest dimensions.

[24k] See ¶ 205, supra.

A further argument that our interpretation is correct can be drawn from a comparison of Article 86 of the EEC Treaty and Article 66 of the ECSC Treaty. Since that article, like Section 7 of the Clayton Act expressly provides for a merger control and no such clause is found in Article 86 of the EEC Treaty, one has to conclude that the member states in establishing the Common Market did not want mergers to fall under this article. This interpretation can also be based on the minutes and governmental comments on the Rome Treaty.[24m]

Illustrations of the abuse that is the object of Article 86 are given in subparagraphs (a) through (d).[24n] All these illustrations point in the same direction as our interpretation of Article 86. None supports the Commission's construction of the words "abusive exploitation." For the requirement of adverse effect upon interstate trade, see ¶ 222, infra.

B. LIST OF ILLUSTRATIONS

I. Article 86(a)

¶ 208   Since purchase and sales prices are mentioned, the subject referred to here is the conduct of the dominant enterprise *toward suppliers and customers;* this is true also of other terms and conditions. Consequently, the dominant enterprise may not exact unfair prices or terms either from its customers or from its suppliers.[25] It is a problem whether it is necessary that a contract be concluded with the supplier or customer. The purchase or sales price is exacted only when a sales contract has been concluded. Before this, there exists only some type of attempt. If the aim is not reached, it may be an indication that the party opposite the dominant enterprise has managed to find alternatives, or in any case, was not forced to capitulate. In our opinion, the mere attempt does not fall under "exaction of prices"; on the other hand, Article 86 (2), subparagraphs a-d, presents only examples.

¶ 209   *Prices* means not only prices in the narrow sense but also their collateral elements (quantity discounts, premiums, cash discounts, etc.), without making it necessary here, in contrast to some provisions of the GWB (e.g., Section 2, paragraph 1), to distinguish neatly between ingredients of price on the one hand and

---

[24m] Burki (footnote 24h) ; Ellis, Enkele Aantekeningen bij Artikel 86 van het EEG Verdrag, 1965, Soc. Econ. Wet., p. 317.

[24n] Illustrations (a)-(d) are similar or identical to those in Article 85 (1) (a), (b), (d), and (e). Hence, compare our comments there (¶ 32 ff., supra).

[25] Accord: von Gamm, p. 37.

terms and conditions on the other, since subparagraph (a) speaks generally of terms and conditions of the transaction and treats price as one of the terms.

¶ 210 Prices and terms are not *unfair* merely by reason of the fact that their value exceeds the counter-value furnished by the dominant enterprise; a fair price is not necessarily the same thing as a just price.[26] Prices and terms will be unfair only where the counter-performance by the dominant enterprise is grossly disproportionate to them; in other words, where they cannot be justified in any manner by the counter-value.[27]

The prices and terms exacted or demanded (see ¶ 35, supra) by the dominant enterprise must be appraised together, in their entirety. What counts is the contract as a whole. However, even normally subordinate conditions, e.g., with regard to jurisdiction for litigation under the contract, play a part because they may contribute to making the agreement as a whole unfair. Similarly, it would not be enough if some important terms, looked at separately, were unfair, but the contract as a whole could still be regarded as fair.

It should be noted that misuse of a dominant position does not follow merely from a higher price for patented products than for unpatented ones. See ¶ 205, supra. According to the European Court's *Parke, Davis* decision (February 29, 1968, ¶ 48 and 50, supra) the sales price of a product manufactured under a procedure protected by a patent may be an indication of misuse. But the Court rightly stresses that there is not necessarily a misuse merely because the price of the product is higher than that of an unprotected product imported from another member state.

¶ 211 The unfair prices or conditions must be *imposed* directly or indirectly by the dominant enterprise. It is immaterial whether the element of compulsion consists of legal measures or of economic pressure.[28]

---

[26] Accord: Wohlfarth/Everling/Glaesner/Sprung, Article 86, note 5. The English term "unfair" is used here in preference to "inequitable," even though the German and French texts employ the literal negatives of "angemessen" and "equitable," respectively (compare ¶ 91, supra), not only because it has greater currency in this connection, but also because it gets even further away from the idea that mere disparity is enough.

[27] Accord: Wohlfarth/Everling/Glaesner/Sprung, *ibid.;* von Gamm, *ibid.;* Kleemann, p. 57. Since what is involved is a consensual transaction between the parties, the term "imposition," which is adopted directly from the French text (the German word being the equivalent of "compelling"), should not, of course, be taken to mean wholly unilateral fiat but, rather, compulsive dictation.

[28] Accord: von Gamm, *ibid.*

It is open to question whether unfair "prices" also include resale prices compelled by a vertical price agreement.[29] Subparagraph (a) speaks only of purchase and sale prices, i.e., of prices which the dominant enterprise concedes to its suppliers or charges to its customers, and thus does not, at least not in terms, refer to prices which it prescribes to its customers for resale. Article 86 may, however, apply, under the heading of unfair conditions, where the dominant firm either legally or in fact sets resale prices[30] and the margin for these customers is fixed "unfairly" low by the dominant enterprise.

It is also questionable whether an exaction exists only when the parties with whom the dominant enterprise deals were aware of the unfairness of the price; such a rule would, in our opinion, lead to unjustifiable distinctions. The dominant enterprise need not be aware of the unfairness; here objective criteria apply (see ¶ 221, infra).

¶ 212   The illustration of abuse in subparagraph (a) accords substantially with Section 22, paragraph 3, No. 1, of the GWB. Under that provision, also, abusive exploitation of market position is seen in demanding unfair prices or conditions, and abuse presupposes an element of compulsion.

II. Article 86(b)

¶ 213   Not every *limitation of production, distribution or technical development* by the enterprise dominant in the market is *eo ipso* an abuse of its dominant position, under this provision. Such a practice must, in addition, be *to the detriment of consumers*. Since in practice any limitation of production, etc., will, or at least may, in some way be detrimental to the consumer, this provision reaches only special detriments and not those which are inherent in any kind of "limitation." The effect of the limitation, therefore, must, at least in essence, be directed at this very detriment to the consumer.[31] Otherwise, a dominant enterprise would be prohibited from taking rationalizing or other managerial measures[32] (for instance, a standardization by elimination of some types within the enterprise)—and, indeed, could be forced to desist from such measures by the imposition of fines under Article 15 (2)(a) of Regulation 17. This is not the

---

[29] For the affirmative: Wohlfarth/Everling/Glaesner/Sprung, *ibid.*
[30] Under German law there must be price competition between similar goods (Section 16 GWB).

[31] Accord: Wohlfarth/Everling/Glaesner/Sprung, Article 86, note 6; Baumbach/Hefermehl, Article 86, margin No. 5; Kleemann, p. 58.
[32] This is rightly pointed out by von Gamm, p. 37.

thrust of Article 86. Rather, the detriment to the consumer must materialize; the danger of a detriment will not suffice (see also ¶ 216, infra).

¶ 214   *Consumer* has the same meaning here as under Article 85 (3), i.e., it is not limited to the ultimate "consumer," but includes every purchaser of the goods[33] (compare also, ¶ 89).

III. Article 86(c)

¶ 215   This provision contains a *prohibition of discrimination* by the enterprise dominant in the market.[33a] Such an enterprise must not, to the detriment of parties with whom it deals in commercial transactions, apply unequal terms to them where they furnish equal considerations. This means:

¶ 216   These parties must not be placed at a disadvantage in their competition with other enterprises on the same functional level, as *customers* or as *suppliers* of the dominant enterprise (this follows from the concept of competition). Such a *disadvantage* must actually materialize. A mere possibility of, or aptness to cause, a detriment will not suffice[34] (see also ¶ 213, supra).

¶ 217   Abusive exploitation of a dominant position within the meaning of illustrative situation (c) will not exist if the application of unequal terms is *justified on the ground of unequal considerations* furnished in return. Even apart from the wording of this provision, abuse will not be involved if the unequal terms are justified objectively on any other ground, even though there may be equivalence of considerations in a literal sense.[35] This is in accordance with the nature of the prohibition. One cannot possibly prohibit the dominant enterprise, e.g., from selling to a customer on the verge of bankruptcy only for cash while giving 30 days for payment to others. This interpretation corresponds to Section 26, paragraph 2 of the GWB, under which the dominant enterprise (as also cartels and suppliers fixing vertical prices) must not treat other enterprises unequally "without justifiable cause." It is in line, further, with American antitrust law where price

---

[33] Accord: Wohlfarth/Everling/Glaesner/Sprung, Article 86, note 6, and Article 85, note 17; Kleemann, p. 57.

[33a] See Antoine Braun/Gleiss/Hirsch, p. 185 ff., particularly footnote 41 *bis* and 43, both on Belgian law.

[34] Accord: von Gamm, p. 38, and probably also Kleemann, p. 58.

[35] Accord: Wohlfarth/Everling/Glaesner/Sprung, Article 86, note 7; Gleiss/Hirsch, AWD 1962, p. 122.

discrimination under Section 2 of the Clayton Act (Robinson-Patman Act) is "unjustified differentiation,"[36] although the theorem that a differential is not *ipso facto* a discrimination is considerably attenuated in practice by the rules governing burden of proof under that statute, and although the American courts have equated discrimination and differentiation with increasing frequency, at least as a matter of semantics.[36a] It bears repetition, however, that neither Article 85 nor Article 86 of the EEC Treaty contains a general prohibition of price or other discrimination, and that Article 86 in particular is limited to monopoly situations akin to those enjoyed by public utilities, where relative or even absolute price or rate regulation is merely designed to compensate for a privileged position.

Possibilities of justifiable cause for unequal terms, in the present connection, include, besides lack of solvency of a customer, limited capacity of the dominant enterprise, its distribution policy, the functional level of the customer, the size of his stock, the bad reputation of the customer, which is detrimental to the good-will of the product and the manufacturer, etc. Whether they justify the difference in treatment must be examined in each particular case.

¶ 218   Illustrative situation (c) does *not* give rise to *compulsory dealing*.[37] A refusal by the dominant enterprise to contract with another is not an "application of unequal conditions." Subparagraph (c) leaves it to the dominant enterprise whether it wishes to have particular dealings or not, and it is only if it decides to enter into an agreement that it must not engage in unjustified differentiation. However, since subparagraphs (a)-(d) list only certain examples of abusive practices, a refusal to deal on the part of the dominant enterprise may still be such a practice under the general prohibition of Article 86. The enterprise may indirectly, through fines imposed under Article 15 (2)(a) of Regulation 17, be compelled to deal with another, but, of course, only if its refusal is without good cause; otherwise, there would be no abuse. The substantive principles are not unlike those applied by the American courts: Although the doctrine of *United States v. Colgate & Co.,* 250 U. S. 300 (1919), reflected also in the Clayton (Robinson-Patman) Act's proviso for selection of customers "in bona fide transactions and not in restraint of trade,"

---

[36] See, e.g., Loevinger, *The Law of Free Enterprise,* New York 1949, p. 133 ff.

[36a] See, e.g., *Federal Trade Commission v. Anheuser-Busch, Inc.,* 363 U. S. 536, 549 (1960).

[37] Von Gamm, *ibid.,* assumes an obligation to deal. Accord with our view: van Hecke in Kartelle und Monopole, vol. I, p. 339.

has been severely limited over the years, it is still true that there is no compulsion to deal in the absence of monopoly or restraint of trade, or, at least, that a refusal to deal may be justified on a variety of grounds.[37a]

IV. Article 86 (d)

¶ 219   There is nothing radically new in this *prohibition of tying*, which corresponds in substance to Section 22, paragraph 3, No. 2, of the GWB. The dominant enterprise's freedom of contract is limited by the rule that it must not make the conclusion of a contract depend upon the acceptance of certain other products or services not related to the subject matter of the contract either intrinsically or by custom of the trade. As already pointed out in connection with Article 85 (1)(e), supra (¶ 71), the Treaty contains no general ban on tying clauses in the fashion of Section 3 of the Clayton Act. Article 86 (d), unlike Article 85 (1)(e), does reach individual tying transactions, but only if engaged in by dominant enterprises, not merely because of potential monopolistic effect of the tying practice itself.

¶ 220   Article 86 (d) does not require that a commercial custom exist in the entire Common Market; such a custom at the place of the dominant enterprise will suffice,[38] since the conduct of the dominant enterprise in this case is that which is usual in its locality. The practice in the customer's locality also suffices, since then the tying-in does not burden him unduly.

C. GENERAL PROHIBITION

I. Interpretation

¶ 221   The most significant item in Article 86 is found in the inconspicuous words introducing subparagraphs (a)-(d): "Such abusive practices may consist, in particular, of the following . . . ". The words "may" and "in particular" emphasize the nature of the preceding clause as a general prohibition of abuse of power by enterprises dominant in the Common Market, regardless of the specific

---

[37a] Pressure from customers who would stop buying if a supplier sold to a certain firm has, however, been held not to justify an otherwise unilateral refusal: *Flintkote Co. v. Lysfjord*, 246 F. 2d 368 (9th Cir. 1957), *cert. den.* 355 U. S. 835 (1957)—a ruling which would be difficult to reach under either Article 85 or Article 86.

[38] Similarly, von Gamm, p. 39.

type of such abuse. The practices listed in subparagraphs (a)-(d) are only illustrative situations and do not purport to give an exhaustive enumeration. Nevertheless, certain standards for other cases of abuse of market power may be deduced from them—broadly speaking, the principle that *abuse* exists only where the dominant enterprise, in a crass manner and without the justification of objective interest, exploits or substantially harms its market partners or consumers,[39] with potential adverse effect upon economic intercourse between member states of the EEC. The question whether there is abuse must be answered by applying not moral but objective economic criteria. This probably is also the position of the Commission.[40] It sees a significant indication of abusive conduct where the practice involved is possible only because of the dominant position of the enterprise. In the Commission's view, one must examine the questions whether the enterprise gains advantages which could not be achieved if there were effective competition, and whether third parties suffer unjustifiable detriments from exploitation of the dominant position. Mere utilization of a dominant position does not constitute an abuse; otherwise, a dominant enterprise would be prohibited from taking advantage of the cost savings resulting from production in large amounts by lowering market prices. The effect might well be that newcomers find market entry difficult, due to their higher prices, but that does not constitute an abuse.

The proposition that specified conduct more readily constitutes an abuse the stronger the position of the dominant enterprise,[41] we deem insupportable in this general form, particularly when the conduct, as such, is neutral.

¶ 222   An abusive practice, even in the cases listed in subparagraphs (a)-(d), is prohibited only "to the extent to which trade between member states is apt to be adversely affected thereby." Although the wording of the German version (literally: "may lead to an adverse effect . . .") varies somewhat from that in Article 85 (1) ("apt to affect adversely"), there is no practical difference; both formulations mean the same thing.[42] This is confirmed by the fact that the French version uses "susceptible" in both places, the difference being one between active and passive voice only. Another vari-

---

[39] For more detailed treatment, see Langen, Marktbeherrschung, p. 49 ff.; von Gamm, p. 37; also the formula used by Kleemann, p. 56.

[40] Guide Lines in their provisional form, although the specific statement to the above effect was omitted in the final version, CMR ¶ 2804.

[41] Accord: Drion, CMLR, Vol. 1, p. 155. Cf. also the tendency in American antitrust law to hold large or established firms to more stringent standards than smaller ones or "struggling newcomers."

[42] Deringer, GRUR AIT 1962, p. 285, evidently sees a difference here. In accord with our view: Baumbach/Hefermehl, Article 86, margin No. 4.

ance between the two articles, existing in all versions, is that Article 85 proscribes agreements, etc., possessing the harmful attribute, i.e., potential adverse effect upon interstate trade, whereas Article 86 prohibits abuse of position only "to the extent to which" it has that attribute; but here again, it is difficult to discover any substantive difference except, perhaps, for the fact that the interstate character or consequences of the practices outlawed by Article 86 might lend themselves more readily to separation from purely local conduct than is the case with the consensual arrangements prohibited by Article 85. A material abuse within the meaning of Article 86 will therefore exist only if it is at least *apt to affect adversely* trade between member states; and adverse effect means some influence which is noticeably unfavorable and is not altogether negligible (see the discussion under Article 85, ¶ 24, supra). If the abuse has effects only in the market of a single member state or only outside of EEC territory, Article 86 will not apply. According to the Commission, a concentration of enterprises, one of which has a dominant position in the Common Market or a substantial part of it, will always be of some significance for interstate trade, so that in concentration cases this prerequisite is not of great importance.[42a] Yet it is always necessary to examine whether the circumstances of a given case confirm this general theory.

II. Consequences of Violation

¶ 223   Every abuse of a dominant position is prohibited, without the necessity of a decision by the Commission. The prohibition is pronounced directly by the law. Article 86 is more severe, in that respect, than the corresponding Section 22 of the GWB, which only gives the cartel authority the right to interdict an abuse (prospectively). Article 86 thus contains more than an administrative control of abuses: The Commission may institute proceedings for a fine against violators of the prohibition (thus also retroactively). Only in this limited sense can one speak of "supervision over abuses"[43] in connection with this provision.

¶ 224   In contrast to Article 85 (2), Article 86 fails to regulate the *consequences of a violation on the civil side.* In that respect, the applicable national law will govern. For the Federal Republic of Germany, this means the following:

[42a] Study on the "Problem of the Concentration of Enterprises" (see ¶ 20, footnote 49a, supra), p. 25.
[43] Thus "Bericht über Anderungen des Gesetzes gegen Wettbewerbsbe- schränkungen" (Report on Amendments to the GWB) of August 22, 1962, Bundestag Printed Document IV/617, p. 74.

¶ 225   As to possible voidness, one would think in the first instance of Section 134 of the BGB, providing that a transaction in violation of a legal prohibition is void unless a different result is called for by the law in question. Article 86 has been a law directly effective in the Federal Republic, and thus a legal prohibition within the meaning of Section 134, at least since March 13, 1962.[44] In spite of this, no invalidity will result from this provision, because there is the reservation in favor of a different result demanded by the prohibitory law itself. The reservation applies here because Article 86, in contrast to Article 85, deliberately fails to decree invalidity. Measures in contravention of Article 86 are therefore not void under Section 134 of the BGB.[45]

Voidness will result in the Federal Republic only if an abuse within the meaning of Article 86 of the EEC Treaty fulfills at the same time the prerequisite of Section 138 of the BGB, i.e., if it is *contra bonos mores.*

¶ 226   Whether violations of the prohibition of Article 86 may give rise to *injunctive relief and claims for damages,* via Section 823, paragraph 2, of the BGB, is questionable.[46] It depends again (compare under Article 85, ¶ 79, supra) on whether Article 86 is a *law for the protection of another* within the meaning of Section 823. This must probably be denied, although Article 86 might furnish a basis for the affirmative in its subparagraphs (a)-(d) somewhat more readily than does Article 85 (compare ¶ 79). The decisive factor is, however, that the main concern of Article 86 is with the proper order of the Common Market which is to be developed and achieved through the rules of competition of the Treaty, and not with the protection of individuals, so that Article 86 is not a protective law within Section 823, paragraph 2 of the BGB.[47] For the different situation in Belgium, see Article 85, ¶ 79, supra.

---

[44] Compare the *Bosch* decision, *ubi supra,* footnote 41 at ¶ 16, discussed under Article 1 of Regulation 17, ¶ 301.

[45] Contra: von der Groeben/von Boeckh, Article 86, note 4, Baumbach/Hefermehl, Article 86, margin No. 6, and Kleemann, p. 60, who see voidness on the basis of Section 134, BGB. Accord with our view: von Gamm, p. 39; see also Spengler, WuW 1961, p. 528.

[46] The affirmative is taken by von Gamm, p. 40; Wohlfarth/Everling/Glaesner/Sprung, Article 86, note 10.

[47] Accord: Spengler, WuW 1961, p. 528, 529; Kleemann, *ibid.* The BGH, in its decision of April 14, 1959, has denied the character of a protective law to the prohibition of discrimination in Article 60, Section 1 of the CST: BB 1959, pp. 576, 578.

¶ 227   The only sanction against violations of Article 86 is there-
         fore the imposition of a *fine*, which the Commission may or-
der under Article 15 (2)(a) of Regulation 17.

¶ 228   *No exemption from Article 86 is possible,* in contrast to Article
         85 (3). In the nature of things, abusive conduct is not a
proper subject for permission[48] (the same rule is contained in the
German GWB). There is no need to call for a rule of reason, since
such considerations will come within the interpretation of the phrase
"abusive exploitation."

---

[48] Accord: Kleemann, p. 57.

Regulation 17

First Regulation
Implementing Articles 85 and 86*

Article 1
BASIC PROVISION

The agreements, decisions and concerted practices referred to in Article 85, paragraph 1, of the Treaty and any abuse of a dominant position on the market within the meaning of Article 86 of the Treaty shall be prohibited, no prior decision to this effect being required; Articles 6, 7 and 23 of the present Regulation shall not be affected by this provision.

I. Legal Effect of Articles 85 and 86 of the EEC Treaty

¶ 301   In legal writing and in the courts, there had for a long time been a conflict of opinion as to the legal effect of Articles 85 and 86. In the main, there were three different views. According to the first, the prohibitions of the two articles pronounced only general principles which still had to be supplemented and made more concrete through the regulations contemplated by Article 87 ,(so-called *program theory*). Under the second view, Articles 85 and 86 were positive law with immediate effect for and against all enterprises in the several member states (*positive law theory*). A third, more or less intermediate, opinion was that Articles 85 and 86, while constituting immediately effective law, nevertheless only empowered the authorities to determine concrete cases according to these provisions (*power theory*). More recent developments in the law have to a large extent rendered this dispute moot. Thus, we indicate only the present state of development.

¶ 302   Article 1 of Regulation 17 declares violations of Articles 85 (1) and 86 to be prohibited, "no prior decision to this effect being required." This has been interpreted[1] to mean that Regu-

---

* Issued by the Council. Dated March 13, 1962, OffJour No. 13/62, p. 204. Translation published in Supplement No. 2, 1962, to the Bulletin of the European Economic Community. It appears at CMR ¶ 2401 et seq.

[1] E.g., by Deringer, WuW 1962, p. 83; Schlieder, BB 1962, p. 306; Obernolte, WRP 1962, p. 104; Weyer, DB 1962, p. 293.

lation 17 has adopted the positive law theory for these provisions, even for the time before the effective date of Regulation 17, i.e., retroactively to January 1, 1958, the effective date of the EEC Treaty.

II.   Legal Situation before March 13, 1962

¶ 303   The interpretation of Article 1 of Regulation 17 which has just been referred to was not, however, adopted by the *European Court* in Luxembourg as far as the period between January 1, 1958, and March 13, 1962 (effective date of Regulation 17) is concerned. Conclusion No. 1 of the *Bosch* decision of April 6, 1962,[2] rendered pursuant to Article 177 of the EEC Treaty upon transmittal of the case from a Netherlands court,[3] makes this clear:

> (1) until the coming into force of the regulation contemplated in Article 87, in conjunction with Article 85, paragraph 3 of the Treaty, Article 85, paragraph 2, thereof takes effect only with respect to agreements and decisions on the subject of which the authorities of the Member States, on the basis of Article 88 of the Treaty, have expressly decided that they come within the provisions of the first paragraph of Article 85 and that they cannot benefit by a declaration contemplated in paragraph 3, or in respect of which the Commission, by a decision taken by virtue of Article 89, paragraph 2, has found that they are contrary to Article 85.

In practical effect, the Court thus adopted the power theory for the period before the effective date of Regulation 17.[4]

¶ 304   In support of its decision, the Court says in substance that Articles 88 and 89 of the Treaty could not have ensured a complete application of Article 85, in the sense of the positive law theory. Article 88, so the Court reasons, provided for a decision by the national authorities only in the event that a cartel was being submitted to them anyway for their decision under the applicable national cartel law. Article 89, by conferring general investigatory and supervisory authority upon the Commission, empowered it only to declare the existence of possible violations of Articles 85 and 86, but did not give it jurisdiction to grant exemptions under Article

---

[2] Printed in BB 1962, p. 467 ff., and AWD 1962, p. 108 ff.; English translation (used for most of the excerpts herein) in CMR, ¶ 8003; annotation by Weyer, BB 1962, p. 469 ff.; Deringer, AWD 1962, p. 109 f.; Gleiss/Hirsch, AWD 1962, p. 125; Menges, DB 1962, p. 661 ff.; Thompson, International and Comparative Law Quarterly, vol. 11, part 3, 1962, p. 712 ff.

[3] For the decision of the trial court, see GRUR AIT 1961, p. 422; for the order of transmittal, BB 1961, p. 883, No. 1757, also GRUR AIT 1961, p. 424.

[4] Accord: Weyer, *ibid.;* Deringer, *id.,* p. 110; Kleemann, p. 97.

85 (3). An interpretation of Article 85 in favor of immediate effectiveness as positive law would therefore, as far as the period before March 13, 1962, was concerned, have led to the "intolerable" result "that these cartels would at first have been void for several years, without any authority ever so declaring, and that this invalidity would subsequently be removed with retroactive effect." It also, says the Court, would conflict with the general principle in favor of the security of legal transactions if certain agreements were deemed void before it had been possible to determine to what agreements Article 85 applied in its entirety, i.e., which agreements fulfilled the conditions for a declaration of exemption under Article 85 (3).

It is questionable to what extent this applies to Article 86,[5] where, in contrast to Article 85 (1), no exemption is possible. Therefore, the reasoning of the *Bosch* decision cannot be transplanted directly into Article 86, even though it would meet a practical need.

III.   Legal Situation on and after March 13, 1962

¶ 305   Nothing is said in the *Bosch* decision as to the effect of Article 1 of Regulation 17 for the time from March 13, 1962. However, the Court's discussion of the *legal situation of old cartels* after the effective date of Regulation 17 shows that the Court regards Article 1 as in harmony with the Treaty from that date on.[6] Conclusions Nos. 2 and 3 of the decision elucidate this:

> (2) other agreements and decisions which come under the prohibition of Article 85, first paragraph, and which were in existence at the time of the coming into force of the first regulation implementing Articles 85 and 86 of the Treaty,[7] should be considered null and void if notification thereof has been given in good time in compliance with Article 5 of the regulation only if the Commission decides that they cannot be the subject of either a decision under Article 85, paragraph 3, or of the application of Article 7, first paragraph, of the regulation, or, further, so far as the authorities of the Member States decide to exercise the powers which have been granted to them by Article 88 of the Treaty in conjunction with Article 9 of the said regulation;

> (3) The agreements and decisions which come under the prohibition of Article 85, paragraph 1, and which, being in existence at the time of the coming into force of the first regulation implementing Articles 85 and 86 of the Treaty, and not falling

---

[5] But see Gerechtshof te Amsterdam, June 28, 1962, WuW/E EWG/MUV 80.

[6] Accord: Deringer, GRUR AIT 1962, p. 284.

[7] For brevity, we use the term "old cartels" for the agreements, etc., antedating Regulation 17.

under Article 5, paragraph 2, have not had notice thereof given in good time in compliance with Article 5, paragraph 1 of this regulation, are null and void from the moment of the taking effect of this regulation.

¶ 306   What the Court says in its reasoning concerning the legal situation of old cartels is not entirely clear. The relevant passages read as follows:

that, so far as the agreements and decisions existing at the coming into force of this regulation are concerned, the nullity *ipso jure* does not come into play for them solely for the reason that they fall under Article 85, paragraph 1;

that these agreements and decisions must be considered as valid when they come under Article 5, second paragraph, of the said regulation; that they should be regarded as provisionally valid when, although they are not entirely within the ambit of this provision, notification of them has been given to the Commission in accordance with Article 5, paragraph 1, of the said regulation;

that this validity is not of a final nature, because the nullity *ipso jure* provided for by Article 85, second paragraph, is effective when the authorities of the Member States exercise the power, conferred upon them by Article 88 of the Treaty, which they retain under Article 9 of the said regulation, to apply Article 85, paragraph 1, and to declare certain agreements and decisions prohibited;

. . . if such [export] prohibitions [as are involved in the case] come within the provisions of Article 85, first paragraph, it cannot be conceded without question that Article 4, paragraph 2, of the first regulation implementing Articles 85 and 86 of the Treaty should be applied to them in such a manner that, by virtue of Article 5, paragraph 2 thereof, they should be exempted from notification and should therefore be considered valid; . . .

¶ 307   For *old cartels requiring notification* (Article 5 (1) of Regulation 17), the decision thus results in the following situation:

They have been void since March 13, 1962, unless the Commission has been notified of them within the periods specified in Article 5 (1) of Regulation 17. It makes no difference whether or not they are capable of receiving an exemption pursuant to Article 85 (3) of the Treaty. This invalidity from March 13, 1962, because of failure to give timely notification, became apparent after the specified periods had expired, i.e., on November 1, 1962, or February 1, 1963, depending upon the case.

If there was notification within these periods, old cartels are provisionally valid.[8] They become definitely valid when the Commis-

---

[8] A kind of "suspended validity," as put by Weyer, BB 1962, p. 470.

¶ 306

sion exempts them under Article 85 (3) from the prohibition of Article 85 (1).

They are void retroactively to March 13, 1962, if the Commission denies them an exemption or if the authorities of a member state[9] declare them to be prohibited by Article 85 (1). Under Article 7 of Regulation 17, the Commission may also provide for invalidity to attach from a later point of time.

In our opinion, "provisional validity" can best be understood as validity subject to a condition subsequent. Thus seen, old cartels requiring notification are valid even after March 12, 1962, but subject to becoming void either through failure of timely notification pursuant to Article 5 (1) of Regulation 17, or through a final denial of exemption under Article 85 (3) of the Treaty and refusal of legalization under Article 7 (1) of Regulation 17. If notification was not given within the time limits of Article 5 (1), in other words, if the first condition subsequent occurred, the old cartel is void retroactively to March 13, 1962. An exemption is no longer available because this would require that the first condition subsequent was finally removed, i.e., that timely notification of the old cartel was given. "Final" validity, in the sense of the decision, thus means nothing less than the final disappearance of all conditions subsequent.

Provisional validity is sometimes understood to mean suspended invalidity, in our opinion wrongly. The *Bosch* decision uses the words "provisionally valid," and that means more than "suspended invalidity." The proposition that "provisionally valid" agreements are effective pending subsequent events, was endorsed by the Bundesgerichtshof ("Trockenrasierer")[9a] with the observation, that the meaning of the expression "provisionally valid" was unambiguous and that a judgment so denominated was enforceable. The Bundesgerichtshof does not elucidate its reasoning, but comes to the same result we do.

The difference between the two interpretations has practical consequences: performance of an agreement that is temporarily invalid may not be obtained, but that of an agreement under a condition subsequent (resolutive) may. Consequently, damages for non-performance may be obtained, but if the condition occurs, their repayment may be demanded. While the agreement is in this provisional stage, the plaintiff may rely on its validity and the defendant may not object on the grounds of invalidity. A stay of the proceeding until a decision from the Commission regarding the application for

---

[9] Pursuant to Article 88 of the Treaty in conjunction with Article 9 (3) of Regulation 17.

[9a] Decision of June 14, 1963, BB 1963, p. 1393; contra: Günther, Festschrift für Böhm, p. 286.

exemption is not necessary and not permissible. Such a procedure would not be in harmony with the concept of the provisional validity of the agreement in question.

"Provisional validity" is also understood in court decisions in other member states to mean that such an agreement contains, in full, the rights and obligations of a normal contract, until an exemption is denied by the Commission according to Article 85 (3).

It is open to question whether provisional validity attaches to agreements which have been notified within the periods specified in Article 5 (1) of Regulation 17, but which are certain not to meet the prerequisites of Article 85 (3). In our opinion, even such agreements are to be treated as being provisionally valid,[10] especially in legal proceedings; the courts would otherwise have to undertake a substantive examination under Article 9 (1) and (3) of Regulation 17. The term provisional validity was finally explained by the European Court in its *Portelange* decision:[10a] provisional validity was held to be full (true) civil law validity. The provisionally valid contract provided all rights given by any other contract, in particular claims for performance and damages because of non-performance (breach of contract).

According to this decision of the Court, the Commission is able to end this full validity: As soon as the Commission has informed the parties by decision according to Article 15 (6) of Regulation 17 that, on provisional examination of the legal and factual situation, an exemption (Article 85 (3) of the EEC Treaty) will not be considered, the parties act at their own risk.[10b] The final refusal of the exemption abolishes the full validity, retroactively to the date of notification.

¶ 308   The *Bosch* decision lacks clarity with respect to *old cartels not requiring notification* (Article 5 (2) in conjunction with Article 4 (2) of Regulation 17) :[11]

In the second paragraph of the quoted reasoning (¶ 306, supra), the Court calls such old cartels "valid." It is doubtful, nevertheless, whether the words "this validity is, however, not of a final nature" in the succeeding paragraph relate to them also, or relate only to

---

[10] Contra: Alexander, CMLR, Vol. 1, p. 453; Scholz WRP 1964, p. 271.
[10a] Decision of July 9, 1969, Case No. 10/69, Recueil Vol. XV, p. 310 ff.; CMR ¶ 8075; annotations by Knöpfle, JZ 1969, p. 788; Nass, EuR 1970, p. 100.

[10b] This view was already advanced in 1963 in the first edition of this commentary.
[11] This has been pointed out by Weyer (*ibid.*), Deringer (AWD 1962, p. 110), Gleiss/Hirsch (*ubi supra*), Kleemann (*ubi supra*), Schumacher (WuW 1962, p. 479).

old cartels requiring and having the benefit of timely notification. Grammatically, "this" validity relates only to the "provisionally valid" old cartels requiring notification. This construction is supported further by the language used in the last-quoted paragraph of the reasoning, in which the Court describes old cartels coming within Article 5 (2) of Regulation 17 as exempt from notification and *therefore* to be considered as *valid*, without qualifying this validity by any other condition.[12] If the Court in fact regarded these old cartels not requiring notification as unconditionally valid, that would mean the following:

They would be unqualifiedly valid even after March 12, 1962, and could be prohibited by the Commission or the national authorities, on account of a violation of Article 85 (1) of the Treaty, only with effect for the future (*ex nunc*). The time limitation provided in Article 7 (2) and the benefits of Article 7 (1) of Regulation 17 would then, according to the decision, be without significance for old cartels not requiring notification because, being invalid only *ex nunc*, they naturally would not be in need of legalization for the past.

We doubt whether these consequences were envisaged and intended by the Court. Arguing against it is not only the fact that the Court did not touch upon the significance of the time limitation in Article 7 (2) and the benefit of legalization under Article 7 (1), but also the import of Article 6 (2) of Regulation 17. According to this provision, the Commission may, in the case of agreements, etc., not requiring notification, make an exemption under Article 85 (3) of the Treaty effective even for the time before notification, i.e., the time from March 13, 1962, in the case of old cartels. This possibility would, however, be meaningless if the agreements would be valid in any event and could be declared void only *ex nunc*.[13] Therefore, it may well be a misinterpretation of the decision to attribute substantive significance to Article 5 (2), and simultaneously also to Article 4 (2) (for new cartels not requiring notification), contrary to the meaning and purpose of these regulations. Rather, *prima facie*, one ought to assume that Articles 4 (2) and 5 (2) of Regulation 17 have no substantive law content and that, accordingly, old cartels not requiring notification, as well as those requiring it, have, since March 13, 1962, been only provisionally valid, i.e., valid subject to a condition subsequent, according to our construction. Since failure to observe the time limit for notification is not involved where notification is not required, that condition, for these old cartels, can only be a

---

[12] This is the interpretation given to the decision by Weyer (*ibid.*), Gleiss/Hirsch (*ibid.*), Menges (DB 1962, p. 664), Kleemann (*ibid.*).

[13] Accord: Menges, *ibid.*

final denial of exemption under Article 85 (3) of the Treaty and refusal of legalization under Article 7 (1) of Regulation 17. As provisionally valid agreements, before denial of an exemption by the Commission according to Article 85 (3), they contain the full measure of
the rights and obligations of the parties.

¶ 309   *New cartels requiring notification:* The *Bosch* decision says
         nothing, either in its reasoning or in its conclusions, with regard
to agreements made after March 12, 1962 (new cartels) ; the reference
to Article 4 (2) in the last-quoted paragraph of the reasoning is not
instructive. However, apart from its Article 7 and the different time
limits for notification set by Article 5 (1), Regulation 17 makes no
distinction between old and new cartels. Therefore, the Commission
and the Court will hardly draw such a distinction either. This means
that, pursuant to the decision of April 6, 1962, new cartels requiring
notification (Article 4 (1) of Regulation 17) are void before notification (Article 85 (2) of the Treaty) and provisionally valid thereafter
(¶ 307, supra). They become finally valid with the grant of an exemption by the Commission under Article 85 (3). If exemption is denied,
they are void with retroactive effect to the day of notification (and,
of course, remain void for any earlier period).

It is somewhat difficult to comprehend that new cartels are thus
void until notification but become provisionally valid upon notification, i.e., that a void transaction is thereby being brought to life. This
dogmatic difficulty must, however, be accepted, the more so since
under German civil law a void legal transaction can become valid
under certain circumstances.

¶ 310   *New cartels not requiring notification:* In its decision of March
         18, 1970 *("Bilger v. Jehle"),*[13a] the European Court has further
clarified the questions arising if a cartel agreement does not require
notification and is not notified: such agreement is fully valid. So
long as the Commission does not proceed against the agreement, national authorities (cf. Article 9 (3) of Regulation 17, infra) may decide that it violates Article 85 (1) of the EEC Treaty. Such a decision
involves invalidity according to Article 85 (2). But in contrast to
provisionally valid agreements, this invalidity does not have retroactive effect.

_____

[13a] Case No. 43/69, AWD 1970, p. 180;   ¶ 8076. See Spormann, AWD 1970, p.
Recueil Vol. XVI, 1970-2, p. 127; CMR   156.

According to the Court's decision, "national authorities" also comprise courts. But it is doubtful whether these courts with their national rules of procedure may decide on such a contravention of Article 85 (1) with legally binding effect.[13b]

The *Bilger-Jehle* decision appears to contradict the *Bosch* decision. In the latter case the Court stated that the agreement could not become invalid (Article 85 (2)) before there had been a decision on the exemption under Article 85 (3). According to the Court's *Bilger-Jehle* decision it is at least theoretically possible that a contract may become invalid even prior to a decision under Article 85 (3). The contradiction can be rendered academic however, since before the national authorities decide that the agreement contravenes Article 85 (1), a party may notify the agreement to the EEC Commission and thereby avoid the national authorities' jurisdiction (cf. Article 9 (3) of Regulation 17, ¶ 401, infra).

Article 2

NEGATIVE CLEARANCE

At the request of the enterprises or associations of enterprises concerned, the Commission may find that, according to the information it has obtained, there are, under Article 85, paragraph 1, or Article 86 of the Treaty, no grounds for it to intervene with respect to an agreement, decision or practice.

¶ 311   This regulation creates the possibility for the Commission, upon application by the parties concerned, to issue a *negative clearance*. This negative clearance is, in contrast to the exemption according to Article 85 (3), not provided for in the Rome Treaty. A legal basis in the Treaty is, however, not necessary, since such a clearance does not encroach upon the rights of those subject to the law of the Community. Thus, legal objections to group negative clearances may not be drawn from the Treaty either.[14]

The Commission may "find" that, on the basis of the facts known to it, there is no occasion for it to take steps against an agreement, decision or practice under Article 85 (1) or 86 of the Treaty. Such a

---

[13b] Thus, on April 9, 1970 (WM 1970, p. 1188), the BGH ruled that in Germany such a decision can be made only by the administrative authorities; a court can be referred to only to check their decisions. This, like de Haecht and Bilger-Jehle, was a case dealing with an exclusive delivery contract between a brewery and an innkeeper.

[14] Cf., Buxbaum, Bulletin, Vol. 9, p. 126.

finding by the Commission may, but does not necessarily (compare ¶ 318, infra), mean that, in its view, the agreement, etc., does not violate either of the cited provisions. This is confirmed by Form A/B, which is prescribed for applications for a negative clearance (Article 4 (1) of Regulation 27). Its Item IV calls for supporting reasons why the prohibition of Article 85 (1) is thought not applicable on factual or legal grounds. According to our view, however, the possibility for a negative clearance extends even further; see below ¶ 318.

¶ 312   The negative clearance requires an *application*, but, notwithstanding the wording of Article 2, not necessarily one from all participants;[15] even a single one of the parties to the agreement, etc., may apply for the clearance. This is shown by Form A/B which expressly provides for this possibility. The other parties must, however, be informed of the application. The validity of the application is not affected by the omission of such notice. Whether an omission has consequences under civil law may be determined only in the particular case (for notice regarding application for exemption, see below ¶ 502 and 503).

¶ 313   The Commission is not under a duty to ascertain the relevant facts on its own motion or even to investigate the facts supplied by the applicant. It is up to the latter to present the facts in his application completely and correctly. Intentionally or negligently false or misleading information may be punished by fines up to $5,000 (Article 15 (1) (a) of Regulation 17).

¶ 314   *The negative clearance has no binding effect on the courts in civil matters*, e.g., in actions for damages.[16] The very phrasing of Article 2 of Regulation 17 speaks against any effect on the civil side. This *greatly reduces the value of the negative clearance;* it does not achieve what appeared at times in the deliberations to be the legislative aim.[17] Ultimately it will be the European Court which will have to decide the matter. Perhaps it will find a constructive solution, as did the Bundesgerichtshof (Federal Supreme Court)[18] when it discovered an exemption in the "Willner letter," although Willner had written expressly that it was not intended to be one.

---

[15] Accord: Kleemann, p. 67.
[16] Accord: Schlieder, BB 1962, p. 308; Obernolte, WRP 1962, p. 108; Weyer, DB 1962, p. 296; Deringer, GRUR AIT 1962, p. 286; Kleemann, p. 66; contra (at an earlier time): Deringer, WuW 1962, p. 90.

[17] For the legislative history of the negative clearance see Deringer, WuW 1962, p. 90; Obernolte, *ibid.*
[18] Decision of December 10, 1957, BB 1958, p. 214 ff., also in WuW/E BGH 205 ff. ("Waldbaur"). Willner was chief of the U. S. decartelization agency in Germany.

¶ 312

¶ 315   In contrast to the courts, particularly the civil courts, *the national cartel authorities are bound by the negative clearance*,[19] albeit not directly, but indirectly, by being deprived of jurisdiction. For, under Article 9 (3) of Regulation 17, they are competent to apply Articles 85 (1) and 86 of the Treaty only so long as the Commission has not commenced a proceeding under Article 2 (for granting a negative clearance). Thus, even the "initiation" of such a proceeding results in taking away the jurisdiction of any national authority to deal with the particular situation involved, and this would be true *a fortiori* of a conclusion of the proceeding by granting the negative clearance.[20] The question whether the national authorities reacquire competence after a change in the facts upon which the Commission had issued a negative clearance probably should be answered in the affirmative.[21]

¶ 316   As far as the language of Article 2 is concerned, the Commission itself is not bound by a negative clearance given by it. This is also the Commission's own view as apparent from the Guide Lines issued by it.[22] Nevertheless, it will feel free to render a different decision, only if the facts on which it issued a negative clearance have changed or if it appears that they have not been fully submitted by the parties.[23] The *binding effect upon the Commission* to that extent rests upon general principles of administrative law which are reflected also in Article 8 (3) (a) and (c) of Regulation 17 and therefore are not alien to the regulation. In the view of the Commission,[24] the negative clearance loses its effect—apart from cases where the basic facts change—if other factors become apparent which were not known when the case was examined or if there is new legislation, possibly even if there has been a change in legal opinion.[25] The Commission may not, however, revoke a negative clearance because of a change in its legal opinion or in relevant court decisions. Under Regulation 17 a negative clearance depends only on the *factual circumstances* known to the Commission. It follows that the Commission may depart from an issued negative clearance only when new facts become known to it; a change in its legal opinion or in court decisions will not suffice. The revocation of a negative clearance has effect only for the future; prosecution for violation of Article 85 (1) or Article 86 prior to the time of revocation is precluded.

[19] Contra: Schlieder, *ibid.* Accord: Deringer, *ibid.*; Obernolte, *ibid.*

[20] Accord: Obernolte, *ibid.*; Gleiss/ Hirsch, AWD 1962, p. 126; Tessin, AWD 1962, p. 130; Deringer in AG 1962, p. 141, and in GRUR AIT 1962, p. 286.

[21] Accord: Deringer, GRUR AIT 1962, p. 286.

[22] Guide Lines, CMR ¶ 2813, 2834.

[23] Accord: Deringer, AG 1962, p. 141.

[24] Guide Lines, *ibid.*

[25] See the answer of the Commission to the inquiry from Deringer, OffJour No. 76/62, p. 2135.

According to the provision's wording, the Commission "may" grant a negative clearance when the prerequisites are met. The use of the word "may" expresses only the legal authority of the Commission to grant such clearances; it does not mean that, when the prerequisites are fulfilled, the grant lies in the discretion of the Commission (regarding the exemption, compare above, ¶ 80 ff.). Rather, a *legal right* to an exemption arises once the conditions are given. Denial of the application is thus a "decision" within the meaning of Article 173 (2) of the Treaty, against which the applicant has a right of appeal. Also a proceeding to compel a decision (Article 175) is permissible if the Commission takes no action.

If an application for negative clearance is granted, the Commission must formally state its reasons. The nature of such clearance is more than a mere legal opinion;[26] it is a decision in the sense of Article 189 (4) of the Treaty. This is also the view of the Commission; it expressly denominates its negative clearances as decisions.[27]

¶ 317   Pursuant to Article 2, the Commission finds that there are no grounds for it to take steps against "an" agreement, decision or practice. However, the singular form need not receive emphasis. In our opinion, the Commission may also, as in the case of group exemptions (Article 85, ¶ 86, supra), define generally for which categories or types of agreements it is granting a *negative group clearance*, e.g., vertical price agreements for brand-name goods as to which there exists horizontal competition, or certain restrictions in license contracts under industrial protective rights.[28] This possibility appears to be confirmed by the language of Regulation 27, Article 1 (3). To be sure, the tenor of Article 2 requires an application for such group clearances also; that could, however, be filed by an association of enterprises, e.g., by a trade association, at least for agreements, etc., made by its members. The theory of group negative clearances, advanced here in the first edition, has found approval in legal literature in the meantime.[29] The Commission in effect issued group clearances[30] in its Official Notices of December 24, 1962.[31] That it envisaged in these Notices a sort of general negative clearance, is shown by the one-month period for parties to state their positions, provided

---

[26] Cf., Schlochauer, JZ 1963, p. 108.

[27] Compare OffJour 1964, p. 916 (Grosfillex); OffJour 1964, p. 1427 (Bendix); OffJour 1964, p. 2287 (Nicholas); OffJour 1964, p. 2761 (DECA).

[28] See Gleiss, Handelsblatt of December 15/16, 1961; Gleiss/Hirsch, *ubi supra*.

[29] See Schlochauer, JZ 1963, p. 108; contra: Deringer, Article 2, Regulation 17, marg. n. 16.

[30] Buxbaum, Bulletin, Vol. 9, p. 137, also sees a type of negative clearance in these two official notices.

[31] OffJour 1962, pp. 2921 and 2922; CMR ¶ 2697, 2698.

for by both previous Official Notices of November 9, 1962,[32] in accordance with Article 19 (3) of Regulation 17. It is notable that there was no application in these cases.

¶ 318   The Commission is not compelled to institute proceedings against violations of Articles 85 (1) and 86 of the Treaty; this is a matter, rather, within its official discretion.[33] It could, therefore, issue a negative clearance even where there is such a violation. In that case, the clearance would be equivalent to a declaration that the Commission would not proceed against the violation. The text of Article 2 of Regulation 17 easily covers this type of "negative clearance" since it does not require that the prohibitions of Article 85 (1) or 86 be inapplicable to the situation involved. This kind of negative clearance, somewhat analogous to the *nolle prosequi* of American criminal procedure, would have practical importance in all cases where the parties are not particularly concerned with validity and enforceability on the civil side. This would be true especially where concerted practices are involved which are not legally binding in any event; but it may be true also where the subject matter is an agreement or decision, especially since here, too, the national authorities would be at least indirectly prevented from prosecution by reason of their loss of jurisdiction pursuant to Article 9 (3) of Regulation 17. The clearance would have still greater significance if, as we believe entirely possible (¶ 317, supra), it were given for certain categories of agreements, in a way perhaps comparable to the announcement by the BKartA that it would not institute proceedings against certain recommendations to dealers.[34] Naturally, no right to such a negative clearance would arise.

¶ 319   The application for a negative clearance may not be construed to include one for an exemption. In contrast to an application for exemption, one for a negative clearance does not protect from *fines;* Article 15 (5)(a) of Regulation 17 does not apply here. If, however, a negative clearance has been issued for a particular agreement, the contracting parties may perform their agreement without risk; even if it was granted erroneously, they are acting without fault (the situation is different, of course, where fraudulent procurement of the clearance is involved). Third parties' damage claims are also precluded for want of fault, at least as a rule.

---

[32] OffJour 1962, pp. 2628 and 2629; CMR ¶ 2711.

[33] This may be implied from Article 15 (2) of Regulation 17.

[34] BKartA Annual Report 1959, p. 44.

¶ 320   The *national authorities* cannot grant negative clearances;[35] such grants would lack substantive significance as well as jurisdictional basis under Article 9 (3) of Regulation 17.

¶ 321   There are *no fees* for the issuance of a negative clearance by the Commission. No fee schedule exists for cartel proceedings before the Commission, nor is there any intention to enact one. This general principle of freedom from charges applies also to proceedings for obtaining exemptions.

¶ 321A   *Commission decisions:* Decisions on requests for negative clearance made by the Commission from February 26, 1968, to June 30, 1970, are:

¶ 321B   *Eurogypsum:* On February 26, 1968, the Commission, pursuant to Article 2 of Regulation 17, granted Eurogypsum, Paris, a negative clearance with regard to its by-laws and activities.[1] Eurogypsum is a non-profit association of individual European gypsum producers and their organizations, which is established for the purpose of promoting production and knowledge of plaster, gypsum, and anhydrite, as well as of the construction materials derived from those products, by joint scientific, technical and legal studies as well as by collective advertising. The results of this work are published or, at least, are made available to all members. None of the members is restricted in its individual research.

This case did not pose any legal problems since a restraint on competition did not exist, either with regard to the objective or with regard to the effect of the association. Also, the case is covered by the "Kooperationsfibel" (i.e., Cooperation Primer, see ¶ 17, supra).[2]

¶ 321C   *Alliance de Constructeurs Français de Machines-Outils:* On July 17, 1968, the Commission granted the Alliance de Constructeurs français de Machines-Outils (Association of French Machine-Tool Manufacturers), Paris, a negative clearance with regard to its by-laws and the agreements made with its shareholders, etc.[3]

---

[35] Accord: Schlieder, BB 1962, p. 310; Gleiss/Hirsch, BB 1962, p. 624; Kleemann, p. 65.
[1] OffJour No. L 57, March 5, 1968; Second General Report on the Activities of the Communities, 1968, p. 46; for more details see CMR ¶ 9220, particularly the section on "slow growth for plaster industry" in which the situation in the EEC is compared with that in Great Britain and the U. S.

[2] As to questions of procedure see Kirschstein, WRP May 1969, pp. 185 ff., particularly regarding application for negative clearance and exemption.
[3] OffJour No. L 201, August 12, 1968, p. 1; Second General Report on the Activities of the Communities, 1968, p. 46; CMR ¶ 9248 and 9249.

The Alliance is a stock corporation entrusted with acting as common export organization for eight small and medium-sized French enterprises manufacturing machine-tools. The organization's share in the export of French machine-tools is about 10%. Their total turnover is FF 129 million. The individual manufacturers, with the Alliance being merely a negotiator, sell their products at their own prices, in their own names and for their own account, and collect payment directly. The Alliance is reimbursed only for its prospecting costs.[3a] In fact, at the time the company was formed, the members of the Alliance were specializing in different machines. Each shareholder agrees not to manufacture or sell machines that might compete with those manufactured by another shareholder.

The Commission, on the basis of these facts, for the most part set forth in its opinion, found two reasons for a restraint on competition within the meaning of Article 85 (1) not being present:

(a) The common export organization serves exclusively to open markets and is not an independent stage in the distribution; the customer's interests are not affected.

(b) The non-competition clause corresponds to the actual situation at the time the agreement was concluded (1961). In any event, in the case of machine-tools, there is a trend toward specialization; hence, there is no reason to expect that one of the members will start manufacturing machines that compete with those produced by the other members.

This last statement is surprising. The Commission's previous attitude would lead one to believe that it would have at least taken potential competition for granted in this case.

We observe that the Commission has found that the members of the Alliance have only a comparatively small share in the machine-tool market within the Common Market, but does not state the actual percentage. Moreover, in one sentence the Commission says that the machines which are the object of the contract do not compete—i.e., that each has a market of its own—whereas elsewhere it declares their share of the French export market to be 10%. Thus, it obviously refers to three different markets.

Under German cartel law the fact that the members are legally bound to sell only through their joint organization would constitute an essential element of a restraint of competition. The same would also seem to be true for EEC law, in the actual circumstances of the case.

[3a] Compare the words "joint selling arrangements" in the Notice of May 27, 1970, ¶ 17, supra.

¶ 321D *SOCEMAS:* On July 17, 1968, the Commission granted
SOCEMAS, Paris, a negative clearance with regard to its by-
laws and activities.[4]

SOCEMAS, a trading and research company of 69 French chain
store enterprises marketing food and related commodities, prospects
foreign markets in order to find articles likely to interest member
firms because of quality and price, such as biscuits, canned fish,
wine, toys. If the number of members interested is large and the
quantity of products to be bought sufficient, SOCEMAS negotiates
with the foreign suppliers the most favorable terms for the transaction, which is then concluded on behalf of the member firms concerned. In 1965, SOCEMAS' imports from other EEC countries
amounted to 0.1% of the total turnover of the associated stores. None
of the products bought through SOCEMAS exceeds 1% of the annual
production of this article in the EEC supplier country concerned.
This was the percentage of canned fish bought from German enterprises in relation to the total German supply of such goods. These
are the facts presented in the Commission decision.

In its reasons the Commission states the following: The by-laws
do not *aim at* a restraint on competition, since the members need not
buy their goods through SOCEMAS, but are completely independent
with regard to their purchases. The by-laws and activities do not
effect any restraint on competition within the meaning of Article
85 (1) since, as the small percentage of purchases made through
SOCEMAS indicates, they do *not perceptibly* influence the position of
the suppliers on the various markets.

We note that here the Commission does not use the term "perceptible" in context with restraint on competition, but, in our opinion
rightly, with the influence on the market, particularly the influence on
the position of the suppliers on the market. It would be helpful if the
Commission would use clearer and more consistent terminology.[4a]

Furthermore, we observe that this is the Commission's first decision on a cooperation between retailers, particularly those acting as
purchasers.

Finally, we would like to point out that the Commission did not
object to the clause according to which the application of outsiders
to become members may be turned down by a SOCEMAS board
which need not give reasons.

---

[4] OffJour No. L 201, August 12, 1968,
p. 4; Second General Report on the
Activities of the Communities, 1968, p.

47; for more details, see CMR ¶ 9248
and 9250.
  [4a] For "perceptible," see ¶ 17A and
22, supra.

¶ 321D

¶ 321E　*Cobelaz-Synthetic Products Manufacturers and Cobelaz-Cokeries:*
In two decisions issued November 6, 1968,[5] the Commission granted the sales associations Cobelaz-Synthetic Products Manufacturers and Cobelaz-Cokeries a negative clearance, after the parties had abolished a number of concerted practices and restraints on competition—among others, a premium paid customers for exclusive dealing.

As a result of these reforms, Cobelaz (Comptoir belge de l'azote), in Brussels, now deals only with the sale, in Belgium and certain countries outside the Common Market, of fertilizers consisting of or containing synthetic ammonium sulfate and ammonium sulfate derived from the production of coke. For these markets, there are quotas and a pooling or equalization of proceeds, and the prices as well as the general sales conditions are determined by Cobelaz. Its members are Belgian enterprises or cooperatives manufacturing fertilizers.

After presenting these facts, the Commission, in its decisions, makes the following statement: The agreements, especially the clause imposing on the manufacturers the obligation to abstain from independent sales of contractual products in Belgium, perceptibly restrict competition within the Common Market. Since, however, according to the Commission's investigations, the agreements and their application are not apt to impair trade between member states, i.e., do not impair the freedom of the members or third parties to import and export within the Common Market, the Commission granted a negative clearance. The restraint, in the Commission's opinion, is mitigated by the fact that the members are free to decide themselves what quantities they wish to sell through the syndicate and what they want to export.

These decisions, which involve very similar facts and reasoning by the Commission, are remarkable in that they concern the first sales syndicates and boldly permit them, notwithstanding the members' obligation to sell, in Belgium, exclusively through these syndicates.

In conclusion, it can be observed that the "bad" part of the agreements is legalized, as is the case in other decisions of the Commission, on the basis of Article 7 of Regulation 17.[6]

---

[5] OffJour No. L 276, November 14, 1968, pp. 13 and 19; Second General Report on the Activities of the Communities, 1968, p. 47; for more details see CMR ¶ 9265 and 9266, particularly ¶ 9265 at II as to procedure, e.g., use of Form B instead of A.

[6] As to procedural problems see Kirschstein, WRP, June 1969, p. 223, asserting, among other things, that the reasons mentioned by the Commission do not bear these decisions.

¶ 321F *Comptoir français de l'azote:* The Commission, also on November 6, 1968, granted a negative clearance for a very
similar agreement between 28 French manufacturers and the *Comptoir
français de l'azote* (CFA), Paris, on the common sale of nitrate fertilizers.[7]

In this case also, the members abolished previously stronger restraints on competition,[8] e.g., the obligation of CFA and the member
manufacturers not to export to the other EEC countries. At present,
CFA is entrusted with the sale, in France and certain countries outside the Common Market, of contractual products manufactured by
its members. According to the facts presented in the Commission's
decision, the manufacturers are even bound exclusively to CFA where
some such countries are involved.

CFA has a certain influence on the production program of the
members. With regard to sales outside France it determines uniform
prices and conditions, but without imposing export prohibitions on
CFA's customers.

In its reasoning the Commission states:

"It is true that, in its present version, the agreement still imposes
perceptible restrictions on the position of distributors within the Common Market. In particular, CFA sets a uniform monthly sales price
scale and uniform sales conditions for the French market which require delivery to be made freight-free to all rail depots of destination, so that French buyers, for the quantities purchased from CFA,
have no opportunity to encourage price competition between French
manufacturers or to profit from any advantage arising out of proximity
to certain plants, thus reducing freight costs. These restrictions of
competition do not, however, justify refusal of the negative clearance,
since according to the facts known to the Commission, it does not appear in the present circumstances that such restrictions, which concern the internal French market, are likely to affect trade between
Member States."[9]

Surprisingly, the Commission here, also, did not grant an exemption but a negative clearance.

In this case, as in the two Belgian fertilizer cases, the Commission does not state whether the members in fact do sell on the domestic market, and, if so, how much they sell.

---

[7] OffJour No. L 276, November 14,
1968, p. 29; Second General Report on
the Activities of the Communities, 1968,
p. 47; for more details, see CMR ¶ 9268.
[8] This was agreed upon orally, a
procedure permissible under EEC law.

[9] Translation taken from CMR ¶ 9268
at II(7). We do not concur with the
word "likely" to affect in the translation
quoted, because Article 85 (1) requires
no more than ability ("aptness") to affect "interstate trade."

¶ 321G   *Rieckermann/AEG-Elotherm:* On November 6, 1968, the Commission granted a negative clearance in the following case:[10]

Under a contract with *AEG-Elotherm* ("AEG"), a German manufacturer, Rieckermann, an export dealer in Hamburg, is bound to promote at his own risk and for his own account the sale in Japan of AEG's equipment for heating, melting and tempering by induction. He is not allowed to sell in other countries, except Korea. He is required to provide post-sale and guarantee services, and may buy equipment for Japan only from AEG. AEG is permitted to distribute its equipment in Japan through Rieckermann exclusively and must see to it that its other customers do not distribute such equipment in Japan. The contract is valid for an unlimited period and may be cancelled by either side.

Based on the statements of the parties to the contract—the only source mentioned in the decision!—the Commission presented the following facts:

AEG sells equipment in the Common Market through representatives who take orders for its account on a commission basis. As a rule, this equipment is not mass-produced, but is made to order on specifications given by the individual clients and according to their technical requirements, so that others cannot make use of the equipment. In Japan, different voltages and often different frequencies are customary, so that the equipment designed for Japan can be used in the Common Market only in exceptional cases, and vice versa. The dealers place an order with AEG only after contacting a customer. Equipment of this kind is offered by quite a few enterprises in the Common Market. (Why doesn't the Commission state at least the approximate figure? Such information could be used as a point of departure in other cases.) Some enterprises are comparable in size to AEG, and the others also distribute their equipment within and outside the Common Market through representatives—either their own branches, commission agencies, or independent dealers.

Rieckermann specializes in export trade, particularly to countries in the Middle and Far East. He does not sell within the Common Market and, therefore, does not have any sales organization there. The export of the contractual equipment requires consultant and post-sale service by a specially trained staff. Rieckermann competes with many enterprises exporting to Japan. He registered the exclusive dealing contract and, even though he considers Article 85 (1) inapplicable, applied for an exemption as a precaution.

---

[10] OffJour No. L 276, November 14, 1968, p. 25; Second General Report on the Activities of the Communities, p. 48; for more details, see CMR ¶ 9267.

In its decision the Commission makes the following statements:

(a) The prohibition imposed on Rieckermann against selling AEG equipment in any country but Japan includes the prohibition against selling such products in the Common Market (sales prohibition). Pursuant to the agreement, Rieckermann is not allowed to sell in Japan equipment competing with the AEG equipment (prohibition to compete). AEG may distribute its equipment in Japan only through Rieckermann (exclusivity clause) and must see to it that its other customers do not sell such equipment there, i.e., it must impose on them a sales prohibition for Japan or have the prohibition imposed on them (absolute *district protection*, designated by the Commission as "sales prohibition to be transferred").

(b) The Commission does not see any reason for assuming that these prohibitions and stipulations *aim at* a restriction, prevention or distortion of competition within the Common Market. This possibility is not always excluded, however, merely because the main purpose is to promote sales in a country outside the Common Market. In the case concerned "there is no evidence that the parties are also pursuing objectives that might prove to have perceptible adverse effects on competition."

We wish to mention here that the Commission does not make it clear that the objective or purpose of the agreement, according to its language, must be a *perceptible* restraint on competition. The terminology is also undesirably vague insofar as the Commission refers to an "impairment" of competition, an expression used by the legislator in Article 85 (1) only in the following context: "apt to impair *trade* between member states."

(c) The Commission then states that the agreement also does not, in *effect,* prevent, etc., competition within the Common Market. Competition has not, in fact, been impaired perceptibly—this is the first indication in the Commission's reasoning that the agreement has already been practiced for some time—and it is not sufficiently probable that a perceptible impairment(!) of competition will follow. The Commission substantiates this by stating that Rieckermann does not have any sales organization in the Common Market and, furthermore, that the equipment is generally made to the customers' specifications. Moreover, AEG and important competitors sell their equipment in the Common Market directly to the users, partly themselves and partly through representatives who act on their behalf, with minimum costs, so that Rieckermann could not compete with them. Besides, there is nothing in the agreement to prevent Rieckermann from selling within the Common Market equipment manufactured by AEG's competitors, if he wished to do so.

¶ 321G

The prohibition to compete, the Commission states further, refers only to Japan, but it means that Rieckermann may not buy any equipment from competitors of AEG for resale there. Thus, demand is also diminished in the Common Market. "The Commission nevertheless has concluded that the prohibition to compete does not *pertain* to a prevention . . . of competition within the Common Market." This is, in our opinion, unclear language which seems to be related to the Commission's incorrect theory that the *purpose* of a restraint on competition is sufficient. In any case, the word "pertain" is not clear. The Commission saves itself by stating that: "There are so many manufacturers of such equipment and so many dealers exporting to Japan that there is no reason to expect any *effect*s of the prohibition to compete on the relationship between supply and demand in the Common Market which might be interpreted as perceptible impairment of competition (!)." (Here again we notice the transition from "purpose" to "effect," which we already criticized in the *Grundig* decision of the European Court; see ¶ 23 ff., supra.) Rieckermann competes with a large number of enterprises that export to Japan. There are no criteria for assuming that AEG's competitors in the Common Market have suffered or would suffer competitive disadvantages with regard to their sales in Japan, that would not have occurred if Rieckermann had also worked for them in Japan. Furthermore, it is questionable (a realistic argument) whether it would be as advantageous to AEG's competitors to be represented in Japan by a joint export dealer, as it would be for them to have their own exclusive dealers (it is rather unusual for the Commission itself to have a good word for exclusive dealing).

AEG's exclusivity clause, according to the Commission, is confined merely to the market of Japan and does not affect the Common Market. The exclusion of other dealers in the Common Market wishing to export to Japan, according to the Commission, is deliberate, "but cannot lead to any perceptible impairment of the relationship between supply and demand in the Common Market."

We note that thus, the purpose alone is not sufficient if perceptible effects or consequences do not follow![10a] In this case the Commission's language is clearer. It states that the export dealers are able to buy equipment from many other manufacturers. The Commission assumes that, because of the technical complexity of the equipment, AEG would employ the services of only *one* "sales promoter" in Japan even if there were no agreement. According to the Commission, this is valid also for the (absolute) sales prohibition to be transferred.

(d) The Commission concludes, therefore, that it need not be assumed that the exclusive dealing contract aims at or effects a pre-

---

[10a] Cf. ¶ 22, supra.

vention of competition within the Common Market; since at least one of the conditions for applying Article 85 (1) is not present, the negative clearance may be granted. The exemption applied for as a precaution was thus considered to be unnecessary.

We observe that, according to the Commission, even an absolute exclusive dealing contract may be permissible, e.g., if a "third country," outside the Common Market, is involved, and, in any event, if there are special circumstances like those prevailing here.

Using this test decision on exclusive dealing contracts concerning export to third countries, the Commission will be able to dispose of approximately 1,100 notifications of such contracts in a simplified procedure.[11] When it issued its decision, the Commission stated further that, in most cases, notification of such contracts would not be necessary and that the parties concerned would not be interested in a negative clearance.

¶ 321H   *Convention Chaufourniers:* On May 5, 1969, the Commission granted a negative clearance for the *Convention Chaufourniers (Limeburners' Agreement)*.[12]

The Commission sets forth the following facts:

Under a contract concluded in 1936 with the Association of Belgian Manufacturers of Artificial Cement, 13 Belgian Limeburners agreed to refrain from producing any cement other than natural cement and to limit their sales of natural cement to a maximum of 2.75% of the artificial cement sold by the members of the Association. The Association agreed to pay the Limeburners, every three months, 0.5% of the total cement sales by its members.

In 1936, 50,000 tons of natural cement and approximately 2,500,000 tons of artificial cement were produced in Belgium. Today, there is only one manufacturer of natural cement in Belgium, and he produces 1,000 tons per year. In 1965, the production of artificial cement rose to 5.9 million tons. This replacement of natural cement is due to the superior qualities of artificial cement.

There were 26 Belgian cement manufacturers in 1935, compared with 9 in 1966, 7 of which make Portland cement. Today, the establishment of new plants is profitable only if their capacity exceeds 200,000 tons annually. A factory costs at least 400 to 500 million BF. The enterprise yields a profit only if the premises and the quarries are

---

[11] See BKartA Annual Report, 1968, p. 94.

[12] OffJour No. L 122, May 22, 1969, pp. 8 ff.; for more details, see CMR ¶ 9303.

¶ 321H

comparatively large. In 1965, 10 Limeburners reached an agreement with the Association and were paid off. The remaining three Limeburners own 15.51 hectares (38.33 acres) of scattered land, 7.63 hectares (18.86 acres) of which are inactive quarries. In contrast, the smallest Belgian Portland cement firm produces on 63.54 hectares (156.94 acres) of contiguous land, 21.16 hectares (52.27 acres) of which are quarries. The industry apparently suffers from over-capacity.

On October 31, 1962, the Association and the Limeburners notified their contract to the Commission pursuant to Article 5 (1) of Regulation 17 (i.e., on the last day of the time-limit). On July 1, 1962, the cement manufacturers had stopped their payments to the Limeburners on the ground that the contract violated Article 85 (1) and was, therefore, void. The Limeburners instituted proceedings at the Commercial Court in Tournai which ruled against the cement manufacturers on April 10, 1964. The Court of Appeals in Brussels reserved its decision "until such time as the Commission finally decides on the application of Article 85 . . . to the disputed convention . . . ."[13]

On the basis of these facts, the Commission granted the negative clearance giving the following reasons :

(a) The obligation of the Limeburners not to produce any *artificial cement* does not, in view of the present circumstances, *aim at or effect* any restraint on competition, at least not a perceptible one. It is probably impossible for the Limeburners to establish new factories on their small and scattered premises, considering the large and modern plants necessary for profitability. Even a concentration of their quarries would be of no use. In 1936, a readjustment of the existing Limeburners' plants would still have been possible. Today it is impossible because the quarries have been closed down and the Limeburners have been eliminated from the market as producers of cement. Hence, they are not even potential competitors for the producers of artificial cement. This seems to be confirmed by the fact that these producers, since 1947, have endeavored to terminate the agreement, so that the Limeburners would be free to produce artificial cement. In no event could the prohibition of production perceptibly restrict competition. The smallest Belgian Portland cement firm, with an annual production of about 65,000 tons, accounts for only 1.5% of total Belgian Portland cement production. Thus, the three

---

[13] For comments on this ruling of the Brussels Court, among others as to problems of procedure, see Gleiss/Hootz, "Vorläufige Gültigkeit von Altkartellen" (Preliminary Validity of Old Cartels), AWD September 30, 1965, pp. 336 ff., particularly pp. 337-339.

Limeburners could by no means ever influence the supply of Portland cement in Belgium, much less in the Common Market.

(b) Because of technical development, the restriction on the Limeburners' sales of *natural* cement has become meaningless. They produce only about 1,000 tons per year, even though under the 1965 agreement they could manufacture 132,000 tons.

(c) The facts known to the Commission do not support the conclusion that the agreement of 1936 aims at or effects a prevention, restriction or distortion of competition within the meaning of Article 85 (1). Hence, at least one prerequisite for the prohibition is lacking, so that the negative clearance may be granted. So much for the Commission's opinion.

The remaining question, which is purely a question of civil law, is whether the Court of Appeals in Brussels will rule against the Association and require it to continue payment to the three Limeburners who have not yet given up the fight, and, if so, how long it will require the Association to do so. It is encouraging that in this case—in contrast to cases like *Grundig-Consten*—the Commission presents the economic circumstances very accurately, in even more detail than we gave them here. Consequently, the reader can form his own opinion. Furthermore, it is gratifying that the Commission's decision was influenced largely by economic considerations, especially since, from a purely legal point of view, the agreement, concluded for an unlimited period, apparently violated Article 85 (1).

¶ 321J *Christiani & Nielsen: Christiani & Nielsen N.V.,* a company in The Hague, requested a negative clearance for an agreement concluded in 1931 and renewed in 1959 between it and its parent company of the same name in Copenhagen, of which it is a wholly owned subsidiary.[14] Under the contract, the Danish construction enterprise is bound to make available to its Dutch subsidiary all the experience, patents, inventions and technical know-how which the parent possesses and, in certain cases, services of its technical division. The parent company may not do business in Holland, and the Hague company may not operate outside Holland without the parent's permission. The Danish company is entitled to appoint the Hague firm's managers and to give them orders.

Christiani & Nielsen, The Hague, is obliged to pay the Copenhagen company compensation for each completed order. If one of the companies makes an invention, it must share it with the other

---

[14] OffJour No. C 37, April 24, 1968, p. 1; CMR ¶ 9231.

one, free of charge. This contract may be terminated only if both parties agree.

Christiani & Nielsen, Copenhagen, has many wholly owned sub-sidiaries, two of which are located in Germany and France. Each subsidiary is, by contract, prohibited from doing any business in a country in which another subsidiary has its domicile. There are many competitors of the group within the EEC.

The Commission, on June 18, 1969, granted a negative clear-ance.[15] In its Christiani & Nielsen decision, the Commission clarified its view with respect to intra-concern restraints, and this view is entirely in line with our thesis (see ¶ 21, supra). The Commission states:

"For Article 85 (1) to be applicable there must be competition between the enterprises concerned that might be restrained. This condition is not fulfilled by enterprises active in the same line of business merely because each of them is a legal entity of its own. It is of decisive importance, however, to determine on the basis of the facts in the individual case, whether the subsidiary is able to take economic actions independently of the parent. For reasons of policy the (Copenhagen) enterprise, whose activities are international, has preferred to establish subsidiaries in the various countries instead of branch offices or agencies. This is a view determined by market strategy, which makes it necessary to recognize that the wholly owned subsidiary and the parent are not to be considered as an eco-nomic unit in which the former is able to compete with the latter. Moreover, Christiani & Nielsen, Copenhagen, is entitled to appoint the management of Christiani & Nielsen, The Hague, and to give orders to this subsidiary. Thus, the latter is an integral part of the economic complex of the Christiani & Nielsen group. The Copen-hagen firm would be able, even without any agreement at all, to determine at any time the behavior of Christiani & Nielsen, The Hague, in which it holds all of the capital. It can be concluded from this that the agreement in question does not aim at or effect a pre-vention, restriction or distortion of competition within the Common Market."

One of these statements should be emphasized, viz., the one beginning with the words *"Moreover,* Christiani & Nielsen, Copen-hagen, is entitled . . ." because these words at least seem to indicate that even if the Copenhagen company did not have the power to appoint management or give orders, there would, in the Commission's

---

[15] OffJour No. L 165, July 5, 1969, p. 12; CMR ¶ 9308.

opinion, be no competition within the meaning of Article 85 (3), since the parent holds all of the subsidiary's capital. In other words, this probably means that if the parent does not hold all of the capital, the other factors mentioned will gain in importance, e.g., the parent's power to appoint the management, etc., but particularly the subsidiary's inability to take—really and fully—independent action.

For the two cases Scott Paper-Continental and Scott Paper-Burgo Scott, see the Commission's announcements of October 1968[16] (for details, see ¶ 465A, infra).

¶ 321K *Pirelli/Dunlop:* On December 5, 1969,[17] the Commission granted a negative clearance for agreements between Pirelli (parent company) and Dunlop Italiana (subsidiary), both in Milan, and Dunlop (parent company) and Pirelli France (subsidiary), both in Paris, which were concluded to facilitate the opening up of the counterpart's home market. Dunlop in France and Pirelli in Italy were obliged to manufacture, against payment, inner tubes for cars, having certain properties required in France and Italy, respectively; the subsidiaries, Pirelli France and Dunlop Italiana, were bound to buy certain minimum quantities of these tubes.

After the parties eliminated the obligations contained in the original agreement of 1959 (not to fit tires on new cars, not to import similar goods from other sources, and not to conclude further contracts with other tube manufactures), the Commission stated that the remaining agreements do not aim at a restraint of competition, since there are technical differences in tires and tubes depending on the make of car and on the roads in France and Italy, and that therefore they do not fall under Article 85 (1).

The Commission refrained from applying Article 85 (1) to the agreements for the period of time prior to their final revision in 1965, because the parties had shown their willingness to adjust their agreements to Article 85. In other words, the Commission saw no need to impose fines.[18]

¶ 321L *VVVF:* On June 25, 1969, the Commission granted the following negative clearance:[19]

---

[16] OffJour No. C 110, October 24, 1968; CMR ¶ 9263.

[17] OffJour No. L 323 (December 24, 1969), p. 21; CMR ¶ 9336. The agreements had been duly notified before October 30, 1962, according to Article 7 (1), Regulation 17.

[18] For the planned merger between Dunlop Co. Ltd. and Pirelli S.p.A., see ¶ 207, supra.

[19] OffJour No. L 168 (July 10, 1969), p. 22; CMR ¶ 9312; WuW/E EV 285.

The Vereniging van Vernis- en Verffabrikanten in Nederland (Association of Varnish and Paint Manufacturers in the Netherlands) was founded in Amsterdam on September 26, 1907, in order to protect the interests of the paint industry, especially of their members. The purpose of the association's Export Committee is, in particular, to protect the good name of the paint products of its members, i.e., practically all the Dutch manufacturers and exporters of ready-mixed paint.

Three of the four obligations imposed on the committee members were, on the Commission's request, abolished insofar as the Common Market is concerned. The content of these obligations is nevertheless of interest because it indicates what the Commission did not tolerate. The members were obliged

(a) to maintain conditions and minimum prices for export fixed by the committee's directors;

(b) to engage one representative only for each country outside of Holland, to fix his sales prices at the minimum level set by the directors and not to grant him compensation higher than that fixed by them;

(c) to inform the committee of all essential details of their export transactions.

The only obligation remaining with regard to the Common Market is the members' obligation to see to it that the products they export meet the minimum quality standards reasonably determined on the basis of the common export program, the name of the goods, the trademark applied to them, the intended use, the price, and other criteria. The members are free to set prices and sales conditions for exports into the member states. In exporting to third countries, they are obliged to maintain minimum prices fixed in the export program and to meet conditions prescribed by the directors. The members have to tolerate an examination of their dealings made by the common secretariat which may take samples of products and have them analyzed. A joint body may fine the members for non-compliance.

The Commission gave the following reasons for granting a negative clearance:

If the members export into other countries of the Common Market products of certain names defined by the group, these products must be up to the minimum quality standards prescribed by the group. The members may export products of lower quality if they do not use the names fixed by the group. Under these given

¶ 321L

circumstances, the Commission states that competition is not restrained.

This was to be expected. We have here a sort of common quality mark, which has always been considered acceptable under European cartel law (for another example, see ¶ 321N, infra). It is more remarkable that the joint fixing of minimum export prices is accepted by the Commission. It could have objected on the basis that the reimport of these products into the Common Market, and thus trade within it, might be impeded. This once more (see ¶ 321P, infra, Kodak) confirms our theory (see ¶ 27 ff., supra) that the Common Market must, in practice, be treated as one block, as a unit, so that restraints on exports to third countries do not affect trade within the Common Market even if it is conceivable that the goods concerned might otherwise be reimported into one member country and sold from there into another one.

The Commission resolves this problem by stating that the minimum prices fixed for export are "rather" (ziemlich) low as compared with the prices actually charged, so that there is still a possibility of price competition both between the members of the group and from third parties. Furthermore, the Commission points to the lively competition actually existing between paint manufacturers in the member states, thus indicating that there would be no perceptible restraint of competition within the Common Market.

This example shows that the Commission is not too reluctant to grant negative clearances even if, according to its own statements, the whole industry of a member state is concerned. In a case like this, of course, there would, in the future, be a very good chance of obtaining at least an exemption under Article 85 (3).

¶ 321M   *SEIFA:* On June 30, 1969,[20] the Commission granted a negative clearance to the Società per lo Sviluppo dei Consumi dei Fertilizzanti, an association for the development of the consumption of fertilizers with headquarters in Milan, founded by a number of Italian producers of fertilizers. Under the altered agreement, the SEIFA company, as an executive organ, sells the goods supplied, without any form of exclusive arrangement, in Italy and in countries outside of the EEC, for the account of the participating enterprises. It is prohibited from exporting to the member states of the EEC. Such exports may be undertaken only by the producers and their resellers on an individual basis. In its capacity as agent, SEIFA sets

---

[20] OffJour No. L 173 (July 15, 1969), p. 8; CMR ¶ 9315. The request for the negative clearance had been made before October 31, 1962.

¶ 321M

the conditions, terms and prices for the sale of the fertilizers supplied by its members. The orders obtained by SEIFA for delivery both on the domestic market and for export outside of the EEC are distributed among the parties according to the characteristics of the product desired, the quantities available in the warehouses, and the location of the factories in relation to the destination of the goods. SEIFA applies to Italian buyers general sales conditions that contain no export ban.

The Commission regarded the terms of the agreement as not coming within Article 85 (1). Since the parties concerned had indicated their intention of altering the old agreement, which had been duly notified before October 31, 1962, in order to comply with EEC cartel law, and since they actually altered it within a reasonable time, the Commission thought it justified not to apply Article 85 (1) for the time prior to October 9, 1968, the date of the alteration.

¶ 321N　*ASBL pour la promotion du tube d'acier soudé électriquement:*
On June 29, 1970,[21] the Commission granted a negative clearance to four Belgian manufacturers of electrically welded steel pipe and to the "Association sans but lucratif pour la promotion du tube d'acier soudé électriquement," founded to promote their pipe and to maintain standards and quality. The association advertises this pipe jointly for all four members, but they are also allowed to advertise on their own. The association has a national and an international trademark. Any enterprise is free to join the association and to use the trademark if it keeps the standards of the International Standard Organization (ISO) for this type of pipe. A member can be expelled only if it does not keep these standards or engages in unfair competition.

The Commission stated that the association was founded by an "agreement between enterprises," and that the rules on using the trademark were set by a "decision of an association of enterprises." But the joint advertising campaign, which is intended only to draw attention to features of a product manufactured by several enterprises, was considered not to affect competition between the members of the association since they can also advertise their products on their own.

Finally, according to the Commission, the use of the common trademark held by the association and the conditions for acquiring the right to use it do not affect competition within the Common

---

[21] OffJour No. L 153 (July 14, 1970), p. 14; CMR ¶ 9380. The request for the negative clearance had been made on October 30, 1962, according to Article 2 of Regulation 17.

Market, since each manufacturer can adjust his products to the standards of the ISO and then join the association.

The Commission is thus of the opinion that *joint advertising* is not a restraint of trade so long as the partners remain free to advertise on their own. This shows that the Commission rightly considers advertising to be a means of competition.

The *trademark* in this case serves as a joint quality mark. The Commission argues that: "The standard measurements are fixed by an international standards organization (ISO) acting in numerous countries. Every pipe manufacturer may therefore adapt his production to satisfy the conditions for obtaining the joint trademark." The Commission uses the word "therefore" without saying that it examined whether every manufacturer is really able to reach the prescribed level.[22]

¶ 321P   *Kodak:* On June 30, 1970,[23] the Commission granted a negative clearance to the national subsidiaries of the American corporation Eastman Kodak for their new terms of business introduced January 1, 1970, in order to comply with the requirements of EEC law. The Commission first examined whether the fact that all Kodak enterprises in the Common Market use identical trading conditions indicates an agreement or concerted practice. Since all subsidiaries completely depend on the parent company which is able to control them and give them exact instructions, it is impossible for a single enterprise to act independently from the others. Thus, there is no agreement or concerted practice within the meaning of Article 85 (1).[24]

The terms become part of the agreements concluded with the customers. In their previous form (export prohibition and obligation to sell Kodak products in recognized shops only) they clearly came under Article 85 (1). The new terms, however, were found not to violate Article 85 (1) since they prohibit only exports to countries outside of the Common Market, deliveries from one member state to another thus no longer being impaired. This prohibition is considered by the Commission not to be apt to affect trade between member states, because it was held to be very unlikely that these goods would be reimported into the Common Market and sold from one member state to another.

---

[22] For joint advertising and joint quality marks as a means of competition, see ¶ 17, supra.

[23] OffJour No. L 147 (July 7, 1970), p. 24; CMR ¶ 9378. The original agreement was notified on May 6, 1963.

[24] See ¶ 9 and 10, supra.

The original obligation not to sell Kodak products except in recognized shops was altered to the effect that these products are to be sold only by trained staff and in business premises which guarantee satisfactory storage, display, and selling conditions. These new terms were considered to be in accord with Article 85 (1), since there is no reason to suspect that the requirements exhaustively enumerated will be used to exclude wholesalers or retailers unless they do not fulfill those requirements.

We conclude from this that the Commission countenances the concert of behavior not only between the parent company and a subsidiary, but also between subsidiaries. Joint control excludes violation of Article 85, but the Commission does not state the degree of dependency necessary.

In our opinion, restraints on exports from the Common Market to a third country do not affect interstate trade (see ¶ 27 ff., ¶ 321L, VVVF, supra). Apparently the Commission does not want to admit this in principle. Instead it argued in *Grosfillex-Fillistorf*[25] that goods exported from France into Switzerland would not be reimported from there into the Common Market because of transport costs and customs barriers. In the Kodak case, the Commission discusses in detail the costs arising from export into a third country, reimport into a Common Market country, and reexport to another member state. Only this third transaction might affect interstate trade. This goes to show that in practice restraints on exports to third countries are irrelevant for interstate trade. Perhaps the most remarkable consequence of the "cleaning" of the old "sales conditions" is that the prices for Kodak products in the six EEC countries will, in the future, move freely, unhampered by any restraints on the subsidiaries' customers as to exports or distribution in general.

¶ 321Q *ASPA:* Also on June 30, 1970,[26] the Commission granted a negative clearance to the Association syndicale belge de la parfumerie (ASPA), an organization of Belgian manufacturers, general agents and sole distributors of perfume and toilet articles, whose purpose is to protect the common interests of its members as well as the quality and reputation of their products, and to avoid unfair competition. Originally, ASPA also supervised the maintenance of prices fixed individually by the members who manufacture or distribute the products concerned. For this purpose, the members were obligated to respect the exclusive rights of licensed manufacturers

---

[25] See ¶ 22, supra.

[26] OffJour No. L 148 (July 8, 1970), p. 9; CMR ¶ 9379. Notification dated October 31, 1962.

¶ 321Q

and agents, and to comply with the general sales conditions concerning fixed prices and imports and exports of the products designated annually by the secretariat of ASPA. They also had to bind their customers to the same obligations. In case of contravention, all ASPA members were obliged to terminate their relations with the defaulter.

The ASPA practices were followed by other enterprises on the Belgian market so that the ASPA rules influenced the Belgian market considerably. The Commission declared that the rules in this form contravened Article 85 (1), without all the prerequisites of Article 85 (3) for an exemption being fulfilled. The agreement was altered several times so that now there are no objectionable clauses left; it no longer aims at price maintenance. If the association wants to prevent unfair competition, it now has to observe the EEC Treaty and regulations. Since the Commission saw no reason to suspect that the agreement has been replaced by concerted practices, Article 85 (1) no longer applies. Insofar as the past contravention of Article 85 (1) is concerned, the Commission thought it justified not to apply the prohibition since ASPA altered its statute within the time limit set by the Commission.

This decision confirms that both joint resale price maintenance[27] and, ordinarily, joint sanctions against unfair competition are prohibited.

Article 3

ENDING OF INFRINGEMENTS

(1) If, acting on request or *ex officio*, the Commission finds that an enterprise or association of enterprises is infringing Article 85 or Article 86 of the Treaty, it can by means of a decision oblige the enterprises or associations of enterprises concerned to put an end to such infringement.

(2) A request to this effect may be submitted by:
(a) Member States;
(b) Natural and legal persons and associations of persons, who show a justified interest.

(3) Without prejudice to the other provisions of the present Regulation, the Commission, before taking the decision mentioned in paragraph 1, may address to the enterprises or associations of enterprises concerned recommendations designed to put an end to the infringement.

[27] Cf. ¶ 37, supra.   [28-35] Reserved.

¶ 321Q

¶ 322   The finding of an infringement by the Commission is a decision within the meaning of Article 189 of the EEC Treaty and it can thus be challenged independently. Before it takes such decision the Commission may, but need not, issue a recommendation that the enterprises end the infringement.

¶ 323   An *application* may be made by a member state or by persons, legal entities or associations who have a legitimate interest.[36] This means a substantiated explication of all facts pertinent to a legitimation of the interest of the applicant; if such party has several grounds for objection, of course only one need be advanced. To "show" is, in our opinion, the same as to "assert"; as a rule, it does not mean that the applicant must establish the credibility of, or prove, his assertions. If, however, they are improbable or untrustworthy, the Commission is authorized to require proof of the allegations. Proper applicants may thus be, e.g., the enterprises against which a competitive restraint, as by a cartel, is directed. As far as the wording of Article 3 is concerned, this includes persons outside the Common Market; in general, however, such persons will have a justified interest only if they have an establishment or perhaps a subsidiary in one or more of the Common Market countries,[37] although the interest, e.g., in importing into a particular member country, of a party outside the Common Market without an establishment there may suffice.

The term "natural and legal persons and associations of persons" means, according to the usage in Regulation 17, those parties not participating in the restraint of competition (compare Article 19 (1) and (2) of Regulation 17; see below ¶ 385). Thus, a participant may not apply to put an end to an infringement. This rule is a justifiable one, since he has other means of advancing his interests, e.g., an action to void his commitment.

Member states need not show a legitimate interest. Their right of application is unqualified; consequently, a member state may make application even if the restraint of competition does not affect its interstate trade. A party not able to show a "legitimate interest," thus has the possibility of enlisting a member state to make application.

For an application for prosecution of a violation, the Commission recommends the use of Form C.[38]

---

[36] Guide Lines, CMR ¶ 2812; also Deringer, AG 1962, p. 141.

[37] Accord: Gleiss/Hirsch, AWD 1962, p. 126.

[38] This form, unlike Forms A and B, is not prescribed by regulation. It is reproduced in CCH translation in CMR ¶ 2693.

¶ 324   The right to file an application concerns the finding of a violation, not its elimination.[39] However, the right to make application is not exhausted, according to its meaning and purpose,
when there is a formal finding of a violation, but rather when the
violation has been eliminated. Nonetheless, an applicant may not demand an immediate decision, i.e., one without a prior recommendation.
In practice, this distinction will not be of much significance because
a finding of a violation will normally be followed by an order that
the enterprises or associations involved cease the violation. It will be
different only where the participants have already abandoned the
violation on the basis of the finding itself or where they follow
recommendations made by the Commission.

It is questionable whether the application obligates the Commission to act or whether it constitutes only a request without
binding effect. The legislative history shows, in our opinion, that a
formal right of application in the former sense was intended.[40] There
is also some doubt as to whether, when the applicant has received a
negative decision, he has an action under Article 173 (2) of the Treaty
to void the decision, or whether he may proceed to compel a decision
(Article 175) should the Commission fail to act on his application.
In our opinion, both questions should be answered in the affirmative.[41]

If the Commission intends to refuse the application, it must communicate its position and reasons therefor and grant the applicant an
opportunity to submit his comments (Article 6 of Regulation 99/63).

The *decision*[42] of the Commission obligates the participants to
cease the "ascertained violation." This means, first of all, that the
participants may not carry on the conduct (Article 85) or prohibited
abuse (Article 86) found to be a restraint of trade. It is questionable
whether the Commission, on finding a violation of Article 85, as a rule
may also require that the underlying agreement, i.e., the cartel agreement, be abrogated, since the cartel is "decontaminated" by the prohibition of its activities (compare the parallel prohibition of "disregarding" the invalidity of an agreement in restraint of trade in Section 38, paragraph 1, no. 1 GWB). In its recommendation to the
"Convention Faience,"[43] the Commission forbade the Convention as
a whole to be practiced and, moreover, suggested that certain parts

---

[39] Probably contra: Deringer, WuW
1962, p. 91; accord: Schlieder, BB
1962, p. 308.
[40] Details in Steindorff, AWD 1963,
p. 353.
[41] *Ibid.*

[42] On the form of the legal act, see
Art. 189 of the Treaty and Everling,
BB 1959, p. 52.
[43] WuW/E EV 60, also in AWD
1964, p. 187.

of the Convention be eliminated; however, this corresponds to the nature of the recommendation under Article 3 (3) of Regulation 17.

The Commission may require the abrogation of agreements only to the extent that their individual provisions violate Article 85. Thus, it may not require a complete abrogation when elimination in part suffices. This is in accord with the European Court's *Grundig* decision (July 13, 1966, CMR ¶ 8046) where the Court stated that only those clauses of an agreement are void under Article 85 (2) which violate Article 85 (1) or "contribute to the infringement."

The content of a decision under Article 3 (1) of Regulation 17 directed against misuse of a dominant position (Article 86) is comparatively easy to define if the abuse consists of a "predatory practice." If a strong enterprise systematically cuts a weak competitor's prices with the aim either of annihilating him or of buying him cheaply, the content of the decision will, of course, be to forbid such underselling, without having to state the minimum price at which the dominant enterprise must sell. Positive instructions to an enterprise as to the conduct of its business have no foundation in Article 3.

Should the Commission try to state other forms of abuse, e.g., in the acquisition of shares, the exchange of shares (particularly with different values or different voting powers), or financial transactions which in our times tend to become more and more refined and complicated, Article 3 does not offer a sufficient legal basis for inventing appropriate countermeasures.

This differs from the legal situation in the United States where the law in fact permits the judge to fashion remedies of his own, which to a European lawyer sometimes seem fantastic. The semantics frequently involved hardly soften the impact of what may actually be the setting of legislative or, at least, administrative policies.

Hence, as we stated above (¶ 207), the acquisition of shares by an enterprise in a dominant position is not an "abusive exploitation." This is confirmed by an analysis of Article 3 (1) of Regulation 17, which does not give the Commission a legal basis for ordering the purchaser, e.g., to sell shares at any price or for setting a deadline for such sale. A sales order without a deadline would be incomplete and without effect.

The Commission may combine its decision with a monetary fine (Article 15 (2)(a) of Regulation 17), but need not do so. Fines may be imposed in an independent decision.

¶ 325   The *decision*[44] of the Commission, by which it orders the participants to desist from the violation found, is subject to

[44] For the different forms of legal acts by the institutions of the EEC, see Article 189 of the Treaty, and Everling, BB 1959, p. 52 ff.

judicial review at their instance. Jurisdiction of such an action for review is in the Court at Luxembourg, pursuant to Article 173 of the Treaty. This means, among other things, that the question of how a certain agreement is to be interpreted and whether Article 85 (1) is applicable to it may be brought before the European Court.[45] This uniform system of administrative decision subject to judicial review contrasts decisively with enforcement procedures under the antitrust laws of the United States, where a similar system prevails only for matters within the jurisdiction of the Federal Trade Commission (which may be exclusive or may be concurrent with that of the Department of Justice as far as the function of prosecutor is concerned). The central provisions of American antitrust law—Sections 1 and 2 of the Sherman Act—are enforced directly by the courts without the intervention of an administrative agency, and in a variety of ways (criminal proceedings, governmental or private injunction suits, treble damage actions) which have no or only limited counterparts in the EEC law.

¶ 326   Decisions of the Commission are to be published (Article 21 of Regulation 17), but not *recommendations* which it may address to the parties concerned for putting an end to a violation (Article 3 (2)). This latter provision, in our view, empowers the Commission to eliminate a violation without any formal proceeding. By the same token, the parties are given the opportunity of adapting themselves to EEC cartel law without making it a matter of public knowledge. This has disadvantages as well as advantages. Advantages, because the parties may reform or adapt themselves without publicity. The principal disadvantage, however, lies in the possibility that they might, from fear of publicity, accept recommendations even where the existence of a violation of Article 85 (1) might be contested on valid grounds. Important legal questions might thus remain unclarified for substantial periods of time because this apprehension of the parties might prevent formal decisions of the Commission which could then be submitted to the European Court for review. Another disadvantage is that in a particular case a benevolent recommendation may in the end prove to be inefficient, and a formal decision may still be needed, so that valuable time may be lost.

There has been little activity of the Commission under Article 3. It has concluded only one proceeding under this provision, the case of "Convention Faience." The Commission, apparently with the concurrence of the participants, issued a recommendation to strike cer-

---

[45] Accord: Deringer/Tessin, NJW 1962, p. 990; Schumacher, WuW 1962, p. 475 ff., 482.

tain obligations from the Convention. Since the participants yielded to this recommendation, the Commission did not need to use the means of a decision to obtain compliance. It is notable that the Commission did not limit itself in its recommendation to proposing that the participants cease practicing their agreement, but suggested the deletion of particular obligations. Furthermore, it is of interest that the Commission rendered a rather detailed statement of the factual circumstances and its legal view.

¶ 327　　On December 2, 1968, the Commission addressed a recommendation to the Agfa-Gevaert AG (Germany) and the Gevaert-Agfa N. V. (Belgium),[46] after a cash and carry firm filed a request under Article 3 of Regulation 17 that the terms of trade of the two enterprises be examined. According to Article 19 (1) of Regulation 17, the Commission stated that it would consider

—the prohibition imposed on customers of the two companies, preventing them from exporting or selling the products bought to exporters;

—in the German terms, the obligation of the customer to stipulate the export prohibition also in reselling the products;

—in the Belgian terms, the obligation of the customer to sell the goods only to certain wholesalers and retailers;

as coming within Article 85 (1), but not Article 85 (3), and that it intended to issue a decision under Article 3 of Regulation 17 requiring the firms to end the contravention.

The terms were said to create distribution systems and prices independent from those in the other state, thereby splitting the Common Market into separate national markets. The legality of a price maintenance system in Germany was held not to justify such export prohibitions. An exemption according to Article 85 (3) was denied because the restraint of trade was not considered necessary for the advantages achieved, since the terms of business had to be viewed in the context of the whole system for distribution of all Agfa-Gevaert enterprises in all member states. Furthermore, the Commission remarked that the other prerequisites of Article 85 (3) were also not fulfilled, in particular because the customers did not get their fair share of the advantages.

We conclude that the Commission will not tolerate vertical export prohibitions and vertical distribution systems creating independent national markets where prices cannot be influenced by imports from other member states.[47]

---

[46] The text of this letter is published in AWD 1970, p. 77.　　[47] Cf. ¶ 37 and ¶ 42.

Article 4

NOTIFICATION OF NEW AGREEMENTS, DECISIONS AND PRACTICES

(1) The Commission shall be notified of any agreements, decisions or concerted practices referred to in Article 85, paragraph 1, of the Treaty which have come into being after the entry into force of the present Regulation and for which those concerned wish to invoke Article 85, paragraph 3. As long as such notification has not taken place, no decision to issue a declaration under Article 85, paragraph 3, may be rendered.

(2) Paragraph 1 shall not be applicable to agreements, decisions and concerted practices where:

(i) enterprises of only one Member State take part and where such agreements, decisions and practices involve neither imports nor exports between Member States;

(ii) only two enterprises take part and the sole effect of these agreements is:

(a) to restrict the freedom of one party to the contract to fix prices or conditions of trading in the resale of goods which have been acquired from the other party to the contract, or

(b) to impose restraint on the exercise of the rights of any person acquiring or using industrial property rights—particularly patents, utility models, registered designs or trademarks—or on the rights of any person entitled, under a contract, to acquire or use manufacturing processes or knowledge relating to the utilization or application of industrial techniques.

(iii) their sole object is:

(a) the development or the uniform application of standards and types,

(b) joint research to improve techniques, provided that the result is accessible to all parties and that each of them can exploit it.

The Commission may be notified of such agreements, decisions and practices.

I. In General

¶ 331   This article concerns only agreements, etc., since the effective date of Regulation 17, i.e., since March 13, 1962 (*"new cartels"*). Agreements, etc., before that date ("old cartels") are dealt with in Article 5.

Article 4, like Article 5, does not establish a compulsory notification. There is no legal duty to notify. Notification is only a prerequisite for an exemption under Article 85 (3) and then only where the agreements require notification (see below ¶ 334).

¶ 331

¶ 332   Article 4 distinguishes between those agreements, decisions and concerted practices which require notification (paragraph 1) and those which do not (paragraph 2). The essential difference is the following:

If the Commission grants an exemption under Article 85 (3) from the prohibition of Article 85 (1) of the Treaty, this action will, in the case of *agreements*, etc., *requiring notification*, have retroactive effect at most to the date of notification (Article 6 (1) of Regulation 17); before that date they are void (Article 85 (2) of the Treaty).[48] For *agreements*, etc., *not requiring notification*, however, the exemption pursuant to Article 85 (3) may be granted also for the period before notification, i.e., retroactively to the time of the agreement, etc., involved (Article 6 (2) of Regulation 17). Due to this possibility of retroactive exemption, these agreements, etc., not requiring notification thus cannot, at least according to German legal concepts, be regarded as void, but at most as invalid in a suspended sense; according to our view, they are provisionally valid (see above ¶ 307, 310).

¶ 333   The categories of agreements, etc., not requiring notification are listed exhaustively in Article 4 (2). This provision has no substantive significance, notwithstanding the decision of the European Court in the *Bosch* case (see ¶ 308, supra). Article 4 (2) cannot, therefore, be interpreted to mean that agreements, etc., coming within it do not violate Article 85 (1) of the Treaty, as a matter of substantive law. It is, thus, incorrect to assert that Article 4 (2) (ii) allows resale price maintenance.[49]

¶ 334   In cases covered by Article 4 (2) of Regulation 17, exemption under Article 85 (3) of the Treaty may be granted even *without notification* having been given to the Commission, e.g., on the application of a third party, upon referral by a national authority or court, or the like. This theory is supported by the language of paragraph (2), the introductory words of which exclude application of the entire preceding paragraph (1), and not only of its first sentence. However, Article 4 (1) provides in its second sentence that, for agreements, etc., requiring notification, an exemption under Article 85 (3) of the Treaty may not be given in the absence of previous notification. Therefore, Article 4 (2) is to be interpreted as excluding from that provision[50] agreements, etc., not requiring notification. The Commission shares this view.[51]

---

[48] This situation was not touched by the *Bosch* decision of April 6, 1962, which concerned old cartels only.

[49] Rinck, Wirtschaftsrecht, p. 201.

[50] Accord: Schumacher, WuW 1962, pp. 478, 480; Kaiser, p. 40. Contra: Schlochauer, JZ 1963, p. 107. In doubt on this point, Weyer, DB 1962, p. 327 and AWD 1962, p. 315; Deringer GRUR AIT 1962, p. 287.

[51] Guide Lines, p. 11; contra: Schlochauer, JZ 1963, p. 107; LG Mannheim, January 22, 1965, AWD 1965, p. 61; refuting them, and correctly so, Niederleithinger, AWD 1965, p. 62.

¶ 335   Here, too, *no fees* are levied for the procedure with the Commission; see ¶ 321, supra.

II. New Cartels Requiring Notification

¶ 336   Agreements, decisions and concerted practices coming into existence since the effective date of Regulation 17, i.e., since March 13, 1962, require notification *if, and to the extent to which*, the parties desire an exemption for them under Article 85 (3) of the Treaty. There is *no legal duty to give notification.* Notification is only a prerequisite to exemption.[52] That there is no obligation to give notification is demonstrated, among other things, by the fact that the Commission cannot impose either penalties or fines on account of failure to notify.[53] However, the prohibition of cartels is self-executing, and agreements requiring notification—their conclusion as well as their performance—are, in the absence of notification, prohibited and void and subject to the imposition of fines under Article 15 of Regulation 17. This has not been changed or affected by the decision in the *Bosch* case (see ¶ 305, ff., supra); "provisional validity" begins only with notification. If the Commission exempts a new cartel, it is valid from the date of notification; if no exemption is granted, it is void retroactively to the date of its origin.

¶ 337   Notification, as shown by Form A/B, actually means an *application* to the Commission for an exemption under Article 85 (3) of the Treaty.

¶ 338   *After notification,* the agreement, etc., requiring it may be performed or practiced by the parties without the risk of fines (Article 15 (5)(a) of Regulation 17), even if exemption is ultimately denied (but cf. ¶ 365, infra).

III. New Cartels Not Requiring Notification

¶ 339   Article 4 (2) exempts from the notification requirements certain competitive restraints stated, in the preamble to Regulation 17, to constitute "less of a threat to the development of the Common Market." It should be noted that Article 4 (2) applies only to those agreements which fall under Article 85 (1) of the Treaty. Agreements not requiring notification naturally may be notified to the Commission at any time; there is no particular period for such

---

[52] This seems to be the generally accepted view; see, e.g., Weyer, *id.* p. 294.

[53] Accord: Weyer, *ibid.*

notification; when notification is made is up to the parties to the agreement (but see Article 7 (2)).

Article 4(2)(i)

¶ 340   This provision applies to so-called "national" agreements, etc., no matter how many enterprises participate. It does not cover agreements in which enterprises from a single member state and enterprises from a country outside the EEC participate, e.g., an agreement between a German and a Swedish enterprise.[54] The language of (i) supports this view. This provision requires that "only" enterprises from one member state be parties. Agreements between enterprises from one member state and from a third country thus must be notified unless they come within one of the exceptions. This is also the view of the Commission.

¶ 341   A further question is, what is meant by *"involve."* Do agreements which have other immediate objectives, but touch trade between member states in an indirect and perhaps rather remote manner, "involve" imports or exports between member states?

The German text does not furnish any clear answer, nor is one to be gained from the other versions. However, if "involve" were to be interpreted as including indirect or remote effects of an agreement, no reasonably defined borderline could be drawn. For, one could say of almost any agreement of some economic impact that it will ultimately have effects upon imports and exports. The exception in Article 4 (2) would thus be so narrowed down as to lose any real significance. This provision, however, ought to be interpreted, as all law, so as not to become nugatory. In our view, therefore, the agreement need only be one which does not *directly* relate to imports and exports between member states, one, in other words, which does not deal with imports or exports as its subject matter. On the other hand, it is immaterial that a direct relation may not have been intended.[55]

---

[54] Thus Deringer, GRUR AIT 1962, p. 294; contra: Schumacher, WuW 1962, p. 480. It should be noted that this interpretation appears to be supported to a greater degree in the English translation, where the "only" precedes "one member state," than by the German text, where the equivalent of "only" precedes "enterprises" and therefore qualifies the phrase "enterprises from one member state" in its entirety.

[55] Kaul, AWD 1962, p. 156, interprets "involve" as meaning "affecting inten-

tionally," in our view erroneously. Probably in accord with us: Schumacher, *ubi supra.* Actually, the German "betreffen" might have been translated by "concern" more accurately than by "involve," but with little difference as far as the question of proximity is concerned. The American lawyer will be reminded here of the long history of developing interstate commerce concepts in the courts and the distinction still drawn between "in commerce" and "affecting commerce" statutes.

However, since an agreement dealing with imports or exports will as
a rule be one affecting them "intentionally," the disputed question is
without great practical importance. For example, if the ten or twenty
independent German dealers of a German enterprise are obligated to
sell its products only in their respective exclusive territories, such an
obligation does not "involve" exports of these products, even though
it may be responsible for the fact that, e.g., the dealer in Aachen (near
the Belgian border) may not sell across the border. It will, however,
be different if the enterprise has an exclusive distributor, say, for
Belgium and obligates him to sell the products only in that country.
This latter obligation does "involve" exports, for it can have no other
purpose than to prevent the Belgian distributor from exporting.

In principle, at least, the Commission has accepted this strict interpretation of "involve." In its Guide Lines (CMR ¶ 2818), it is stated
that "national" agreements touching imports or exports only indirectly,
such as agreements on specialization or exclusivity, or on prices or
limitation of production without (direct) involvement of imports or
exports, are within the exception of Article 4 (2)(ii); whereas even
"national" agreements prohibiting reimports or providing for joint
purchasing in another member state, i.e., agreements thus regulating
imports or exports in a direct sense, would be subject to the notification requirement.

Article 4(2)(ii)(a)

¶ 342   *Only two enterprises* can be parties to an agreement within
this exception, but it is immaterial here whether they are
from one or from two member states or from one member state and
a third country.

Nor does it matter that one enterprise, e.g., the supplier in the
case of a vertical price agreement, may conclude separate agreements
on the same terms with a large number of other enterprises;[56] subparagraph (ii)(a) is also intended to cover such cases of multiple
vertical price and terms agreements.[57] The Munich Landgericht failed
to recognize this in a case[58] in which it had to decide whether a
vertical export prohibition, which was part of a vertical price agreement, had been timely notified to the Commission. The decision was
rightly held to be incorrect by commentators;[59] the Court of Appeals
for Munich set it aside.[60]

[56] Accord: European Court, decision of June 30, 1970, Case No. 1/70, *Marcel Rochas.*
[57] Accord: Schumacher, *ubi supra.*
[58] Decision of January 14, 1963, BB 1963, p. 167.
[59] Compare the remarks on this decision by Hellmann/Pfeiffer, BB 1963, p. 169; Benisch DB 1963, p. 301, and Basson, MA 1963, p. 124.
[60] Decision of May 30, 1963, BB 1963, p. 745. See ¶ 46, supra.

The concept of enterprise is, of course, the same here as in Article 85 (1) (see Article 85, ¶ 1 ff., supra). Consequently, where two member companies of a concern (Konzern) are parties to an agreement on the same side, the agreement is one between more than two enterprises and therefore not within this exception.

On the other hand, the view that *vertical agreements giving exclusive distribution rights or restricting a distributor as to territory or customers* are covered by (ii)(a), because such matters are frequently contained in the terms and conditions of a distribution contract and are themselves "conditions" in the broader sense,[61] cannot be reconciled with either the language or the purpose of this provision.

¶ 343   Its language includes only such restrictions as prescribe for the obligated party certain terms (prices or conditions) to be observed in the resale of the products supplied to him by the other party. In the case of exclusive distributorship agreements and restrictive agreements as to a distributor's territory or customers, however, the matter at issue is not the contents of resale transactions stipulated in the contract between supplier and distributor, but the question whether such transactions may take place at all. The text of (ii)(a) thus covers only the cases of Section 15 GWB (the "how" of the contract), but not those of Section 18 GWB[62] (the "if" of the contract).

The history of this provision also shows that its purpose was only to exempt the imposition of certain resale terms, in the narrow sense stated above. There is no room here to recount that history in detail.[63] It should be observed, however, that the draft of Regulation 17 prepared by the Commission would have exempted in the then Article 5 (3), in addition to vertical stipulations regarding conditions and prices,[64] also vertical exclusive distribution rights and territorial or customer restrictions. Upon a French request, this was later deleted, for the stated purpose of not treating such competitive restraints more mildly than others.[65] Subparagraph (ii)(a), therefore, does not cover such exclusive rights and sales restrictions.[66]

---

[61] Thus Hellmann/Pfeiffer in "Volkswirt" 1962, p. 233, and the editor of MA in an annotation to the *Bosch* decision, MA 1962, p. 498, 499.

[62] Accord: Tessin, AWD 1962, p. 130; Kaul, *ubi supra*, p. 157; Deringer, GRUR AIT 1962, p. 294.

[63] For details see Kaul, *ibid.*

[64] In literal conformity, to that extent, with the final Article 4 (2)(ii)(a).

[65] Accord: Kaul, *ibid.;* Weyer, DB 1962, p. 294; Schlieder, BB 1962, p. 309, footnote 33; Deringer, *ibid.*

[66] This is also the view of the Commission, as apparent from Guide Lines, CMR ¶ 2818, and even more clearly from the implicit subjection of exclusive distributorship agreements to the notification provisions of Article 4 of Regulation 27, albeit simplified ones for certain such agreements: see the discussion there, ¶ 501 ff., infra.

It is true, however, that notification is not necessary for the obligation of a customer—indispensable to a vertical price system— to resell the goods supplied by the price stipulator only to dealers who will in turn agree to observe the prescribed price. To be sure, this also is a restriction as to customers. However, it has no independent significance, but merely forms a part of the resale price system and ensures the completeness necessary to its operation. If it required notification, then the exception of (ii)(a) would make no sense because no vertical price or terms agreement can dispense with this or a similar clause. This clause, therefore, does not of itself subject the agreement to notification requirements;[67] otherwise, the statutory exception would be narrowed down to the point of virtual ineffectiveness.

¶ 344   *Not all vertical price and terms agreements are excepted from notification requirements* by the text of (ii)(a). Such agreements are not within this exception if, for example, they concern goods not bought by the customer from the contracting supplier. Separate identity of contracting party and supplier of the goods in the resale of which the customer is to be bound is, however, immaterial if the contracting party is merely acting for the supplier, e.g., as trustee, and establishes the vertical price and terms system for him. Branded goods, within the meaning of Section 16 of the GWB (or of the so-called fair trade legislation in the United States), need not be involved; the exception applies also to unbranded products.

As far as its wording is concerned, (ii)(a), like Section 16 of the GWB, covers vertical price and terms agreements only for goods and not for commercial services, and it is obvious that services, e.g., repair services in the automobile trade, are not being supplied to and resold by the dealer. Nevertheless, to the extent that future rendition of such services is included within the terms on which the dealer sells the automobile bought from the manufacturer, stipulations by the latter regarding the terms of such services will concern "conditions of trading in the resale of" the automobile, so as to exempt them from the notification requirement.[68]

¶ 345   The exception exists only for agreements that "solely" restrict a customer in his freedom to determine prices and terms of resale. If an agreement contains more, e.g., an export prohibi-

---

[67] Accord in result, although not in reasoning, Kaul, *id.*, p. 158.

[68] An exception may, of course, be claimed for commercial services of any kind under Article 4 (2)(i), if the parties belong to the same member state.

tion or other restrictions on distribution by the customer, the exception is not available. In that case, and unless another exception applies, notification is required for the agreement in its entirety and not only for the contractual obligations beyond the observance of resale prices and terms.[69]

Article 4(2)(ii)(b)

¶ 346   This provision deals with license agreements concerning industrial protective rights and gives four illustrations. Also included under the term are design rights *(Ausstattungsrechte)*, legally protected "know-how," legally unprotected inventions, production processes, constructions, etc. Copyrights and publication rights do not belong in this category.

This provision concerns only license agreements with restrictions on the licensee that are *not* within the scope of the licensed protective right.[70] If the protective area covers the restrictions in question imposed upon the licensee, the agreement does not fall under Article 85 (1) of the Treaty in the first place, so that there is no occasion to apply Article 4 of Regulation 17. Throughout this topic, reference should therefore also be made to the discussion under Article 85, ¶ 49-59, supra. As to "know-how," in particular, compare Article 85, ¶ 52. An agreement regarding the use of a trademark, in our opinion, comes within subparagraph (ii) (b) when an enterprise could for legal reasons prohibit another from using a particular trademark (e.g., danger of confusion), but contractually permits such use, thereby imposing certain restrictions on the user.

This is particularly clear in the case of patent licenses, where the Commission regards certain provisions as being outside of Article 85 (1), in most cases for the reason that they are held to be within the scope of the patent monopoly. It is true that the Commission's Official Notice on the subject states expressly that it is not to affect the interpretation of Article 4 (2)(ii)(b) of Regulation 17—the provision now under discussion. Yet, where the Commission in its Notice has characterized certain restrictions on the licensee (e.g., as to technical application or geographical area) as "covered by the patent" and therefore not reached by Article 85 (1) of the Treaty, it is difficult to see how a different position could be adopted for the purposes of Article 4 of Regulation 17; in other words, it seems clear that paragraph (2)(ii)(b) will have nothing to operate on in such a case.

---

[69] Accord: Deringer, *ubi supra;* the Commission, too, holds this view: Guide Lines, CMR ¶ 2818.

[70] Accord: Deringer, *id.,* p. 293; Schumacher, WuW 1962, p. 481; still undecided: Gleiss/Hirsch, AWD 1962, p. 126.

Moreover, it seems highly unlikely that certain other restrictions upon or obligations of the licensee (e.g., marking duty, imparting of know-how) which, even though not covered by the patent in a direct sense, have yet passed muster in the Notice as having none of the effects prohibited by Article 85 (1), could be given a different status here. The real significance of the Commission's above statement may therefore be seen in its aspect as a disavowal of any *limiting* effect of the Notice upon the interpretation of the present provision, quite in line with the simultaneous reservations in the Notice to the effect that the enumeration of restrictions within the scope of the patent monopoly is not intended to be exhaustive and, even more generally, that the Notice is not to affect the legal status of any patent license provisions not listed therein.

¶ 347   Subparagraph (ii)(b), like (ii)(a), is applicable only where *but two enterprises take part* in the agreement (for the meaning of "enterprise", see above ¶ 1 ff.). It does not include agreements among a larger number of parties, e.g., when the licensors are two different enterprises, perhaps joint patentees, but will cover the situation where the licensor makes separate contracts with several or many individual licensees. It is immaterial if such agreements are circumstantially related, e.g., if they provide for an exchange of know-how among licensees, so long as the agreements are legally independent of one another. Again, it is immaterial from which state or states the two parties are or where they have their headquarters. This provision applies also, and perhaps particularly, to international license agreements. If one or both contracting parties are located outside the Common Market, the agreement will often lack the "aptness" to affect adversely interstate trade.

¶ 348   The restrictions must be imposed upon the licensee *in relation to the exercise of the licensed rights*. What restrictions this includes is doubtful. The expression does not mean only such restrictions as are indispensable for the exercise of the licensed right. Such a view would not be in accord with the language of subparagraph (ii) (b) (not only in the German version). Rather "relative to the exercise" means merely that the restriction must be inherently related to such exercise, not that it must be indispensable. Whether a particular restriction is indispensable, is determined in the exemption process according to Article 85 (3) of the Treaty. The Commission now shares this view. In its Guide Lines, it assumes that "relative to the exercise" means every such restriction imposed which has a direct relation to the exercise of the protective right.

Thus, in our view, all those obligations imposed on the licensee, which restrict him in the utilization of the licensed right and/or the exploitation (including distribution) of the protected articles, are meant by the expression "relative to the exercise".[71] The same applies to a transfer of the protective rights, as distinguished from a license thereunder.

¶ 349   Among restrictions coming within Article 4 (2)(ii)(b) would be the licensee's obligation to sell the goods produced under the licensed right only to certain customers. This *restriction on distribution* is thus privileged, as compared to other exclusivity agreements and restraints on distribution.[72]

The provision covers, furthermore, an obligation of the licensee to sell the products made under the licensed right only at *prescribed prices*[73] (if, indeed, such an obligation were to fall under Article 85 (1) of the Treaty in the first place : compare Article 85, ¶ 56, supra). In our view, it covers also an obligation of the licensee to prescribe to his customers certain resale prices for these goods, since such an obligation is still intrinsically related to utilization of the protected articles.

"Restrictions relative to the exercise" of the protective rights also includes the duty to affix to the products made under the license a reference to the license, a patent notice, or a particular trademark, if the licensee is prohibited from adding his own name or trademark. If, however, the licensee may mark such products with a reference to himself as manufacturer, according to the view of the Commission, no restraint of competition is presented by the additional obligation to affix a reference to the patent.[74] In such a case, the obligation does not violate Article 85 (1), so that subparagraph (2) (ii) is manifestly not applicable.

"Restrictions relative to the exercise" also covers purchase obligations of the licensee. In the Commission's view, an obligation to purchase restricts the licensee "relative to the exercise" of the protective right only when it concerns raw materials that are indispensable to the exploitation of the licensed right.[75] Since the licensee may utilize the right only in connection with the prescribed materials, in our opinion, the obligation to purchase always restricts him in the exercise of the licensed protective right, without regard to indis-

---

[71] Deringer, Article 4, Regulation 17, marg. n. 18, holds a narrower view. Compare also, Weiser, WuW 1964, p. 732.
[72] Accord: von Gamm, WRP 1962, p. 81; Tessin, AWD 1962, p. 130; Kaul, AWD 1962, p. 158.

[73] Accord: Deringer, GRUR AIT 1962, p. 294.
[74] Official Notice Concerning Patent Licensing Agreements, Off Jour of December 24, 1962, I B; CMR ¶ 2698.
[75] Provisional Guide Lines, p. 19.

pensability of the materials. Consequently, even agreements containing such obligations do not require notification. The Commission's "Official Notice Concerning Patent Licensing Agreements" of December 24, 1962,[76] indicates in effect that the Commission no longer regards its prior view as correct. In this Official Notice (see Section I C), it was stated that obligations of the licensee concerning the quality of product or sources of supply were not covered by the prohibition of Article 85 (1) of the Treaty "insofar and so long as they were indispensable in the interest of technically unobjectionable exploitation of the invention." Since, however, subparagraph (ii)(b) and, indeed, all of Regulation 17, may be applied only to such restrictions as fall under Article 85 (1) of the Treaty, it is evident that an "indispensable" obligation concerning quality or sources of supply is not covered by subparagraph (ii)(b). On the contrary, that provision includes only those obligations concerning quality or sources of supply which are *not* indispensable, but which the licensor considers necessary or desirable for business reasons (in this connection, see above ¶ 54 ff.).

¶ 350   On the other hand, (ii)(b) does not cover an obligation of the licensee not to make or distribute *competing products.* Such a stipulation has no intrinsic connection with the exercise of the protective right but restrains the licensee in his freedom to compete.[77]

No longer "relative to the exercise" is the imposition of restrictions on the licensee beyond the termination of the protective right, for, in the nature of things, he will then no longer be exercising that right.[78]

¶ 351   Complications are presented by the question whether the licensee's obligations to *exchange know-how* and to *grant cross-licenses under his own inventions* (especially under improvement patents) are still "restrictions relative to the exercise" of the licensed rights; and the same applies to *obligations not to contest* those rights.[79] As for these obligations, the following applies:

In the view of the Commission,[80] Article 85 (1) of the Treaty is *not* violated when a licensee need grant only *simple* licenses on patents for new uses and/or improvements and when there is a reciprocal obligation on the licensor (Section I D of the Official Notice; see above ¶ 58). Consequently, there is, under these presuppositions, no

---

[76] CMR ¶ 2698.
[77] The Commission shares this view, Guide Lines CMR ¶ 2819; accord: Deringer, *ibid.*
[78] Also the view of the Commission, *ibid.*

[79] See Deringer, *ibid.* Know-how imparting and improvement licensing obligations imposed on patent licensees have been declared to be *dehors* Article 85 (1) by the Commission, but only if there is nonexclusiveness and reciprocity.
[80] See footnote 74 above.

violation of Article 85 (1) of the Treaty, so that subparagraph (ii)(b), which includes only prohibited restrictions of the licensee, is no longer applicable (see above ¶ 346).

In our opinion, this interpretation is too narrow (see above ¶ 58). The obligation of the licensee to grant simple licenses under his new-use and/or improvement patents does not violate Article 85 (1) of the Treaty, even if the licensor is not under a "reciprocal" obligation; consequently, here too, subparagraph (ii)(b) finds no application.

The situation is different where the licensee must grant *exclusive licenses* under his patents on new use and/or improvement patents, or where he must also license under patents on parallel inventions. In such cases, it depends on whether the licensee is restricted "relative to the exercise" of the licensed right. Thus, the decisive question is whether the obligation relates inherently to the licensed right or not. If the licensee is obligated to exchange know-how and to grant cross-licenses for the experience gained and inventions made in the course of exploitation of the licensed right, he is restrained "relative to the exercise" of that right. The legal situation differs, in our view, when he must also communicate other know-how or license further protective rights. Then he is no longer restricted only "relative to the exercise" of the *licensed* right, so that subparagraph (ii)(b) of Article 4 does not apply, i.e., there is no exception from the notification requirement.

The same is true, in our opinion, of obligations of the licensee not to contest. The licensee may be said to be restricted "relative to the exercise" of the protective right if he must not contest the validity of that specific right. This requirement is certainly not met, however, if he is obligated not to contest other protective rights of the licensor not contained in the license. On the other hand, it is difficult to deny that the obligation not to contest is not connected with the exercise of the licensed protective rights; at least there is an indirect relation to the extent that a successful attack upon the validity of the protective right would make further exercise impossible. In doubtful cases, notification would be indicated, just to be on the safe side.

¶ 352   If the agreement contains restrictions that come within Article 85 (1) of the Treaty and are not imposed "relative to the exercise" of the licensed right, the alleviation of (ii)(b) will not apply. The agreement then requires *notification in its entirety,* as follows cogently from the "sole" preceding this provision;[81] thus, not only the particular clauses concerned are to be notified.

---

[81] Accord: Deringer, *ibid.*

The same is true if the agreement contains also restrictions upon the *licensor* which come within Article 85 (1). Such restraints are not covered by (ii)(b), as shown conclusively by its text.

Article 4(2)(iii)(a)

¶ 353   The number of parties to the agreement, etc., is immaterial here, as is also their location. The agreement, etc., must, however, be limited to the *development or uniform application of standards and models.*[82] If it goes beyond this, e.g., by stipulations for specialization, it requires notification. The provision, however, is applicable only if the parties are under an obligation to employ the agreed-upon standards and types or do so on the basis of concerted behavior. Otherwise, there is no restraint on competition, so that the prohibition of Article 85 (1) does not apply.

Article 4(2)(iii)(b)

¶ 354   This provision is concerned only with those agreements that are limited to joint research; this follows from its wording. If, in addition, an agreement restricts the participants in their production and/or distribution, the exception will not apply, unless such restrictions are still inherently related to the understanding concerning joint research. If such a relation exists, these restrictions also are covered by the exception. Whether this still holds true when other restrictions are only prerequisites for the decision to participate in the joint research,[83] we deem questionable. In our opinion, the question of "indispensability" is, rather, to be answered under Article 85 (3) of the Treaty.

According to the language, the exception is limited to joint "technical" research. Agreements concerning other joint research, e.g., market research or—perhaps in the cigarette industry—medical research, are therefore not covered.

With good reason the question was raised whether, in light of the wording of the provision, the joint research had to be limited to "improvements" in products already in existence. This question should be answered in the negative, for, in our opinion, the "technical

---

[82] On this subject, compare the literature and the practice of the BKartA concerning Section 5, paragraph 1, of the GWB.

[83] See Deringer/Tessin, DB 1964, p. 872.

improvements" of (iii)(b) are inherently equivalent to the "promotion of technical progress" mentioned in Article 85 (3) of the Treaty. Thus, joint research that is aimed at the development of new products, e.g., synthetic fibers, also is covered by the exception of (iii)(b); there is no substantial ground for treating such joint research less favorably.

The essential requirement is that the *results* of the joint research must be *accessible to all parties* and may be exploited by all of them. In our opinion, however, this does not mean that all parties must also be joint owners of protective rights which may result from the research. Rather, such rights may belong to one of them or to a third party, as long as the others receive at least licenses thereunder.

¶ 355   Subparagraph (iii)(b) does not say that utilization must be permitted free of compensation. The provision will therefore still apply where certain parties may utilize the results of the research only *for compensation,* provided only that the latter must not be prohibitive. The amount of compensation may vary, e.g., according to the measure of contribution or utilization.[84]

¶ 356   *"Exploit,"* in our view, is to be interpreted to mean that the parties themselves may utilize the results of the research. It is not necessary, however, that they exploit those results also by granting licenses to third parties; on the contrary, they may be forbidden to do so, since the grant of the right to use need not be unrestricted. As a result, the participants may place restrictions on themselves in the utilization of the results, e.g., each participant may make use of the research results only in his native country or only in specified technical fields, so long as such restrictions are not prohibitive.

¶ 357   Like all of these exceptions, (iii)(b), too, applies only if there is a competitive restraint on the parties, e.g., if they are obligated to refrain from research outside of the joint undertaking, or if they are restricted concerning the communication of research results to third parties.[85]

IV.   Relationship of the Exceptions Inter Se

¶ 358   *None of the exceptions* of Article 4 (2) *has precedence* over the others. It therefore is possible that certain agreements, etc.,

---

[84] Compare Honig / Brown / Gleiss / Hirsch, p. 55. Accord: Deringer/Tessin, DB 1964, p. 872.

[85] Compare in detail, Deringer/Tessin, DB 1964, p. 870.

may come within several of these provisions. For example, a license agreement may be covered by the specific exception for such agreements (subparagraph (ii)(b)) and at the same time by the exception for single-nation agreements not involving imports or exports (subparagraph (i)). A vertical price agreement may come within that latter provision and simultaneously within the exception made particularly for agreements fixing resale prices or terms (subparagraph (ii)(a)). It is possible, further, that a license agreement is not covered by the specific exception for agreements of that type (subparagraph (ii)(b)), e.g., because it contains collateral restrictions on the licensee to which Article 85 (1) of the Treaty applies, but is covered by the exception for single-nation agreements (subparagraph (i)). Of course, this latter possibility does not exist for international license agreements, where the parties are not from a single member state.

In fine, however, it is necessary only that the agreement, etc., in question fulfill the prerequisites of one of the exceptions. If so, it does not require notification, even though it may appear to belong to a group covered by another exception.

V. Legal Remedy

¶ 359   Against the granting as well as against the denial of an exemption by the Commission, there exists recourse by action in the Court at Luxembourg. For details see ¶ 369 ff., under Article 5 of Regulation 17, infra.

VI. Future Development

¶ 360   On May 29, 1970, the Commission[85a] submitted to the Council a draft regulation exempting certain agreements on research, development and specialization from the necessity of being notified under Article 4 (1) of Regulation 17. Simultaneously, the Commission submitted to the Council another draft empowering the Commission to issue group exemptions in the field of cooperation (standards and types, research and development, specialization, joint purchase and sale). It will probably take some time for these draft regulations to be passed by the Council.[85b]

[85a] OffJour No. C 92 (July 20, 1970), p. 14. Cf. ¶ 17, supra.

[85b] On the recent improvements of cooperation facilities in the EEC cartel law, see Benisch, DB 1970, p. 1363.

Article 5

NOTIFICATION OF EXISTING AGREEMENTS, DECISIONS AND PRACTICES

(1) The Commission must be notified before November 1, 1962, of any agreements, decisions and concerted practices referred to in Article 85, paragraph 1, of the Treaty which are already in existence at the date of entry into force of the present Regulation and in respect of which those concerned wish to invoke Article 85, paragraph 3, of the Treaty. However, as an exception to the preceding provision, notification of agreements, decisions and concerted practices in which only two enterprises participate must be given before February 1, 1963.

(2) Paragraph 1 is not applicable where the said agreements, decisions and concerted practices fall within the categories referred to in paragraph 2 of Article 4; the Commission may be notified of these.

¶ 361   This provision concerns only agreements, etc., existing since before the effective date of Regulation 17, i.e., before March 13, 1962 ("old cartels"). The validity of these old cartels under national law is not a prerequisite, since national and Common Market cartel law are applied side by side and independently.

¶ 362   Article 5 was amended by Regulation 59 of July 3, 1962;[86] the amendment has been in effect since July 11, 1962. The time period provided in the first sentence of paragraph (1) originally was to expire on July 31, 1962; the second sentence of paragraph (1) was added by Regulation 59.

¶ 363   Article 5 (1) offers for old cartels the *possibility of notification* to the Commission. Here, too, as in the case of Article 4 (1), no genuine legal duty is involved.[87] Notification cannot be compelled. It is merely a prerequisite to an exemption under Article 85 (3) of the Treaty, and he who desires an exemption must give notification. In the absence of notification, the Commission cannot grant an exemption for agreements that do not fall under Article 5 (2), not even on the application of a third party or upon referral from a national court.

---

[86] OffJour, No. 58/62 of July 10, 1962.   1962, p. 294; Gleiss/Hirsch, AWD 1962,
[87] This is the generally accepted view   p. 162; Deringer, GRUR AIT 1962,
among writers: see, e.g., Weyer, DB   p. 287.

¶ 364   Notification had to be effected within the prescribed *time period*, i.e., on or before October 31, 1962,[88] and in the case of agreements, etc., between but two parties, on or before January 31, 1963. In a decision of June 30, 1970,[88a] the European Court held that in applying Article 5 an exclusive distributorship contract between two enterprises has to be considered as an agreement in which only two enterprises participate, even if the contract belongs to a system of parallel contracts. The time of receipt by the Commission was determinative (Article 3 of Regulation 27). If notification was by registered letter, the postmark of the place of mailing was decisive (*ibid.*). Thus, notifications by registered letter mailed on October 31, 1962, or on January 31, 1963, respectively, were timely even though they reached the Commission only later. The notification constitutes at the same time an application that the Commission grant an exemption under Article 85 (3) of the Treaty, i.e., that it exempt the notified agreement, etc., from the prohibition of that provision.[89]

¶ 365   If the notification reached the Commission in time, the agreement notified became therewith *provisionally valid,* according to conclusion No. 2 of the decision in the *Bosch* case[90] (see ¶ 307, supra). Until the Commission's decision on the application for exemption under Article 85 (3), the parties may continue to perform the agreement; fines may not be imposed upon them on that account (Article 15 (5)(a) of Regulation 17). Of course, their acts must be covered by the notification (*ibid.*). These activities may not be continued if and when the Commission has informed the parties, on the basis of a preliminary examination of the matter, that the notified agreement, etc., violates Article 85 (1) and cannot be exempted under Article 85 (3). In case of continued activities after such a communication, the Commission may impose fines (Article 15 (6) of Regulation 17).

If the Commission issues a declaration pursuant to Article 85 (3) of the Treaty, i.e., if it exempts the notified agreement from the prohibition of Article 85 (1), the agreement becomes finally valid, and this retroactively to March 13, 1962, back beyond the time of notification. Here, in the case of old cartels requiring notification, the

---

[88] Not, as so often stated erroneously, within the period until November 1, 1962.

[88a] Case No. 1/70, "Parfums Marcel Rochas," OffJour No. C 97 (July 29, 1970) p. 11.

[89] The application for exemption is to be made on the official form for the notification, as appears from Guide Lines, CMR ¶ 2814 ff.

[90] *Ubi supra,* footnote 41 at ¶ 16. The European Court held in its "Parfums Marcel Rochas" decision that due notification of a model contract before March 13, 1962, suffices for the provisional validity of a corresponding individual contract concluded after that date which is not notified.

limitation of retroactive effect to the date of notification, provided in Article 6 (1) of Regulation 17, does not apply (Article 6 (2)). The Commission's declaration is binding upon the national authorities and courts.

¶ 366   If the Commission *denies exemption,* the notified agreement thereupon becomes *null and void* with retroactive effect to March 13, 1962.[91] The parties may not, however, be fined for having performed the agreement before the Commission's decision (Article 15 (5)(a) of Regulation 17); fines may be imposed only for activities thereafter *(ibid.).*

¶ 367   Retroactive invalidity from March 13, 1962, occurred also if *notification* of an agreement, etc., was not given to the Commission, or *was not given to it in time.*[92] It is immaterial in this connection whether the conditions for exemption under Article 85 (3) were or were not fulfilled.[93] If the parties were still performing the non-notified agreement after March 12, 1962, the Commission may impose fines upon them on that account (Article 15 (2).(a) of Regulation 17), and it is of no consequence whether or not an exemption might or might not have been granted upon proper notification.[94]

¶ 368   Agreements of which timely notification was not given may still be notified *after the expiration of the time periods* specified in Article 5 (1) of Regulation 17,[95] and the Commission may still grant an exemption for them; Article 85 (3) of the Treaty does not make exemption dependent upon notification within a fixed time. In such a case, however, the Commission's declaration pursuant to Article 85 (3) will have no retroactive effect to March 13, 1962, but at most to the date of notification;[96] these agreements of which there is late notification are thus treated like new cartels requiring notification.[97] Accordingly, they remain void at least to the date of notification, even if the Commission grants the exemption after the late notification.[98]

---

[91] Unless the Commission makes use of Article 7 (1) of Regulation 17: see conclusion No. 2 of the *Bosch* decision, *ubi supra.*

[92] See conclusion No. 3 of the *Bosch* decision, *ubi supra.*

[93] Gleiss/Hirsch, AWD 1962, p. 125; Schumacher, WuW 1962, p. 479.

[94] Article 15 (2)(a) in connection with 15 (5)(a). Accord: Weyer, *ibid.;* Obernolte, WRP 1962, p. 104; Deringer, *ibid.*

[95] This appears also from Guide Lines, CMR ¶ 2824.

[96] Article 6 (1) of Regulation 17; also the view of the Commission, Guide Lines, *ibid.*

[97] Gleiss/Hirsch, AWD 1962, p. 127; also Deringer, GRUR AIT 1962, p. 289. Not only is this true as a practical matter, but it also accords with the German legal notion that a transaction once void cannot become valid but must be "confirmed," i.e., established anew, within the meaning of Section 141 of the BGB; such a novation really makes it a "new cartel."

[98] Also the Commission's view, Guide Lines, *ibid.*

The administrative permissibility of notification after expiration
of the time periods must not lead to overlooking the problems arising
under civil law. Under German civil law, a void legal transaction
cannot be validated, although this is a principle to which exceptions
are possible[99] (see above, ¶ 309). Consequently, an agreement tendered
for notification after the time period has run out must be "confirmed" within the meaning of Section 141 BGB, i.e., must be executed anew. This "confirmed" agreement is then a "new cartel,"
since it has been executed (again) after March 12, 1962, (compare
¶ 331); it is thus correctly treated as such (compare the previous
paragraph). The requisite confirmation may be seen in the contracting parties' assent to the late notification.

¶ 369   *If the Commission denies an exemption* pursuant to Article 85
         (3), the applicants (notifying parties) may institute an *action*
against this decision *in the Court at Luxembourg* (Article 173 of the
Treaty). Furthermore, this right is given not only to the parties who
gave the notification and thereby applied for the exemption; rather,
as appears from Article 173, any person to whom the decision is of
"direct and individual concern" is entitled to bring the action, and that
includes all other parties. It is also possible that one party to an
agreement gives the notification and the other institutes the action
against the denial of the exemption.

¶ 370   *If the Commission grants an exemption*, a proper party to bring
         action is again anyone who is affected by the decision "di-
rectly and individually." Depending on the circumstances, such persons may be, e.g., distributors who, because of an exclusive franchise
given to another, may no longer be supplied, customers of a cartel, etc.

¶ 371   The *time limitation for commencement of the action* is two
         months (Article 173 of the Treaty). Depending on the case,
it begins to run with the publication of the Commission's decision, its
service upon the plaintiff, or, in the absence of both, the time when
the plaintiff obtains knowledge of the decision. Since the decisions
of the Commission are to be published (Article 21 (1) of Regulation
17), it will, in case of doubt, be the time of such publication.[1]

¶ 372   Whether the voidness of an agreement, etc., may give rise
         to *claims for damages* depends upon the applicable national
law.[1a] Under German law it turns upon whether Article 85 (1) is a

---

[99] See Enneccerus/Nipperdey, Lehrbuch des Bürgerlichen Rechtes, 15th
Edition 1960, Vol. I, p. 1211 ff.
[1] Accord: Deringer, *id.*, p. 290.

[1a] Cf. the Commission's study "Schadensersatzansprüche bei einer Verletzung
von Art. 85 und 86 EWGV," Series:
Competition, Vol. 1, 1966.

protective law within the meaning of Section 823, paragraph 2, of
the BGB. In our view, this is not the case, because Article 85 (1) is
not aimed at the protection of individuals or limited groups. It has
already been so held by the BGH with regard to Article 60 of the Coal
and Steel Treaty.[2]

¶ 373   *Article 5 (2)* exempts certain agreements, etc., from the no-
         tification requirement and thereby from the time limitations
of Article 5 (1). For details, see the discussion under Article 4 (2),
supra. As to the time limitation provided in Article 7 (2) for such
old cartels not requiring notification, see the discussion under that
provision, infra.

Article 6

DECLARATIONS PURSUANT TO ARTICLE 85 (3)

(1) When the Commission decides to issue a declaration
under Article 85, paragraph 3, it shall indicate the date from
which the decision shall take effect. This date shall not be prior
to the date of notification.

(2) The second sentence of paragraph 1 shall not be applicable to the agreements, decisions and concerted practices referred to in Article 4, paragraph 2, and Article 5, paragraph 2,
nor to those which are referred to in Article 5, paragraph 1, and
of which the Commission has been notified within the time-limit
fixed therein.

¶ 374   This provision governs the point of time as of which an ex-
         emption granted by the Commission takes effect. The *prin-*
ciple is contained in the second sentence of paragraph 1 : An *exemption*
does not cover the time before notification, i.e., the time before the date
on which the notification reaches the Commission, or the date of the
postmark in the case of registered letters (Article 3 of Regulation 27).

¶ 375   The *Commission* is *not compelled* by Article 6 (1) to make the
         exemption effective from the date of notification. It *may* fix a
later point of time. However, if the Commission fixes a later time for
effectiveness of the exemption, it will thereby depart from the legislative intent to create continuity, and it consequently ought to have
special and cogent reasons for such a course.

[2] See the decision of the BGH of   and see in general Article 85, ¶ 79, and
April 14, 1959, BB 1959, pp. 576, 578;   Article 86, ¶ 226, supra.

¶ 376   The principle of Article 6 (1), second sentence, applies to all
          cases under Article 4 (1) of Regulation 17, i.e., to all *new
cartels requiring notification*. It further applies to those *old cartels requiring notification* for which notification was not given within the
time limitations of Article 5 (1).[3] All these cartels thus are void at
least until the date of notification, and possibly even for a longer period, pursuant to Article 85 (2) of the Treaty, but in the case of old
cartels not notified in time only on and after March 13, 1962.[4]
Their activities before the time fixed by the Commission for the
effectiveness of the exemption may be punished by fines (Article
15 (2) (a) of Regulation 17). For new cartels requiring notification,
this applies naturally only from the date of their conclusion.

¶ 377   Article 6 (2) makes an important *exception* to the general
          rule of Article 6 (1), second sentence: The Commission may
make the exemption effective *even for the time before notification* in the
cases of new cartels not requiring notification, old cartels not requiring notification, and old cartels requiring and having received timely
notification.

          This may mean, for new cartels, validity from the time of origin,
and, for old cartels, validity on and after March 13, 1962. It may
and normally ought to mean continuous validity of all of these agreements, since old cartels were valid until March 12, 1962, in any case.

¶ 378   It should be observed here, too, that the *Commission* is *not
          compelled* by Article 6 (2) to grant the exemption for the pe-
riod before notification. As for exemption effective on a date later
than notification, see above ¶ 375.

Article 7

SPECIAL PROVISIONS FOR EXISTING AGREEMENTS, DECISIONS AND PRACTICES

          (1) Where agreements, decisions and concerted practices al-
ready in existence at the date of the entry into force of the present
Regulation and of which the Commission has been notified within
the time limitations provided by Article 5, paragraph 1, do not
meet the requirements of Article 85, paragraph 3, of the Treaty,
and where the enterprises and associations of enterprises con-

---

[3] See Gleiss/Hirsch, AWD 1962, p. 127; Deringer, GRUR AIT 1962, p. 289.

[4] This results from conclusion No. 1 of the *Bosch* decision, *ubi supra*, foot-note 41 at ¶ 16.

¶ 376

cerned put an end to them or modify them so that they no longer fall under the prohibition laid down in Article 85, paragraph 3, the prohibition laid down in Article 85, paragraph 1, shall be applicable only for a period fixed by the Commission. A decision by the Commission pursuant to the foregoing sentence cannot be invoked against enterprises or associations of enterprises which have not given their express assent to the notification.

(2) Paragraph 1 shall be applicable to agreements, decisions and concerted practices which are already in existence at the date of the entry into force of the present Regulation and which fall within the categories referred to in Article 4, paragraph 2, provided that notification shall have taken place before January 1, 1964.

The date in paragraph 2 of this provision was originally January 1, 1964. However, the time period was extended for three years by Regulation 118/63 of the Council on November 5, 1963; the reason was the overwhelming number of notifications to the Commission, especially on January 31, 1963. It was intended that such a flood of notifications should not be increased even more.

¶ 381   This provision constitutes a *transitional regulation for old cartels*, i.e., for agreements, etc., already in existence on March 13, 1962, the effective date of Regulation 17. New cartels are not affected by this article. Its first paragraph provides, in rather a cumbersome manner, as follows:

¶ 382   The Commission may annul the prohibition of Article 85 (1) of the Treaty retroactively[5] for those old cartels of which notification was given within the periods specified in Article 5 (1) of Regulation 17, but which do not fulfill the requirements for an exemption. The prerequisite for application of Article 7 (1) is that the parties either do not continue acting under the agreement, etc., in question or alter it so that it no longer falls under the prohibition of Article 85 (1) of the Treaty or so that it at least meets the conditions for an exemption. The parties need not have made these changes before the notification. It suffices if they do so later, e.g., when the Commission informs them that, in the light of a preliminary examination, the conditions for an exemption do not exist.

The Commission may render a decision on its own instigation; however, as a rule it will decide only upon application which, in our opinion, must be made in the notification under Article 5 of Regulation 17. By this notification, the applicants request a declaration of the non-applicability of Article 85 (1) of the Treaty to their agreement, at least for a certain time period.

---

[5] ". . . shall be applicable only for a period fixed by the Commission. . . ."

¶ 383   The first sentence of Article 7 (1) thus enables the Commission to legalize even non-exemptible old cartels on the basis of "active reform."[6] This action is a bonus, intended to encourage adaptation to the law. This method corresponds to the one used concerning notification : the party not notifying agreements that require it receives no exemption.

In the literature on the subject,[7] doubts have been expressed whether this power of the Commission is covered by the EEC Treaty. In any event, it answers a practical need because, before the effective date of Regulation 17, there could be no certainty whether an agreement fulfilled the prerequisites for an exemption pursuant to Article 85 (3) of the Treaty.

By a decision of the Commission according to Article 7 (1), an agreement becomes fully valid for the period for which the Commission declares the prohibition of Article 85 (1) inapplicable and, thereby, unaffected by Article 85 (2), which would render it void.

¶ 384   The second sentence of Article 7 (1) limits the *consequences* resulting for *private interests* from retroactive legalization of a non-exemptible agreement. Such legalization might otherwise be detrimental to those parties who had ceased to act under the agreement even before the Commission's decision. It might result in claims for damages against them by the other parties for breach of contract, claims for specific performance for the past, claims for contractual penalties, and the like. Such claims are excluded by the second sentence of Article 7 (1), unless the enterprises against which they are made have expressly consented to the notification and thereby to the application for exemption.[8] Those parties, therefore, who have renounced an agreement, etc., can, by failing to give their assent to the notification, protect themselves against damage claims of the other parties in the event of subsequent legalization by the Commission. Conversely, an express assent to the notification implies under the law a conclusive election to abide by the agreement, with the result of liability for nonperformance, etc. In the limitation of the consequences of legalization, a differentiation is made between retroactive legalization and exemption under Article 85 (3) of the Treaty from which automatic consequences for the participants follow.

---

[6] Accord: Deringer, WuW 1962, p. 89; Schlieder, BB 1962, p. 307; Weyer, DB 1962, p. 295; Obernolte, WRP 1962, p. 107.

[7] See Deringer, *ibid.*

[8] Accord: Schlieder, *ibid.;* Weyer, *ibid.;* Obernolte, *ibid.;* Deringer/Tessin, NJW 1962, p. 991; Deringer, GRUR AIT 1962, p. 289.

¶ 383

¶ 385   The view has been expressed that subsequent legalization is effective also as against third parties,[9] so that, as far as they are concerned, the legalized agreement is to be deemed valid except for any period of invalidity fixed by the Commission. Third persons, e.g., customers or outsiders, thus could not claim damages from the parties on the theory that the agreement was a prohibited cartel. There is some doubt whether this view is really supported by Article 7 (1), second sentence. The wording of this provision does not fit the cases in question unless third parties had the opportunity of assenting to the notification. That opportunity, however, is open only to the parties to the agreement, etc. (see Article 1 of Regulation 27); and assent to the notification by third parties, or lack thereof, is without legal significance. Moreover, no cogent reason can be adduced from other language in this provision for precluding third parties' claims. In Article 7 (1), sentence 2, "enterprises and associations of enterprises" are mentioned, meaning—throughout Regulation 17—the participants in an agreement, whereas third parties are denominated "natural and legal persons and associations of persons" (see, e.g., Articles 3 (2) (b) and 19 (2) of Regulation 17).[10]

If the Commission has already imposed penalties or fines on the parties to an agreement and later declares Article 85 (1) of the Treaty inapplicable to the period in question, it must suspend the penalties or fines.

¶ 386   Article 7 (2) offers the possibility of subsequent legalization also for *old cartels not requiring notification,*[11] *for which notification is in fact given on or before December 31, 1963.* Delay beyond that time will result in losing the benefit of Article 7(1).

Article 8

PERIOD OF VALIDITY AND POSSIBILITY OF REVOCATION OF DECLARATIONS PURSUANT TO ARTICLE 85 (3)

(1) A decision to issue a declaration under Article 85, paragraph 3, of the Treaty shall be valid for a specified period and may have certain conditions and stipulations attached.

(2) The decision may be renewed on request provided that the conditions laid down in Article 85, paragraph 3, of the Treaty continue to be fulfilled.

---

[9] Weyer, *ibid.;* Deringer, *ibid.*
[10] Deringer apparently misses this, Article 7, Regulation 17, marg. n. 6.
[11] Article 5 (2) in connection with Article 4 (2) of Regulation 17.

(3) The Commission may revoke or alter its decision or prohibit those concerned from taking certain courses of action:

(a) where the *de facto* situation has changed with respect
to a factor essential in the granting of the decision;

(b) where those concerned infringe a stipulation attached to the decision;

(c) where the decision is based on false information or
has been obtained fraudulently; or

(d) where those concerned abuse the exemption from
the provisions of Article 85, paragraph 1, of the Treaty
granted to them by the decision.

In the cases covered by subparagraphs (b), (c) and (d),
the decision can also be revoked with retroactive effect.

¶ 387   This provision is concerned with the period of validity of an
             exemption under Article 85 (3).

¶ 388   Article 8 (1) requires that an exemption must in every case
             be limited in time. The *length of that period* is within the dis-
cretion of the Commission. In the Transocean Marine Paint case
(¶ 119, supra), the Commission granted an exemption for six and a
half years, while the contract as concluded was to be renewed after
twenty years.

¶ 389   The Commission may attach *conditions and obligatory terms*
             (the English term "stipulations" used in the translation seems
too ambiguous) to the exemption. Each of these concepts has its
technical legal meaning: a condition postpones the effectiveness of
an exemption, but does not force the parties to do anything; if they
do not meet the condition, the exemption does not become effective.
In contrast, the obligatory term must be fulfilled by the participants
and under it the exemption comes into effect immediately. The participants may avoid the consequences of the obligatory term by aban-
doning their plan. By the nature of the condition, it is difficult to
tell when it is fulfilled and, thus, whether the exemption comes into
effect. This uncertainty does not exist under the obligatory term.
If the parties wilfully or negligently violate such an obligation, the
Commission may impose fines on them (Article 15 (2) (b) of Regulation 17). Violation of a condition, on the other hand, does not subject them to a fine, and a fine would be quite unnecessary in that case.
For, if the parties fail to comply with a condition precedent to the
exemption, the latter, on general principles, will simply not become
effective. If a condition subsequent materializes, the exemption loses
its validity. However, it naturally remains a violation of Article
85 (1) when the participants perform their agreement before the

condition precedent has been fulfilled or after the condition subsequent has materialized, since, then, there is no exemption. The contents of the conditions and terms are within the discretion of the Commission. The right to an exemption may not, however, be restricted thereby. Examples of an obligatory term (stipulation) would be the duty to strike certain terms of delivery, or to make annual reports to the Commission on the performance of the agreement (cf. the conditions imposed on the Transocean Marine Paint Association, ¶ 119, and on ACEC/Berliet, ¶ 120).

¶ 390   After the expiration of the period fixed pursuant to Article 8 (1), the parties may reapply for exemption (paragraph (2)). The Commission is bound to grant a renewal if the conditions specified in Article 85 (3) of the Treaty still exist. The parties must make a showing that this is the case.[12]

¶ 391   In certain cases enumerated in the third paragraph of Article 8, the Commission may revoke or alter the declaration of exemption—in cases (b), (c) and (d) even with retroactive effect. It may also prohibit the parties from doing certain things.

¶ 392   A particular problem is raised by subparagraph (d), since "abuse" of the exemption is not further defined (as is also true of Section 12 (1), No. 1, of the GWB). Here, the practice of the Commission and judicial pronouncements of the European Court will have to develop the necessary standards. An "abuse" will have to be determined not from subjective, but from objective circumstances (see above ¶ 221).

¶ 393   *Retroactive revocation* is designed to enable the Commission to deprive an exemption of its effect from the time as of which it was not or was no longer justified on account of the conduct of the parties, e.g., in the case of fraudulent procurement, from the outset.[13] Retroactive revocation of an exemption has important legal consequences as a matter of private law, since it results in retroactive voidness. It, therefore, is justified only where the exemption "is based on false information or has been obtained fraudulently" (subparagraph (c));[14] in the other cases it would not comport with the principle of security of legal transactions, in the absence of particularly grave circumstances.

---

[12] Accord: Schlieder, *ibid.*, who emphasizes that this does not impose a burden of proving negatives.
[13] Accord: Obernolte, WRP 1962, p. 106.

[14] Obernolte, *ibid.*, regards retroactive revocation as intrinsically justified also in other cases; as here, however, Deringer, WuW 1962, p. 87.

The enumeration in paragraph (3) is exhaustive; the Commission may not base its revocation or denial on other grounds. But the enumerated grounds are so comprehensive and vague that the Commission has ample discretion.

If an exempted agreement is changed, it does not automatically mean the end of the exemption. The termination of an exemption is not possible, according to Article 8 of Regulation 17, without a decision from the Commission (disregarding the running of the time period and materialization of a condition subsequent). According to our interpretation, for *changes in an agreement,* the following holds true:

If the change brings an easing of the restraint of competition in the agreement, the participants need not do anything. A revocation of the exemption for the original agreement would be unwarranted; the prerequisites for a revocation are naturally not met, since the easing of the restraint is in accord with the legislative intent of Article 85, paragraph (1), and paragraph (3) as well. In such a case, the change is not "essential." Changes in an agreement that lead to less restraint of competition are always permissible and covered by the exemption for the original agreement (for comparison, see Section 9, paragraph 2 GWB).

However, if the change leads to a new restraint of competition or to a strengthening of the old one, it is not covered by the exemption for the original agreement. If the new restraint of competition in the agreement contains an *independent* violation of Article 85 (1), according to the general rules a separate exemption must be applied for, or the change will be legally invalid. In its examination, the Commission must, of course, consider and respect the agreement as a whole. Exemption of the altered agreement is, thus, possible only when the agreement in its entirety still fulfills the prerequisites of Article 85 (3) of the Treaty. If this is no longer the case, an exemption may not be granted for the alteration; however, this does not affect the exemption for the original agreement. Revocation of the exemption in such a case would be unjustified.

It may be different in those cases in which new restraints of competition are concluded which, regarded independently, present no violation of Article 85 (1) of the Treaty, i.e., are manifestly valid. Such restraints of competition, however, together with the originally concluded restraints, may constitute an alteration of the actual circumstances in an "essential factor" and consequently—unless the parties abandon the changed agreement—entitle the Commission to revoke the exemption granted for the original agreement (subparagraph (3) (a)). Revocation with retroactive effect (last sentence of subparagraph (3) (b)) is, as a rule, not possible even in such cases.

¶ 393

Article 9

JURISDICTION

(1) Subject to review of its decision by the Court of Justice, the Commission shall have sole competence to declare Article 85, paragraph 1, inapplicable pursuant to Article 85, paragraph 3, of the Treaty.

(2) The Commission shall have competence to apply Article 85, paragraph 1, and Article 86 of the Treaty, even if the time-limits for notification laid down in Article 5, paragraph 1, and Article 7, paragraph 2, have not expired.

(3) As long as the Commission has not initiated any procedure pursuant to Article 2, 3 or 6, the authorities of the Member States shall remain competent to apply Article 85, paragraph 1, and Article 86 in accordance with Article 88 of the Treaty, even if the time-limits for notification laid down in Article 5, paragraph 1, and Article 7 have not expired.

¶ 401   Under paragraph (1), the Commission has *exclusive jurisdiction of exemption grants,* subject only to review by the Court in Luxembourg (Article 173 of the Treaty); consequently, national authorities and, of course, national courts may not grant exemptions. It is clear, although not stated in paragraph (1), that a declaration under Article 7 (1) of Regulation 17 (subsequent legalization) also may be made only by the Commission. Of course, national authorities have jurisdiction to apply national cartel law (cf. Introduction, B, IV, and ¶ 81, supra, on the *Tar-Colors* case).

¶ 402   Paragraph (2) had significance only for the *transitional period until December 31, 1963.* It made clear that the Commission could prosecute violations of the prohibitions of Articles 85 (1) and 86 of the Treaty even before that time had expired.

¶ 403   Of greater importance is the *distribution of jurisdiction* made in paragraph (3) *between the Commission and the national cartel authorities:*

¶ 404   The national authorities may apply only the prohibitions of Articles 85 (1) and 86, but not Article 85 (3) of the Treaty. They have no jurisdiction over exemptions, as follows from paragraph (1).

¶ 405   However, the fact that the national authorities may not grant exemptions does not prevent them from declaring certain agreements, etc., to be prohibited by Article 85 (1) or 86. This was confirmed by the *Bosch* decision.[15]

¶ 406   This decision contains important guides for the scope of jurisdiction of the national authorities. As provided in Article 9 (3) of Regulation 17, they may apply Articles 85 (1) and 86 of the Treaty only "in accordance with Article 88" thereof. This means that this preservation of their jurisdiction is subject to the limitations placed thereon before March 13, 1962, by Article 88 of the Treaty, and their acts under Article 9 (3) must remain within those limits.

¶ 407   Under Article 88 of the Treaty, the national authorities were by no means generally authorized to apply Article 85 (1), as seen from the reasons given in support of conclusion No. 1 of the *Bosch* decision. Rather, they were authorized to do so only if a cartel[16] was submitted to them for approval pursuant to the applicable national cartel law.

Consequently, the national authorities may apply Articles 85 (1) and 86 only in the course of a proceeding which is pending before them under national cartel law independently from EEC law. They may not prosecute violations of those prohibitions *ex officio* or on their own motion.[17]

Since Article 86 will hardly ever be applicable in an approval proceeding instituted independently under national law, the jurisdiction of the national authorities to apply that article is largely theoretical.

¶ 408   Regulation 17 in substance leaves no room for the national authorities to apply EEC cartel law. In greater detail, the situation is as follows:

¶ 409   *Old cartels requiring and having received timely notification:* The notification of these agreements, etc., constitutes at the same time an application for exemption.[18] Therefore, at the latest with confirmation of receipt of the notification, the Commission has initiated a proceeding pursuant to Article 6 of Regulation 17. There-

---

[15] *Ubi supra,* footnote 41 at ¶ 16; for details, see Gleiss/Hirsch, BB 1962, p. 623.

[16] I.e., an agreement, decision or concerted practice.

[17] Accord: Weyer, DB 1962, p. 326.

[18] It is true that item IV of Form A/B calls for a statement from the parties of reasons why the agreement, etc., is thought not to fall under Article 85 (1). This, however, is not in issue here, where we are interested only in agreements, etc., which violate the cited article.

after, the national authorities no longer have any jurisdiction. They, therefore, may not apply Article 85 (1) to old cartels requiring and having received timely notification.

¶ 410   *Old cartels requiring notification, but not notified in time:* Lapse of the period for notification resulted in voidness of these old cartels on and after March 13, 1962.[19] This voidness occurred by operation of law (Article 85 (2) of the Treaty), without the need of any order of the Commission or of the national authorities. The authority given to the latter to apply Article 85 (1) to these old cartels thus is an empty gesture. They can only enunciate what the legal situation is. Their "application" of Article 85 (1) plays no more than a merely declaratory role.

Nor may the national authorities take any steps against parties to a void old cartel who act under it and thereby violate Article 85 (1). This is again the effect of Article 88 of the Treaty. It gives no independent prosecuting powers to the national authorities.[20] Thus, they cannot impose fines upon the parties under Article 15 of Regulation 17.[21] Nor can they exercise any other powers under Regulation 17, even if the Commission has not yet initiated any proceeding.[22] The very language of Article 9 (3), like that of Article 15 (fines), excludes jurisdiction on their part; it reserves to the national authorities only such competence as they had under Article 88 of the Treaty, which confers no genuine powers on them.

Under Article 88, the national authorities are to apply Article 85 "in accordance with the law of their countries." This reference to national cartel law offers the possibility, e.g., for the Bundeskartellamt to prosecute violations of Article 85 (1) of the Treaty conformably to the GWB.[23] This authority is, however, without practical value, for the following reasons:

A proceeding for the imposition of a fine on account of an infraction of Article 85 (1) is possible under Section 38 (1), No. 4, of the GWB only if there is an intentional or negligent violation of a final order of the BKartA based on Section 12 of the GWB. A proceeding for a fine presupposes, therefore, in the first instance, that there be a valid cartel agreement under Section 2 (terms and conditions), Section 3 (discounts), Section 5 (1) (standards and types), Section 5 (4) (uniform methods of making offers) and Section 6 (1) (export cartels without domestic restraints). Second, these cartels must be in violation of Article 85 (1) of the Treaty. Third, the

---

[19] Conclusion No. 3 of the *Bosch* decision, *ubi supra.*
[20] Accord: Weyer, *ibid.*
[21] Accord: Schlieder, BB 1962, p. 310.
[22] Accord: Schlieder, *ibid.*
[23] Accord: Schlieder, *ibid.*

BKartA must have ordered the participating enterprises to cease and
desist from the abuse of the domestic cartel considered in violation
of Article 85 (1). Finally, this order must have become final, i.e., not
subject to further review. Then only, and exclusively in connection
with the cartel agreements just enumerated and not in cases of other
restraints on competition, may the BKartA consider punishment of
a violation of Article 85 (1) through the imposition of fines.

Thus, no fines may be imposed by the national authorities, either
under Article 15 of Regulation 17 or directly under Article 88 of the
Treaty, for acting under an old cartel which is void. These authorities
may prosecute such a violation of Article 85 (1) only "in accordance
with" their national cartel law. For the BKartA this means, as a
practical matter, that it cannot initiate a proceeding under the German statute for that purpose.

¶ 411   *Old cartels not requiring notification:* According to the *Bosch*
         decision, these cartels remain valid even after March 12, 1962.
To them, therefore, the national authorities could apply Article 85 (1).
However, here again they cannot proceed on their own motion but
only within the confines of a proceeding under national law.

Furthermore, they must not interfere with the exclusive jurisdiction of the Commission over exemption grants, also bearing in mind
that such exemptions may be granted with retroactive effect. The
Bosch decision means that an agreement may not *finally* be declared
invalid unless the possibility of an exemption could be examined
first.[24] For this, however, the national authorities are not competent.
It would be intolerable if they could make a final declaration that a
cartel is prohibited and therefore void, and could thus foreclose the
opportunity of applying for an exemption. To be sure, it is up to the
parties, and not the national authorities, to make such an application.
The latter may therefore limit themselves to ordering the parties to
seek an exemption from the Commission within a certain time, on
pain of applying Article 85 (1) in case of refusal or failure. If the
parties do apply for exemption or negative clearance, this will amount
to the initiation of a proceeding pursuant to Article 6 or Article 2 of
Regulation 17. Thereupon, the Commission acquires exclusive jurisdiction, leaving no room for further steps by the national authorities.
The Kammergericht (Court of Appeals in Berlin) recognized this
view in its decision of May 4, 1962. It held a discount cartel based
on total volume of the customers' purchases possibly to constitute a

---

[24] Accord: Weyer, BB 1962, p. 470;
Gleiss/Hirsch, BB 1962, p. 625.

violation of Article 85 (1) of the Treaty, since it did not include in its calculations the volume of customers' orders placed with suppliers in other countries of the Common Market. The BKartA and the court, however, were prevented from applying Article 85 (1) of the Treaty, since the cartel had been notified and, thus, the Commission had the power to grant an exemption retroactively. The court felt it could not interfere with the Commission's jurisdiction.

If the parties do not apply to the Commission for exemption or negative clearance, the national authorities may declare the agreement to be prohibited by Article 85 (1). However, since the latter may not limit the time for applications to the Commission in a way contrary to Regulation 17, the parties can deprive them of jurisdiction even now, through filing such an application for exemption or negative clearance after the time set by the national authorities. Since Article 9 (3) contains nothing to the contrary, this will, in our view, be possible even in the judicial stage of the case.

To sum up, in the case of old cartels not requiring notification, the national authorities may apply Article 85 (1), but without prejudice to possible exemption by the Commission. Moreover, the parties are in a position throughout the proceeding to deprive the national authorities of jurisdiction by means of filing an application for exemption or negative clearance.

¶ 412   *New cartels requiring notification:* These new cartels are void under Article 85 (2) of the Treaty before notification. Application to them of Article 85 (1) by the national authorities would serve only the purpose of clarification. After notification, a proceeding by the Commission has been "initiated" within the meaning of Article 9 (3) of Regulation 17 (since notification involves an application for exemption: see ¶ 337 and 409, supra), so that the Commission has sole jurisdiction.

¶ 413   *New cartels not requiring notification:* What has been said regarding the situation of old cartels not requiring notification (¶ 411, supra) applies in substance to these new cartels also, and again regardless of the exact nature of their status under the *Bosch* decision. The national authorities may apply Article 85 (1), but without prejudice to the possibility of an exemption, and their jurisdiction can be cut off at any time by the initiation of a proceeding by the Commission on application made by the parties.

¶ 414   *Initiation of a proceeding:* In view of the extremely limited
         jurisdiction of the national authorities, the question of when
the Commission has "initiated" a proceeding within the meaning of
Article 9 (3) is not of great practical importance. One finds some
opinion to the effect that this occurs as early as the time when the
Commission acquires knowledge of a set of facts which is to be judged
by EEC cartel law.[25] With this we agree where the Commission obtains such knowledge from a national authority, e.g., by transmittal
of the matter to it. In such a case, it is not necessary that the Commission engage in visible external activity such as investigation,
requests for information, etc. Its internal occupation with the matter,
within its own organization, suffices, and it will occupy itself at least
internally with all matters submitted to it by national authorities.

Mere knowledge on the part of the Commission is not, however,
sufficient, in our view, where it is obtained from enterprises, associations and the like. Otherwise, any mere "denunciation" with the
Commission would already mean the initiation of a proceeding. This
is not in accord with either the letter or the purpose of Article 9 (3).
In such cases, a proceeding will be "initiated" only when there is a
visible reaction from the Commission, e.g., inquiries addressed by it
to parties or governmental authorities, or even just a confirmation of
receipt or communication of a file number, i.e., some manifestation of
its intention to proceed. Only then can one avoid the situation
where a national authority still asserts its jurisdiction while the Commission has already commenced a proceeding. A like danger normally
will not exist in the case of transmittal of a matter by a national
authority. It is too extreme, in our opinion, to regard a proceeding
as "initiated" only when the Commission begins to deal with the
merits of the case in an externally perceivable manner. If this
were true, then the numerous notifications in the hands of the
Commission would still not be sufficient to initiate a proceeding
when, as is the practice in nearly all cases, the response from the
Commission is only a confirmation of receipt and a file number. Such
procedure would not constitute treatment of the merits of the case.
The result that in all these cases the national authorities would still
have jurisdiction would, however, be in patent contradiction to the
purpose of Article 9 (3). The Commission itself gives notice of the
initiation of a proceeding in its routine printed acknowledgement of
receipt.

---

[25] Thus Ewald, Frankfurter Allgemeine Zeitung of April 24, 1962.

¶ 414

¶ 415   The *national courts* for civil matters are not excluded from jurisdiction by Article 9 (3), in our opinion.[25a] Article 9 (3) merely introduces a demarcation of the jurisdiction of various administrative authorities; this allocation makes sense only when made between them, since the courts and administrative authorities have significantly different tasks. While Article 9 (3) might be taken to mean that courts, too, must stay proceedings in all cases, such a construction is not required by its terms. Consequently, the courts are subject only to the general limitation of Article 177 of the Treaty (duty of national courts of last resort to refer certain matters to the European Court). However, the question has not yet been definitely clarified. The Court of Appeals (Cour d'Appel) in Paris, in its decision of January 26, 1963, was of the opinion that, when the Commission has initiated a proceeding within the meaning of Article 9 (3), courts, as national authorities, must suspend their proceedings. For this reason, the Court of Appeals stayed the case. The same view was expressed in the decision of May 9, 1963, by the Court of Appeals in Amiens.[26] On the other hand, the High Court of Appeals in Turin[27] rendered a decision under Article 88 of the Treaty, under which provision the same problem arises in an analogous manner, that courts were not included under the term "authorities of the Member States"; decisions in the Netherlands have held to the same effect.[28] The German Federal Supreme Court, in its "Electric Razor" decision,[29] saw no hindrance in dealing with the validity of re-export prohibitions that were notified to the Commission; thus, presumably it also did not consider courts to be national authorities under Article 9 (3).[29a]

Article 10

LIAISON WITH THE AUTHORITIES OF THE MEMBER STATES

(1) The Commission shall transmit without delay to the competent authorities of the Member States copies of the requests, applications and notifications together with copies of the most important documents which have been sent to it with the purpose of establishing the existence of infringements of Article 85 or Article 86 of the Treaty, or with the purpose of obtaining negative clearance or a decision to issue a declaration under Article 85, paragraph 3.

[25a] Cour d'Appel de Bruxelles, June 25, 1964, AWD 1965, p. 336.
[26] See Mezger, AWD 1963, p. 180.
[27] CMR ¶ 2011.57.
[28] See Gerechtshof te Amsterdam, June 28, 1962, WuW/E EWG/MUV 88.

[29] Of June 14, 1963, BB 1963, p. 1393, also in NJW 1964, p. 152.
[29a] This opinion is confirmed in BGH decision, WM 1970, p. 1188, ¶ 310, footnote 13b, supra.

(2) It shall carry out the procedures mentioned in paragraph 1 in close and constant liaison with the competent authorities of the Member States; and these authorities may submit their views on the said procedures.

(3) A Consultative Committee on Cartels and Monopolies shall be consulted prior to any decision consequent upon a course of procedure referred to in paragraph 1 and prior to any decision concerning the renewal, the alteration or the revocation of a decision to issue a declaration under Article 85, paragraph 3, of the Treaty.

(4) The Consultative Committee shall be composed of officials competent in the field of cartels and monopolies. Each Member State shall appoint one official to represent it, who, if he is prevented from attending, may be replaced by another official.

(5) The consultation shall take place at a joint meeting called by the Commission; the session shall take place fourteen days at the earliest after dispatch of the convocation letter. This letter shall be accompanied by an exposition of the case to be considered, indicating the most important documents, and a preliminary draft of the decision shall be enclosed.

(6) The Consultative Committee may render an opinion even if some members are absent and have not been replaced by another official. The result of the consultation shall be set out in a written statement which shall be attached to the draft of the decision. It shall not be made public.

¶ 416   This provision regulates only the *technical cooperation* between the Commission and the authorities of the member states (compare Section 45, paragraph 1 GWB: notice of all administrative and fine assessment proceedings of the Federal Cartel Authority to the highest Land authority having local jurisdiction; and *vice versa,* Section 45, paragraph 2 GWB). A matter for some concern is the fact that the close cooperation between these agencies will inevitably lead to delay, since the "Consultative Committee on Cartels and Monopolies" must be heard before any important decisions of the Commission are to be made (paragraph (3)). However, only consultation is required, and the Commission need not adopt the position of the Committee. The Commission may also guard against undue delay by holding the joint session at or right after the minimum of fourteen days from sending out the call for it together with an exposition of the facts and the Commission's proposed decision (paragraph (5)); with that session, the consultative proceeding is concluded.

The Consultative Committee is not to be heard before all proposed actions of the Commission, but rather, as seen from the language of paragraph (3) of Article 9, only before decisions *terminating a proceeding.* Not belonging in this category is a recommendation of the

Commission under Article 3 of Regulation 17 to put an end to violations of Articles 85 or 86 of the Treaty. Also excluded is notice, according to Article 15 (6) of Regulation 17, to the effect that after a preliminary examination of the matter, an exemption under Article 85 (3) of the Treaty for a notified agreement, etc., will not be warranted.

Article 11

REQUESTS FOR INFORMATION

(1) In the execution of the duties assigned to it by Article 89 and by provisions pursuant to Article 87 of the Treaty, the Commission shall have power to seek all necessary information from the Governments and competent authorities of the Member States as well as from enterprises and associations of enterprises.

(2) When sending a request for information to an enterprise or association of enterprises, the Commission shall at the same time address a copy of this request to the competent authority in the Member State in the territory of which the principal place of business of the enterprise or the association of enterprises is situated.

(3) In its request the Commission shall indicate the legal basis and the purpose of the same, and the penalties for supplying false information laid down in Article 15, paragraph 1, subparagraph (b).

(4) Information must be supplied on request by the owners of the enterprises or by their representatives and, in the case of legal persons, of companies or of associations without legal personality, by the persons responsible for representing them according to the law or the memorandum or articles of association.

(5) Where the enterprise or association of enterprises does not supply the information required within the time-limit set by the Commission, or supplies incomplete information, the Commission's request for information shall be made by means of a decision. This decision shall specify the information requested, fix an appropriate time-limit within which it is to be supplied and specify the sanctions applicable under Article 15, paragraph 1, subparagraph (b), and under Article 16, paragraph 1, subparagraph (c), and shall indicate that there is a right to institute proceedings against the decision before the Court of Justice.

(6) The Commission shall at the same time send a copy of its decision to the competent authority of the Member State in the territory of which the principal place of business of the enterprise or association of enterprises is situated.

¶ 421   This provision gives to the Commission far-reaching *rights to obtain information,* from the governments and authorities of the member states as well as directly from enterprises and associations thereof. The Commission may seek all "requisite" information (a term which corresponds more closely to the German "erforderlich" and which is somewhat broader than the "necessary" used in the translation). Its right to information thus is quite extensive, finding its limits only in the general principle that its exercise must serve performance of the tasks imposed upon the Commission by Article 89 of the Treaty and by Regulation 17.[30] From this it follows that the Commission may demand information concerning the economic circumstances of the enterprises only when it is necessary in order to determine whether a violation of Article 85 (1) or 86 has been committed. The Commission must have some indications of violations before it can require information; in our opinion, it is not entitled to demand information merely to obtain such indications. The Commission may demand information not only from enterprises involved in a violation of Article 85 (1) or 86, but also from any others.

¶ 422   The *procedure for the information request* has two stages: In the first place, the Commission addresses an *informal request* to an enterprise or association (paragraph (2)), in which it will indicate the legal basis and the purpose of the request and also the consequences of giving false information (paragraph (3)). Notwithstanding the peremptory language of paragraph (4) (the information "must" be supplied, or, closer to the German original, the owners, etc., are "obligated" to supply the information), the enterprise need not give the information in this first phase. It cannot be compelled by fines or penalties to do so. However, if it does supply information voluntarily, it must be accurate; the giving of false information may be punished by fines (Article 15 (1)(b) of Regulation 17). If the enterprise gives no information or does not do so within the time fixed by the Commission, the second stage of the information proceeding begins.

The Commission now demands the information by means of a *decision* and fixes an adequate period of time for compliance. Against this decision, the enterprise concerned may, within two months from the notice thereof given to it, institute an action in the European Court at Luxembourg (Article 173 of the Treaty). But even during the pendency of such an action, the Commission may compel the giving of information through fines or penalties (Articles 15 (1)(b) and 16 (1)(c) of Regulation 17), because an action against its decisions does not operate as a suspension or stay thereof (Article 185 of the Treaty). On the other hand, the Court may, if it deems it necessary or appropriate, stay the execution of a decision (*ibid.*).

---

[30] Accord: Schlieder, BB 1962, p. 310.

¶ 423   There is at present *no right to refuse* to give information, not
          even where there is danger of self-incrimination. This is
objectionable on general principles and under existing notions of the
rule of law.[31] However, the right to refuse to give information is
slated to become the subject of a special regulation;[32] it has still not
been issued.

As for the protection of secrets, see Article 20 of Regulation 17.

Article 12

INQUIRIES BY ECONOMIC SECTORS

(1) If in any sector of the economy the trend of trade between Member States, price movements, inflexibility of prices or
other circumstances suggest that in the economic sector concerned
competition is being restricted or distorted within the Common
Market, the Commission may decide to conduct a general inquiry
in the course of which it may request enterprises in the sector
concerned to supply the information necessary for giving effect
to the principles laid down in Articles 85 and 86 of the Treaty
and for carrying out the tasks entrusted to the Commission.

(2) The Commission may in particular request any enterprise or group of enterprises in the sector concerned to communicate to it all agreements, decisions and concerted practices which
are exempted from notification by virtue of Article 4, paragraph
2, and Article 5, paragraph 2.

(3) When making inquiries as provided for in paragraph 2,
the Commission shall also request enterprises or groups of enterprises whose size suggests that they occupy a dominant position
within the Common Market or within a substantial part thereof
to supply any particulars relating to the structure of the enterprises and to the conduct of their affairs necessary to appraise
their situation in the light of Article 86 of the Treaty.

(4) Article 10, paragraphs 3 to 6, and Articles 11, 13 and 14
shall be applied *mutatis mutandis.*

¶ 431   This provision, the heading of which could be translated more
          meaningfully as "Investigation of Particular Industries,"
gives the Commission the *right to investigate entire industries or branches*

---

[31] Compare *Malloy v. Hogan*, 378 U. S.
1 (1964). Contra: Schlieder, *id.* pp. 310,
311, especially footnote 37, who sees
no legally valid objection to the lack
of such a right.
[32] As to the general principles governing the limits of governmental de-

mands for information, see Thomae,
"Auskunfts- und Betriebsprüfungsrecht
der Verwaltung" (Rights of the Administrative to Information and Examination of Business Establishments),
Heidelberg 1955.

of industry, independently of any concrete case and notably, in contrast to Articles 11 and 14 of Regulation 17, independently of any concrete suspicion of a violation of Article 85 or 86 of the Treaty. The prerequisites to this astonishingly broad right of investigation are only vaguely defined in paragraph (1) (note: "or other circumstances"). Nevertheless, from the illustrations in paragraph (1) as well as the import of a general investigation of an industry, it is evident that weighty circumstances must be present to justify such an investigation.

The reference to Article 10, paragraphs (3) through (6), of Regulation 17 means that the Commission may decide to investigate an industry or branch of an industry only after having heard the opinion of the Consultative Committee. To this extent, a precautionary measure has been provided.

The investigation need not cover all enterprises in an industry or branch; a representative *selection* will suffice. The investigation may, under some circumstances, concern only the largest enterprises in an industry or branch, e.g., in order to pursue questions that arise especially or only there (e.g., accumulation of patents).

¶ 432   The reference in paragraph 4 to Article 11 of Regulation 17 means that such a general investigation, too, is divided into *two procedural stages* (compare Article 11, ¶ 422, supra). Both an informal request for information and a formal decision that information be furnished are, however, based on the resolution of the Commission to institute an investigation of an industry or branch. No one is obligated to disclose information by reason of this resolution only; rather, individual decisions according to Article 11 (4) of Regulation 17 (requests for information) or Article 14 (3) of Regulation 17 (investigating powers) are necessary to achieve such an effect. Since the resolution, however, constitutes the legal basis for a request for information or an individual decision, an internal act of the Commission will not suffice. The parties affected by the resolution must have an opportunity to examine it; consequently, it must be communicated to them.[33]

¶ 433   The *information obtained* in the course of a general investigation may be used only for the purposes pursued by the investigation (Article 20 (1)). The Commission, the national authorities

---

[33] Accord: Deringer, Art. 12, Reg. 17, marg. n. 4.

and their employees are put under an obligation of secrecy (Article 20 (2))—a provision which, in view of the large circle of persons who share in the information, offers but little security. The information may, however, be utilized and published in general form, e.g., in statistical surveys (Article 20 (3)).

Article 13

INVESTIGATION BY AUTHORITIES OF THE MEMBER STATES

(1) At the request of the Commission, the competent authorities of the Member States shall carry out the investigations that the Commission considers appropriate under Article 14, paragraph 1, or which it has ordered by a decision taken pursuant to Article 14, paragraph 3. The servants of the competent authorities of the Member States carrying out this investigation shall exercise their powers on production of a written warrant issued by the competent authority of the Member State in the territory of which the investigation is to be carried out. This warrant shall indicate the subject and the purpose of the inquiry.

(2) The servants of the Commission may, at its request or at that of the competent authority of the Member State in the territory of which the investigation is to be made, assist the servants of this authority in the execution of their duties.

¶ 434   The national authorities may not act upon their own motion.

A *request from the Commission* is required, which it may make when it considers such a step appropriate. The reference to Article 14 means that the prerequisites of that article must be met; only when the investigations requested by the Commission are "necessary" (requisite), may it deem them "appropriate." Whether it may be concluded from the relation of Articles 13 and 14 that the investigations are as a rule primarily the responsibility of the national authorities and not the Commission, we regard as a doubtful proposition. The language of those provisions discloses nothing in support of such a conclusion; as a practical matter, however, it will likely be so interpreted.

Competent authorities of member states are usually the national cartel authorities. Requests to them from the Commission are made, due to the nature of the Community, not through various diplomatic channels, but directly. It is self-evident that the Commission must indicate in its request the subject and purpose of the inquiry. The national authority will then act under the doctrine of "aiding another administrative body." Under German law, this means that it may not, as a rule, examine the question of the legal validity of the request ;[34] consequently, refusal is justifiable only if the Commission pursues aims manifestly contrary to the purpose of the proceeding, if a proceeding under Article 14 is obviously not permissible, or if the Commission has tendered its request to an authority patently lacking the requisite jurisdiction. The Commission may not render impossible the exercise of the national authority's right of investigation; therefore, it must at least inform the authority that the prerequisites of Article 14 are not obviously wanting.[35]

The request of the Commission may not be challenged by the party affected by the investigation, although he may bring an action against the administrative act by which the national authority orders the investigation. Such an action would be governed by national law. The issue of whether the prerequisites of Article 14 have been fulfilled may be presented to the European Court under Article 177 of the Treaty.

In which manner the national authorities comply with the request of the Commission for an inquiry is also a question governed by national law. In this connection, paragraph (1) should be noted. According to it, the national authorities must present their servants with a warrant indicating the subject and purpose of the inquiry.

Article 14

INVESTIGATING POWERS OF THE COMMISSION

(1) In execution of the duties assigned to it by Article 89 and by provisions laid down pursuant to Article 87 of the Treaty, the Commission may conduct all necessary investigations into the affairs of enterprises and associations of enterprises.

To this end the servants authorized by the Commission shall be vested with the following powers:

(a) to examine the books and other business documents;

(b) to make copies of, or extracts from, the same;

(c) to ask for verbal explanations on the spot;

(d) to have access to all premises, land and vehicles of enterprises.

(2) The servants authorized by the Commission for these investigations shall exercise their powers on production of a written warrant stating the nature and purpose of the inquiry

---

[34] This is the prevailing view; compare here and in the following text, Peters, Lehrbuch der Verwaltung, p. 60 f.

[35] For more stringent requirements, see Deringer, Art. 13, Reg. 17, marg. n. 3.

¶ 434

and the fines provided for in Article 15, paragraph 1, sub-paragraph (c), in the event of incomplete submission of the books or other business documents required. The Commission shall in good time advise the competent authority of the Member State in the territory of which the investigation is to take place, of this investigation, stating the name and office of the authorized servant.

(3) The enterprises and associations of enterprises must submit to the investigations ordered by a decision of the Commission. The decision shall state the subject and purpose of the inquiry, fix the date when it is to begin and call attention to the sanctions provided for under Article 15, paragraph 1, subparagraph (c), and Article 16, paragraph 1, subparagraph (d), and shall indicate that there is a right to institute proceedings against the decision before the Court of Justice.

(4) Before taking the decisions referred to in paragraph 3, the Commission shall consult the competent authority of the Member State in the territory of which the investigation is to be carried out.

(5) The servants of the competent authority of the Member State in the territory of which the investigation is to be carried out may, at the request of this authority or of the Commission, lend assistance to the Commission's servants in the execution of their duties.

(6) Where an enterprise resists an investigation ordered pursuant to the present Article, the Member State concerned shall lend the servants authorized by the Commission the assistance necessary to enable them to carry out their investigation. The Member State shall, after consulting the Commission, take the necessary measures for this purpose before October 1, 1962.

¶ 441   The Commission may conduct directly (Article 14), or cause to be conducted by the competent authorities of the member states (Article 13), all "necessary" (requisite) "investigations" (inspections or examinations) of enterprises or associations thereof. As the right to information, this right to examination is limited only by the principle that it must serve the performance of the Commission's duties under Article 89 of the Treaty and Regulation 17. Mere expediency will not suffice; rather, here again the Commission must already have some indications of violations of Article 85 or Article 86 of the Treaty (see above, ¶ 421).[36]

¶ 442   Since the Commission does not have its own administrative organization in the member states, it will as a rule request the national authorities to carry out the examinations ordered by it. The national authorities may move only upon such a request; they

---

[36] Compare Würdinger, WuW 1964, p. 582.

do not have visitatorial rights of their own. In performing their task, they must respect the national laws.[37] However, the Commission may itself engage in an examination. In such a case, the authority of its servants is carefully circumscribed in paragraph (1) ; the Commission may not exceed this limit in the warrant issued to them. Article 14 (6) indicates that, in such a case also, conflicts with national laws are to be avoided wherever possible, through measures taken by the member states before October 1, 1962. In this connection it might have been provided, e.g., for the Federal Republic, that searches may be undertaken only upon a judicial order ;[38] however, no provisions of this character have been made by it as yet.

¶ 443   Like the procedure for obtaining information (see Article 11, ¶ 422, supra), that governing inspection and examination has two stages.

In the first phase, the enterprises or associations concerned are under no duty to submit books, records, etc. However, if they do so voluntarily, compliance must be complete, or else fines may be imposed (Article 15 (1)(c)).

If voluntary submission is refused, the Commission may order the examination by decision (Article 14 (3)). In the decision, the subject, purpose and starting time of the examination must be stated and attention must be called to the right of the party concerned to institute an action against the decision within two months from notice thereof in the European Court at Luxembourg (ibid., and Article 173 of the Treaty). But even if such an action is brought, the Commission may compel submission to the examination by penalties and fines (Articles 16 (1)(d) and 15 (1)(c) of Regulation 17), without there being a right to resist inspection or to refuse required explanations.

If the investigation is ordered by decision, the member state in whose territory the investigation is to take place is obligated to lend its assistance. This duty does not exist in the first phase, although this conclusion follows more from the purpose of paragraph (6) than from the language. As long as a party may refuse (first phase) to produce records, etc., the assistance of the member state is without purpose.

If the Commission can reach its aim by either a demand for information (see above, Article 11) or an investigation, the question arises whether the less drastic method of a request for information must prevail as a consequence of the rule of *proportionality of means*. Ac-

---

[37] Accord: Schlieder, BB 1962, p. 311;   [38] Accord: Weyer, DB 1962, p. 327.
Deringer, GRUR AIT 1962, p. 291.

¶ 443

cording to the decisions of the European Court, the answer is in the negative; in its decision of April 4, 1960,[39] concerning Article 47 of the Coal and Steel Treaty, it stated that the High Authority could choose either a demand for information or an investigation, whichever was more expedient. Consequently, one must assume that also under Regulation 17, the Commission may select one or the other means at its discretion.[40]

The servants of the Commission must (compare paragraph (2)) have a written warrant stating the subject and purpose of the investigation. In the above decision, the European Court assumed under Article 47 (1) of the Coal and Steel Treaty that the High Authority need not precisely disclose in advance which topics the investigation was to cover. Regarding Article 14 (2) of Regulation 17, this does not mean that the servants may institute investigations outside the scope of their warrant; on the contrary, the investigation must be necessary for the fulfillment of the warrant. The warrant must not transgress the limits of the law.

Article 15

FINES

(1) The Commission may by means of a decision impose on enterprises and associations of enterprises fines of from one hundred to five thousand units of account where, wilfully or through negligence:

(a) they supply false or misleading information in an application submitted pursuant to Article 2 or in a notification made pursuant to Articles 4 and 5;

(b) they supply false information in reply to a request made pursuant to Article 11, paragraph 3 or 5, or to Article 12, or do not supply information within a time-limit fixed by a decision taken under Article 11, paragraph 5; or

(c) they submit in incomplete form, on the occasion of investigations carried out under Article 13 or Article 14, the books or other business documents required, or decline to submit to an investigation ordered by means of a decision taken pursuant to Article 14, paragraph 3.

(2) The Commission may by means of a decision impose on enterprises and associations of enterprises fines of from one thousand to one million units of account: this last figure may be increased to 10% of the turnover of the preceding business year of each of the enterprises having taken part in the infringement where these enterprises, wilfully or through negligence:

---

[39] Case No. 31/59, *Recueil* Vol. VI, pp. 155, 173.

[40] Accord: Deringer, Art. 14, Reg. 17, marg. n. 1; Würdinger, WuW 1964, p. 581.

(a) have infringed the provisions of Article 85, paragraph 1, or of Article 86 of the Treaty, or

(b) have infringed a stipulation made under Article 8, paragraph 1.

In determining the amount of the fine the duration of the infringement shall be considered in addition to its gravity.

(3) Article 10, paragraphs 3 to 6, shall apply.

(4) The decisions taken under paragraphs 1 and 2 shall have no penal character.

(5) The fines provided for in paragraph 2, subparagraph (a), may not be imposed for actions taking place:

(a) after the notification to the Commission and prior to its decision regarding the application of Article 85, paragraph 3, of the Treaty, in so far as these actions do not go beyond the limits of the activity described in the notification;

(b) prior to the notification of and within the framework of the agreements, decisions and concerted practices existing at the date of entry into force of the present Regulation, provided that this notification has been made within the time-limits laid down in Article 5, paragraph 1, and Article 7, paragraph 2.

(6) Paragraph 5 shall not apply once the Commission has informed the enterprises concerned that after a preliminary examination it considers that the conditions of Article 85, paragraph 1, of the Treaty have been fulfilled and that application of Article 85, paragraph 3, is not warranted.

¶ 444   See comments following Article 16.

Article 16

PENALTIES

(1) The Commission may by means of a decision impose on enterprises or associations of enterprises penalties of from fifty to one thousand units of account per day of delay, reckoned from the date fixed in its decision, in order to oblige them:

(a) to put an end to an infringement of Article 85 or Article 86 of the Treaty in conformity with a decision taken pursuant to Article 3;

(b) to discontinue any action prohibited under Article 8, paragraph 3;

(c) to supply completely and truthfully any information which it has requested by a decision taken under Article 11, paragraph 5;

(d) to submit to any investigation it has ordered by a decision taken pursuant to Article 14, paragraph 3.

(2) When the enterprises or associations of enterprises have fulfilled the obligation which it was the object of the penalty to enforce, the Commission may fix the final amount of the penalty at a figure lower than that which would result from the initial decision.

(3) Article 10, paragraphs 3 to 6, shall apply.

¶ 451   The terminology of *"fines"* and *"penalties,"* employed in the English translation of Articles 15 and 16, respectively, is somewhat imprecise since a fine is itself a penalty in the ordinary sense of the latter term. As here used, "fine" has its normal meaning of a monetary punishment for an offense (even though not technically of a criminal character: Article 15 (4)). "Penalty," as here employed, should not be understood to mean a punitive imposition, but merely a compulsory sanction (used, as Article 16 (1) itself says, "in order to oblige" to, or to enforce, compliance with legal duties). The wording of both of these articles ("The Commission may . . .") makes it clear that the Commission is not compelled to impose either fines or penalties. This is less obvious with regard to fines for violations of Article 85 (1) or 86 of the Treaty than it is with regard to compulsory sanctions. However, this *discretionary principle* gives the Commission the opportunity of leaving trifling matters to one side and following up only violations of real interest to it.[41] It would be a constructive use of this broad discretion if the Commission were to announce that, until further notice, fines would not be imposed for certain defined infractions of Article 85 (1) (compare the discussion in connection with negative clearance, Article 2 of Regulation 17, ¶ 317 ff., supra).

¶ 452   Under Article 15, the Commission may fix fines against enterprises and associations up to $1,000,000; or,[42] beyond this, up to 10% of the turnover (sales) during the preceding business year of the individual enterprises participating in a violation of Article 85 (1) or 86, if they did so intentionally or negligently or if they acted contrary to obligatory terms imposed by the Commission (see Article 8 (1), ¶ 389, supra).

---

[41] Similarly to Section 81, paragraph 2, of the GWB, under which the cartel authority applies for the imposition of a fine only if it deems prosecution to be in the public interest.

[42] Weyer (DB 1962, p. 325) and Deringer (AG 1962, p. 142), without explanation, substitute the word "and" for "or" (in the German text of Article 15 (2)). This may create the impression that $1,000,000 and 10% of annual turnover may be fixed cumulatively as a fine.

This was not the legislative intention, as seen perhaps most clearly in the Italian text: "ad un massimo di un millione, con facolta di aumentare quest' ultimo importo fino al 10 per cento . . ." (up to a maximum of one million, with authority to increase this latter amount up to 10% . . .). This means that, above $1,000,000, 10% of the turnover is the absolute upper limit of a fine. The English translation of Article 15 (2), also, poses no problem in this respect.

¶ 453   Fines and penalties require a formal *decision* of the Commission, which is subject to judicial review (Article 17). They may be imposed in conjunction with a decision under Article 3 (1) of Regulation 17 ordering the parties to put an end to the violation, but they may also be imposed in a separate decision.

Shortly after imposing fines for the first time in the *quinine cartel case* on June 16, 1969 (which has meanwhile been upheld in principle by the European Court),[42a] the Commission made a second decision on July 24, 1969,[42b] in which it fined ten producers of *tar colors* a total oi $490,000 for concerted practices fixing the price-raising indices and terms in 1964, 1965, and 1967.[42c]

The Commission may also impose fines on enterprises in third countries, if they are doing business within the Common Market, even if this is done by subsidiaries. But this question is debated.[42d]

¶ 454   Article 15 (4) declares that a fine does *not* have the character of *punishment for crime* under penal law. The violations subject to fine thus are comparable to the "breaches of order" (Ordnungswidrigkeiten) under German law.[43] The reason for this disposition was that the Council of Ministers of the EEC was willing to give to the Commission authority to impose sanctions, but no punitive powers.

¶ 455   *Instigating or abetting* violations of Articles 85 (1) and 86 does not entail fines, and the Commission cannot punish such activities.[44]

¶ 456   The Commission is *not under any duty to issue a warning* to the enterprises or associations concerned before it imposes fines, although it may do so (Article 3 (3), ¶ 326, supra). Before notification according to Article 15 (1), in our opinion, the Commission is obligated, however, to grant the parties a hearing, since the notification is not a mere declaration of intent, but a decision with legal consequences (see Article 1 of Regulation 99/63). Therefore, we are of the opinion that an action may be instituted against such notification and the European Court may annul the decision if the factual and legal circumstances do not support the "view" of the Commission.

Our view that the communication of the Commission under Article 15, paragraph 6, is a decision that may be appealed to the

---

[42a] For the Commission decision and the Court's ruling, see ¶ 459, infra.

[42b] OffJour No. L 195 (August 7, 1969), p. 11; CMR ¶ 9314.

[42c] Cf. also the preceding *Tar-Colors* decision of the European Court, Introduction, footnote 6a, supra.

[42d] Cf. Written Question No. 219/70 put to the Commission by Mr. Glinne on August 24, 1970.

[43] See Section 38 ff. of the GWB; accord: Weyer, *id.*, p. 326.

[44] Accord: Kleemann, p. 81.

Court, has been approved by the Court in its *Noordwijks* decision of March 15, 1967.[44a] The Court also deems it decisive that the "blue letter" removes any protection of parties to the agreement from fines. For the Commission, this means that it must support its notification with reasons.

If notification of an agreement to the Commission has been made, the parties may perform it without fear of fines (Article 15 (5) (a) of Regulation 17); this protection is also accorded by a late notification. The protection from fines provided by notification ceases when notice under Article 15 (6) has been given.[44b] However, this does not mean that the Commission may assess fines against the parties before its final decision on the merits of the notification, i.e., whether an exemption under Article 85 (3) is warranted. Rather, the notice under Article 15 (6) merely gives the Commission the opportunity, at the time of its final decision on the merits (or thereafter), to impose fines also for violations occurring before this decision. Under civil law, the notice of Article 15 (6) means nothing; the agreement does not become retroactively void because of it. The attendant difficulties of the opposite interpretation, especially if an exemption were to follow a notice under Article 85 (3), could hardly be solved under German law (see also, Article 1 of Regulation 99/63).

Article 17
REVIEW BY THE COURT OF JUSTICE

The Court of Justice shall have full jurisdiction within the meaning of Article 172 of the Treaty to adjudicate on proceedings instituted against the decisions by which the Commission has fixed a fine or a penalty; it may cancel, reduce or increase the fine or the penalty imposed.

¶ 457 The fines and penalties, assessable by the Commission only by means of decisions (Articles 15 and 16), may be brought for review before the European Court, by an action filed within two months from notice of the decision (Article 173 of the Treaty).

¶ 458 In contrast to the rule of Article 173, however, Article 17 of Regulation 17 gives the Court the power of unrestricted revision of the Commission's exercise of discretion. The Court may cancel or reduce, but may also increase the fine or penalty fixed by the Commission. It thus may substitute its own discretion for that of the Commission. There is no bar to revision making the decision less favorable to the complainant. An action in the Court against a de-

---

[44a] Annotations by Fuss/Burkhard, Europarecht 1967, p. 232; Torelli, Revue du Marché Commun 1968, p. 979.

[44b] Cf. van den Heuvel, CMLR Vol. 4 (1966), p. 192.

cision of the Commission does not have the effect of a stay .(Article 185 of the Treaty).

¶ 459   On July 16, 1969, the European Commission for the first time imposed fines for violations of Article 85 of the EEC Treaty.[44c] The firms involved were the six members of an international quinine cartel. The following fines were imposed:

210,000 units of account ($) on the Dutch company Nedchem;

190,000 units of account on the German company Boehringer GmbH;

65,000 units of account on the German company Buchler & Co.;

12,500 units of account each on the two French companies Pointet Girard and Nogentaise;

10,000 units of account on the French company Pharmacie Centrale.

The Commission stated that the members of the cartel, during the period from 1962 to the beginning of 1965, by means of agreements and concerted practices (secret gentlemen's agreements), jointly determined and applied selling prices for quinine and quinidine, established export quotas and market shares, protected home markets against imports of other cartel members and regulated the manufacture of quinidine. Nedchem, Boehringer, and Buchler filed appeals against the imposition of fines with the European Court, whereas the French cartel members accepted the fines. The European Court confirmed the Commission's decisions but decreased the plaintiffs' fines by 10,000 units of account each.[44d] The Court's rulings against the three enterprises have the same legal content.

The following details of the Court's substantiation are legally the most interesting:

The question of prescription which was raised by the enterprises is of no relevance. The Treaty does not provide for any period of limitation. In order to guarantee legal security, the period of limitation has to be fixed in advance. It is up to the legislator of the Community to decide on its length and on details for its application.

With regard to the legal nature of the proceedings for imposing a fine, the Court said that the proceedings in application of Article 85 of the EEC Treaty were of an administrative character. In such proceedings it is not objectionable if the members of the Commission who have to decide on the fine are merely informed of the hearing of the enterprises concerned; it is not necessary that they hear them personally.[44e]

[44c] OffJour No. L 192 (August 5, 1969), p. 5; English translation, CMR, ¶ 9313.

[44d] See CMR ¶ 8083-8085.

[44e] Contrast this with *Morgan v. United States*, 298 U. S. 468, 481 (1936): "The one who decides must hear."

The European Court repeatedly stressed that there must be sufficient proof of the contravention. It states in connection with Article 15 (2) of Regulation 17: "In deciding on the gravity of the contravention in order to determine the amount of the fine, one has to take into account, in particular, the kinds of restrictions on competition, the number and the importance of the enterprises involved, the market shares controlled by them in the Community, and the situation on the market at the time of the contravention."

Fines which have been imposed on the enterprises in third countries (e.g., the U. S.) may not be deducted from the fines under EEC law, since those penalties concern restraints on trade outside of the Common Market. There is therefore no reason to take them into account in the proceedings under Regulation 17.

Article 18

UNIT OF ACCOUNT

For the purposes of Articles 15 to 17 the unit of account shall be that adopted for drawing up the budget of the Community in accordance with Articles 207 and 209 of the Treaty.

¶ 460   Unit of account is, at least in substance, the present United States dollar (0.88867088 grams of pure gold). Fines and penalties under Articles 15 and 16 may therefore be extremely high, considering that the exchange rate for the dollar is in any case a multiple, although in greatly varying proportions, of the currencies of the member states.

Article 19

HEARING THE PARTIES CONCERNED
AND THIRD PERSONS

(1) Before taking decisions as provided for in Articles 2, 3, 6, 7, 8, 15 and 16, the Commission shall give the enterprises or associations of enterprises concerned an opportunity to express their views on the points objected to which have been taken into consideration by the Commission.

(2) So far as the Commission or the competent authorities of the Member States consider it necessary, they may also hear other natural or legal persons or associations of persons. If natural or legal persons or associations of persons who show that they have a sufficient interest ask to be heard, their request shall be granted.

(3) When the Commission intends to give negative clearance pursuant to Article 2 or to render a decision applying Article 85,

¶ 460

paragraph 3, of the Treaty, it shall publish the essential content of the application or notification, inviting all interested third parties to submit their observations within a time-limit which it shall fix and which shall not be less than one month. Publication shall respect the justified interest of enterprises that their business secrets should not be divulged.

¶ 461   Before the Commission renders decisions on negative clearances (Article 2 of Regulation 17), obligations to discontinue violations of Article 85 or 86 of the Treaty (Article 3 of Regulation 17), exemptions pursuant to Article 85 (3) of the Treaty (Article 6 of Regulation 17) or their revocation (Article 8), subsequent legalization in case of active reform (Article 7), or fines (Article 15) and penalties (Article 16), it must grant a hearing to the enterprises or associations concerned by the decision. Article 19 (1), therefore, guarantees the *opportunity of being heard* in the legal sense before all important decisions, particularly those of substantive significance.

The requirement contained in paragraph (1) may lead to technical difficulties if the number of participants is large. This can be the case where form agreements involving thousands of participants, e.g., contractual export prohibitions, are concerned. In such a case, the opportunity to be heard may be given, in some circumstances, by publication in the Official Journal.

The hearing of participants and third parties (Article 19 (1) and (2)) in a proceeding before the Commission is the subject of detailed regulations contained in the so-called *Regulation Concerning Hearings* (Regulation 99/63).

¶ 462   In Form A/B (application for negative clearance or for exemption pursuant to Article 85 (3) of the Treaty), introduced by Regulation 27,[45] supporting reasons are to be furnished for the application. Here, the applicant enterprises have a chance to explain their position. This alone, however, does not satisfy the requirement in Article 19 (1) of Regulation 17 of an opportunity of being heard in the legal sense, since, at the time of being called upon to furnish supporting reasons, the position of the Commission regarding the particular application, in the nature of things, cannot yet be known to the applicants. Therefore, if the Commission wishes to deny an application, it cannot let it go at the statements contained in the form, but must give the parties a new opportunity to argue their position. (Article 2 of Regulation 99.) In doing so, it is under an

---

[45] OffJour No. 35/62 of May 10, 1962, p. 1118 (Article 4). Regulation 27 is based upon Article 24 of Regulation 17.

obligation also to indicate its possible objections, doubts, etc., for the applicants must be enabled to express themselves "on the points objected to which have been taken into consideration by the Commission" (paragraph (1)).[46] If complaints are involved which have been raised with the Commission by third persons, the opportunity of being heard must be given to the parties regardless of whether or not the Commission intends to rely upon such complaints to their disadvantage.[47] However, if the Commission is determined to ignore a complaint in any event, e.g., because of manifest baselessness, it need not hear the parties on that particular matter;[48] but if it changes its position later, it must grant a hearing at that time.

¶ 463   Concerning *third parties'* "sufficient *interest*" *in being heard* (paragraph (2)), an economic interest is, in our view, enough. One who is affected by a restraint on competition has the right on that account to take part in a proceeding before the Commission.

¶ 464   Article 19 (3) governs the *publication of applications for negative clearance or exemption.* As there provided, they do not have to be published in every case, but only if the Commission intends to grant them. With the publication, the Commission is to join an "invitation" to all "interested third parties" to "submit their observations," i.e., to take a position in respect of the application, within a fixed period of time, which must not be less than one month. The "invitation" does not, of course, oblige, but merely affords the chance to, third persons to take a position. (This is already implied in the English translation by use of the term "inviting"; the German original sounds somewhat more peremptory. On the other hand, "interested third parties" appears somewhat too liberal a translation of what is really third persons "concerned" or "affected," unless it is remembered that "interested" in the legal sense is a rather narrow concept and would not include, e.g., a purely intellectual as distinguished from a pecuniary concern.)

¶ 465   At first it appeared that the Commission was prepared to publish these applications not only in cases where it intended to grant them. This was indicated by the "Fifth General Report of the EEC Commission on the Activities of the Community."[49] In the

---

[46] Accord: Kleemann, pp. 73, 74. Contra: Weyer, DB 1962, p. 327, who, in our view erroneously, relates the quoted language only to complaints made to the Commission by third persons.

[47] Accord: Weyer, *ibid.*
[48] Accord: Weyer, *ibid.*
[49] For the period from May 1, 1961, to April 30, 1962.

meantime, it has become evident from the practice of the Commission that its publications are in accord with the law.

The Commission may not indiscriminately publish trade secrets. Such a practice is prevented by the last sentence of paragraph (3) (compare Article 21 (2) of Regulation 17).

Not only non-patentable know-how falls under the heading of trade secrets; other trade facts, e.g., the sales volume or customer lists of an enterprise, may also come within this category; for details, see Article 2 of Regulation 99/63. If the facts that an enterprise wishes kept secret are of common knowledge or, at least, available to the public, trade secrets are no longer involved.

When a trade secret exists, the Commission must determine whether the interest of the enterprise in protecting it is "justified." We deem the answer to be in the affirmative as a general rule, since it is not possible to differentiate between trade secrets of the first and second degree. The interest in secrecy would be unjustified only in exceptional cases, e.g., when a violation of a provision of the Treaty is the subject of the secret.

Even if there is a justified interest in doing so, the Commission may in no case disclose the secret to the public, not even when its publication is rendered incomprehensible.[50] Article 19 (3) does not grant the Commission any area of discretion for weighing the private interest in secrecy against the public interest in publication of the intended decisions;[51] the law contains no reference to a "preponderant" interest in secrecy.

¶ 465A   We will now present some examples of Commission publications under Article 19 (3).

In one case[51a] the *Scott Paper Company*, Philadelphia, U. S. A. ("Scott") has, by contract, granted to its wholly-owned subsidiary, *Scott Continental S.A.*, Brussels ("Continental"), licenses to manufacture and sell free of charge in the Common Market, except Italy, absorbent paper products, such as napkins and tissues, as well as water-repellent paper used for packaging. Continental is free to manufacture goods of the same type and quality under its own trademarks, both in and outside the contract area, but not in violation of Scott's industrial property rights or know-how.

---

[50] In favor of publication of the secret in these cases, Deringer, Art. 21, Reg. 17, marg. n. 6.

[51] Thus, however, Deringer, *ibid*.

[51a] The text of the announcement is printed in OffJour No. C 110 (October 24, 1968), p. 2 (CMR ¶ 9263).

¶ 465A

Scott has to make available to Continental, without charge, all technical knowledge, including licenses on industrial property rights, manufacturing procedures, sales methods, etc. Both parties are bound to secrecy with respect to know-how, information, etc., obtained from the other. The licensee cannot contest Scott's trademark rights.

The contract between Scott and its subsidiary *Burgo Scott* S.p.A., Turin ("B.S."), in which it holds a 50 percent interest, is essentially the same. The other parent of B.S. is *Cartiere Burgo* S.p.A. ("Burgo"). In this case the contract is concluded between the three firms. Scott alone is the licensor, and B.S. is the licensee. The license area includes Italy, France, Germany, Austria, Switzerland and Liechtenstein. In this case, the subsidiary is equally dependent on both parents, also with regard to personnel. Neither Scott nor Burgo are able to exert a prevailing influence on B.S.

Although the licenses granted in both cases are non-exclusive, Scott has not granted any trademark licenses to any other enterprise in the contract areas. Only in France and Italy are both licensees entitled to use Scott's trademarks. In the Benelux countries and in Italy only B.S. may do so. Continental and B.S. guarantee that they will not hinder Scott articles marketed by the sister firm.

In the final paragraph, the Commission announced its intention, which is usually the case in these announcements under Article 19 (3) of Regulation 17, to take a favorable decision. It is very probable that it will grant a negative clearance in the Continental case because of Scott's 100 percent interest there. In the Burgo Scott case, however, it will be very interesting to see if the Commission grants an exemption and if so, to study the reasons.

Another example of a publication made by the Commission is that in the *MAN-SAVIEM* case.[51b]

A French truck manufacturer, the Société Anonyme de Véhicules Industriels et d'Equipements Mécaniques (SAVIEM), Suresnes, a subsidiary of Renault and therefore essentially state owned, and a German truck manufacturer, the Maschinenfabrik Augsburg-Nürnberg AG, Munich (MAN), have agreed to cooperate. The objective of the contract concluded between them is to research, design and develop jointly a line of medium and heavy trucks for civilian use, and to manufacture, assemble and distribute them. After-sale service is also covered by the contract. Basically, the medium-weight trucks, i.e., those having a gross weight of more than 7.5 tons and self-con-

---

[51b] OffJour No. C 75, June 14, 1969, p. 2 (CMR ¶ 9306).

¶ 465A

tained vehicles of not over 12 tons, are the business of the French firm, while heavy-weight trucks in the 12 to 24 ton range are the business of the German company. Sales to third parties are restricted and, as a rule, have to be approved by the other partner. Each party handles assembly, distribution and service in its own country. SAVIEM will make engines for medium-weight trucks under a license from MAN. Each party may subcontract the manufacture of components, etc., in its range, but it has to grant the other party priority. MAN had previously concluded a licensing agreement with SAVIEM's parent, the Régie Nationale des Usines Renault, and this agreement is confirmed in the MAN-SAVIEM contract. The parties are free in their price policy but are enjoying a most-favored-client clause. Exports to countries outside France and Germany are made by the party doing the assembling. Trucks that are subject to the contract will carry combinations of the trademarks MAN-Renault-SAVIEM. There are also clauses on industrial property rights. The parties may cooperate in a similar way with third parties, subject to the approval of the other partner, which can be denied only for cogent reasons (for further details, see CMR ¶ 9306). The Commission again announced its intention to take favorable action.

Article 20
PROFESSIONAL SECRETS

(1) Information gathered pursuant to Articles 11, 12, 13 and 14 may not be used for any purpose other than that for which it was requested.

(2) Without prejudice to the provisions of Articles 19 and 21, the Commission and the competent authorities of the Member States as well as their officials and other employees may not disclose matters which have come to their knowledge through the application of the present Regulation and which by their nature are professional secrets.

(3) The provisions of paragraphs 1 and 2 shall not hinder the publication of general surveys or reviews not containing information relating to particular enterprises or associations of enterprises.

¶ 466   A *duty of secrecy* is imposed upon officials and employees even after they have retired from the service of the Commission or of the national authorities (Article 214 of the Treaty). A breach of this duty entails disciplinary measures. In our opinion, there is also the possibility of claims for damages by the injured party against the Commission (Article 215 (2) of the Treaty). Claims of that nature on account of indiscretions of officials of the German national authority would be governed by Section 839 of the BGB, providing for liability of a public officer for intentional or negligent breach of official duty owed to a third person, and by various provisions of German law substituting the employing government as the party liable directly to third persons, with a possible right of action against the officer.

Notably lacking in this provision are criminal sanctions against violations of the duty of secrecy such as, for instance, those in Section 47 GWB (imprisonment up to two years). This gap should be closed promptly.

The national authorities' duty of secrecy also covers knowledge disclosed in the notification forms. Consequently such knowledge may not be used by the national authorities to punish violations of national law, since such action would also constitute a breach of the duty of secrecy.

Article 21

PUBLICATION OF DECISIONS

(1) The Commission shall publish the decisions which it takes pursuant to Articles 2, 3, 6, 7 and 8.

(2) The publication shall name the parties concerned and give the essential content of the decisions; the justified interest of the enterprises that their business secrets should not be divulged shall be respected.

¶ 471   The Commission must *publish all decisions of substantive content*. To be published are not only the conclusions or closing portions of the decision, and names and addresses of the parties, but also the essential reasons for the decision.[52] This is to be applauded in the interest of harmonious development and certainty of the law.

Business secrets of the parties, of course, must not be disclosed in the process (paragraph (2)); this would be a violation also of Article 20 (2). For details regarding the prohibition of publication of trade secrets, see above ¶ 465.

¶ 472   Decisions fixing fines (Article 15) or penalties (Article 16) or requesting or ordering information, investigations or examinations (Articles 11, 12, 14), as well as notice under Article 15 (6), are *not subject to the publication requirement*.

---

[52] Article 21 thus goes further than Section 58 of the GWB, which provides for publication only of the "dispositions" or orders of the cartel authorities in certain matters.

¶ 472

¶ 473   *Against all decisions* of the Commission, the enterprises or
         associations concerned may institute an *action in the European
Court at Luxembourg* (Article 173 of the Treaty). Standing to sue
extends also to persons who are directly and individually affected by
a decision, even though it may not be directed to them (Article 173
(2)). Proper grounds for an action for review are lack of jurisdiction,
disregard of essential requirements as to form, violation of the Treaty
or of implementing regulations, and abuse of discretion. The French
version of the Treaty speaks in this connection of a "détournement
de pouvoir" (misuse of power); the Conseil d'Etat has created an
extensive amount of judicial precedent regarding this term which
might well be of some influence here. Violation of essential requirements as to form would include a denial of the right to be heard,
guaranteed by Article 19 (1) of Regulation 17.

¶ 474   The *time limitation for commencing an action* is *two months*
         (Article 173 of the Treaty). This period runs from publica-
tion of the decision, from notice of it given to the plaintiff, or—in the
absence of both of these events—from the time at which the plaintiff
obtains knowledge of the decision. If a decision is published pursuant
to Article 21 of Regulation 17, this is publication within the meaning
of Article 173 of the Treaty. Publication thus starts the period
running as against persons who had not been parties to the proceeding theretofore; as against the parties themselves, on the other hand,
it will normally be the notice given to them of the decision, because
this will as a rule precede publication.

¶ 475   According to Article 185 of the Treaty, actions against deci-
         sions of the Commission *do not operate as a stay.* It is a matter
of doubt, however, whether this is true in cases involving a denial of
exemption, for the following reasons:

    If the Commission denies an exemption, this means that the
agreement for which the exemption was sought becomes retroactively
void pursuant to Article 85 (2). If the Court were now, in an action
by the parties, to declare the denial of exemption null and void
(Article 174 (1)), this holding ought likewise to have retroactive
force, i.e., the agreement which had become void would again become
valid. This is an impossibility according to the German legal view
(and the *Bosch* decision argues somewhat analogously when it characterizes as "inadmissible" a situation where agreements wholly void
ab initio could be retroactively validated). Therefore, in our opinion,
the action in the Court does have the effect of staying the decision
in such a case, contrary to the provision of Article 185. It is no valid

argument against this view that the Court has power under Article 186 to order interim measures, since such dispositions also could only retroactively remove the voidness *ab initio* of the agreement, entailed by the denial of exemption; moreover, it cannot be assumed that the Court is to take such action—as it would have to—separately and affirmatively in each individual case.

An action against a decision imposing fines, on the other hand, will probably not have any suspending effect. It is not an immutable principle of the legal order that fines may be collected only on the basis of final decisions. Moreover, here the Court can give effective relief in individual cases by interim measures under Article 186 or by granting a stay of execution under Article 185 of the Treaty. These considerations apply even more strongly to actions against decisions imposing penalties.

¶ 476   The Court may, if it deems it necessary, *stay* the execution or operation of measures ordered by decisions of the Commission (Article 185); it may require the giving of security in that connection. Complementary to this authority is the Court's power to take necessary interim measures (Article 186).

Article 22

SPECIAL PROVISIONS

(1) The Commission shall submit to the Council proposals for making certain categories of agreements, decisions and concerted practices such as are referred to in Article 4, paragraph 2, and Article 5, paragraph 2, subject to the notification provided for in Articles 4 and 5.

(2) Within one year from the entry into force of the present Regulation the Council shall examine, on a proposal of the Commission, any special provisions which could be made in derogation from the provisions contained in this Regulation with respect to the agreements, decisions and concerted practices referred to in Article 4, paragraph 2, and Article 5, paragraph 2.

¶ 477   The *provision* in paragraph (1) directs the Commission to prepare proposals for subjecting to the notification requirements of Articles 4 (1) and 5 (1) of Regulation 17 certain additional categories of agreements, decisions and concerted practices for which Articles 4 (2) and 5 (2) now provide only for optional notification. Article 22 thus aims at a tightening of the present provisions. Here, too, classification into "categories" must be by abstract criteria, similarly to group exemption under Article 85 (3) of the Treaty and to the negative group clearance which we have suggested (see Article 2 of Regulation 17, ¶ 317, supra). The difference between paragraph (1) and paragraph (2), apart from the reference in paragraph (1) to "certain categories," is not quite clear. Evidently the Commission under paragraph (1) may propose only that notification be introduced for some or all of the agreements, etc., which up to now are excluded from notification (Articles 4 (2) and 5 (2) of Regulation 17). Apparently, the Commission is allowed more leeway by paragraph (2), under which it could propose other regulations as well. If that is so, the time period of paragraph (2) would not apply to paragraph (1), a conclusion not precluded by the language of the two paragraphs.

The Commission made no proposals under paragraph (2) within the first year. Rather, it informed the Council in that year that such proposals could not yet be presented since the notification deadline of January 31, 1963, had passed just prior thereto and the materials received in the notifications could not be evaluated in time. Which importance the time period in paragraph (2) still has is an open question. It is certain, however, that the Commission still may submit proposals under paragraph (1) to the Council.

Article 23

TRANSITIONAL RULES FOR EARLIER DECISIONS OF AUTHORITIES OF MEMBER STATES

(1) Agreements, decisions and concerted practices referred to in Article 85, paragraph 1, of the Treaty to which, before the entry into force of this Regulation, the competent authority of a Member State has declared Article 85, paragraph 1, to be inapplicable pursuant to Article 85, paragraph 3, shall not be subject to the notification provided for in Article 5. The decision of the competent authority of the Member State shall be considered a decision within the meaning of Article 6; its validity shall expire at the latest on the date which the said authority has fixed, but may not exceed a duration of three years reckoned from the entry into force of the present Regulation. Article 8, paragraph 3 shall apply.

(2) Applications for renewal of the decisions referred to in paragraph 1 shall be settled by the Commission in accordance with Article 8, paragraph 2.

¶ 478   This was a *transitional provision of minor importance*. It was
designed to vest jurisdiction for exemptions pursuant to Article 85 (3) of the Treaty in the Commission, ultimately in every case (compare also Article 9 (1) of Regulation 17, supra). The

national authorities made little use of the opportunity to grant exemptions; only the Bundeskartellamt issued declarations under Article 85 (3) for five licensing agreements and one cartel agreement. These exemptions lost their validity at the latest on March 13, 1965, or sooner if the BKartA itself had limited them to a shorter period. However, the Commission could have revoked them even earlier if grounds therefor had existed under Article 8 (3) of Regulation 17 (see discussion of that provision, ¶ 391, supra). Applications for renewals of such exemptions had to be made to the Commission, which could grant them if it was shown that the conditions for exemption continued to exist (Article 8 (2)).

Article 23 applies only to those proceedings that resulted in an exemption. Article 9 of Regulation 17 applies to proceedings that are still pending before the national authorities. Under the latter provision, these authorities may still apply Articles 85 (1) and 86 so long as the Commission has instituted no proceeding; however, they may no longer grant exemptions.

Article 24

IMPLEMENTING PROVISIONS

The Commission shall have authority to lay down implementing provisions concerning the form, content and other details of applications submitted pursuant to Articles 2 and 3 and of the notification provided for in Articles 4 and 5, and to lay down those concerning the hearings provided for in Article 19, paragraphs 1 and 2.

The present Regulation shall be binding in every respect and directly applicable in each Member State.

¶ 479   The first implementing provisions are contained in Regulation 27 (OffJour No. 35/62 of May 10, 1962, p. 1118), with details governing form and procedure of notification. See ¶ 501 ff., infra.

The other two regulations issued by the Commission under its implementing authority are also of importance:

In Regulation 153 of December 21, 1962 (OffJour No. 139, December 24, 1962, p. 2918), the Commission supplemented Article 4 of Regulation 27 by easing the notification requirements for certain exclusive distributorship agreements.

July 25, 1963, the Commission issued Regulation 99 (OffJour No. 127, August 20, 1963, p. 2268), the so-called Hearings Regulation (*Anhörungsverordnung*), which provides for details of the proceeding regarding cartel matters before the Commission and assures the interested parties of the proper legal hearing.

Regulation 27
First Regulation
Implementing Regulation 17*

Article 1
RIGHT TO FILE APPLICATIONS AND NOTIFICATIONS

(1) An application pursuant to Article 2 and a notification pursuant to Articles 4 and 5 of Regulation 17 may be filed by any enterprise which is a party to agreements, decisions or practices specified in Article 85 or 86 of the Treaty. If only some of the enterprises involved file the application or the notification, they shall inform the other enterprises involved.

(2) Where representatives of enterprises, associations of enterprises, or legal or natural persons sign the applications and notifications provided for in Articles 2, 3, paragraphs 1 and 2b, and in Articles 4 and 5 of Regulation 17, they must furnish written evidence of their authority.

(3) In case of group applications or notifications a common representative shall be designated.

¶ 501   Paragraph 1 of this article makes clear that each individual enterprise which is a party to an agreement, decision or concerted practice may file a notification for itself, even if the other enterprises fail to do so and even if they object to notification. However, if the Commission grants an exemption pursuant to Article 85 (3) of the Treaty upon *notification by a single party,* the exemption will be effective also for or against the parties who have not given or joined in the notification. With the exemption, the agreement, etc., acquires legal validity in its entirety. An exception exists only where the transitional provisions of Article 7 (1) of Regulation 17 are applied. There, subsequent legalization in case of "active reform" does not operate in favor of or against parties who have not expressly assented to the notification (see discussion of Article 7 (1), supra).

¶ 502   Article 1 (1) leaves open the form in which the enterprise filing the notification or application is to inform the other parties to the agreement. Therefore, an *informal communication will be sufficient.* However, the Commission must be told in what manner the

* Issued by the Commission. Dated   1118. CCH translation, CMR ¶ 2651
May 10, 1962, OffJour No. 35/62, p.   et seq.

other parties have been informed (see Item I 2 in Form A/B). If
the application or notification blanks disclose how they were informed, the Commission will let the matter rest. If not, the Commission will demand the supplementary information. If, contrary
to what he has told the Commission, the notifying party has not
informed the other parties, Community law provides for no sanctions.
Regardless of claims that these other parties may have against the
notifying party, the Commission has a moral obligation to provide
them with information upon request. Otherwise, the purpose of the
provision would be thwarted.

As indicated in the preamble to Regulation 27, the giving of notice to the other parties is to afford them an opportunity of protecting
their interests in the matter. Thus, no party to the agreement should
initiate a proceeding without his partners being notified at once.

¶ 503   Notice to the other parties is unnecessary if the notified
          agreement is a *standard contract* (see Items I 2 and II 1 (b) in
Form A/B). Here, a requirement to inform the other parties would frequently entail a disproportionate expenditure of time and money for
the party filing the notification or application; e.g., in the case of
export prohibitions imposed upon the customers of an enterprise, notice to hundreds of thousands of customers might be necessary. However, the parties to the individual agreements represented by the
standard contract may state their positions to the Commission (Article 19 (1) of Regulation 17).

¶ 504   The two remaining paragraphs of Article 1 contain routine
          requirements. A simple power of attorney suffices as *proof
of representative authority;* in contrast to Section 9 (5) of the GWB, it
need not be certified by a public official. The proof of authority to
represent is necessary, in our opinion, only for representatives appointed by private agreement, not for those receiving their powers
by operation of law (statutory representatives). Thus, when the
statutory representative of a legal person notifies the Commission,
he need not prove his authority by extracts from the Commercial or
Association Register. The reason for this is that the statutory representative must be designated in Item I 1 of the notification form
anyway. Incorrect or misleading information there is subject to the
fines of Article 15 (1) of Regulation 17, so that the designation in
the form has the same practical effect as proof of authority.

Paragraph (3) is designed to simplify the administrative procedure, but it is not mandatory. This provision is reminiscent of the
cartel representative (person to be appointed by each cartel to repre-

sent it before the cartel authority and reviewing courts) under Section 36 of the GWB, an institution which has worked well in practice, from the point of view of the public authorities as well as of the private interests involved.

Article 2

FILING OF APPLICATIONS AND NOTIFICATIONS

(1) The applications and notifications as well as their annexes shall be filed with the Commission in seven copies.

(2) Annexed documents shall be filed in the original or in copy. Where a copy is filed its conformity to the original must be certified.

(3) The applications and notifications must be worded in one of the official languages of the Community. Documents must be filed in their original language. If the original language is not one of the official languages, a translation into one of the official languages must be attached.

¶ 505   *Documents* that must be submitted as exhibits to an application for negative clearance or a notification include, of course, primarily any written agreements or decisions involved. They must as a rule be submitted in their entirety and not merely in the form of excerpts. An exception is made only for license agreements (see Article 4 (2)(ii)(b) of Regulation 17), where descriptions of technical manufacturing processes may be left out (Item II 1 (c) of Form A/B). Parts of an agreement that must be kept secret due to public law reasons, e.g., because of military secrets, may also be omitted (compare also Article 223 (1) (b) of the Treaty).

¶ 506   No particular form is prescribed for the certification of conformity of a copy to the original. Thus, the certificate of a lawyer, or even of the notifying party himself, will suffice.

¶ 507   No certification is necessary for translations required by Article 2 (3).

¶ 508   One of the prescribed seven copies of the application or notification goes to the competent national authorities of each member state, a practice that may cause some apprehension notwithstanding the obligation of secrecy imposed by Article 20 (2) of Regulation 17 also upon the national authorities and their employees, especially since there are no penalties for violations.

Article 3

EFFECTIVE DATE OF APPLICATIONS AND NOTIFICATIONS

The application or the notification shall take effect at the time when it is received by the Commission. However, where the application or the notification is sent by registered mail, it shall take effect at the time indicated by the postmark of the place of mailing.

¶ 509   This provision has some substantive importance with regard to observance of the time limitations in Articles 5 (1) and 7 (2) of Regulation 17 (see discussion under Article 5 (1), ¶ 364, supra). It probably should find analogous application to questions of observance of time periods fixed by the Commission, e.g., under Article 8 (1) or 11 (5) of Regulation 17.

Article 4

CONTENTS OF APPLICATIONS AND NOTIFICATIONS

(1) The applications referred to in Article 2 of Regulation 17, implementing Article 85, paragraph 1, of the Treaty, and the notifications referred to in Article 4 or Article 5, paragraph 2, of Regulation No. 17, must be made on Form A/B, which is reproduced as an annex.

(2) The applications and notifications must contain the information called for on Form A/B.

(3) Several participating enterprises may make an application or a notification on a single form.

(4) The applications referred to in Article 2 of Regulation 17, implementing Article 86 of the Treaty, must give full details. They must state in particular the practice involved and the position occupied by the enterprise or enterprises on the Common Market or on a substantial part thereof for the product or service to which the practice refers.

¶ 511   This provision *requires the use of Form A/B.* If an application for negative clearance or a notification is submitted in another form, it is, by implication from Article 5 of Regulation 27, out of order and therefore without effect.

¶ 512   *Form A/B* is prescribed for *applications for negative clearance* pursuant to Article 2 of Regulation 17 and for *applications for exemption* pursuant to Article 85 (3) of the Treaty. If both a negative clearance and, perhaps as a secondary alternative, an exemption are sought for an agreement, Form A/B may be used. Item IV in this form enables the applicant to give the reasons for which he feels the agreement does not fall under Article 85 (1). If he does this and makes the statements necessary for Items I-III, he has done everything required by the form. If negative clearance and exemption are applied for, the Commission is not obliged to examine first whether it can give a negative clearance. It would be at liberty to do just the opposite—process the application for exemption first, and then grant a negative clearance if it finds that Article 85 (1) does not apply. The Commission indicated at one time that it would regard the notification, i.e., application for exemption, as filed only subsidiarily, and would investigate it only if the negative clearance were refused; but this statement in the provisional form of the Guide Lines was not adopted in their final form.

¶ 513   The *facts* must be presented completely and accurately. For information which is wilfully or negligently false or misleading, fines of from $100 to $5,000 may be imposed (Article 15 (1) (a) of Regulation 17).

¶ 514   No detailed reasons, indeed, *no reasons* at all beyond what is called for in the form, *need be given* in support of an application for negative clearance or exemption. A statement of reasons *in extenso* is not necessary under Regulation 17, so that it is not required but merely contemplated as possible in Form A/B. A complete statement of supporting grounds will, however, tend to shorten the proceeding. Supplying them at a later time is also possible (see Item VI of the form, and see discussion under Article 19 of Regulation 17, ¶ 462, supra).

¶ 515   *Form A/B* (for English translation of the form, see CMR ¶ 2659) :

Under *Item I*, complete information is to be given regarding the participants; under *Item II*, information regarding the agreement, decision or concerted practice involved.

¶ 516   *Item II 1 (b)* contains a definition of *"standard contract."* In spite of its wording ("which the *applicant* concludes regularly . . ."), it need not be understood to mean that negative clearance or exemption for a standard contract may be applied for only by the contracting enterprise itself and not, e.g., by an authorized agent. The definition merely seems to take it for granted that the contracting party will normally also be the applicant, but its wording was not meant to exclude situations where such identity is lacking.

Agreements following a standard contract, e.g., a manufacturer's contract with a number of dealers, may be filed for negative clearance or exemption also by enterprises with whom they are concluded, e.g., the dealers. However, since the latter do not themselves conclude standard contracts with other parties, they cannot make application for clearance or give notification of such individual agreements as if they were standard contracts, but must do so in the regular manner, separately for each agreement. Thus, they must inform the other party of the application or notification.

¶ 517   *Item III* calls for a *description of specific provisions in restraint of competition.* It will be sufficient compliance with this requirement if the substance of these provisions is set forth in summary form and reference is made for the rest to the text of the agreement, etc., provided that the latter is in writing. Word-for-word copying of these provisions is not necessary and would be sheer formalism, in our view. On the other hand, if the agreement, etc., in question has not been reduced to a writing, the specific restrictions on competition must be set forth as accurately and comprehensively as possible.

¶ 518   *Item IV* of the form provides for a statement of why the applicant or notifying party believes that the agreement, etc., does not fall within Article 85 (1) of the Treaty. This is a matter of course as far as applications for negative clearance are concerned, but it may seem somewhat surprising for an application for exemption. The form, however, excludes an admission, which might otherwise be implied, that the agreement, etc., in question violates Article 85 (1). The Commission, too, does not regard use of the form as an admission that Article 85 (1) is applicable in the first instance.

¶ 519   *Item V* calls for grounds in support of the application for exemption pursuant to Article 85 (3). Even though Articles 4 (1) and 5 (1) of Regulation 17 speak only of notification, this item in the form shows that notification operates in substance also as an application for exemption. Although not required in the application (see ¶ 514, *supra*), it may be advisable to include supporting reasons *in extenso.* Otherwise, the Commission might, on the basis of a preliminary examination, reach the conclusion that Article 85 (1) applies and that, at the same time, the conditions for an exemption are not fulfilled. If the Commission then informs the parties of this, any further action under the agreement, etc., is subject to fine (Article

15 (2) (a) and (6) of Regulation 17). The Commission also warns against letting this situation arise.

¶ 520   An *acknowledgment of receipt* by the Commission is a part of the procedure. At the latest with this acknowledgment, the Commission will have "initiated" a proceeding within the meaning of Article 9 (3) of Regulation 17 (see discussion there, especially ¶ 414). In the acknowledgment, the Commission will give the file number assigned to the matter.

Article 5

TRANSITIONAL PROVISIONS

(1) The applications and notifications filed prior to the coming into force of this regulation without use of the forms are deemed to be sufficient for purposes of Article 4 of this regulation.

(2) The Commission may request that a form duly filled out be filed with it within a period fixed by it. In this case the applications and the notifications are deemed to be in order only if the forms are filed within the set period in accordance with the provisions of this regulation.

¶ 524   These provisions, being only of a transitional nature, have relatively little importance. With regard to observance of time limits fixed under paragraph (2), attention should be paid to Article 3 of Regulation 27, supra.

Article 6

EFFECTIVE DATE

This regulation shall enter into force the day after its publication in the *Official Journal of the European Communities.*

This regulation is binding in all its parts and directly applicable in each Member State.

¶ 525   Regulation 27 became effective on May 11, 1962.

Regulation 26
Application of Rules of Competition
to Agricultural Products*

Article 1
RULES OF COMPETITION APPLICABLE IN GENERAL

From the coming into force of this regulation, Treaty Articles 85 to 90, inclusive, as well as the provisions made for their application, shall apply to all the agreements, decisions and practices referred to in Article 85 (1), and in Article 86 of the Treaty and relating to the production of and trade in products enumerated in Annex II of the Treaty, subject to the provisions of Article 2.

I. General Observations

¶ 531　　Until the middle of 1962, Articles 85 ff. of the Treaty were not applicable to agricultural products (Article 42 of the Treaty). Since July 1, 1962, however, the "rules of competition" of the Treaty have been extended to include these products also. This is the substance of Regulation 26 of April 4, 1962. The products covered are listed exhaustively in Annex II of the Treaty (English translation in CMR ¶ 995). They include, among other things, live animals, meat, milk, vegetables, fruits, cereals, products of the milling industry, margarine, sugar, tobacco, and wine.

Regulation 26 has not been altered by the numerous regulations in the agricultural sector, except for Regulation 159/66[1] which gave a special interpretation of "organization of producers" with regard to its purpose and the duties imposed on it.

II. Basic Principle of the New Regime

¶ 532　　Since July 1, 1962, Articles 85-90 of the Treaty and the implementing regulations thereunder have been applicable to agreements, decisions and concerted practices which concern the production of, or the trade in, agricultural products.

¶ 533　　Thus, for these products also, there is now prohibited any cooperative action in restraint of competition which is apt

---

* Issued by the Council. Dated April 4, 1962, OffJour No. 30/62, p. 993. CCH translation, CMR ¶ 915 et seq.

[1] OffJour No. 192 (October 27, 1966) p. 3287; CMR ¶ 586.

adversely to affect trade between member states and which has as its purpose or effect the prevention, restriction or distortion of competition within the Common Market (Article 85 (1)).

Likewise prohibited is the abuse of a dominant position in the Common Market or a substantial part thereof, to the extent to which such abuse may adversely affect trade between member states (Article 86).

¶ 534   The provisions of the implementing regulations under Articles 85-90, i.e., Regulations 17, 153, 99/63, and 27, now govern the application of Articles 85 and 86 to agricultural products also.

Regulation 17 distinguishes between "old" and "new" cartels;[1a] the critical date is March 13, 1962. This date is of no consequence for Regulation 26 since until July 30, 1962, cooperative action concerning production of and trade in agricultural products was permitted without limitations. It was clearly so provided in Article 42 of the Treaty, which reserved to the Council the power to determine when and to what extent the cartel provisions should become applicable to such products. This was done only through Regulation 26. Thus, as far as it is concerned, the critical date is July 30, 1962. Whatever took place prior to that date is "old", whatever after, "new." "Old" cooperative action requiring notification must therefore have been notified by either October 31, 1962, or January 31, 1963.

Article 2

EXCEPTIONS

(1) Article 85 (1) of the Treaty shall not apply to the agreements, decisions and practices referred to in the preceding Article which are an integral part of a domestic organization of the market or which are necessary for the fulfillment of the objectives set forth in Article 39 of the Treaty. In particular, it shall not apply to the agreements, decisions and practices of farmers, farmers' associations or unions of farmers' associations under the jurisdiction of one Member State only, insofar as they affect the production or sale of agricultural products or the use of common installations for storage, treatment or processing of agricultural products, without entailing the obligation of charging a certain price, unless the Commission finds that competition is thus being excluded or that the objectives of Treaty Article 39 are being endangered.

(2) After having consulted the Member States and heard the enterprises or associations of enterprises concerned, as well as any other individual or corporation which it considers neces-

[1a] See Articles 5 and 4 of Regulation 17.

sary to hear, the Commission, subject to the control of the Court of Justice, shall have the exclusive authority to determine by a published decision which of the agreements, decisions and practices have met the conditions set forth in paragraph (1).

(3) The Commission shall proceed to such verification either as a matter of routine, or at the request of a competent authority of a Member State or of an enterprise or association of enterprises concerned.

(4) The publication shall mention the parties concerned and the main point of the decision; it must take into account the legitimate interests of the enterprises so that their business secrets are not revealed.

I. General Observations

¶ 541   Article 2 provides for certain *exceptions* to the general rule of applicability of Article 85 (1) of the Treaty, laid down by Article 1.

The prohibition of Article 85 .(1) does *not* apply to cooperative restraints which are an "essential part of a national system of marketing" (so translated in preference to the translation, "integral part of a domestic organization of the market," and to the U.K. translation of the almost identical critical term in Article 46 of the Treaty, "national marketing organization"). A *system of marketing backed by the sovereign power of a member state* must be involved, as distinguished from private organizations. It is not necessary, however, that the system be introduced by statute. A "national" system of marketing will also exist, e.g., when, even though agreed upon by producers or producer associations, it has been sanctioned by the member state. "System of marketing" probably means the same as it does under Article 46 of the Treaty (where, however, the term is likewise used without being defined). According to the wording of the provision, the cooperative restraint must be an "essential" part of a national system of marketing; mere connection will therefore not suffice.

¶ 542   The cartel prohibition furthermore does not apply to cooperative restraints which are "necessary for accomplishment of the objectives of Article 39 of the Treaty." Those *objectives* are: Increase of agricultural productivity, fair standard of living for farmers, stabilization of markets in agricultural products, assurance of adequate supplies, and fair prices to the consumer. This leaves a large area for cooperative restraints immune from prohibition, even though they must be *necessary* for the achievement of the named objectives and mere usefulness or aptness will not be sufficient. Permissible restraints thus may include, e.g., agreements on minimum prices (fair standard of living for farmers), but also agreements on maximum prices (fair prices to the consumer). Whether such agreements are "necessary" will have to be answered according to the circumstances of the particular case. The Commission affirmed the permissibility of a minimum price cartel of Dutch sugar-beet growers.

On the other hand, no special legislation applies to the opposite side of the market. If, for instance, manufacturers of cigarettes or sugar wish to join the above-mentioned minimum price cartel of growers it would be possible only through an exemption under Article 85 (3), since the advantages of Regulation 26 are not available to them.

¶ 543   Finally, the cartel prohibition does not apply to cooperative restraints practiced by *farmers, (simple) farmers' associations, and (syndicated or central) associations of the latter in a single member state,* so long as they concern the production or distribution, or the use of common installations for the storage, treatment or processing, of agricultural products, and *do not fix prices to be charged.* While the "in particular" introducing this exception would normally indicate it to be merely illustrative of one or the other of the preceding ones, this is not the case here, and we are dealing with a true third exception independent of the others. This is evident particularly from the renewed reference to Article 39 of the Treaty following it, which would make no sense if affirmative necessity for the objectives of Article 39 would have to exist in the first instance for the exception to apply.

¶ 544   The terms *"farmers," "farmers' associations"* and *"associations of farmers' associations"* are the same as in Section 100 of the GWB and should probably be given the same meaning, with the qualification that the definition of "farmers" in Section 100 (6) of the GWB (establishments which produce or derive certain agricultural products, including also plant nurseries) can be taken over only by analogy (since the definition of agricultural products in Section 100 (5) is not as inclusive as the list in Annex II of the Treaty).

¶ 545   Farmers within the meaning of Article 2 of Regulation 26 thus are establishments which produce or derive the products listed in Annex II of the Treaty. Associations of farmers would include farmers' cooperatives; and associations of farmers' associations would include regional or national organizations of farmers.

¶ 546   Farmers or their associations must not fix prices for agricultural products through cooperative restraints, as far as the exception presently discussed is concerned. On the other hand, an agreement is permissible under which, e.g., certain products may be sold only through a cooperative organization (*common sales agency*), or under which a common installation, e.g., for tobacco curing, must, in the interest of rational utilization, be used by all participants (*compulsory use*), and the like. A common agency may even fix uniform selling prices.

¶ 547   Narrower limits are set to cooperation between associations of farmers' associations, as they must be from a single member state of the EEC. This condition is stated somewhat ambiguously both in the original languages and in the English translation, in that it is not entirely clear whether it qualifies only these syndicated associations or also farmers themselves and their simple associations. The first alternative would seem to recommend itself more strongly, as a matter both of literal construction and of legislative purpose.

¶ 548   Legality of cooperative restraints coming within the general exception is, however, subject to a sub-exception. Such restraints are prohibited and therefore void under Article 85 of the Treaty if competition is thereby excluded *or* if the above-listed objectives of Article 39 of the Treaty are thereby imperiled (endangering one of those objectives probably being sufficient). Under which circumstances the objectives of Article 39 of the Treaty are endangered can be answered only in the individual case, but even then not with certainty. The Commission has an extremely broad area of discretion[2] for its assessment which may be reviewed only by the European Court.

Competition is "excluded" only if it is eliminated entirely (compare Article 85 (3)(b) of the Treaty, ¶ 111, supra—there seems to be no difference of substance between "eliminate" there and "exclude" here, or between their counterparts in the official languages) ; mere restriction or distortion of competition is not enough since this is inherent in every type of restraint within the main exception. Similarly, mere aptness to exclude competition will not suffice.

Whether the conditions for application of the sub-exception are fulfilled is decided by the Commission. Its decision is subject to review by the Court in Luxembourg (Article 173 of the Treaty).

¶ 549   *Abusive exploitation of a dominant position* is prohibited outright, and no exceptions are provided in Regulation 26 to the prohibition of Article 86 of the Treaty. Enterprises dominant in

---

[2] Ditges/Ehle AWD 1963, p. 300 and Deringer, Art. 2, Reg. 26, marg. n. 29 have reservations as to the legality of this provision.

the Common Market or a substantial part thereof will, of course, hardly ever be individual farmers, but rather organizations such as governmental tobacco monopolies or combinations.

II.   Legal Nature of the Exceptions

¶ 550   The formulation of Article 2 (1) differs significantly from that of Article 85 (3) of the Treaty. The latter provision begins with the phrase that the prohibition of Article 85 (1) "may . . . be declared inapplicable." In contrast, Article 2 of Regulation 26 provides that Article 85 (1) "shall not apply . . ." This is not a mere difference in form. Agreements, etc., that may be exempted from the prohibition of Article 85 (1) pursuant to Article 85 (3)—which may, in other words, be permitted—are in principle void in the absence of such a permission, and become valid only with the grant of permission. Not so agreements that come within the exceptions of Article 2 of Regulation 26. To them, the prohibition of Article 85 (1) of the Treaty simply does not apply, i.e., they are valid on the basis of the law itself, so to speak automatically, without any permission from the Commission. Article 2 of Regulation 26 thus grants to certain types of competitive restraints the benefit of a *statutory exception*[3] (as distinguished from an administrative exemption), so that no disposition or decision is necessary in the particular case.

This appears also from the second paragraph of Article 2. Under this provision, it is for the Commission to "determine" whether the conditions of the first paragraph are fulfilled. This, too, shows that the Commission does not grant a permission here, but determines validity under the law.

¶ 551   However, the Commission may apply *Article 85 (3) of the Treaty* to cooperative restraints not excepted by Article 2 of Regulation 26, in other words, it may grant an exemption, provided that the conditions of Article 85 (3) exist. This appears, first of all, from the language of Article 1 of Regulation 26, which makes Articles 85-90 applicable in their entirety, without excluding Article 85 (3). Here, the language is unambiguous. Apart from this admittedly somewhat formalistic argument, applicability of Article 85 (3) is confirmed by the basic principles deductible from the *Bosch* decision of the European Court of April 6, 1962 (see discussion under Article 1 of Regulation 17, ¶ 303 ff., supra). For, the conclusion may be drawn from that decision that an agreement, etc., may not be finally declared prohibited under Article 85 (1) of the Treaty unless the pos-

---

[3] See Gleiss/Hirsch, AWD 1962, p. 160.

sibility of exemption pursuant to paragraph (3) at least *could* be examined first.[4] For this reason, also, Article 1 of Regulation 26 ought to be interpreted as leaving open the possibility of exemptions under Article 85 (3) of the Treaty.

Naturally, negative clearances (Article 2 of Regulation 17) are also possible, e.g., when a price cartel of German tobacco growers is not apt to affect adversely interstate trade to a perceptible degree.

III. Legal Validity of Paragraph (1)

¶ 552   Sentence 2 of Article 2 (1) makes an exception from Article 85 (1) only for decisions, etc., of farmers' associations and associations of farmers' associations. Thus, it applies in effect only to farmers' cooperatives and not to enterprises that merely deal in agricultural products. For this reason, actions were brought in the European Court by French and German food wholesalers to have sentence 2 of Article 2 (1) declared void.[5] The Court rejected the petitions on the grounds that Article 2 (1) of Regulation 26 was a regulation and, as such, an action against its validity could not be instituted by natural and legal persons under Article 173 (2) of the Treaty. Thus, the question of whether Article 2 (1) violates the Treaty by disadvantaging ordinary commercial enterprises as opposed to agricultural cooperatives and is consequently void, is still open.[6]

IV. Jurisdiction

¶ 553   The Commission has *exclusive jurisdiction* to determine whether a cooperative restraint is covered by one or the other exception in Article 2. Paragraph (2) expressly so provides. According to the preamble to Regulation 26 (CMR ¶ 915), this exclusive jurisdiction is designed to prevent failure in the development of a common agricultural policy, to assure certainty in the law, and to prevent discriminatory treatment of the enterprises concerned.

¶ 554   On the other hand, Regulation 26 contains no special provisions regarding jurisdiction to apply Articles 85 ff. to cooperative restraints not covered by an exception. This matter is governed by the provisions of Regulation 17, a conclusion compelled by the reference in Article 1 of Regulation 26 to the regulations implement-

---

[4] Gleiss/Hirsch, BB 1962, pp. 623, 625.

[5] This result reached by, among others: Ditges/Ehle, AWD 1963, p.

300, setting forth some noteworthy reasons.

[6] For the legislative history on this article, see Deringer, Art. 2, Reg. 26, marg. n. 24.

---

ing Articles 85-90 of the Treaty. This means *exclusive jurisdiction of the Commission also for the granting of exemptions* pursuant to Article 85 (3) (see Article 9 (1) of Regulation 17). The authorities of the member states are, however, competent to apply the prohibitions of Articles 85 (1) and 86 of the Treaty, so long as the Commission has not initiated a proceeding under Article 2 (negative clearance), Article 3 (ending of violations) or Article 6 (exemption) of Regulation 17 (see Article 9 (3) of Regulation 17 and discussion there).

The jurisdiction of the national authorities has little, if any, practical significance. Among other things, they may apply Article 85 (1) of the Treaty only in a proceeding pending under the national cartel law anyway, and not spontaneously. Since the national authorities, moreover, may not determine under Regulation 26 whether an agreement, etc., is within the exceptions there provided, their jurisdiction means even less here than in non-agricultural cases, as this determination must regularly be made before considering the application of Article 85 (1) or 86.

If the participants invoke the statutory exception of Article 2 (1) in a proceeding before a national authority or a national court, the court or authority must stay its proceeding due to the exclusive jurisdiction of the Commission.

V. Procedure

¶ 555   Procedural details are supplied by Regulation 26 only for the determination of whether an agreement, etc., comes within the exceptions of Article 2 (1). The Commission may make this determination either on its own motion or upon application (Article 2 (3)). Entitled to apply are competent authorities of the member states and the enterprises or associations of enterprises concerned. These parties need not all join in the application; even a single one may file it. Before making the determination, the Commission must hear the member states and the parties (Article 2 (2)). Whether all EEC member states or only those concerned by the agreement, etc., must be consulted cannot be answered definitely from the text of this provision. We assume, according to its letter, that *all* of the member states are meant.

¶ 556   Further, the Commission *may* hear any other person or legal entity if it deems it necessary.

¶ 557   The *decision* of the Commission is to be *published*. Parties and substance of the decision must be given; the Commission must, however, in this connection also respect the justified interests of the parties in the protection of their business secrets (see above, ¶ 465).

As far as the text of Article 2 (2) goes, only affirmative determinations that an exception is satisfied must, or at least need be, published; not, however, negative decisions denying applications for such a determination. This interpretation appears reasonable, too, because the general public naturally has a particular interest in learning which cartels do lawfully exist. A similar provision for publication is contained in Article 19 (3) of Regulation 17, which notably deals only with publication of applications. According to its language, however, publication even of negative decisions is not totally precluded.

Article 3

DUMPING PRACTICES

(1) Without prejudice to the provisions of Article 46, Article 91 (1) of the Treaty shall apply to trade in the products enumerated in Annex II of the Treaty.

(2) Taking into account the provisions of the Treaty regarding agriculture and, in particular, those of Article 39, the Commission shall appraise all the causes which are at the root of indictable practices, particularly the price level at which imports from other sources have been made into the market under consideration. Pursuant to such appraisal, it shall send recommendations and authorize the protective measures referred to in Article 91 (1) of the Treaty.

¶ 558   This is a declaration that Article 91 (1) of the Treaty is applicable to trade in agricultural products. Pursuant to that provision, the Commission, if it finds *dumping practices* to exist in the Common Market on the part of member states or enterprises, is to make recommendations to the party engaged in such practices, designed to put an end to them. If its recommendations are not heeded, the Commission is to empower the adversely affected member state to take protective measures designated in detail by the Commission. Under Article 3 (2) of Regulation 26, the Commission may issue such recommendations and authorize such protective measures only after appraising all the causes of the dumping and after taking account of the provisions of Article 39 of the Treaty regarding the common agricultural policy. In addition, Article 46 of the Treaty remains fully applicable, i.e., the member states may impose equalizing duties against imports from other EEC countries with a national system of marketing.

¶ 558

Article 4

SUBSIDIES

The provisions of Article 93 (1) and (3), first sentence, of the Treaty shall apply to subsidies granted in favor of the production of or trade in products enumerated in Annex II of the Treaty.

¶ 559   This makes Article 93 (1) and (3), first sentence, of the Treaty applicable to the production of or trade in agricultural products. This means that the Commission, in cooperation with the member states, is to examine existing systems of granting subsidies, and further, that the Commission is to be informed of future introduction or modifications of such systems in time to be able to submit its comments thereon.

Article 5

EFFECTIVE DATE

This regulation shall come into force on the day following its publication in the *Official Journal of the European Communities*, except the provisions of Articles 1 to 3, inclusive, which shall come into force on July 30, 1962.

This regulation shall be binding in all its parts and immediately applicable in all member states.

¶ 560   Article 4 became effective on April 21, 1962.

Regulation 19/65
Application of Article 85, Paragraph 3, of the Treaty to Groups of Agreements and Concerted Practices*

Article 1

TYPES OF AGREEMENTS SUBJECT TO GROUP EXEMPTION

(1) Without prejudice to the application of Council Regulation 17, the Commission may, through a regulation and in accordance with Article 85, paragraph 3, of the Treaty, declare that Article 85, paragraph 1, is not applicable to groups of agreements, in which only two enterprises take part and

(a) —under which one enterprise agrees in respect of the other to deliver certain products to the latter only, for resale in a specified part of the territory of the Common Market, or

—under which one enterprise agrees in respect of the other to purchase certain products from the latter only, for the purpose of resale, or

—under which exclusive agreements with regard to delivery and purchase as described in the two preceding subparagraphs have been concluded, for the purpose of resale, and

(b) that include restrictions imposed in connection with the acquisition or use of industrial protective rights—particularly patents, utility models, designs and models, or trademarks—or with rights flowing from contracts assigning or licensing manufacturing processes or know-how relating to the use and application of industrial techniques.

(2) The regulation must include a definition of the groups of agreements to which it applies and specify, in particular:

(a) what restrictions or clauses may not appear in the agreements;

(b) what clauses must appear in the agreements or what other conditions must be fulfilled.

(3) Paragraphs 1 and 2 shall apply by analogy to groups of concerted practices in which only two enterprises take part.

¶ 601   Article 1 (1) authorizes the Commission to issue group exemptions under Article 85 (3) for certain types of agreements.

* Issued by the Council. Dated March 1965, p. 533. CCH translation, CMR 2, 1965, OffJour No. 36, March 6, ¶ 2717 et seq.

The Commission earlier felt that it was competent to issue group exemptions directly. In two communications on the application of Article 85 of the EEC Treaty to certain exclusive distributorship agreements and patent licensing agreements,[1] it announced its intention to issue group exemptions for these agreements which at first were to be limited to three years. According to Article 19 (3) of Regulation 17, it invited interested parties to submit their comments within a period of one month. The Commission's plan, however, ran into political objections in the Council of Ministers. The announced group exemptions, therefore, were not issued.

The Commission then sought general authorization by the Council of Ministers. It submitted a draft regulation on the subject to the Council.[2] The Parliament and the Economic and Social Committee, which were heard by the Council, in essence agreed to the regulation.[3] The Council nevertheless hesitated to issue the regulation. After lengthy deliberations in the Council's committee of experts, this limited authorization finally remained.

The Italian Government brought suit against the Council of Ministers before the European Court of Justice, requesting that Regulation 19/65 be declared null and void. The Court in a decision of July 13, 1966,[4] rejected the suit.

¶ 602   The Commission, under Regulation 19/65, may, through a regulation, issue group exemptions for certain exclusive dealing and licensing agreements in which only two enterprises take part, namely:

agreements imposing exclusive supply or purchase obligations or both;[5]

agreements including restrictions in connection with the acquisition or use of industrial protective rights (for example, patents, registered designs, design patents, trademarks), of manufacturing processes or of know-how relating to the application of industrial techniques.

¶ 603   The agreements imposing exclusive supply and/or purchase obligations are the same as those that could be notified on a simplified form under Regulation 153.[6]

---

[1] OffJour No. 113, November 9, 1962, p. 2628 and 2629; CMR ¶ 2711.
[2] Document VI/KOM (64) 62 (final); for the text see OffJour No. 197, November 30, 1964, page 3319.
[3] Parliament: OffJour No. 81, May 27, 1964, p. 1275; Economic and Social Committee: OffJour No. 197, November 30, 1964, p. 3318, particularly 3320 f.

[4] Recueil Vol. XII-4, p. 563; CMR ¶ 8048.
[5] The Commission has meanwhile exempted certain groups of exclusive dealing agreements in Regulation 67/67 of March 22, 1967 (OffJour No. 57, March 25, 1967, p. 849 f.; CMR ¶ 2727).
[6] OffJour No. 139, December 24, 1962, p. 2918.

¶ 604   The regulation does not set forth in detail which restrictions in licensing agreements may be exempted by the Commission. The limits are drawn both by the scope of application of Article 85 (1) and by the conditions of Article 85 (3).

The only restrictions involved, therefore, are those going beyond the protective right or the legally unprotected process.[7] Hence, the conditions of Article 85 (1) must always be met first, then the conditions of Article 85 (3). In case of a group exemption it is obviously impossible to determine concretely in the individual case that these conditions are fulfilled; an abstract, general determination only can be made. Regarding paragraph 3 it is sufficient, therefore, if the fulfillment of its conditions is guaranteed as much as possible.[8]

For the most part, the following restrictions, in particular, could be involved:

restrictions which the Commission listed in the Official Notice Concerning Patent Licensing Agreements[9] and which, in its opinion, are no longer covered by the protective right, namely

the obligation to affix patent information on the product;

obligations of the licensee concerning the quality of product or sources of supply, insofar and so long as they are indispensable in the interest of technically unobjectionable exploitation of the invention;

obligations to exchange know-how and grant licenses on improvements or on new uses; these, however, are permissible obligations of the licensee only if they are not exclusive and if the licensor has assumed similar obligations;

obligations of the licensor not to authorize any other person to utilize the invention and/or not to use the invention himself (exclusive license);

furthermore, corresponding restrictions in agreements concerning other protective rights as well as manufacturing processes and industrial techniques that do not need to be secret.

With regard to these restrictions in patent licensing agreements the Commission assumed that they did not restrain competition deserving of protection or, considering the present situation, were not apt to affect adversely trade between member states. Since the Commission limited its Official Notice on Patent Licensing Agreements,

---

[7] See ¶ 49, supra.
[8] See ¶ 86, supra.
[9] OffJour No. 139, December 24, 1962, p. 2922 (CMR ¶ 2698); the Commission, in the reasons to its draft regulation—Document VI/KOM (64) 62 (final), p. 2—stated that it was considering group exemptions primarily for these restrictions.

and the courts, in any event, are not bound by this declaration, a group exemption here seems to us to be desirable in the interest of legal security.

Moreover, in our opinion, price agreements, certain restrictions on distribution, and other obligations of the licensee, e.g., agreements not to compete, can and should be exempted through group exemptions. No reasonably germane restriction is of a nature that could prevent it from being included in a group exemption. This is also true for restrictions of the licensor. Under Article 1 (1) it is necessary only that the restrictions be imposed in connection with acquisition or use, etc. Any restriction can fulfill this requirement. According to the regulation the connection also does not need to be close. The following are examples: price-maintenance duty for the licensor; the duty to inform the licensor of improvements; restrictions extending beyond the duration of the licensed right.

¶ 605   Article 1 (2) sets forth details of the regulations to be issued to enable the Commission to grant group exemptions. These regulations must indicate what clauses may not be contained in the agreements, what clauses must appear, and/or what other conditions must be fulfilled. Thus, they make it easier for the interested parties to determine whether they can make use of the group exemption.

Article 1 (3) makes it clear that the Commission may also grant group exemptions for concerted practices.

In the future the Commission might be empowered by the Council to grant further group exemptions for certain kinds of cooperation (standards and types, research and development, specialization, joint purchase and sale); cf. ¶ 360, supra.

Article 2

AMENDMENT OR REPEAL OF REGULATIONS

(1) A regulation adopted pursuant to Article 1 shall be issued for a limited period of time.

(2) It may be repealed or modified where the situation has changed with respect to a factor essential in its adoption. In such case, provision shall be made for a period of adjustment for the agreements and concerted practices covered by the earlier regulation.

¶ 606   Article 2 corresponds to the provision on individual exemptions,[10] except for certain deviations which the subject re-

---

[10] Article 8, Regulation 17.

quires. The Commission may issue the group exemption for a limited period of time only, but can renew it as often as it desires. This possibility was provided in drafts and was struck out. This, however, does not alter the fact that the very nature of the matter indicates that renewal must be possible.

If the situation essential for the group exemption has changed, the Commission may *ex nunc* repeal or modify the exemption. It must grant the parties concerned a period of adjustment.

Article 3

RETROACTIVE EFFECT OF REGULATIONS

A regulation adopted pursuant to Article 1 may apply retroactively to agreements and concerted practices which, at the time it comes into force, could have benefitted by a decision having retroactive effect pursuant to Article 6 of Regulation No. 17.

¶ 607   Group exemptions in principle become effective at the time the Commission regulation granting them takes effect or at the time indicated in the regulation.

They can, if the conditions are fulfilled, apply retroactively to the date from which the Commission could have issued an individual exemption (under Article 6 of Regulation 17).

All agreements requiring notification which were notified to the Commission are included here. The exemption for these agreements may be issued any time after the notification. In the case of so-called old cartels which had to be notified and were notified on time, the exemption may even be retroactive to the date the agreement was concluded, at the earliest to January 1, 1958.

The group exemption for agreements not requiring notification may be retroactive to the date the agreements, etc., were concluded, at the earliest to January 1, 1958.

Agreements requiring notification that were not notified on time may not be exempted retroactively.

This is, of course, also true for concerted practices.

Article 4

EXEMPTION OF OLD AGREEMENTS

(1) A regulation adopted pursuant to Article 1 may provide that the prohibition laid down by Article 85, paragraph 1, of the Treaty shall not apply, for a period of time which it shall fix, to

agreements and concerted practices in existence on March 13, 1962, that do not fulfill the conditions of Article 85, paragraph 3:

—if, within three months from the date the regulation comes into force, they are modified so as to meet such conditions in accordance with the provisions of the regulation, and

—if the modifications are made known to the Commission within the time limit fixed by the regulation.

(2) Paragraph 1 shall not apply to agreements and concerted practices that were to be notified before February 1, 1963, pursuant to Article 5 of Regulation No. 17, unless they were notified before that date.

(3) It shall not be possible to invoke the provisions adopted by virtue of paragraph 1 in actions pending on the date a regulation issued pursuant to Article 1 comes into force, or to invoke them as a basis for a claim for damages against third parties.

¶ 608   Article 4, corresponding to Article 7 of Regulation 17, contains a transitional regulation. Agreements in existence on March 13, 1962, that do not fulfill the conditions of Article 85 (3) of the EEC Treaty can be exempted with retroactive effect if, according to the regulation to be issued, they are modified to meet such conditions within three months from the date the regulation comes into force, and if the Commission is informed of the modifications within a certain period of time. The Commission determines the scope of the exemption. If the agreements were to be notified under Article 5 of Regulation 17, a retroactive exemption is possible only if notification was given within the time limit provided.

Agreements concluded after March 13, 1962, or not notified on time cannot be exempted with retroactive effect. The group exemption applies to them only after they have been modified to meet the necessary conditions.

The effect of this transitional regulation is slight. Litigation pending on the date the group exemption takes effect is not, according to Article 4 (3), affected by the retroactive exemption. Claims for damages against third parties may not be based on the exemption for the time preceding modification to meet the necessary conditions. For example, a claim for damages may not be brought against a third person who earlier induced a party to breach an agreement that was not yet exempted. Claims of the partners against each other as well as third persons, in contrast, are extinguished as a result of the retroactive group exemptions. They can protect themselves against this effect only by bringing suit at the proper time.

Article 5

THIRD-PARTY COMMENTS

Before issuing a regulation, the Commission shall publish a draft of that regulation, inviting any interested parties to submit their observations within a time-limit which it shall fix and which shall not be less than one month.

¶ 609   The provision corresponds to Article 19 (3) of Regulation 17. It is intended to help preserve the rights of interested parties. The Commission must publish its draft before it issues group exemptions. The interested parties then have an opportunity to submit their comments within a certain period of time. The concept "interested parties" does not mean much, since anyone can express his opinion. The Commission will evaluate the importance of the comments. The decisive factor is that Article 5 does not entail a right to be heard. The Commission need not, therefore, decide on the comments. They are merely suggestions.

The Regulation Concerning Hearings (Regulation 99/63), in our opinion, does not apply here. This regulation refers to Article 19 of Regulation 17 and governs the procedure which that article provides. Article 19, however, prescribes hearings prior to decisions, not regulations. This distinction (see Article 189 of the EEC Treaty) is so important that direct and even analogous application of the Regulation Concerning Hearings is precluded, apart from the fact that its application would also lead to practical difficulties that could not be solved.

Article 6

CONSULTATION OF COMMITTEE ON CARTELS AND MONOPOLIES

(1) The Commission shall consult the Consultative Committee on Cartels and Monopolies:

(a) before publishing the draft of a regulation,

(b) before issuing a regulation.

(2) Article 10, paragraphs 5 and 6, of Regulation No. 17, relating to the consultation of the Consultative Committee, shall apply by analogy, it being understood that the joint meetings with the Commission shall take place no sooner than one month after the letter calling the meeting has been sent.

¶ 609

¶ 610   This provision prescribes a double hearing of the Consultative Committee on Cartels and Monopolies,[11] thereby ensur-
ing a particularly close connection between the committee and the
Commission. This may lead to a thorough examination of all aspects
but will also cause a delay. This provision might be based on the
Council's efforts not to allow the Commission too much latitude.

Article 7

WITHDRAWAL OF EXEMPTION

If the Commission finds, on its own motion or upon request
of a Member State or of natural and legal persons or associations
of persons showing a legitimate interest, that in a specific case
agreements or concerted practices defined by a regulation adopted
pursuant to Article 1 nevertheless have certain effects that are
incompatible with the conditions set forth in Article 85, paragraph 3, of the Treaty, it may, while withdrawing the benefit of
that regulation, take a decision pursuant to Articles 6 and 8 of
Regulation 17, without the requirements of the notification provided for under Article 4, paragraph 1, of Regulation 17.

¶ 611   The group exemption is naturally granted in general; the
Commission cannot guarantee in each individual case that
the conditions of Article 85 (3) are fulfilled. Article 7, therefore, authorizes the Commission, on its own motion or upon request, to
withdraw the benefits of the group exemption for an agreement and
to decide on such agreement as an individual case. In particular, it
may subject the individual exemption to certain conditions or stipulations. In this connection, it proceeds under Articles 6 and 8 of Regulation 17. Notification of the agreement under Article 4 of Regulation
17 is not required for this procedure.

Member states as well as natural and legal persons or associations of persons may ask the Commission to withdraw the exemption.
As the comparison with Article 19, Regulation 17, indicates, these
persons are outsiders who are not parties to the agreement, etc. They
must, therefore, in contrast to the member states, have and prove a
legitimate interest.[12] Otherwise they do not have a right to request
the Commission to withdraw the exemption and also cannot enforce
their request before the Court of Justice.[13] The Commission can,
however, also proceed on its own motion in these cases. If, in contrast, a legitimate interest is shown and the Commission denies the

---

[11] See Article 10(4) to (6), Regulation 17.
[12] See also Article 3, Regulation 17.

[13] See also the commentary to Article
3, Regulation 17.

request, this, in our opinion, is a decision that may be contested before the Court of Justice. The same is true if the Commission fails to act on the request.

Article 8

AMENDMENT

Before January 1, 1970, the Commission shall submit to the Council a proposal for a regulation amending this regulation through such modifications as appear necessary in the light of experience acquired.

This regulation is binding in all its parts and directly applicable in each Member State.

¶ 612   The Commission must first acquire experience and examine whether the authorization in this regulation is practicable and sufficient or whether and which modifications are necessary. It should, if necessary, have proposed such modifications to the Council prior to January 1, 1970, but did not do so. It is desirable that the Council authorize the Commission to issue further group exemptions. For the Commission's drafts, see ¶ 360, supra.

Regulation 67/67
Application of Article 85, Paragraph 3, of the Treaty to Exclusive Dealing Agreements*

¶ 701   Regulation 67/67 was issued by the Commission on the basis of Articles 85 and 155 of the Treaty. According to Regulation 19/65, Article 1, the Commission may declare the prohibition in Article 85 (1) to be inapplicable to certain groups of agreements, i.e., those containing exclusive supply or purchase obligations (in short, exclusive dealing agreements or clauses). Regulation 67/67 grants the first general exemption to this group of contracts. Prior to this regulation, the European Court had, at least in outlines, clarified in three decisions how such contracts stand under the law. These are the decisions of June 30, 1966, in Case No. 56/65, *Maschinenbau Ulm,*[1] of July 13, 1966, in combined Cases Nos. 56 and 58/64, *Grundig-Consten,*[2] and, again, of July 13, 1966, in Case No. 32/65, *Italian Government.*[3]

¶ 702   Regulation 67/67 builds on these three decisions. It contributes few new points of view for the legal treatment of exclusive dealing obligations.[3a] The regulation was issued in the interest of legal security (*Rechtssicherheit*) to give the economy a foothold for concluding interstate exclusive dealing agreements.

The regulation had to keep within narrow limits (see Regulation 67/67, Article 6) because, under Regulation 19/65, the Commission has to keep within the framework of Article 85 and cannot exempt agreements except in accordance with Article 85 (3).

¶ 703   Agreements not protected under Regulation 67/67 may still be exempted by the Commission in each individual case (Regulation 19/65, Article 1 (1)).

¶ 704   Regulation 67/67 became effective May 1, 1967.

---

* Issued by the Commission. Dated March 22, 1967, OffJour No. 57, March 25, 1967, page 849. CCH translation, CMR ¶ 2727.

[1] Recueil Vol. XII-4, page 337; CMR ¶ 8047. See ¶ 16, supra.

[2] Recueil Vol. XII-4, page 429; CMR ¶ 8046. See ¶ 12, 14, 16, supra.

[3] Recueil Vol. XII-4, page 563; CMR ¶ 8048. See ¶ 601, supra.

[3a] Champaud, CMLR, Vol. 5, p. 23; Kirschstein, WuW 1967, p. 373.

Article 1

AGREEMENTS COVERED

(1) Article 85, paragraph 1, of the Treaty shall, in accordance with Article 85, paragraph 3, and under the conditions set forth in this regulation, be declared inapplicable until December 31, 1972, to agreements in which only two enterprises take part and in which:

(a) one of the parties agrees to deliver certain products only to the other party for resale within a specified area in the Common Market, or

(b) one of the parties agrees to purchase for resale certain products only from the other party, or

(c) exclusive supply and purchase for resale agreements within the meaning of subparagraphs (a) and (b) have been concluded between the two parties.

(2) Paragraph 1 shall not apply to agreements in which only enterprises of one Member State take part and which concern the resale of products within that Member State.

¶ 705   In accordance with the three decisions of the European Court just mentioned, the Commission starts from the supposition that even agreements between enterprises standing on different steps of the economic ladder (vertical agreements) fall under Article 85. Regulation 67/67 exempts a certain group of vertical agreements: those containing exclusive supply or purchase obligations. This does not mean that all such agreements would otherwise be prohibited under Article 85. The "Group Exemption Regulation" need not expressly pronounce on agreements not fulfilling the conditions of Article 85 (1), e.g., because they do not perceptibly affect (adversely) interstate trade or competition.[4]

¶ 706   Regulation 67/67 applies to agreements in which only *two enterprises* participate. "Enterprise" here has the same meaning as in Article 85 (1), (Article 85, ¶ 1 ff., supra and Regulation 17, Article 4, ¶ 342). *Participation* within the meaning of Article 1 is given only if the two enterprises do take part in the agreement on the exclusive dealing obligation itself. If, however, a third party guarantees the contractual obligations of an exclusive dealer, this party is not a participant of the agreement, even if the guarantee is part of the same contract, written on the same paper.

---

[4] European Court of Justice, *Italian Government* decision, Recueil Vol. XII-4, page 563; CMR ¶ 8048.

¶ 707   Regulation 67/67 is not applicable to agreements between enterprises in the same member state which concern the distribution of goods within this state (Article 1 (2)). The Commission believed there was no need for a group exemption for these national contracts because they could affect interstate trade only in exceptional cases. Whether they fall under the prohibition is a question to be answered in the individual case. There will seldom be a perceptible effect on interstate trade and a perceptible restraint of competition.

¶ 708   Since, according to Article 1 (2), the group exemption is applicable to all agreements between enterprises not belonging to the same member state, Regulation 67/67 applies to agreements between enterprises in a member state and enterprises in a *third country,* i.e., outside the Common Market.[4a]

¶ 709   The *result* of this solution (¶ 707 and 708, supra) is somewhat *paradoxical,* because two enterprises are worse off if they are both located in one member state than if only one were located inside and the other outside the state. If two enterprises in the same state want legal security they must specifically ask the Commission for an individual exemption, in spite of the fact that their agreement actually will be less likely to violate Article 85 (1).

Thus, the contract between the brewery Brasserie de Haecht and the tiny little village "café" Wilkin-Janssen (¶ 45, supra), concerning 42 hectoliters out of 11.7 *million* hectoliters of beer sold on the market in Belgium and Luxembourg, was not exempted by Regulation 67/67 since both contracting partners were Belgian.

¶ 710   An agreement *concerns* resale inside one member state within the meaning of Article 1 (2) if its object is trade in that country (Regulation 17, Article 4, ¶ 341, supra). If a national agreement indirectly has some repercussions on trade with other member states this does not result in making the regulation applicable. Thus, an exclusive dealing contract, for example, in which a manufacturer ties up the only potential customer for certain products in his country, thereby preventing imports from other member states, is not exempted (Article 85, ¶ 14 ff. and 28). Such contract concerns resale within only one member state even if it contains ancillary clauses on sale in other member states, e.g., if advertising is prohibited there.

[4a] Regulation 17, Article 4, ¶ 340, supra ;
Niederleithinger, WRP 1967, p. 198, 199.

¶ 710

¶ 711   Article 1 (1) grants exemption to three types of contracts:
         those by which the manufacturer binds himself exclusively
to supply a given enterprise (alternative a) ; those by which a dealer
(wholesale or retail) binds himself to purchase exclusively from an
enterprise .(alternative b) ; and those containing both obligations (alternative c). The wording closely follows Article 1 (1)(a) of Regulation 19/65.

¶ 712   The manufacturer's and the dealer's exclusive obligations
         must concern goods destined *for resale*. Thus, if commercial
consumers are limited in their freedom to buy and sell or are granted
exclusive rights, Article 1 (1) does not apply, e.g., if a French manufacturer of machines is obliged to purchase raw material exclusively
from a German dealer, or if the dealer is obliged to supply such material exclusively to this French manufacturer, the regulation is inapplicable. The power granted the Commission in Article 1 of Regulation 19/65 was limited correspondingly.

         We do not see a sufficient reason for this limitation and consider
it to be unjustified in all three alternatives.

         If the parties to the contract do not aim at resale, but at industrial
use, Article 85 (1) may apply. It is necessary, however, to examine
whether its requirements are met.

¶ 713   It must be the parties' intention (Article 1 (1)(a)) that the
         goods be resold within a limited area of the Common Market.
Which area does not matter. In view of the wording of the provision
resale in such an area only is of importance, and not the dealer's
domicile, which could be outside the Common Market. The latter
case will, of course, occur infrequently. Even the supplier's, particularly the manufacturer's domicile may be outside the Common
Market.

         The parties' intention has to be directed towards resale within a
specified area of the Common Market as far as exclusive supply agreements, although not exclusive purchase agreements are concerned.
Thus, supply contracts for resale in the Common Market as a uniform
economic bloc are not exempted.[4b] However, such contracts, in most
cases, will not fulfill the conditions of Article 85 (1) (Article 85,
¶ 30, supra).

¶ 714   Articles 1-7 of Regulation 67/67 deal with *agreements* (equiv-
         alent to contracts). According to Article 8, these provisions
apply correspondingly to concerted practices.

[4b] Accord: Niederleithinger, WRP
1967, p. 198-200.

According to Article 1 (1), the group exemption is granted until December 13, 1972. At the end of that day the general exemption will end if it is not extended.

Article 2

OTHER AUTHORIZED RESTRICTIONS ON COMPETITION

(1) Besides the obligations named in Article 1, the only restrictions on competition that may be imposed on the exclusive dealer shall be:

(a) the obligation not to manufacture or distribute, during the life of the contract or for one year following the expiration of the contract, products competing with the products under contract;

(b) the obligation not to advertise the products under contract, not to establish a branch, and not to maintain a distribution warehouse outside the contract territory.

(2) The following obligations on the part of the exclusive dealer shall not prevent Article 1, paragraph 1, from being applicable:

(a) the obligation to purchase complete lines of products or minimum quantities;

(b) the obligation to undertake certain sales promotion measures, in particular:

—to advertise,

—to maintain a sales network or stock,

—to assume responsibility for customer service and guarantees,

—to employ personnel having specialized or technical training.

¶ 715   The principle is that no further restraints of competition may be imposed on the *exclusive dealer* than those mentioned in Articles 1 and 2. Obligations that do not restrain competition within the meaning of Article 85 (1) may, of course, be contained in the contract without endangering the advantages of the exemption. Thus, agreements on exchange of experience, on comparison of costs or operations as well as genuine price notification systems are permitted.

¶ 716   There is, furthermore, no exemption for *concerted practices* not covered by Articles 1 and 2. It does not follow from the wording of Article 2 (1) or from the reasons given by the Commission for the regulation ("obligations restraining competition") that only contractually binding restraints are harmful. This follows from Article 8.[4e]

[4e] Contra: Niederleithinger, WRP 1967, p. 200.

¶ 717   Article 2 (1) (a) permits an *obligation not to compete* for the
         life of the contract or for one year after its expiration. Both
these obligations may be combined. The agreement may prohibit
the manufacture and sale of goods competing with the goods which
are the object of the agreement. Potential competition is enough.
That it is permissible to prohibit the purchase of such goods from
third parties so long as the contract lasts follows from Article 1 (1) (b).

¶ 718   The exclusive dealer may be prohibited from *advertising* the
         contract goods, from establishing branches, or from main-
taining a distribution warehouse *outside his district.* But he must not
be prohibited from delivering there. Absolute territorial protection,
thus, is not exempted; neighboring exclusive dealers cannot be protected against such deliveries.

¶ 719   According to Article 2 (2) certain further obligations of the
         exclusive dealer do *not* stand *in the way of the exemption,* viz.,
the obligation to purchase a complete line of products, to buy minimum quantities, to sell the products with a trademark or in a package
prescribed by the manufacturer, or the obligation to take certain steps
furthering the sale. The wording in paragraph 2 that deviates from
paragraph 1 is explained by the fact that such obligations as a rule
are not restraints of competition within the meaning of Article 85 (1).
Paragraph 2, in other words, merely clarifies the legal situation prevailing as a rule. If, however, in an exceptional case there is a restraint of competition, it is exempted.

It is not an obligation to buy a complete line of products if the
exclusive dealer is bound to deal only in accessories and spare parts
manufactured by his suppliers. This is, however, an exclusive purchase obligation within the meaning of Article 1 (1) (b), also covered
by the exemption.

¶ 720   Article 2 deals only with restraints of competition or other
         obligations of the *exclusive dealer ("concessionaire exclusif").*
This term is not exact. The restrictions of Article 2 may also be
imposed on a dealer who is not given exclusive selling rights, but is
bound to buy exclusively.

¶ 721   Article 2 does not concern restraints of competition imposed
         on the manufacturer. He may be subjected only to the exclusive

supply obligation of Article 1 (1) (a). Agreements or concerted practices restraining competition that go further than that must be exempted by the Commission.

Article 3
PROHIBITED CLAUSES

Article 1, paragraph 1, of this regulation shall not apply when:

(a) manufacturers of competing products grant each other the exclusive dealership for such products;

(b) the contracting parties make it difficult for middlemen and consumers to obtain the products under contract from other dealers in the Common Market, particularly when the contracting parties

1. exercise industrial protective rights to prevent dealers from obtaining in other areas of the Common Market supplies of the products under contract properly marked and marketed, or from selling them in the contract territory;

2. exercise other rights or take measures to prevent dealers or consumers from obtaining the products under contract from other sources in the Common Market or from selling them in the contract territory.

¶ 722   Article 3 contains two barriers to the application of Regulation 67/67.

Letter a does not exempt contracts in which competing manufacturers make each other exclusive dealers of their products. It is irrelevant whether this is done in one contract or in several. This follows from the wording of the provision.

Article 3 (a) denies exemption only to mutual exclusive dealing agreements between manufacturers, not between dealers or between manufacturers and dealers. If manufacturers do not grant exclusive dealership to each other but to a subsidiary of either one of them dealing in distribution, Article 3 (a) does not apply. Legally independent members of a concern are to be treated as different enterprises (Article 85, ¶ 1 ff., supra).

Article 3 (a) presupposes that the goods which are the object of exclusive dealing contracts are in competition with each other.

¶ 723   Furthermore, the regulation is not applicable if the partners to the agreement hinder dealers (the word "middlemen" does not mean anything else) or consumers in procuring the relevant goods from other dealers in the Common Market (Article 3 (b)). To hinder or "to make it difficult" here, in our opinion, means creating legal bars

¶ 723

only, and not mere economic impediments, e.g., higher costs in buying from other sources. This is true since an economic difficulty of one sort or another for any buyer may or will always occur. That this is not enough follows from the examples in Nos. 1 and 2. The Commission in its "reasons" expressly speaks of *misuse* of industrial protective rights or other rights.

¶ 724   Article 3 (b) intends to prevent *absolute territorial protection* in favor of the exclusive dealer. This is in accord with the European Court of Justice's *Grundig-Consten* decision.[5] The possibility of bringing about parallel imports is always to be preserved. Whether such imports actually take place or not is not essential.

¶ 725   Article 3 mentions, as an example of inadmissible hindering, the *use of industrial protective rights* to prevent dealers or consumers from buying in other parts of the Common Market the goods involved, legally marked or legally brought to the market, or from selling such goods in the district covered by the contract. What is required, thus, is the *exercise* of the protective rights. This is in conformity with the European Court of Justice's *Grundig-Consten* decision where it is said that Article 85 does not affect the existence of industrial protective rights but merely their exercise or use. It is essential that in using their rights the parties act with the intention of preventing parallel imports. It does not matter whether they have other aims besides this, or whether a law suit based on the protective rights would be successful under national law. There must be an impediment, though; this might possibly also be found in an unjustified suit. Obviously, industrial protective rights may be used as a defense against imports of goods illegally marked.

¶ 726   The parties to an agreement must not use any other rights or take *measures* to prevent parallel imports, e.g., claims arising from the law against unfair competition, if the position of the exclusive distributor is endangered by third parties (in France, for instance, the exclusive dealer's rights grant *opposabilité aux tiers*).

The examples in Nos. 1 and 2 show that undue hindering within the meaning of Article 3 (b) presupposes that a partner to the contract takes measures against parallel imports. These measures may even be found in agreements to prevent parallel imports, e.g., in prohibiting third parties from importing into the contract district. Legal proceedings need not have been initiated. The mere existence of

[5] Recueil Vol. XII-4, page 429; CMR ¶ 8046. ¶ 12, 14, 16, supra.

¶ 724

contractual export prohibitions may in certain circumstances mean an impediment, e.g., if the partners expressly and formally inform all potential parallel importers of the contract.

¶ 727   Normally, it will be clear if an exclusive dealing contract falls under Article 3 (b). If this is the case, such contract is not exempted. It is also possible, however, that a contract is covered by Regulation 67/67 to begin with, and that Article 3 becomes applicable afterwards because, e.g., the parties only later use industrial protective rights. In such case the exemption for this particular agreement does not become void automatically, but Regulation 19/65, Article 7, applies. The Commission may, for this contract, issue a declaration according to Regulation 17, Articles 6 and 8; it may, in particular, revoke the exemption.

Article 4

RETROACTIVE EFFECT OF EXEMPTION

(1) For agreements that were in existence on March 13, 1962, and were notified before February 1, 1963, the inapplicability of Treaty Article 85, paragraph 1, referred to in Article 1, paragraph 1, shall apply retroactively to the time as of which the conditions for the application of this regulation were fulfilled.

(2) For all other agreements that were notified before this regulation comes into force, the inapplicability of Article 85, paragraph 1, referred to in Article 1, paragraph 1, shall apply retroactively to the time as of which the conditions for the application of this regulation were fulfilled, but not to a date preceding the date of notification.

¶ 728   Regulation 67/67 became effective May 1, 1967. Article 4, based on Regulation 19/65, Article 3, makes the exemption *retroactive* for certain older agreements and concerted practices.

¶ 729   Agreements existing prior to March 13, 1962, and notified before February 1, 1963, are exempted retroactively from the date on which they fulfilled the requirements of Regulation 67/67. It is unessential whether they were notified on Form B or B1.

Agreements notified later are exempted as of the same date, but not earlier than the date of notification.

Contracts concluded before May 1, 1967, but not notified, are exempted as of May 1, 1967, if they satisfy the requirements of Regulation 67/67.

¶ 729

Agreements concluded after Regulation 67/67 became effective (May 1, 1967) and fulfilling its requirements are exempted from the day they are concluded.

Article 5

MODIFIED AGREEMENTS

For agreements that were in existence on March 13, 1962, were notified before February 1, 1963, and were modified before August 2, 1967, so that they fulfill the conditions set forth in this regulation, the prohibition of Article 85, paragraph 1, of the Treaty shall not apply, for the period preceding the modification, if the Commission was notified before October 3, 1967, that the agreement has been modified. The notice shall be effective as of the time of receipt by the Commission. If the notice is sent by registered mail, the date of cancellation at the place from which it was mailed shall be considered the date of receipt.

¶ 730   Article 5 is based on Regulation 19/65, Article 4. It says:
Agreements existing on March 13, 1962, and notified before February 1, 1963, are not prohibited by Article 85 (1) if they were modified before August 2, 1967, so that they fulfill the conditions of Regulation 67/67, and if the Commission was informed thereof before October 3, 1967.

¶ 731   If a contract is not protected by Regulation 67/67 because the parties actually hinder parallel imports by the use of industrial protective rights or other rights (Article 3 (b)) "modification" is made by giving up this *practice*. No formal alteration of the contract is needed if its wording does not stand in the way of the application of Regulation 67/67.[6]

¶ 732   The effects of Article 5 are limited. The retroactivity may not be asserted in law suits pending when Regulation 67/67 became effective. Nor can claims for damages by third parties based on the retroactivity be valid (Regulation 19/65, Article 4 (3)).

¶ 733   If the parties missed the deadlines of Article 5 or if they refuse to modify the agreement, they may still ask the Commission for an exemption under Regulation 17 (Regulation 19/65, Article 1 (1)). It is advisable, as a matter of precaution, to notify agreements if it is uncertain whether they fulfill the requirements of Regulation 67/67. Here, Article 7 must be observed.

---

[6] Accord: Niederleithinger, WRP 1967, p. 198-202.

Article 6

EXAMINATION BY COMMISSION

The Commission shall examine whether Article 7 of Regulation 19/65 is applicable in a specific case, particularly if there is reason to suspect that:

(a) the products under contract are not exposed in the contract territory to the competition of products which are to be considered by the consumer as similar because of their characteristics, their price, and the use for which they are intended;

(b) it is impossible for other manufacturers to sell, at the same trading level and in the contract territory, products similar to those of the exclusive dealer;

(c) the exclusive dealer is making improper use of the exemption by:

1. preventing, for no objectively justifiable reason, the products under contract from being delivered in the contract territory to groups of buyers who cannot obtain them from other sources under suitable conditions;

2. selling the products under contract at unreasonably high prices.

¶ 734   Under Article 7 of Regulation 19/65 the Commission may withdraw the advantages following from the regulation on group exemptions if it finds that an agreement, to which the regulation applies, still does not meet the conditions of Article 85 (3). Then an individual procedure is initiated.

¶ 735   Article 6 lists types of cases in which the Commission intends to examine whether a procedure according to Article 7 of Regulation 19/65 will be initiated. The Commission must not withdraw the advantages of Regulation 67/67 solely for the reason that the case fits one of the examples of Article 6. It must be found that in the particular case an exemption under Article 85 (3) cannot be granted. So long as the advantages of Regulation 67/67 have not been withdrawn the agreement in question remains exempted. Nevertheless, the examples in Article 6 show the cases in which the Commission believes that an agreement containing exclusive supply and/or purchase obligations will not meet the conditions of Article 85 (3).

This is the case if the goods subject to the contract are not exposed to competition from similar goods, or if manufacturers of such goods are unable to sell them to dealers at the same level as that of the exclusive dealer, or, finally, if the exclusive dealer misuses the group exemption by discriminatingly refusing supply or by charging prices disproportionately high.

¶ 735

Article 7

NOTIFICATION REQUIRED

(1) Article 4, paragraph 2a, of Regulation 27 of May 3, 1962, as amended by Regulation 153, is rescinded.

(2) A notification on Form B1 of an exclusive dealing agreement that does not fulfill the conditions set forth in Articles 1 and 3 of this regulation must, insofar as it is not adjusted to those conditions, be supplemented before October 3, 1967, by submitting Form B together with the annexes thereto in accordance with the provisions of Regulation 27.

¶ 736   Article 4 (2a) of Regulation 27 provided a simplified notification for "exclusive distributorship contracts" imposing exclusive supply and/or purchase obligations to which only two enterprises were parties. Such agreements could be notified on the simpler Form B1 instead of Form B (Article 4 (2), Regulation 27).

The exclusive dealing agreements, theretofore to be notified on Form B1, for the most part met the conditions of Regulation 67/67. Therefore, Article 7 abolished the simplified way of notifying (based on Article 4 (2a), Regulation 27).

¶ 737   Insofar as a contract notified on Form B1 meets the conditions of Regulation 27, it had to be notified anew on Form B, including the annexes, before October 3, 1967. Otherwise, the advantages of notifying, particularly the preliminary validity, were lost.

Article 8

CONCERTED PRACTICES

Articles 1 through 7 of this regulation shall apply by analogy to concerted practices of the type defined in Article 1, paragraph 1.

¶ 738   Articles 1-7 of Regulation 67/67 aim at agreements (or contracts). They are to be applied correspondingly to concerted practices. Restraints of competition not declared unobjectionable in Articles 1 and 2 bar an exemption not only if they are based on a binding agreement, but also if they are based on concerted practices.

Article 9

EFFECTIVE DATE

This regulation shall come into force May 1, 1967.

This regulation is binding in all its parts and directly applicable in each Member State.

¶ 739   Regulation 67/67 became effective on May 1, 1967.

¶ 736

Table of Court and Agency Decisions Cited

GERMAN AND OTHER EUROPEAN

Arrondissements Rechtbank te Breda (Netherlands)
December 31, 1968 (GRUR AIT 1969, p. 203 ff.)

Arrondissements Rechtbank te Rotterdam (Netherlands)
October 26, 1960 (*Bosch v. de Geus*) (GRUR AIT 1961, p. 442 ff.; BB 1961,
p. 883, No. 1757)

Bundesgerichtshof (Federal Supreme Court of Germany)
June 1, 1951 (NJW 1951, p. 836; BB 1951, p. 623, No. 1616)
January 8, 1952 (NJW 1952, p. 299)
December 10, 1957 (BB 1958, p. 214 ff.; WuW/E BGH 205 ff.)
April 14, 1959 (BB 1959, p. 576 ff.)
October 26, 1959 (WuW/E BGH 359; BB 1959, p. 1274 f.)
October 26, 1961 (NJW 1962, p. 247 ff.; BB 1962, p. 7 ff.)
June 7, 1962 (BB 1962, p. 936 f.)
June 14, 1963 (BB 1963, p. 1393; NJW 1964, p. 152)
January 22, 1964 (Vol. 41, p. 84 ff.)
October 18, 1967 (Vol. 22, p. 293 ff.)
February 5, 1968 (WuW/E BGH 907)
February 27, 1968 (BB 1969, p. 692 ff.)
February 28, 1968 (AWD 1968, p. 152 ff.)
July 7, 1969 (WuW/E BGH 1039)
November 12, 1969 (WuW/E BGH 1054)
February 26, 1970 (WuW/E BGH 1081; BB 1970, p. 683)
April 9, 1970 (WM 1970, p. 1188 ff.; AWD 1970, p. 417 f.)

Bundeskartellamt (German Federal Cartel Office) Beschlussabteilung
(Decisions Section)
February 19, 1959 (WuW/E BKartA 25 ff.)
August 23, 1960 (WuW/E BKartA 241 ff.)
December 12, 1960 (WuW/E BKartA 337 f.)
August 11, 1961 (BB 1961, p. 1255 No. 2389; WuW/E BKartA 427)
November 29, 1961 (WuW/E BKartA 400 ff.; BB 1962, p. 77 f.)
September 2, 1963 (WuW/E BKartA 741 f.)

Bundeskartellamt (German Federal Cartel Office), Einspruchsabteilung
(Appeals Section)
May 9, 1959 (BB 1959, p. 540 No. 941; WuW/E BKartA 50 ff.)

Bundesverfassungsgericht (German Federal Constitutional Court)
October 18, 1967 (Vol. 22, 1968, p. 293 ff.)

Commission of the EEC
March 11, 1964, negative clearance for Grosfillex Co. (OffJour No. 58, April
9, 1964, p. 915)
June 1, 1964, negative clearance for S. A. Mertens & Straet (OffJour No.
92, June 10, 1964, p. 1426)
July 30, 1964, negative clearance for S. A. Nicholas Frères (OffJour No.
136, August 26, 1964, p. 2287)
September 23, 1964, Grundig-Consten agreement (CMR ¶ 2743; WuW/E
EV 60; AWD 1964, p. 187)
October 22, 1964, negative clearance for DECA (OffJour No. 173, October
31, 1964, p. 2761)

Commission of the EEC—Continued

    July 8, 1965, exemption for DRU-Blondel (OffJour No. 131, July 17, 1965, p. 2194; CMR ¶ 9049)

    September 17, 1965, exemption for Hummel-Isbecque (OffJour No. 156, September 23, 1965, p. 2581; CMR ¶ 9063)

    December 17, 1965, exemption for Maison Jallatte (OffJour No. 3, January 6, 1966, p. 37; CMR ¶ 9083)

    June 27, 1967, exemption for Transocean Marine Paint Association (OffJour No. 163, July 20, 1967, p. 10; CMR ¶ 9188)

Commission of the European Communities

    February 26, 1968, negative clearance for Eurogypsum (OffJour No. L 57, March 5, 1968; CMR ¶ 9220)

    July 17, 1968, negative clearance for Alliance de Constructeurs français de Machines-Outils (OffJour No. L 201, August 12, 1968, p. 1; CMR ¶ 9249)

    July 17, 1968, negative clearance for SOCEMAS (OffJour No. L 201, August 12, 1968, p. 4; CMR ¶ 9250)

    July 17, 1968, exemption for ACEC-Berliet (OffJour No. L 201, August 12, 1968, p. 7; CMR ¶ 9251)

    November 6, 1968, negative clearance for Cobelaz-Synthetic Products Manufacturers (OffJour No. L 276, November 14, 1968, p. 13; CMR ¶ 9265)

    November 6, 1968, negative clearance for Cobelaz-Cokeries (OffJour No. L 276, November 14, 1968, p. 19; CMR ¶ 9266)

    November 6, 1968, negative clearance for Rieckermann/AEG-Elotherm (OffJour No. L 276, November 14, 1968, p. 25; CMR ¶ 9267)

    November 6, 1968, negative clearance for Comptoir français de l'azote (OffJour No. L 276, November 14, 1968, p. 29; CMR ¶ 9268)

    March 13, 1969, exemption for CECIMO (OffJour No. L 69, March 20, 1969, p. 13; CMR ¶ 9295)

    May 5, 1969, negative clearance for Convention Chaufourniers (OffJour No. L 122, May 22, 1969; CMR ¶ 9303)

    June 18, 1969, negative clearance for Christiani & Nielsen (OffJour No. L 165, July 5, 1969, p. 12; CMR ¶ 9308)

    June 25, 1969, negative clearance for VVVF (OffJour No. L 168, July 10, 1969, p. 22; CMR ¶ 9312)

    June 30, 1969, negative clearance for SEIFA (Società per lo Sviluppo dei Consumi dei Fertilizzanti) (OffJour No. L 173, July 15, 1969, p. 8; CMR ¶ 9315)

    July 16, 1969, fines for quinine cartel (OffJour No. L 192, August 5, 1969, p. 5; CMR ¶ 9313)

    July 22, 1969, exemption for Clima Chappée-Buderus (OffJour No. L 195, August 7, 1969, p. 1; CMR ¶ 9316)

    July 22, 1969, exemption for Jaz-Peter (OffJour No. L 195, August 7, 1969, p. 5; CMR ¶ 9317)

    July 24, 1969, fines for tar color producers (OffJour No. L 195, August 7, 1969, p. 11; CMR ¶ 9314)

    December 5, 1969, negative clearance for Pirelli/Dunlop (OffJour No. L 323, December 24, 1969, p. 21; CMR ¶ 9336)

    June 29, 1970, negative clearance for ASBL pour la promotion du tube d'acier soudé électriquement (OffJour No. L 153, July 14, 1970, p. 14; CMR ¶ 9380)

    June 30, 1970, negative clearance for Kodak (OffJour No. L 147, July 7, 1970, p. 24; CMR ¶ 9378)

    June 30, 1970, negative clearance for ASPA (Association syndicale belge de la parfumerie) (OffJour No. L 148, July 8, 1970, p. 9; CMR ¶ 9379)

    October 28, 1970, exemption refused for Julien/Van Katwijk (OffJour No. L 242, November 5, 1970, p. 18; CMR ¶ 9395)

    October 28, 1970, exemption for Omega (OffJour No. L 242, November 5, 1970, p. 22; CMR ¶ 9396)

Conseil d'Etat

    March 1, 1968 (Recueil Dalloz 1968, p. 286)

Cour d'Appel (Court of Appeals) Amiens
    May 9, 1963 (Recueil Dalloz 1963, p. 556)

Cour d'Appel (Court of Appeals) de Bruxelles
    June 25, 1964 (AWD 1965, p. 336)

Cour d'Appel (Court of Appeals) Paris
    January 26, 1963 (Recueil Dalloz 1963, p. 189)

Court of Justice of the European Communities (Luxembourg)
    July 17, 1959, Cases Nos. 32 and 33/58 (Recueil Vol. V, p. 275 ff.)
    April 4, 1960, Case No. 31/59 (Recueil Vol. VI, p. 151 ff.)
    March 22, 1961, Cases Nos. 42 and 49/59 (Recueil Vol. VII, p. 101 ff.)
    April 6, 1962, Case No. 13/61 (*de Geus v. Bosch*) (CMR ¶ 8003; Recueil Vol. VIII, p. 89 ff.)
    May 18, 1962, Case No. 13/60 (Recueil Vol. VIII, p. 165 ff.)
    July 17, 1963, Case No. 13/63 (*Italian Refrigerators*) (CMR ¶ 8014; Recueil Vol. IX, p. 335)
    June 30, 1966, Case No. 56/65 (*Maschinenbau Ulm*) (CMR ¶ 8047; Recueil Vol. XII-4, p. 337 ff.)
    July 13, 1966, Cases Nos. 56/64 and 58/64 (*Grundig-Consten*) (CMR ¶ 8046; Recueil Vol. XII-4, p. 429 ff.)
    March 15, 1967, Cases Nos. 8-11/66 (*Noordwijks Cement Accoord*) (CMR ¶ 8052; Recueil Vol. XIII-1, p. 93 ff.)
    December 12, 1967, Case No. 23/67 (*Brasserie de Haecht*) (CMR ¶ 8053; Recueil Vol. XIII-5, p. 525 ff.)
    February 29, 1968, Case No. 24/67 (*Parke, Davis & Co.*) (CMR ¶ 8054; Recueil Vol. XIV-2, p. 81 ff.)
    February 13, 1969, Case No. 14/68 (*Tar Colors*) (CMR ¶ 8056; Recueil Vol. XV, p. 1)
    July 9, 1969, Case No. 5/69 (*Konstant*) (CMR ¶ 8074; Recueil Vol. XV, p. 295)
    July 9, 1969, Case No. 10/69 (*Portelange*) (CMR ¶ 8075; Recueil Vol. XV, p. 309)
    March 18, 1970, Case No. 43/69 (*Bilger-Jehle*) (CMR ¶ 8076; Recueil Vol. XVI, p. 127)
    June 15, 1970, Case No. 44/69 (*Quinine Cartel*) (CMR ¶ 8084)
    June 30, 1970, Case No. 1/70 (*Parfums Marcel Rochas*) (OffJour No. C 97, July 29, 1970, p. 11)

Gerechtshof te Amsterdam (Netherlands)
    June 28, 1962 (WuW/E EWG/MUV 80)

Gerechtshof te 's-Gravenhage (Netherlands)
    February 20, 1963

High Court of Appeals Turin
    June 28, 1963 (CMR ¶ 2011.57)

Hoge Raad (Netherlands)
    January 12, 1939 (Nederlandse Jurisprudentie 1939, No. 535)

Kammergericht (Court of Appeals in Berlin)
    January 12, 1960 (BB 1960, p. 385 f.; WuW/E OLG 322 ff.)
    May 4, 1962 (BB 1962, p. 859 f.)

Landgericht (District Court) Bochum
    April 20, 1964 (AWD 1964, p. 369)

Landgericht (District Court) Mannheim
    January 22, 1965 (AWD 1965, p. 61)

Landgericht (District Court) Munich
    January 14, 1963 (BB 1963, p. 167) reversed by OLG Munich, May 30, 1963 (CMR ¶ 8020; BB 1963, p. 744)

Oberlandesgericht (Land High Court of Appeals) Celle
  February 15, 1963 (BB 1963, p. 1113)

Oberlandesgericht (Land High Court of Appeals) Düsseldorf
  October 21, 1958 (BB 1958, p. 1110 No. 1933; WuW/E OLG 262 ff.)
  March 29, 1963 (BB 1963, p. 489)
  July 14, 1964 (AWD 1964, p. 262)

Oberlandesgericht (Land High Court of Appeals) Frankfurt a.M.
  January 19, 1962 (BB 1962, p. 735)

Oberlandesgericht (Land High Court of Appeals) Karlsruhe
  April 23, 1968 (WuW/E OLG 951)

Oberlandesgericht (Land High Court of Appeals) Munich
  May 30, 1963 (CMR ¶ 8020; BB 1963, p. 744)

Oberlandesgericht (Land High Court of Appeals) Stuttgart
  May 17, 1961 (WuW/E OLG 426 ff.)

Tribunal de Commerce (Commerce Court), Seine
  May 21, 1962 (AWD 1962, p. 206) reversed by Cour d'Appel of Paris, First
  Chamber (see Handelsblatt of February 6, 1963)

AMERICAN

Supreme Court of the United States
  Albrecht v. Herald Co., 390 U. S. 145 (1968)
  American Tobacco Co. v. United States, 328 U. S. 781 (1946)
  Apex Hosiery Co. v. Leader, 310 U. S. 469 (1940)
  Brown Shoe Co. v. United States, 82 S. Ct. 1502 (1962)
  Bruce's Juices v. American Can Co., 330 U. S. 743 (1947)
  Federal Trade Commission v. Anheuser-Busch, Inc., 363 U. S. 536, 549 (1960)
  Flintkote Co. v. Lysfjord, 246 F. 2d 368 (9th Cir. 1957), *cert. den.* 355 U. S.
    835 (1957)
  Kelly v. Kosuga, 358 U. S. 516 (1959)
  Kiefer-Stewart Co. v. Seagram & Sons, Inc., 340 U. S. 211 (1951)
  Lear, Inc. v. Adkins, 395 U. S. 653 (1969)
  Malloy v. Hogan, 378 U. S. 1 (1964)
  Morgan v. United States, 298 U. S. 468, 481 (1936)
  Standard Oil Co. v. United States, 221 U. S. 1 (1911)
  Swift & Co. v. United States, 196 U. S. 375 (1905)
  Theatre Enterprises, Inc. v. Paramount Film Distributing Corp., 346 U. S. 537
    (1954)
  United States v. American Tobacco Co., 221 U. S. 106 (1911)
  United States v. Colgate & Co., 250 U. S. 300 (1919)
  United States v. duPont Co., 351 U. S. 377 (1956)
  United States v. First National Bank and Trust Company of Lexington et al.,
    376 U. S. 665 (1964)
  United States v. Griffith, 334 U. S. 100 (1948)
  United States v. Socony-Vacuum Oil Co., 310 U. S. 150 (1940)
  United States v. United Shoe Machinery Co., 247 U. S. 32 (1918)
  United States v. United States Steel Corp., 251 U. S. 417 (1920)
  United States v. Yellow Cab Co., 332 U. S. 218 (1947)

United States Court of Appeals, Second Circuit
  United States v. Aluminum Co. of America, 148 F. 2d 416 (C. C. A. 2, 1945)

United States District Court for the District of Massachusetts
  United States v. United Shoe Machinery Corp., 110 F. Supp. 295 (D. Mass.
    1953), affirmed *per curiam,* 347 U. S. 521 (1954)

Table of Other Authorities Cited

GERMAN AND OTHER EUROPEAN

Alexander

Annotation to the *Parke, Davis* decision, Cahiers de Droit Européen 1968, p. 307 ff.

"Article 85 of the EEC Treaty and the Exclusive License to Sell Patented Products," CMLR Vol. 5, p. 465 ff.

"The Domestic Courts and Article 85 of the Rome Treaty," CMLR Vol. 1, p. 431 ff.

Barnikel

"Die Abgrenzung des relevanten Marktes" (Delimitation of the Relevant Market), WuW 1961, p. 246 ff.

Basson

"Preisbindung, Exportverbot und EWG-Kartellrecht" (Price Maintenance, Export Prohibition and EEC Cartel Law), annotation to LG Munich decision of January 14, 1963, MA 1963, p. 122 ff.

Baumbach/Hefermehl

Kommentar zum Wettbewerbs- und Warenzeichenrecht (Commentary on the Law of Competition and Trademarks), 8th Ed. 1960

Baumbach/Hueck

Kommentar zum Aktiengesetz (Commentary on Law of Corporations), 13th edition, 1968

Benisch

Annotation to LG Munich decision of January 14, 1963, DB 1963, p. 301

Commentary on Sections 34-37 GWB in Gemeinschaftskommentar 63

"Kartellfreie Kooperation im Gemeinsamen Markt. Bemerkungen zur Bekanntmachung der EWG-Kommission vom 29. 7. 1968" (Cartel-free Cooperation in the Common Market. Remarks on the Notice of the EEC Commission of July 29, 1968), WuW 1969, p. 1 ff.

"Kooperationserleichterungen im Kartellrecht der EWG" (Measures to Facilitate Cooperation in EEC Cartel Law), DB 1970, p. 1363

Bericht

see Deringer

Bodenhausen

"Der EWG-Vertrag und der gewerbliche Rechtsschutz" (The EEC Treaty and Industrial Legal Protection), GRUR AIT 1958, p. 218 ff.

Bollack

"Das marktbeherrschende Unternehmen im EWG-Recht" (The Dominating Enterprise in EEC Law), Kartellrundschau, Vol. 8, p. 223 ff.

Borchardt/Fikentscher

"Wettbewerb, Wettbewerbsbeschränkung, Marktbeherrschung" (Competition, Competitive Restraint, Market Dominance), Articles Covering the Entire Commercial, Civil and Bankruptcy Law, Supplement 24 to "Zeitschrift für das gesamte Handelsrecht und Konkursrecht" (Review for the Entire Commercial and Bankruptcy Law), Stuttgart 1957

Brugger
WuW 1959, p. 467

Bundeskartellamt (German Federal Cartel Office)
Letter of August 6, 1962 (BB 1962, p. 978 No. 1617)

Reports for the Years 1959, 1961, 1963, and 1968, Bundestagsdrucksachen
(Federal Parliament Printed Matter) No. 1795, 3rd Electoral Period, No.
IV, 378, 4th Electoral Period, No. IV, 2370, 4th Electoral Period, and
No. V, 4236, 5th Electoral Period, cited as "BKartA Annual Report 1959,"
"BKartA Annual Report 1961," "BKartA Annual Report 1963," and
"BKartA Annual Report 1968," respectively

Bundestag (German Federal Parliament)
"Bericht über Änderungen des Gesetzes gegen Wettbewerbsbeschränkungen"
(Report on Amendments to the GWB) of August 22, 1962, Bundestag
Printed Document IV 617

Burki
"Le problème de l'abus des positions dominantes des grandes entreprises
dans le marché commun" (The Problem of Abuse of Dominant Positions
by the Large Enterprises in the Common Market), 1968

Canellos/Silber
"Concentration in the Common Market," CMLR Vol. 7, p. 138 ff.

Catalano
"Manuel de droit des Communautés Européennes" (Manual of the Law
of the European Communities), 2nd ed., 1964

Champaud
"The Group Exemptions of E.E.C. Regulation 67/67," CMLR Vol. 5, p. 23

Commission of the EEC
Answer to Inquiry from Deringer, OffJour No. 76/62, p. 2135

Answer to Inquiry from Nederhorst, OffJour No. 37/61, p. 736

"Das Problem der Unternehmenskonzentration im Gemeinsamen Markt"
(The Problem of Concentration of Enterprises in the Common Market),
Series: Competition, Vol. 3, 1966

Eighth General Report on the Activities of the Community, for the period
from April 1, 1964, to March 31, 1965

Faïence Convention, CMR ¶ 2741; WuW/E EV 60; AWD 1964, p. 187

Fifth General Report on the Activities of the Community, for the period
from May 1, 1961, to April 30, 1962

Merkblatt zu Artikel 85 und 86 des EWG-Vertrages und ihren Durchfüh-
rungsverordnungen (Guide Lines regarding Articles 85 and 86 of the EEC
Treaty and Implementing Regulations Thereunder), issued by the Commission of the EEC (English translation in CMR ¶ 2801 ff.), cited as
"Guide Lines"

Official Notice Concerning Exclusive Representation Contracts with Commercial Agents, OffJour of December 24, 1962, p. 2921 (English translation in CMR ¶ 2697)

Official Notice Concerning Patent Licensing Agreements, OffJour of December 24, 1962, p. 2922 (English translation in CMR ¶ 2698)

Policy proposals concerning the application of Article 85 of the Treaty to
certain exclusive distributorship agreements and to certain patent licensing
agreements, OffJour No. 113/62, p. 2627 (English translation in CMR
¶ 2711 et seq.)

Commission of the EEC—continued
"Schadensersatzansprüche bei einer Verletzung der Art. 85 und 86 des Vertrages zur Gründung der EWG" (Claims for Damages in Case of a Violation of Articles 85 and 86 of the EEC Treaty), Series: Competition, Vol. 1, 1966

Commission of the European Communities
Answer to Inquiry from Deringer, OffJour No. C 71, July 17, 1968, p. 1

Answer to Inquiry from Glinne, OffJour No. C 138, November 18, 1970, p. 8; CMR ¶ 9397

Answer to Inquiry from Westerterp, OffJour No. C 20, February 14, 1970, p. 3

First General Report on the Activities of the European Communities, for the period from April to December, 1967

Notice concerning agreements, decisions and concerted practices in cooperation between enterprises, OffJour No. C 75, July 29, 1968, p. 3 (English translation in CMR ¶ 9248)

Notice relating to Agreements, Decisions and Concerted Practices of Minor Importance Not Coming within Article 85 (1) of the EEC Treaty, OffJour No. C 64, June 2, 1970, p. 1 (English translation in CMR ¶ 9367)

Second General Report on the Activities of the European Communities, for the period from January through December, 1968

Dabin
"Les concentrations d'entreprises et le droit de la concurrence" (The Concentration of Enterprises and Competition Law), paper at seminar held in Rome

van Damme
"La mise en oeuvre des articles 85 et 86 du traité de Rome" (The Enforcement of Articles 85 and 86 of the Treaty of Rome), cah. dr. eur., 1966, p. 300

Deringer
"Alleinvertriebsabkommen mit Gebietschutz nach EWG-Wettbewerbsrecht" (Exclusive Distributorship Agreements Entailing Territorial Protection under EEC Competition Law), MA 1965, p. 113

Annotation to *Bosch* decision, AWD 1962, p. 108 ff.

Annotation to German Federal Constitutional Court's decision of October 18, 1967, NJW 1968, p. 338

Bericht (Report) in the name of the Internal Trade Committee for Consultation of the European Parliament by the Council of the European Community, concerning a first implementary regulation to Articles 85 and 86 of the EEC Treaty (Document No. 104/1960-61), Session Documents of the European Parliament, Document No. 57 of September 7, 1961, cited as "Bericht"

"Das Wettbewerbsrecht des Europäischen Wirtschaftsgemeinschaft" (The Competition Law of the European Economic Community), Düsseldorf 1962/1963/64. Translation into English published by Commerce Clearing House, Inc.

"Die erste Durchführungsverordnung zu den Artikeln 85 und 86 des EWG-Vertrages" (The First Implementing Regulation to Articles 85 and 86 of the EEC Treaty), WuW 1962, p. 81 ff.

Deringer—continued
"Europäisches Wettbewerbsrecht im Werden" (European Law of Competition in the Making), AG 1962, p. 139 ff.

"Inhalt und Auswirkungen der ersten Kartellverordnung der Europäischen Wirtschaftsgemeinschaft" (Contents and Effects of the First Cartel Regulation of the European Economic Community), GRUR AIT 1962, p. 283 ff.

"Zwei Jahre Europäische Kartellpolitik" (Two Years of European Cartel Policy), in "Europäische Wirtschaft" (The European Economy), 1960, p. 66 ff.

Deringer/Tessin
"Das erste Kartellgesetz des Gemeinsamen Marktes" (The First Cartel Statute of the Common Market), NJW 1962, p. 989 ff.

"Forschungsgemeinschaften im EWG-Kartellrecht" (Joint Research Organizations in EEC Cartel Law), DB 1964, p. 870 ff.

Ditges/Ehle
"Rechtswidrigkeit des 'Genossenschaftsprivileges' in Art. 2 Abs. 1 der VO 26 über die Anwendung der EWG-Wettbewerbsregeln auf landwirtschaftliche Erzeugnisse" (Illegality of the "Association Privilege" in Article 2, paragraph 1, of Regulation 26 Concerning the Application of the EEC Rules of Competition to Agricultural Products), AWD 1963, p. 300 ff.

Drion
"Restraint of Buyer's Freedom under Article 85," CMLR Vol. 1, p. 148 ff.

Editor of MA
Annotation to *Bosch* decision, MA 1962, p. 495 ff.

Ellis
"Enkele Aantekeningen bij Artikel 86 van het EEG Verdrag" (Some Comments on Article 86 of the EEC Treaty), 1965 Soc. Econ. Wet., p. 317 ff.

Ellis/van den Heuvel
"Europees Mededingings- en Kartelrecht—EEG en EGKS" (Competition and Cartel Law—EEC and ECSC), Alphen aan de Rijn 1963

Enneccerus/Nipperdey
"Lehrbuch des Bürgerlichen Rechtes" (Manual of Civil Law), 15th edition 1960, Vol. 1, p. 1211 ff.

Everling
"Die ersten Rechtsetzungsakte der Organe der Europäischen Gemeinschaften" (The First Legislative Acts of the Organs of the European Communities), BB 1959, p. 52 ff.

Ewald
"Der Alleinvertretervertrag unter der Sicht des Artikels 85 EWGV" (The Exclusive Agency Agreement from the Viewpoint of Article 85 of the EEC Treaty), MA 1965, p. 113

"Nationales und Europäisches Kartellrecht" (National and European Cartel Law), Frankfurter Allgemeine Zeitung, April 24, 1962

Fikentscher
Annotation to BGH decision of October 26, 1959, WuW/E BGH 365

Festschrift für Alfred Hueck zum 70. Geburtstag (Publication in Honor of Alfred Hueck's 70th Birthday), 1959

Festschrift für Böhm, p. 270 ff.

Fikentscher—continued

"Neue Entwicklungen der Theorie zum Tatbestandsmerkmal der Wettbewerbsbeschränkung § 1 GWB" (New Developments of Theory Regarding the Criterion of Competitive Restraint under § 1 of the GWB), WuW 1961, p. 788 ff.

"Unternehmenskonzentration und Meldepflicht nach den Regeln des EWG-Vertrages" (Concentration of Enterprises and the Obligation to Notify Them under the Rules of the EEC Treaty), DB 1966, p. 689 ff.

Fischer

Annotation to German Federal Constitutional Court's decision of October 18, 1967, NJW 1968, p. 322

Frankfurter Kommentar
see Kaufmann/Rautmann/Strickrodt

Fuss/Burkhard

Annotation to the *Noordwijks Cement* decision, Europarecht 1967, p. 232 ff.

Gadow/Heinichen

Kommentar zum Aktiengesetz (Commentary on the Law of Corporations), 11th Ed. 1961

Gambrell

"Patents and Antitrust: An Integrated Approach in the EEC," Boston College Industrial and Commercial Law Review, Vol. 6 (1968), p. 541 ff.

von Gamm

"Das Kartellrecht im EWG-Bereich" (Cartel Law in the Area of the EEC), issue No. 3 of the "Kartellrundschau" (Cartel Review), 1961, cited as "von Gamm"

Gemeinschaftskommentar
see Müller-Henneberg/Schwartz

Gleiss

Annotation to *Brasserie de Haecht* decision, WuW 1968, p. 206
Annotation to *Parke, Davis* decision, WRP 1968, p. 143
"Ein Vorschlag zum Kartellrecht" (A Proposal Concerning Cartel Law), Handelsblatt (Journal of Commerce), December 15/16, 1961

"Gefahren des US-Antitrustrechts für europäische Unternehmen" (Dangers of U. S. Antitrust Law for European Enterprises), AWD 1969, p. 499

"Zwei bedeutsame Urteile des Europäischen Gerichtshofes" (Two Significant Decisions of the European Court of Justice), WRP 1967, p. 163 ff.

Gleiss/Hirsch

"Das erste Negativattest der EWG-Kommission" (The EEC Commission's First Negative Clearance), NJW 1964, p. 1605

"Das Kartellrecht der Europäischen Wirtschaftsgemeinschaft" (The Cartel Law of the European Economic Community), AWD 1962, p. 121 ff.

"EWG-Kartellrecht und Zuständigkeit nationaler Behörden" (EEC Cartel Law and Jurisdiction of National Authorities), BB 1962, p. 623 ff.

"Landwirtschaftliche Erzeugnisse und EWG-Kartellrecht" (Agricultural Products and EEC Cartel Law), AWD 1962, p. 159 ff.

Gleiss/Helm

"Berücksichtigung von Parallelverträgen bei Ausschliesslichkeitsverträgen im Gemeinsamen Markt" (Are Parallel Contracts to Be Taken into Account in the Evaluation of Exclusivity Contracts in the Common Market?), NJW 1968, p. 1553

Gleiss/Hootz
  "Alleinverträge mit absolutem Gebietsschutz und EWG-Kartellrecht" (Ex-
  clusive Agreements with Absolute Territorial Protection and EEC Cartel
  Law), AWD 1966, p. 307 ff.

  Annotation to BGH decision of Oct. 26, 1961, NJW 1962, p. 391 ff.

  Annotation to the *Tar-Colors* decision, WRP 1969, p. 218

  "Keine Gruppenfreistellungen nach EWG-Kartellrecht für Alleinvertriebs-
  und Patentlizenzverträge" (No Group Exemptions under EEC Cartel
  Law for Exclusive Distributorship and Patent Licensing Agreements),
  NJW 1963, p. 230 ff.

  "Vorläufige Gültigkeit von Altkartellen" (Preliminary Validity of Old
  Cartels), AWD 1965, p. 336 ff.

Gleiss/Kleinmann
  "Keine Verjährung von Ordnungswidrigkeiten im europäischen Kartell-
  recht" (No Statute of Limitations for Violations of European Cartel Law),
  NJW 1967, p. 2092

Gotzen
  "Gewerblicher Rechtsschutz und Gemeinsamer Markt" (Industrial Legal
  Protection and the Common Market), GRUR AIT 1958, p. 224 ff.

Graupner
  "The Treaty of Rome—Articles 85-90. The Substantive Law of the Rules
  of Competition," 1962 Law Gazette, p. 377 ff.

von der Groeben
  "Die Wettbewerbspolitik als Teil der Wirtschaftspolitik im Gemeinsamen
  Markt" (Competition Policy as Part of Economic Policy in the Common
  Market), speech in the European Parliament in Strasbourg on June 16,
  1965, published as a separate print by the Commission

von der Groeben/von Boeckh
  Kommentar zum EWG-Vertrag (Commentary on the EEC Treaty), vol. I,
  Baden-Baden, Bonn and Frankfurt 1958

Guide Lines
  see Commission of the EEC

Günther
  "Die Regelung des Wettbewerbes im Vertrag zur Gründung der Europäischen Wirtschaftsgemeinschaft" (The Regulation of Competition in
  the Treaty Establishing the European Economic Community), WuW
  1957, p. 276 ff.

  Festschrift für Böhm, p. 286 ff.

  "Relevanter Markt im Recht der Wettbewerbsbeschränkung" (Relevant
  Market in the Law of Restraints on Competition). No. 17 of the article
  series of the Juristische Studiengesellschaft (Society for Legal Studies),
  Karlsruhe 1960, cited as "Relevanter Markt"

Gutzler
  "Neuere Entwicklungen in der praktischen Wettbewerbspolitik der Europäischen Kommission" (Recent Developments in the European Commission's Practice of Competition Policy), WRP 1969, p. 220 f.

Haberkorn
  "Behandlung von Konzernunternehmen nach Artikel 65 des Montanunionvertrages"
  (Treatment of Concern Enterprises under Article 65 of the Coal and
  Steel Treaty), NJW 1960, p. 86 f.

van Hecke
"Das Diskriminierungsverbot des Vertrages über die Europäische Wirtschaftsgemeinschaft" (The Prohibition of Discrimination in the Treaty on the European Economic Community), in Kartelle und Monopole, vol. I, p. 335 ff.

van Hecke/Suetens
in Journal des Tribunaux, 1962, p. 364

Hefermehl
Festschrift für Nipperdey, 1965, p. 771 ff.

"Unternehmenszusammenschlüsse im Lichte der Artikel 85 und 86" (Mergers of Enterprises in Light of Articles 85 and 86), Studien-Vereinigung Kartellrecht, Kooperation und Konzentration im Gemeinsamen Markt, 2. Kartellrechtsforum, Brussels 1967 (1968), p. 59 ff.

Heine
"Bezugsverpflichtungen in Lizenzverträgen" (Obligations Regarding the Obtaining of Supplies in License Agreements), GRUR 1960, p. 265 ff.

Hellmann/Pfeiffer
"EWG-Kartellverordnung, um Interessenausgleich bemüht, die Regelung für horizontale und vertikale Absprachen" (EEC Cartel Regulation Endeavoring to Balance Interests—The Regulation of Horizontal and Vertical Agreements), in "Volkswirt" (Political Economist) 1962, p. 233

"Zum Einfluss des EWG-Kartellrechtes auf innerstaatliche Preis und Vertriebsbindungen" (Concerning the Influence of EEC Cartel Law on National Price and Distributorship Agreements), annotation to LG Munich decision of January 14, 1963, BB 1963, p. 167 ff.

van den Heuvel
"Some Unsolved Problems in Community Law concerning Restrictive Trade Practices," CMLR Vol. 4, p. 192 ff.

High Authority of the European Coal and Steel Community
Fourth General Report on the Activities of the Coal and Steel Community, April 11, 1955–April 8, 1956

Homburger/Jenny
"Internationalrechtliche Aspekte des EWG-Wettbewerbsrechts" (International Law Aspects of EEC Competition Law), 1966

Honig/Brown/Gleiss/Hirsch
"Cartel Law of the European Economic Community," London 1963

Hootz
Annotation to the *Tar-Colors* decision, Europarecht 1969, p. 151

"Stellungnahme der Kommission zur Kooperation und 'Folgetheorie'" (Commission's Opinion on Cooperation and "Folgetheorie"), WRP 1968, p. 383 ff.

Hug
"Die Anwendbarkeit der kartellrechtlichen Bestimmungen des Montanvertrages und des Vertrages über die Europäische Wirtschaftsgemeinschaft auf in Nichtmitgliedstaaten veranlasste Beschränkungen des Wettbewerbs im Gemeinsamen Markt" (Applicability of the Cartel Law Provisions of the Coal and Steel Treaty and of the Treaty on the European Economic Community to Restraints on Competition in the Common Market Caused in Non-member States), in Kartelle und Monopole, vol. II, p. 603 ff.

Immenga
Annotation to German Federal Constitutional Court's decision of October 18, 1967, NJW 1968, p. 1036

Ipsen
  Annotation to German Federal Constitutional Court's decision of October 18, 1967, EuR 1968, p. 137

Jannse/Oudemans/Wolterbeek
  "Der Einfluss der Wettbewerbsregeln des EWG-Vertrages auf die gewerblichen Schutzrechte" (The Influence of the Rules of Competition of the EEC Treaty on Industrial Protective Rights), GRUR AIT 1961, p. 276

de Jong
  "Concentration in the Common Market," CMLR Vol. 4, p. 166 ff.

Kaiser
  "Zur Anwendung von Art. 85, Abs. 3 des EWG-Vertrages auf Gruppen von Kartellverträgen" (Concerning Application of Article 85 (3) of the EEC Treaty to Groups of Agreements), Cologne 1964

  "Kartelle und Monopole im modernen Recht"
  Cartels and Monopolies in Modern Law, being contributions in the field of supranational and national European and American law on the occasion of the International Cartel Law Conference in Frankfurt a.M. 1960, edited by the Institute for Foreign and International Economic Law at the University of Frankfurt a.M., Karlsruhe 1960, cited as "Kartelle und Monopole"

Kartte
  "Zum Begriff marktbeherrschendes Unternehmen in § 22 Abs. 1 GWB" (On the Concept of Market-Dominant Enterprise in § 22 Para. 1 of the GWB), DB 1962, p. 1133 ff.

Kaufmann/Rautmann/Strickrodt
  Kommentar zum Gesetz gegen Wettbewerbsbeschränkungen (Commentary on the Law against Restraints on Competition), 1960, cited as "Frankfurter Kommentar"

Kaul
  "Zur Anmeldung von Ausschliesslichkeits- und Vertriebsbedingungen nach dem EWG-Kartellrecht" (On Notification of Terms Regarding Exclusivity and Distribution under the EEC Cartel Law), AWD 1962, p. 156 ff.

Kellermann
  "Der Einfluss des Gesetzes gegen Wettbewerbsbeschränkungen auf die Verwertung von gewerblichen Schutzrechten" (The Influence of the Law against Restraints on Competition upon the Exploitation of Industrial Protective Rights), GRUR 1959, p. 569 ff.

Kirschstein
  Annotation to BGH decision of February 5, 1968, WRP 1968, p. 211

  Annotation to *Parke, Davis* decision, Europarecht 1968, p. 306 ff.

  "Beurteilung von Alleinvertriebsverträgen nach EWG-Kartellrecht" (Evaluation of Exclusive Distributorship Agreements under EEC Cartel Law), WuW 1966, p. 777 ff.

  "Die ersten kartellrechtlichen Entscheidungen des EWG-Kommission" (The First Cartel Law Decisions of the EEC Commission), WRP 1965, p. 77 ff.

  "Die Gruppenfreistellungsverordnung der EWG-Kommission für Alleinvertriebsvereinbarungen" (The EEC Commission's Group Exemption Regulation for Exclusive Distributorship Agreements), WuW 1967, p. 373

  "Entscheidungen der Kommission der Europäischen Gemeinschaften zum EWG-Kartellrecht im Jahre 1968" (Decisions of the Commission of the European Communities on EEC Cartel Law in 1968), WRP, May 1969, p. 185; June 1969, p. 223

Kleemann
"Die Wettbewerbsregeln der EWG" (The Rules of Competition of the EEC), Baden-Baden 1962

Knoepfle
Annotation to the *Portelange* decision, JZ 1969, p. 788

"Der Rechtsbegriff 'Wettbewerb' und die Realität des Wirtschaftslebens" (The Legal Concept "Competition" and the Reality of Economic Life), 1966, p. 222

NJW 1968, p. 1037

"Zum Wettbewerb im Sinne des § 1 GWB" (On Competition within the Meaning of § 1 of the GWB), WuW 1962, p. 159 ff.

Koch
"Das Verhältnis der Kartellvorschriften des EWG-Vertrages zum Gesetz gegen Wettbewerbsbeschränkungen" (The Relation of the Cartel Provisions of the EEC Treaty to the Law against Restraints on Competition), BB 1959, p. 241 ff.

Kommentar
see Langen

Kracht
"Einwand des Kartellverstosses gegen Kaufpreisforderungen grundsätzlich unzulässig" (Cartel Violation Not Permissible in Principle as Defense against Claims for Purchase Price), WuW 1959, p. 546 ff.

Krawielicki
"Das Monopolverbot im Schumanplan" (The Prohibition of Monopoly in the Schuman Plan), Tübingen 1952, cited as "Monopolverbot"

Kunschert
"Die nationalen Warenzeichen in der Europäischen Wirtschaftsgemeinschaft" (National Trademarks in the European Economic Community), DB 1960, p. 485 ff.

Langen
Kommentar zum Kartellgesetz (Commentary on the German Cartel Law), 3rd Ed. 1958, cited as "Kommentar"

"Marktbeherrschung und ihr Missbrauch nach Artikel 86 des EWG-Vertrages" (Market Domination and Its Abuse under Article 86 of the EEC Treaty), No. 2 of "Studien zum Europäischen Wirtschaftsrecht" (Studies in European Economic Law), 1959, cited as "Marktbeherrschung"

Lutz/Basson
"Re-Importverbot und EWG-Vertrag" (Reimport Prohibition and EEC Treaty), NJW 1961, p. 385 ff.

Magen
"Lizenzverträge und Kartellrecht" (Licensing Agreements and Cartel Law), Heidelberg 1963

Markert
"Beurteilung von Unternehmenszusammenschlüssen und Gemeinschaftsunternehmen als Kartelle" (Evaluation of Corporate Amalgamations and Joint Ventures as Cartels), AWD 1964, p. 186

Marktbeherrschung
see Langen

Menges
> "Auswirkungen des ersten Urteils des Europäischen Gerichtshofes zur An-
> wendung von Artikel 85 des EWG-Vertrages" (Effects of the First De-
> cision of the European Court Involving Application of Article 85 of the
> EEC Treaty), DB 1962, p. 661 ff.

Mestmäcker
> Festschrift für Hallstein, 1966, p. 322 ff.

Meyer-Cording
> "Die Grundbegriffe des Wettbewerbsrechts" (The Basic Concepts of the
> Law of Competition), WuW 1962, p. 461 ff.

Mezger
> "Verbot der Lieferverweigerungen und seine Auswirkungen auf Alleinver-
> triebsverträge in Frankreich" (Prohibition of Refusals to Deliver and Its
> Effects on Exclusive Distributorship Agreements in France), annotation
> to Cour d'Appel Amiens decision of May 9, 1963, AWD 1963, p. 180 f.

Mok
> "The Cartel Policy of the EEC Commission 1962-1967," CMLR Vol. 6, p.
> 67 ff.

Monopolverbot
> see Krawielicki

Mulert
> "Die Wettbewerbsbeschränkung zwischen verbundenen Unternehmen" (Restraint
> of Competition between Combined Enterprises), Schriftenreihe Wirtschaft und
> Wettbewerb, Pamphlet No. 13, 1970

Müller
> "Zur arbeitsrechtlichen Problematik der Rechtsbeziehungen beim Spitzenfilmdar-
> steller" (On Labor Law Problems in the Legal Relations of the Film
> Star), UFITA vol. 28, p. 134 f.

Müller-Henneberg/Schwartz
> Kommentar zum Gesetz gegen Wettbewerbsbeschränkungen (Commentary
> on the Law against Restraints on Competition), 1958, cited as "Gemein-
> schaftskommentar"

Nass
> "Probleme des europäischen Kartellverfahrens" (Problems of the European Car-
> tel Law Proceedings), EuR 1970, p. 100

Neumann
> "Versicherungs- und Kreditwirtschaft in der Wettbewerbsordnung" (Insur-
> ance and Credit Institutions under the Rules of Competition), WuW
> 1956, p. 585 ff.

Niederleithinger
> Annotation to LG Mannheim decision of January 22, 1965, AWD 1965,
> p. 61 f.

> Annotation to the *Tar-Colors* decision, BB 1969, p. 1185

> "Die erste Gruppenfreistellung der EWG-Kommission für Alleinvertriebs-
> vereinbarungen" (The EEC Commission's First Group Exemption for
> Exclusive Dealing Agreements), WRP 1967, p. 198 ff.

Nissen
> "Beschlüsse von Unternehmensvereinigungen im Kartellrecht der Europäischen
> Gemeinschaften" (Decisions of Associations of Enterprises in the Cartel
> Law of the European Communities), WuW 1960, p. 250 ff.

Obernolte
"Die erste Durchführungsverordnung zu den Artikeln 85 und 86 des EWG-Vertrages" (The First Implementing Regulation to Articles 85 and 86 of the EEC Treaty), WRP 1962, p. 103 ff.

"Preisbindung der zweiten Hand im gemeinsamen Markt" (Price Fixing for Indirect Customers in the Common Market), in "Europäische Wirtschaft" (The European Economy) 1960, p. 465 ff.

Omneslaghe
"Anwendung der Artikel 85 und 86 des Rom-Vertrages, Beiträge zum EWG Kartellrecht" (Application of Articles 85 and 86 of the Rome Treaty, Contributions to EEC Cartel Law), 1967

Peters
"Lehrbuch der Verwaltung" (Administration Manual), Göttingen—Berlin 1949

Picker
Annotation to BGH decision of February 5, 1968, WuW/E BGH 929

Rasch
"Deutsches Konzernrecht" (German Concern Law), 4th ed. 1968, p. 357

Relevanter Markt
see Günther

Rinck
"Wirtschaftsrecht" (Business Law), 1963

Rittner
Annotation to Court of Justice decision of April 6, 1962, MA 1965, p. 97

Samkalden/Druker
"Legal Problems Relating to Article 86 in the Rome Treaty," CMLR Vol. 3, p. 158 ff.

Samwer
"Auswirkungen der Territorialität des Patentrechts im EWG-Bereich" (Effects of the Territorial Principle of Patent Law in the EEC), GRUR AIT 1969, p. 1 ff.

Schatz
"Die Erschöpfung des Patentrechts im Recht der Mitgliedstaaten der Europäischen Wirtschaftsgemeinschaft" (The Exhaustion of Patent Law in the Law of the Member States of the European Economic Community), GRUR AIT 1970, p. 207

Scheufele
"Über den sogenannten Relevanten Markt" (On the So-called Relevant Market), AWD 1969, p. 169-178

"Zur Spürbarkeit der 'Marktbeeinflussung' und der 'Wettbewerbseinschränkung'" (On the Perceptibility of the "Influence on the Market" and the "Restraint of Competition"), AWD 1970, p. 385

Schlieder
"Die Anwendung der Artikel 85 und 86 des EWG-Vertrages nach dem Erlass der ersten Durchführungsverordnung" (The Application of Articles 85 and 86 of the EEC Treaty after the Issuance of the First Implementing Regulation), BB 1962, p. 305 ff.

Schlochauer
"Anwendung von Wettbewerbsregeln der Europäischen Wirtschaftsgemeinschaft"
(Application of the Rules of Competition of the European Economic
Community), JZ 1963, p. 105 ff.

Schmidt
"Relevanter Markt, Marktbeherrschung und Missbrauch in § 22 GWB und
Art. 86 EWGV" (Relevant Market, Market Domination and Abuse in
§ 22 GWB and Art. 86 of the EEC Treaty), WuW 1965, p. 453

Scholz
"Vorläufige Gültigkeit—Ein Freibrief für Verbotswidrige Wettbewerbsbeschränkungen?" (Provisional Validity—A Carte Blanche for Illegal Restraints
on Competition?), WRP 1964, p. 264 ff.

Schumacher
Annotation to the *Tar-Colors* decision, AWD 1969, p. 85 ff.

"Die Durchführung der Artikel 85 und 86 des Rom-Vertrages" (The Implementation of Articles 85 and 86 of the Rome Treaty), WuW 1962,
p. 475 ff.

"Rechtliche Probleme bei der Anwendung des EWG-Kartellrechts durch
nationale Behörden und Gerichte" (Legal Problems in the Application
of EEC Cartel Law by National Authorities and Courts), AWD 1965, p. 405

Schwartz, G.
"EWG-Vertrag und vertikale Bindungen" (EEC Treaty and Vertical Agreements), MA 1959, p. 317 ff.

Schwartz, I.
"Anwendbarkeit nationalen Kartellrechts auf internationale Wettbewerbs-
beschränkungen" (Applicability of National Cartel Law to International
Restraints on Competition), in Kartelle und Monopole, vol. II, p. 673 ff.

Schwenk
"Der Marktbegriff" (The Concept of Market), WuW 1960, p. 3 ff.

Seidl-Hohenveldern
"Kartellbekämpfung im Gemeinsamen Markt und das Völkerrecht" (Com-
bating of Cartels in the Common Market and the Law of Nations), AWD
1960, p. 225 ff.

Skaupy
"Know-how-Vereinbarungen und Kartellrecht" (Know-how Agreements and
Cartel Law), GRUR 1964, p. 539

Sölter
"Die Ausnahmevorschrift des Art. 85 Abs. 3 EWG-Vertrag" (The Exemption Provision of Article 85 (3) of the EEC Treaty), WuW 1961, p. 665 ff.

Spengler
"Abgrenzung zwischen dem GWB und den 'Vorschriften für Unternehmen'
im EWG- Vertrag" (Delimitation between the GWB and the "Provisions
for Enterprises" in the EEC Treaty), WuW 1958, pp. 74 ff., 461 ff.

"Das marktbeherrschende Unternehmen im EWG-Vertrag" (The Market-
Dominant Enterprise in the EEC Treaty), WuW 1961, p. 510 ff.

"Die Behandlung des gewerblichen Rechtsschutzes im Rahmen des EWG-
Vertrages" (The Treatment of Industrial Legal Protection within the
Frame of the EEC Treaty), GRUR AIT 1958, p. 321 ff.

in Gemeinschaftskommentar, Appendix to § 101 No. 3 GWB

Spengler—continued
"Nationales und übernationales Kartellrecht im EWG-Vertrag" (National and Supranational Cartel Law in the EEC Treaty), MA 1960, p. 881 ff.

Spormann
"Die Aufweichung des Kartellverbotes im Europäischen Wettbewerbsrecht" (Relaxing of the Cartel Prohibition in European Law), WuW 1970, p. 459 ff.

"Die Entwicklung der europäischen Wettbewerbspolitik" (The Development of the European Competition Policy), AWD 1970, p. 156

"Kommission der Europäischen Gemeinschaften erleichtert Kooperation" (Commission of the European Communities Facilitates Cooperation), AWD 1968, p. 285

Steindorff
"Das Antragsrecht im EWG-Kartellverfahren und seine prozessuale Durchsetzung" (The Right to Initiate Proceedings under EEC Cartel Law and Its Enforcement in Court), AWD 1963, p. 353

"Das Verbot von Wettbewerbsbeschränkungen in der Anfangszeit der Europäischen Wirtschaftsgemeinschaft" (The Prohibition of Restraints on Competition during the Initial Period of the European Economic Community), BB 1958, p. 89 ff.

"Das Wettbewerbsrecht der Europäischen Gemeinschaften und das nationale Recht" (The Law of Competition of the European Communities and National Law), in Kartelle und Monopole, vol. I, p. 157 ff.

Teichmann
"Die Zwischenstaatlichkeitsklausel in Artikel 85 (1) EWG Vertrag" (The "Interstate" Clause in Article 85 (1) of the EEC Treaty), WuW 1969, p. 671

Tessin
"Alleinvertriebsverträge im Wettbewerbsrecht des Gemeinsamen Marktes" Exclusive Distributorship Agreements in the Law of Competition of the Common Market), AWD 1962, p. 128 ff.

"EWG-Kommission erteilt erstes Negativattest" (EEC Commission Issues First Negative Clearance), AWD 1964, p. 114

"Neue Entwicklungen im EWG-Kartellrecht" (New Developments in EEC Cartel Law), NJW 1968, p. 2173

van Themaat
"Competition and Restrictive Business Practices in the European Economic Community." Proceedings of the 1960 Institute on Legal Aspects of the European Community, Washington, D. C., 1960, p. 99 ff.

Thiesing
"Concentration dans le marché commun" (Concentration in the Common Market), RMC 1968, p. 289 ff.

Thomae
"Auskunfts- und Betriebsprufüngsrecht der Verwaltung" (Rights of the Administrative to Information and Examination of Business Establishments), Heidelberg 1955

Thompson
International and Comparative Law Quarterly, vol. II, part 3, 1962, p. 712 ff.

Torelli
Annotation to the *Noordwijks Cement* decision, RMC 1968, p. 979 ff.

Ulmer

"Der Unternehmensbegriff im Vertrag der Europäischen Gemeinschaft für Kohle und Stahl" (The Concept of Enterprise in the European Coal and Steel Community Treaty), Heidelberg 1960, cited as "Unternehmensbegriff"

"Die Stellung von Konzernunternehmen im Montanvertrag" (The Position of Concern Enterprises under the Coal and Steel Treaty), BB 1961, p. 1020 ff.

"Europäisches Kartellrecht auf neuen Wegen" (European Cartel Law in a New Direction), AWD 1970, p. 193 ff.

"Wettbewerbsbeschränkende Absprachen im Rahmen von Unternehmenszusammenschlüssen" (Agreements in Restraint of Competition within the Frame of Mergers of Enterprises), WuW 1960, p. 163 ff.

Unternehmensbegriff
see Ulmer

Weiser

"Antitrustpolitik und gewerbliche Schutzrechte in der Europäischen Wirtschaftsgemeinschaft" (Antitrust Policy and Industrial Property Rights in the European Economic Community), WuW 1964, p. 719 ff.

Wertheimer

"National Trademark Law and the Common Market Rules of Competition," CMLR Vol. 4, p. 308 ff.

Weyer

"Bemerkungen zum Merkblatt über das EWG-Kartellrecht" (Commentary on the Guide Lines to EEC Cartel Law), AWD 1962, p. 315

"Die erste Durchführungsverordnung zu den Artikeln 85 und 86 des EWG-Vertrages" (The First Implementing Regulation to Articles 85 and 86 of the EEC Treaty), DB 1962, pp. 293 ff., 325 ff.

"EWG-Vertrag und Ausfuhrverbot" (EEC Treaty and Export Prohibition), BB 1962, p. 467 ff.

Wohlfarth/Everling/Glaesner/Sprung

"Die Europäische Wirtschaftsgemeinschaft, Kommentar zum Vertrag" (The European Economic Community, Commentary on the Treaty), Berlin and Frankfurt 1960

Wolf

Report of August 23, 1962, delivered before the International Law Association at Luxembourg

Würdinger

"Aktienrecht" (Law of Corporations)

"Aktien- und Konzernrecht" (Law of Corporations and Concerns), 2nd edition, 1966

"Räumlicher Geltungsbereich des Gesetzes gegen Wettbewerbsbeschränkungen" (Territorial Area of Application of the GWB), WuW 1956, p. 775 ff.

"Zum Auskunftsrecht der Organe der EGKS und der EWG gegenüber privaten Unternehmen" (Concerning the ECSC and EEC Institutions' Right to Information as against Private Enterprises), WuW 1964, p. 579 ff.

Zeitler

"Der Konzernrabatt" (The Concern Discount), WuW 1959, p. 621 ff.

Zimmermann
   "Beiträge zum EWG Recht" (Contributions to EEC Law), International
   Cartel Law Forum in Brussels, 1960, p. 200

AMERICAN

Baker
   "Combinations and Conspiracies—Is There a Difference?" 14 Antitrust
   Bulletin 1969, p. 71 ff.

Becker
   "The 'Antitrust' Laws of the Common Market," American Bar Association
   Antitrust Section Reports, vol. XVII, p. 456 (1960)

Brewster
   "Antitrust and American Business Abroad," New York 1958

Buxbaum
   "Patent Licensing: A Case Study on Antitrust Regulation Within the European Economic Community," Antitrust Bulletin, Vol. 9, p. 101 ff.

Commerce Clearing House, Inc. (CCH)
   Common Market Reporter (CMR), Loose-Leaf Reporter in English

Devine
   "Foreign Establishment and the Antitrust Law: A Study of the Antitrust
   Consequences of the Principal Forms of Investment by American Cor-
   porations in Foreign Markets," 57 Northwestern Law Review 400 (1962)

Fugate
   "Foreign Commerce and the Antitrust Laws," Boston 1958

Galbraith
   "American Capitalism: The Concept of Countervailing Power," Boston 1956

Graham
   "Antitrust Problems of Corporate Parents, Subsidiaries, Affiliates and Joint
   Venturers in Foreign Commerce," American Bar Association Antitrust
   Section Reports, vol. IX, p. 32 (1956)

Haight
   "Some Aspects of United States Antitrust Laws and Foreign Commerce,"
   in "Doing Business Abroad," Practising Law Institute, New York 1962,
   vol. I, p. 266

Kelleher
   "The National 'Antitrust' Laws of Europe," American Bar Association
   Antitrust Section Reports, vol. XVII, p. 506 (1960), reprinted in "Doing
   Business Abroad," Practising Law Institute, New York 1962, vol. I, p. 286

Ladas
   "Antitrust Law in the Common Market with Special Reference to Industrial
   Property Agreements," 23 Ohio State Law Journal, p. 709-751

   "Trademark Agreements in the Common Market," 52 TMR p. 1165 f.

Loevinger
   "The Law of Free Enterprise," New York 1949

Maddock
   "Know How Licensing under the Antitrust Laws of the United States and
   the Rome Treaty," CMLR Vol. 2, p. 36

van Notten
   "Know-How Licensing in the Common Market," 38 N. Y. L. R., p. 531

Riesenfeld
   "The Protection of Competition" in "American Enterprise in the Common
   Market: A Legal Profile," University of Michigan Law School, Ann
   Arbor 1960

Sprunk
   "Intra-Enterprise Conspiracy," American Bar Association Antitrust Section
   Reports, Vol. IX, p. 20 (1956)

Turner
   "The Definition of Agreement under the Sherman Act: Conscious Parallelism and Refusals to Deal," 75 Harvard Law Review 655 (1962)

Underwood
   "Combinations in Restraint of Trade: Are They No Longer Synonymous
   with Conspiracies?" 18 Journal of Public Law 1969, p. 135 ff.

Van Cise
   "The Application of the United States Antitrust Laws to the European
   Community," Institute on Legal Aspects of the European Community,
   Federal Bar Association, Washington 1960, p. 140

List of Abbreviations

AG	"Die Aktiengesellschaft" (The Corporation) (year and page)
AktG	Aktiengestez (German Corporation Law) of January 30, 1937
AWD	Aussenwirtschaftsdienst (Foreign Trade Service) of the BB (see below) (year and page)
BB	"Der Betriebs-Berater" (Business Counselor) (year and page)
BGB	Bürgerliches Gesetzbuch (German Civil Code) (section numbers)
BGH	Bundesgerichtshof (Federal Supreme Court of Germany)
BKartA	Bundeskartellamt (German Federal Cartel Office)
CCH	Commerce Clearing House, Inc.
CMLR	Common Market Law Review (volume and page)
CMR	Common Market Reporter by CCH (paragraph numbers)
CST	Treaty Establishing the European Coal and Steel Community
DB	"Der Betrieb" (The Business Establishment) (year and page)
ECSC	European Coal and Steel Community
EEC	European Economic Community (Common Market)
EuR	Europarecht (European Law) (year and page)
GRUR	"Gewerblicher Rechtsschutz und Urheberrecht" (Industrial Legal Protection and Copyright Law) (year and page)
GRUR AIT	same, Auslands- und Internationaler Teil (Foreign and International Part) (year and page)
GWB	Gesetz gegen Wettbewerbsbeschränkungen (German Law against Restraints on Competition) of July 27, 1957 effective January 1, 1958
HGB	Handelsgesetzbuch (German Commercial Code) (section numbers)
JZ	"Juristenzeitung" (legal periodical) (year and page)
LG	Landgericht (German District Court)
MA	"Der Markenartikel" (The Brand-Name Product) (year and page)
Mitt.	Mitteilungen der deutscher Patentanwälte (communications of German patent attorneys)
NJW	"Neue Juristische Wochenschrift" (New Lawyers' Weekly) (year and page)
N.Y.L.R.	"New York University Law Review" (volume and page)
OffJour	Official Journal of the European Communities (number and page)
OLG	Oberlandesgericht (German Land High Court of Appeals)
RGZ	Reichsgericht in Zivilsachen (Official German Supreme Court Reporter in civil matters until 1945)

RMC   Revue du Marché Commun (Review of the Common Market)
               (year and page)

TMR   "The Trademark Reporter" (volume and page)

TZ   Textziffer (margin number)

UFITA   "Archiv für Urheber-, Film-, Funk- un Theaterrecht" (Archive
               for the Law of Authors, Film, Radio and Theatre) (volume
               and page)

WM   "Wertpapier-Mitteilungen" (Securities Bulletin) (year and page)

WRP   "Wettbewerb in Recht und Praxis" (Competition in Law and
               Practice) (year and page)

WuW   "Wirtschaft und Wettbewerb" (The Economy and Competi-
               tion) (year and page)

WuW/E   WuW Entscheidungssammlung zum Kartellrecht (Cartel Law
               Decisions)

Topical Index

References are to paragraph numbers.

C

Calculation
. cost calculation or comparison, cartel for...17, 36
. elements of price, cartel fixing...36

Cartel—see also New cartel, Old cartel, and other appropriate headings
. competition, effect on...22
. general prohibition...32-71
. trade, effect on...23-26

Category
. group exemption...86
. group negative clearance...317

Commercial agent
. contracts with...45
. distinguished from independent trader...45

Commercial custom not required... 71, 219, 220

Commercial services
. elimination of competition...107
. improvement of production or distribution of goods...95
. notification requirements...344
. subjects of trade...3

Commission houses and commission men—see Commercial agent

Commission, jurisdiction of—see Exclusive jurisdiction of Commission; Jurisdiction

Common installations for agricultural products...543, 546

Common Market—see also Outside of Common Market
. dominant position in...206
. effects of restraint within...22
. elimination of competition within ...108
. restraints on competition within... 14-21
. substantial part of...206

Common sales agency—see also Joint purchase or sale syndicate...546

Competing products, prohibition of manufacture or marketing of... 55, 65, 350

Competition
. agricultural products, production and trade in...531-560
. definition...14

Competition—continued
. elimination...106-112, 548
. market domination, measured by ...205
. media of...15
. not deserving of protection...19
. potential, restraints on...18
. prevention, restriction or distortion of, generally...14-21
. unfair, not deserving of protection ...19

Competitive disadvantage of customers or suppliers...68, 216

Compulsory dealing in case of abuse of dominant position...218

Compulsory license for entire Common Market...50

Compulsory use of common installation for agricultural products...546

Concern (Konzern)
. defined...1
. dominant enterprise(s)...202
. intra-concern agreements...21
. members of, as enterprises...342
. protective rights, applicability...48, 48A
. restraint on competition within... 21

Concerted practices
. concept...12
. conscious parallelism, distinguished from...11
. exemptions...81
. legally binding basis not required ...12
. origin of term...10, 11
. recommendation as...13
. uniform conduct, distinguished from...12, 13

Conditions—see also Terms and conditions
. attached to exemption...389
. granting of exemption...87, 88

Conscious parallelism distinguished from concerted practices...11

Consideration—see Equivalent considerations

Consolidation—see also Merger
. not restraint on competition...20
. notification not required...207

Consultative Committee on Cartels and Monopolies...416, 431, 610

References are to paragraph numbers.

References are to paragraph numbers.

References are to paragraph numbers.

References are to paragraph numbers.

References are to paragraph numbers.

References are to paragraph numbers.

References are to paragraph numbers.

Uniform conduct distinguished from
concerted practices...12

Uniform standards and types
. agreements...40, 96
. application or development of...353
. development...353

Union not enterprise or association...
7, 8

Unit of account...460

Utility models—see also Licensee;
Licensor; Protective rights
. licenses...50-65, 346-352

V

Validation of old cartels...381-386

Validity, legal
. agricultural exceptions...552
. Articles 85 and 86 under German
Basic Law...1

Vertical restraints on competition...
16, 37, 42, 327

Violation
. abetting or instigating...455
. Article 85 or 86
. . breach of order...454
. . fine...72, 227, 452
. order to end
. . application
. . . filing...505-508, 524
. . . right to file. 323, 324, 501
. . Commission authority...322, 324
. . hearing requirement...461
. . judicial review...325
. . legal consequences...324
. . publication...326
. . recommendations...326
. per se...33, 53

Voidness
. abusive practices...225
. new cartels...75, 309, 310, 332, 336
. old cartels   74-79, 307, 308,
366-368, 372
. partial...73, 77

Volume discounts—see Discounts

W

Warning before imposition of fine...456

Warranty
. cartel regulating...36